W9-CKS-862

LEANING ON THE WIND

LEANING ON THE WIND

UNDER THE SPELL
OF THE
GREAT CHINOOK

SID MARTY

~

HarperCollins*PublishersLtd*

LEANING ON THE WIND:
UNDER THE SPELL OF THE GREAT CHINOOK
Copyright © 1995 by Sid Marty.
All rights reserved. No part of this book may be used or reproduced
in any manner whatsoever without prior written permission
except in the case of brief quotations embodied in reviews.
For information address HarperCollins Publishers Ltd,
Suite 2900, Hazelton Lanes, 55 Avenue Road,
Toronto, Canada M5R 3L2.

Part opener illustration by Paul Marty

First Edition

Canadian Cataloguing in Publication Data

Marty, Sid, 1944–
Leaning on the wind : under the spell of the great Chinook

Includes bibliographical references.
ISBN 0-00-255059-8

1. Marty, Sid, 1944–   — Homes and haunts —
Canada — Rocky Mountains.
2. Folklore — Canada — Rocky Mountains.
3. Authors, Canadian (English) — 20th century — Biography.*
I. Title.

PS8576.A795L4 1995   C813'.54   C95-930441-X
PR9199.3.M37L4 1995

95 96 97 98 99 ❖ HC 10 9 8 7 6 5 4 3 2 1

Printed on 20% (post-consumer) recycled paper
Printed and bound in the United States

To Jesse and Orland, for life and a love of story. In remembrance of Robert and Alice whom I never knew, and John and Ora whom I knew and loved. And for Myrna, who invokes a chinook in my heart, and makes it all worthwhile.

Our guide also told us that as we approached these mountains of snow we should find the weather become milder, this we could not believe, but it was so, and the month of November was full as mild as the month of October at the trading house we left to the eastward.

David Thompson's Narrative of his Explorations in Western America, 1784–1812

Shams and delusions are esteemed for soundest truths, while reality is fabulous.

Thoreau, *Walden*

CONTENTS

ACKNOWLEDGEMENTS

*A*lberta, a Natural History is the best overall guide I know on the subject, and "Record of the Rocks" by Charles R. Stelck was a valuable guide to Alberta's geologic history. It was augmented here by the work, among others, of the late R.J.W. Douglas, which was originally done virtually in my back yard. A constant reference on Alberta geomorphology is Chester B. Beaty's excellent book. Brian O.K. Reeves answered questions on Alberta archeology. Jack Ondrack's book put elk hunting in historical perspective for me and provided some facts not found in the standard references. Thanks to cowboy poets Jim Ross, Mike Logan, Bryn Thiessen and Lloyd Dolen for permission to excerpt their poems, and to Don Wudel for his advice. The stanza from "Oh Prairie Lands" by Anon. is as given in Margaret MacLeod's book, *Songs of Old Manitoba*.

The history I have presented here is of necessity limited in scope. In writing the human history sections, a number of works were consulted. For a comparative analysis of Alberta/Montana cultural differences and similarities prior to 1874, I am indebted to the monumental work of Paul F. Sharp in *Whoop-Up Country*. There is no dodging Sharp's analysis. He offers, for example, the most detailed account I have discovered of the Cypress Hills Massacre. His book is a valuable guide to original source material that greatly advances the research efforts of the amateur historian of Chinook Country. Information made available by the staff at Fort Walsh National Historic Site afforded details of the massacre that have come to light in more recent years. Joel Overholser's book was a valuable source of information, including raw data on Missouri steamboat traffic, the trade in hides, the "Blackfoot War," the whiskey traders and early mountain men. Harold Troper's work set the historical stage on which my own ancestors played a small part. Similarly, the works of David C. Jones helped me in setting the particular hardships of my own family into the historical context of the Prairie Dryland Disaster, while R. Douglas Francis shed a Canadian light on some aspects (raised earlier by Walter Prescott Webb, most notably) of the Great Plains experience. The books of both Francis and Jones directed me to pertinent source material. The work of J.F. Conway, for me at least, pointed strongly at the socio-economic realities faced by early settlers in the West.

Hugh A. Dempsey generously shared his researches on the Massacre Butte episode, including American reactions to the affray. His insights were of great assistance. The courteous, professional staff at the Glenbow Archives always manage to make research less arduous.

Eric Schwartz's article was a starting point in my attempts to understand health effects of chinook winds. Lawrence C. Nkemdirim, a foremost Alberta authority on this subject, kindly helped to direct my enquiries to some papers I might otherwise have missed. Diane Warnock, emergency room nurse, related her experience with health problems related to chinook wind activity. Ursula Wiese explained cloud structure and thermals in the field. Tony Burton, Bruce Hea, Dick Mamini and Rob Young answered technical questions about sail planes and soaring, while Dale Johnson, president of Wind Power Inc., answered questions about recent improvements in wind machine technology.

Warren Harding was my main guide to the physical principles of chinook winds arising in Alberta and Montana, supplemented by a number of other authorities listed below; Richard A. Kerr's fascinating article clarified the idea of chinook air flow resembling water flow.

Ursula Wiese's book was an education on gliding history and a biography of the lee wave, and the source of a Blackfoot story about the chinook wind. There I first encountered Peter F. Lester's description of lee waves. Dick Mamini pointed me to Lester's work on turbulence, which was an education, for this non-pilot, on lee waves, rotors and thermals.

Some of this material has appeared in an earlier form in the following publications: *Equinox* magazine, *Canadian Geographic* magazine, the Canadian edition of *Reader's Digest* and the *Calgary Herald*. An excerpt from my poem "Mountains" was first published in *Ride off any horizon*, NeWest Press, Edmonton, 1983. Excerpts from Peter Fidler's journal are published by permission of the Hudson's Bay Company Archives. Letters from the John Maclean Papers are published by permission of the United Church Archives.

Any book is a tribute to the work of others who have blazed the way, and I am grateful for the scholarship, expertise and generous assistance given by all those mentioned above and to any that I may have inadvertently omitted in the course of this long and arduous endeavour.

I wish to thank the Province of Alberta for financial support provided by the Alberta Foundation for the Arts, a beneficiary of Alberta Lotteries.

Several personal and place names in this book are inventions, out of respect for the fiercely guarded privacy of an endangered species—the good neighbour—and to safeguard one of this western variety's already threatened habitats from the onrushing forces of darkness and dullness known as Development.

THESE EDENS
UNDER OUR FEET

1

AN ARROWHEAD

~

I live in the montane, a land of giant forms, of mountain, foothill, prairie and sky. The east slope montane, as biologists call it, lies between two worlds—mountain and prairie—and composed of the two it makes a smaller world of its own, a narrow band of high, bald-headed hills and timbered whalebacks in the southwest angle of Alberta, backed by the front range of the Rocky Mountains and forming part of the watershed of the Oldman River.

We are on the east slope of the Rocky Mountains, not far north of the Crowsnest Pass, which shelters the coal-mining towns of Hillcrest, Bellevue, Blairmore and Coleman.

Pincher Creek, a farming and ranching community, is a thirty-minute drive to the southeast; Calgary is two hours north but creeping closer every day. We are some fifteen miles east of the Great Divide, which separates the waters of the Columbia River system flowing into the Pacific from the waters of the Saskatchewan drainage flowing, eventually, into Hudson Bay.

Above our house, a long rocky ridge, 5,700 feet at its summit, studded with tough bullpines, runs north and south down into the valley of a meandering stream. Running down from the ridge are coulees and in these sheltered nooks, just in the lee of the wind, there are stands of Douglas fir trees hundreds of years old and six to eight feet in circumference. In this semi-arid climate, trees qualify as old growth at a fraction of that size. Our house sits on the 4,700-foot contour of this mini-mountain that shoots up from our back yard.

This is ranching country, but our place is a mere ranchette. Some of the surrounding ranches cover several sections of ground—a section being 640 acres. In the West, you don't ask a rancher how big his (or her) spread is, because the amount of land owned is too much a measure of personal worth. When asked to describe the size of our ranchette and its agricultural potential, a friend said, "Put it this way. A grasshopper could traverse it in a day—if it packed a lunch." Most of our land is in the sky, broken with rocky outcroppings forming short cliffs, and growing as much juniper and bearberry as it does grass. Riding by the place once with Frank Halek, the Local Oracle, I pointed out our hill: "Frank, look at that valuable agricultural property." Frank thought I was serious, and he had to pull over so he could laugh in safety.

Our house is wedged into this incline, protected from the ubiquitous chinook wind by a grove of aspens. It began life as a two-room cabin in 1939, then expanded in four directions as a series of afterthoughts until 1960 when it assumed its current, asymmetrical shape. Below the house is a small meadow, well watered by springs, which grows enough hay to keep our two horses, Taj and Candy, fat all year.

Aspen trees creep uphill from the main grove, gaining ground on the wind in every pocket they can find. It is the kind of terrain that cougars feel at home in, and there are mule deer, moose, elk and white-tailed deer to keep them fed. During hunting season, the odd moose hides out in our willows, sometimes stepping casually over the fence to push our horses off their hay rations.

We came here to Aspen Valley twelve years ago, after a winter spent hibernating in an old prairie schoolhouse south of Fort Macleod. Before that, we had lived in Canmore and in Banff, where I was a park warden in Banff National Park.

*   *   *

Sometimes at night, a trail unwinds in my head; every stream crossing remembered, every section of riprap, every rockcut. Once again I am riding in to the Amethyst Lakes north of Jasper. And my wife, Myrna, seven months pregnant, riding a horse named Seldom Swift, lets the packhorses pass her, knowing they will pull up at the hitching rail in front of the cabin. She pulls up beside me; our stirruped legs rub together. The Rampart range jumps up straight from the edge of blue waters far below. We are both twenty-seven years old, but old hands at being together. Below us is an Alberta Shangri-la, the Tonquin Warden station: log house, corral, tack shed. Our temporary home in paradise.

So many trails in the backcountry of Yoho, Jasper and Banff National Parks keep unwinding in my dreams. I don't dream about the bad times any more. I don't see Four-Toes, the seven-hundred-pound grizzly bear that my partner and I trapped at Stoney Warden cabin on the Cascade River, nor hear the metallic crash when Four-Toes hits the barred gate of the culvert trap, trying to get at us. I don't see how he looks dead quite as often now; sometimes I forget why he was not allowed to live, in the one place left where grizzly bears are supposed to be protected. "The parks are hereby dedicated to the people of Canada, to be left, unimpaired, for future generations." It was an ideal that we lived by, when we could. A bit of it died with each passing year, as the railway twinners, highway twinners and real estate developers pursued their politically approved destruction of the Bow Valley. A bit of that idealism died week by week with every game animal crushed under the wheels of progress in Banff National Car Park. A bit of it died in me, every day.

It is a good thing that writers have such a consuming appreciation for irony. After the publication of *Men for the Mountains*, an account of the park warden's life and some of the problems afflicting Canada's first national park, I received a lot of friendly mail from concerned citizens. Our great panjandrum, the Assistant Deputy Minister for Parks Canada, sent congratulations and added, "Your writing will do more for the National Parks and the things we strive for than all our work in Ottawa."

My overseers in Banff and Calgary could not have disagreed more with the ADM's statement, or my public criticisms of their failure to stand up and fight for park values. I had broken the code of silence, that peaceful void in which promotions are nurtured. Parks Canada (or whatever its latest name is) is an organization programmed to eat its own young. I felt as if I were being "nibbled to death by ducks." One day I found myself offering to defenestrate a particularly irritating supervisor (which would have definitely improved the office decor). I saw the light. I turned in my badge and resigned. There are many fine, dedicated people in the Warden Service. Some urged me to reconsider. "I used to have a grip on reality," I told them, "but I broke the handle."

But those memories of the best days, those days in the backcountry of Jasper and Yoho, had just about ruined me for coping with the real world, the modern industrial world. The little mining town of Canmore, where we lived in 1980, was quickly ballooning into a copycat suburb of Calgary. At the same time, mortgage rates had shot up to 19 percent. As a family of four, we could not afford to live in those mountains on the income of a freelance writer who wrote about mountains. But surely, Myrna and I told ourselves, there was yet one place in southern Alberta where greed was held in check, where people lived at peace with the land. Maybe there was even a mountain near by. We were determined to find that Great Good Place, and raise our sons there.

*   *   *

The mountain I mentioned is a part of the Rocky Mountain front ranges. Call it the Livingstone Range; it rises 2,000 feet higher than its foothills. Call the mountain Cirque Peak, the valley Aspen Valley; call the creek the creek.

Cirque Peak rises abruptly from the meadows and forests of Aspen Valley and makes a skyline of rock above the shanty where I work. Myrna and I built the shanty back in 1982 from rough fir boards and beams purchased at auction. I call it the Wheelhouse: there is an old iron wheel bolted to the wall by the entrance. It's a relic from an old horse-drawn hay rake I found half-buried in the willows along our north fence. Give this good Earth a chance, and it will bury all our improvements—amen. I think of it now as a ship's wheel, bolted permanently on a course that steers this shanty into the prevailing southwest wind. The Wheelhouse sits on an old road right-of-way above our house that we are slowly reclaiming. Its lares and penates keep changing. Right now they are the golden eagles that fly low over its roof, the little brown bats that summer under its board-and-batten siding, the antique white mare, Candy, who likes to scratch her buttocks on its corners, and

the chinook, which likes to grab the Wheelhouse in its paws occasionally and shake it like a Christmas present, to see what might rattle out
and run for cover. At times like that I often remember the warning
given by the Local Oracle, when he first set eyes on the building. "Better sink some deadmen and cable that shack down, or the wind's
gonna blow it away." I used to smile at such statements; I used to think
they were exaggerations, just chinook yarns.

The Wheelhouse is my lookout tower on the world. From the east
window, I look over the top of the aspens down the U-shaped valley of
the creek to where the brief interlude of foothills ends and the prairie
might be said to begin. But that first patch of distant prairie downhill
from here is just an inlet of cultivated land twelve miles wide, stretching
between the foothills and the black (from this distance) forests of a singular elevation named the Porcupine Hills. Farther east by south, the
outliers of those hills, named for the stickleback of firs on their crests,
trail off southward in a series of glacier-rounded buttes. Sighting over
the scalloped expanse of cultivated land at their southern end, I can
glimpse the greater prairie lying eastward, the prairie oceanic. As it
sweeps back up the creek valley toward me, it forms narrow embay-
ments surrounded on three sides by steep hillsides, where the August
grass gives way at last, like a dun-coloured surf breaking through the
trees to lap against the rimrock and the clouds.

My south window overlooks the creek, where my neighbour's wide-
armed hills, covered in pines and spruce, have gathered in some mean-
ders of that diminutive stream, lined in pussy willows. But what
dominates the sky southwestward is Cirque Peak (8,400 feet) on the
Livingstone Range, whose bare limestone summit ridge sweeps away
northwest, out of sight behind our hill.

When mountains close in on you, you climb them. The view west
from Cirque Peak takes in the dome and towers of Crowsnest Mountain
and the main ranges of the Great Divide. Crowsnest Mountain marks
the mining towns of the Crowsnest Pass. The Pass, as it's known locally,
is a picturesque assortment of mountain towns overlooking a blue-eyed
river, but it is haunted by its tragic history. Over the years, five hundred
men have died in mining disasters there. The worst in Canadian history
took place on June 19, 1914, when 189 miners died in the Hillcrest
mine. The underground mines are all closed now. As a former collier
once summed it up for me, "We don't dig our own graves any more."

From Cirque Peak's knife-edge summit, one can see Turtle Mountain near the entrance to the Pass, and the white scar of another mini-apocalypse, the monstrous Frank Slide, the worst rockfall disaster in Canadian history. Even after ninety years of weathering, the scar looks fresh. Life, green and rooted, takes hold very slowly in this stone.

The borders of the montane life zone, as ecologists call it, are ragged at times: the wild rose, our provincial flower, grows in the prairie coulee and on these mountainous hills, along with windflowers (crocuses) that every prairie child remembers. There is rough fescue grass here, a parkland type, but mixed grasses of the true prairie, such as spear grass, intrude in patches. Sagebrush is supposed to grow from Lethbridge, a hundred miles away, east, but I know a place where tall sagebrush grows on the slope of the Livingstone Range a few miles south of my house, transplanted, perhaps, by the Peigan time out of hand. (It is a cleanser and a purifying agent in the sweat lodge.)

The bullpine, or limber pine, a wind-fighting tree that is the spirit of the east slope montane, does not grow on the prairie. It is a plant that loves the thinner air of the ridgetops, and it only grows where there is bedrock, as if disdaining the anchorage of mere soil in the windswept heights when there is solid stone to cleave to.

Some bullpine in our area are over five hundred years old.

The bullpine inspires me to persevere, to strive, to endure. It is at war with the wind, but it contemplates the rock of the infinite. The sedentary life of a writer goes very much against my grain at times, and then I climb up among the bullpine, into the teeth of the wind. The one force fills me with the fierce breath of creation; the other gives me purchase, bears me up, stiffens my resolve.

Our sons, Paul and Nathan, were boys when we moved here. They have grown into young men in these last few years. Both are musicians; Paul is a talented visual artist, Nathan threatens to become a writer despite my manic and generally impecunious example. The excitements of the city have lured them away for now, and Myrna and I are left to puzzle out a life as a duo again, after two decades as a foursome.

It isn't easy, this transition. The boys were never really a duo; they were a platoon on furlough, a rock band, a gypsy camp. I go into their empty bedrooms, the one slowly being taken over now by piles of Myrna's sewing, the other becoming her office space. I look at the empty bunks, the posters of Rush and Sting on the walls, and I cannot understand where the years flew off to. In the night I look north to that amber glow in the sky that is the city, and sometimes I feel we two are retreating into darkness as if the night were a river carrying us away.

Then the boys come crashing back in for the weekend and the old life resumes as if there had never been an interruption. Tottering piles of dirty dishes fill the sink; tools in my workshop grow legs and run away and the stereo erupts with rutting cries and jungle drums. This morning I wake to the boys' voices echoing across the little valley between our ridge and Whitford's Ridge a half mile to the east, and feel how deep is that silence we have endured since they left.

I'm consoled by their happiness as they roam these hills again. They say this will be Marty land forever. This pleases me, and I've often wondered aloud if the emotion might inspire them to action—fixing fences, say, or shingling the barn. But the subject changes as they hurriedly don boots and slink off into the willow scrub.

They have gone up to Cougar Notch, a tiny gap in the rimrock beloved by moose, deer, elk and ambushed mountain lions. Footing the notch there is a bare depression, stony-bottomed, where water used to collect in a pool five feet deep, fed by a small spring. The Whitford kids (rancher neighbours) used to ride on horseback up to this spot to swim. But after a seismic outfit came through and set off a series of subterranean explosions the spring dried up. Some small gate in the earth had trembled shut. Now the basin holds meltwater for only a few weeks each season, and the swimming is no more.

Paul and Nathan used to go and camp there overnight when they were small boys, anytime from spring to snow-fly. They have gone up there in March through a chinook gale that bent the aspens half over above their heads, and found a pocket of calm below the rimrock. Sometimes they merely threw their sleeping bags down under the stars, then built a fire from gnarly, bleached bullpine scrags. They would roast strips of elk backstrap filched from our winter meat supply, or heat cans of beans in the coals. Usually they would sleep in a strange hovel they had built over the years out of broken sandstone blocks, roofed with dead branches and heavy sheets of shale. A home for troglodytes, or a war camp for wandering horse thieves.

Looking up from the house, we would see a red glow reflected on the rimrock that marked their fire. The coyotes encircled them with eerie music, and Jupiter blinked back at their blaze. In a shelter of their own, they were teaching themselves how to live without us. But through those years, lying naked on the warm sandstone that carries the sun's heat into the darkness, what soaked into their bones was the country-man's love of place.

* * *

This afternoon, Paul came shouldering through the house, calling me with that voice that makes the tea tins rattle on the wood stove, and thrust out his closed fist, grinning.

"What is it?"

He opened his hand, and there, sharp and bright against the pink flesh, was a perfect arrowhead fashioned from ivory-coloured chert. "I found it up at the notch."

We grinned at each other. "Man, what luck!" I exclaimed. I felt the edges; still as sharp as the day some long-ago hunter knapped them off with an antler pick. How often I have felt the presence of ghostly hunters up at that spot, a prickly, though not unpleasant, emotion: here was the evidence that confirmed the feeling.

"How old do you think it is?"

"I'd just be guessing." I dug out *Alberta Archaeology* by D.R. King, and turned to the section on projectile points. With growing excitement we read the descriptions on point forms, and checked the ears, notches and outline of the little arrowhead with a magnifying glass.

"It's either a High River point," I said, "or a Besant."

"Besant is fifteen hundred years old!" exclaimed Paul, reading the entry. "I didn't know the Blackfoot were here that long."

"The Blackfoot maintained that they were always here. Now the linguistic experts and the archeologists are starting to believe them."

Paul's friends called him away and I was left pondering the arrowhead. I turned it over in my hand, thinking how few are the non-native Albertans who can trace their roots in this province further back than 1883 and the coming of the railway. Those who had the claim on antiquity here, those who should have been embraced as true ancestors and the beginning of our nation's story, were shunted off and corralled in reserves. Their advice was ignored. The newcomers brought a vision of rose gardens and cricket pitches to the wilderness, and filtered western experience through the sieve of European culture, discarding whatever did not fit.

The Kootenay word for the mountain above Frank, Alberta, meant "The-Mountain-That-Moves." That mountain nation had been watching it for hundreds of years. In 1880, a Euro-whiteman galloped onto the scene, glanced at the unusual shape of the peak, and renamed it Turtle Mountain. By 1901, men were tunnelling into the rock to mine for coal; they built a town at its foot and named it for the mine's financial backer, an American, one H.L. Frank, who said it would be "another Pittsburgh." Two years later, at 4:09 a.m., April 29, 1903, The-Mountain-That-Moves dropped 90 million tons of limestone on the ramshackle town of Frank and took seventy-five lives. But men are slow learners. The Hillcrest mine disaster took place within a rifle shot of Turtle Mountain.

Every book has its daemon. This book's daemon fell upon the prairie earth one January, ate up the scant snow down to the topsoil, then lifted the topsoil above the earth in a Black Blizzard. I stood staring out the Wheelhouse window as the sky turned blacker than a Hutterite's jacket; blacker than a cowboy's sense of humour. Tendrils of dust danced in fantastic shapes, and a picture as if from a history book took vague shape in my head: grey, weathered farmhouses banked to the windows with blown dirt. Dust piling up in the corner of an empty room; dust piling up across the road that day, on my neighbour's tractor.

When I think of my ancestors, I picture Ora Belle Marty and J.C. Marty plowing up the prairie wool with two horse-drawn plows. He turns to her, calls out a warning. A black wall of cloud approaches them, higher than any tidal wave, dwarfing the tiny buildings in the foreground. They turn their teams, shaking their reins, forcing the workhorses into a trot . . .

I closed my eyes, trying to focus the memory. And over the distant voice of the wind, I heard a human voice. "Well, nephew," it said, "are you any wiser now?"

Now where, I wondered, did that memory come from? I recognized the voice; the edgy humour in it was that of "Sis," my aunt Sylvia, the Marty family's childless matriarch. It was a question she once asked, after answering some idle question of mine about her homestead days. I had not thought of her for a long time. But I realized then the pictures in my memory were first put there by Sylvia's words, by my father Orland's words. Stories of how they broke the desert prairie of Palliser's

Triangle, called by the western boosters of the day "The Last Best West." They were stories of how the land, and the wind, broke so many men and women of my grandfather's generation in revenge for their plundering of the earth, their pillage by tillage. The sight of that black blizzard had brought my own ancestors back to mind.

They were Americans, drawn into the stricken Palliser's Triangle of southeastern Alberta by our government's offer of free land. But ambition does not rule the drylands. The sun and the wind rule the drylands. The sun shrivelled up my ancestors' dreams, and the wind blew them off the land like so many tumbleweeds: "It blew away everything except the mortgage," as the homesteaders used to say.

Are we any wiser? Sometimes we are, though the monocultural mind-set remains the same, with some exceptions. Farmers have developed many ways of dealing with severe winds and drought since the nineteen hundreds. Yet sometimes wind and drought combine to create conditions no technology can overcome, and the soil takes wing, the farm moves to Saskatchewan, or North Dakota. The truth is, like many truths, outrageously simple, which means it will never be accepted: this semi-arid land was made to grow grass, not wheat.

To the east lies the prairie where I was raised. Although I have done some travelling, I find that after all I am a native son. I have settled down for good within two hundred miles of the place where I spent my childhood—Medicine Hat. Something has operated in me to tie me to this land, yet I remain an outsider among the people who live here. I know the why of it, it is the how of it that eludes me: how I came to be so separate, like a strangerstone on the prairie.

I had turned my back on those sodbusters, because the blowing topsoil of the chinook belt that I had seen so often was a legacy I did not wish to acknowledge as my own. I did not care to understand their motives then. Their whole way of being in this arid plain had been a mistake. I saw only that their history could not be my history. My ancestors had sown the wind, and reaped the whirlwind. So I thought, when I was younger. Their sacrifices had escaped notice of written history for decades: the Prairie Dryland Disaster that swallowed their life's investment has yet to be mentioned in *The Canadian Encyclopedia*. I never heard a word about it during my own school days. But much later in life, in reading such books as *Empire of Dust* and *Men Against the Desert*, I learned that their agony was shared by over a hundred thousand forgotten western settlers whose hopes were burnt out by the sun, blasted out by the hot chinook wind of summer, and decimated by plagues of pests between 1916 and 1929.

And I resolved some day to tell a bit of their story, and so contribute to the record of what historian David C. Jones has referred to as "the monumental blunder of western colonization, of an unprecedented diaspora, of drought and infestation, of suffering and deprivation." They had fought the wind; now I must make the peace with it they never found, and get to know them better, and hence myself. For our ancestors' lives are written on our faces; their history echoes through our genes. Until we know what they suffered and what they rejoiced in, know the connections that join us to them, or that set us apart from them, the mirror confronts us with the face of a stranger.

"*Time,*" sang the wind. "*Mine,*" it sang. It was my neighbour's land that was in motion just then, and the Wheelhouse was inside its hourglass, a world of whirling topsoil.

The door burst open as Myrna came in with a thermos for our morning coffee break, wiping our neighbour's topsoil from her eyes. The wind slammed the door shut behind her. She shook her fist comically at the ceiling and shouted "Damn the CPR." It was an old prairie joke. We had lived in the mountains so long, I had forgotten it.

She was laughing, but her face was streaked with tears.

The wind closed around us again, and began to sing its story into my ears. Its song is the story of Chinook Country of which it is the daemon. It was telling this story to the mountains long before it spoke to men. And it will be telling it to the mountains again, after we are gone.

"*Well, nephew,*" asks the voice of my Aunt Sis again, "*are you any wiser now?*"

Probably not, Aunt Sis. It's true that stripping topsoil is not always feasible in the montane zone: the topsoil is often too thin to strip, but that doesn't stop us from clear-cut logging clear to the Great Divide. The coal boom in the Crowsnest Pass subsided to a rumble by 1980. But another kind of boom is under way, fuelled by Alberta's burgeoning natural gas industry. Amoco Petroleum is snooping around looking for natural gas. The country I love is threatened by tremendous changes. For decades, we have been an undiscovered jewel in a forgotten corner of the province. Our unfashionable reputation as an enclave of rednecks, hillbillies and coal miners helped to protect us from some of the developmentalist forces that have destroyed the ranching and farming opportunities closer to Calgary. But recently, Highway 22 to Calgary, once a local road used by ranchers, has been paved, and the floodgates are opening wide. Now the urbanites are snooping around Pincher Creek looking for "recreational property." A local campground owner wants to turn his operation into a brand-new town of cottages, condos and mobile homes.

Hell is not other people, as Sartre suggested: Hell is too many other people. There are 2.7 million people in Alberta, which is probably about one million too many for the resources available. I don't expect people to leave this paradise; I only ask that they stop paving it.

In this Land of Boomers, I can hear the chainsaws idling and popping; I can feel the earth move as bulldozers mate in the compounds late at night, while the guard dog sleeps with one eye open. If there is anything that words can do to breast the force of this fresh assault on the land, then let me ready my arsenal now. A great urgency compels me to capture the life of this place and the people who lived here long before the Boomers discovered it. It should be a baseline, this picture, in the way an ecological reserve is a baseline to scientists, used to understand what can be lost by too rapid development.

In the end, perhaps I am telling this story to myself. I need to see what I have learned about ancestry in all its guises, about these mountains and prairies and all the new strangers who seem to be more at home than I am in southwest Alberta, though many of them are dangerous to the earth and to their own descendants, whose birthright they are consuming with their own. The Boomer Creed—"Buy cheap, strip it bare, sell as high as you can and leave the mess for the government to clean up"—is the very spirit of the frontier. And in this corner of the world, there is a mute consensus, a mass delusion by which frontier times and frontier attitudes linger on far into the space age. If the land has a voice, the Boomers have not heard it yet. If, in these pages, I can sometimes hit the notes that echo and harmonize with that sustaining voice, I will be satisfied.

What next, then? A sharp pain in my hand startled me, and I saw that I had my fist clenched tight around the arrowhead. Still sharp after centuries, it had pricked a tiny jewel of blood from my palm. The arrowhead gleamed in the glow of my reading light. Chert is an opaque quartz-like rock found locally clumped along the bedding planes of limestone strata. The man who made it, pricked by the need to provide for his loved ones, fashioned a weapon from the very rocks he walked upon. He knew his ground well, and thereby defended it and kept it whole. Citizen, you and I, usurpers by inheritance, can do no less if we are to have the moral right even to speak about this land. There, beyond my window, rise the stony pillars of the earth's household. Look how the ancient threshold makes a ladder to the stars by which gods might descend to walk this earth, a ladder that we might choose to ascend—or pull down into Eden, which is here and now, borne up by ten thousand Edens buried under our forgetful feet.

2

How the Ocean Got Up in the Sky

~

Canada is a young country. Alberta, as a political entity, is only ninety-five years old (and acts as if it were sixteen most days), not even a blink of Time's eye. The white man is a Johnny-come-lately compared to the descendants of the Clovis and Folsom people, here thousands of years before us. What we call the New World was to them merely an extension of the Old; another month on the trail of the woolly mammoth. But the fragmented archive in the rocks tells us that species came and went here for millions of years before the first bipeds shambled this way over the land bridge of Beringia. Though the Cenozoic era, the age of mammals, is 63 million years old, it represents only one percent of geologic time. The fossil record, expressed as a fraction of geologic time, amounts to forty days, according to my old 1964 geology textbook. Modern man by comparison has been on this earth for only five minutes.

In the four billion years before his arrival, the earth's crust, rising and sinking by turns, caused the oceans to advance during some periods and retreat at others. The continents were rafts floating over the earth's mantle; not even the equator was permanent. Gradually, between inundations, a lush flora and fauna developed here. Geologists have found fossilized figs, magnolia and sycamore leaves in the rocks of the Porcupine Hills and the Cypress Hills, a testament to tropical conditions long ago. Most famous witnesses to ancient banana belts are the skeletons of *Tyrannosaurus rex*, mined from the cretacious formations of the Red Deer River badlands near Drumheller, Alberta, and Eastend, Saskatchewan. These animals, the ultimate triumph of stomach over brain, lived on the margins of the Bearpaw Sea, which connected southern Alberta to the Gulf of Mexico 75 million years ago. The shoreline must have edged this region, for the fossilized tracks of dinosaurs have been found a few miles downstream from the highway bridge over the Oldman River, a fifteen-minute drive from my home. Indeed, a Tyrannosaurus skeleton was found in the banks of the Crowsnest River, just above its confluence with the Oldman, in 1982. (The site of the find is buried again now, this time under the waters of the Oldman River Reservoir, a $400-million trap for silt in the theatre of the absurd known as provincial politics.)

The front ranges of the Rocky Mountains are known to Montanans and Albertans as "The East Slope." The first fur traders to set eyes upon them called them the "Shining Mountains"; the Blackfoot, in possession of this region before the Europeans arrived, called these mountains "The Backbone of the Earth." This rocky backbone joins together three countries on one continent.

The Rocky Mountains are sedimentary in structure, something that is obvious at first glance, because the rock is stratified, layered like wedding cake, the different strata are readily distinguished by the naked eye even at several miles' distance. These layers of sediments were deposited in vanished oceans, or in immense brackish swamps and freshwater lakes. Then, as now, the wind acted as a primal shifter of soil, scooping it up in one place and depositing it in aeolian dunes somewhere else. Much of the sediment came from the erosion of earlier landforms, the detritus eventually metamorphosing into mudstone, sandstone and shale. Buried swamps, cooked by the earth's body heat and squeezed in its immense presses, have produced coal, and left reservoirs of oil at Leduc, Alberta, whose discovery changed the entire economic outlook of Alberta. Chinook Country has rich natural gas reservoirs such as the Shell Waterton Field south of Pincher Creek, and the Savannah Field, west of the Livingstone Range. The petroleum, being lighter than water, migrates upward through the earth's crust until it reaches some final collection point and forms a subterranean reservoir. There it waits until multinational corporations have collected enough royalty holidays, tax concessions and exploration grants to coax it upward again.

Coal, some of it formed from ginkgoes, ferns and early conifer trees pickled in humic acid, is in great abundance in this area. Its tilted beds have been bisected by Highway 3 in the Crowsnest Pass, where so many men died over the years while hacking coal out of gas-choked shafts in the Kootenay formation.

Limestone by contrast is made of lime deposited by organisms feeding on carbon dioxide, whose abundance in prehistoric seas is staggering to contemplate. I have fed some of it to our chickens. Prehistoric oyster shell formed such thick deposits that it is mined and sold to poultry farmers for chicken gravel. Another formation well known to petroleum geologists is composed mainly of fossilized fish scales. The Rundle formation, which towers above the town of Banff and above Aspen Valley also, consists mainly of fossil sea lilies, small marine creatures of the Paleozoic.

Without the animate, there would be much less inanimate mass. Life piled on life makes mountains higher where new life forms find a niche. The mountain goat walks on a sea floor raised into the clouds.

What raised it up, from 70 to 55 million years ago, was tectonic activity in the earth's crust. According to one theory, mountain building here is a result of a collision between the North American plate and the Pacific plate. As the Pacific plate was driven inexorably under the North American plate, the west coast and adjacent plains of North America were uplifted in a wide highland. Eventually, vast amounts of molten magma, triggered originally by the collision of the plates, rose up through heavier formations nearer the surface and further raised the highland. Under tremendous pressure, upper sedimentary layers broke away downslope, and an entire skyline from British Columbia to California answered ponderously to the call of gravity.

The front ranges of the Rockies were displaced along faults (fractures that allow masses of rock to slide past each other), such as the great

Lewis Overthrust of Montana and Alberta. In some cases mountains are said to have moved as much as fifty miles east of the location where their sediments were first laid down. Older formations of limestone were pushed over younger sandstones to create bizarre rock sandwiches, reversed chronologies. The foothills were formed at the same time under the same impetus, and being less lofty, reflect where the force subsided. Mountains and foothills form long ridges parallel with each other, running northwest and southeast. Topographically, the effect (to speak very generally) has been compared to shingles on a roof. From the Great Divide, the roof slopes gradually downward to the northeast. The butt ends of the shingles are the steeper east faces of the mountain ranges, such as the Livingstone Range, and higher foothills; the formations subside eastward into the first prairie steppe, the western Alberta plains. The slope is hardly noticeable as one reaches the eastern plains, which lie at altitudes of 2,000 to 3,000 feet above sea level. In reality, deep valleys, containing streams and rivers such as the Columbia, run along those cordilleran faces. A few of the rivers, such as the Bow, the Oldman, Marias and Yellowstone, cut across the mountains at right angles to debouch on the plains.

The extent of this uplift, the power of the forces that caused it, is easy to describe, harder to believe. These southern Rocky Mountains, reaching altitudes of from 8,000 to 12,000 feet above the sea, and with their massive east faces exposed for 1,500 to 5,000 feet, offer mute but irrefutable witness. Look at them close up and you will see expressed a power that can take limestone strata hundreds of feet thick and bend it into wave-like crests (anticlines) and troughs (synclines) that look like they were mortared into the rock by some Brobdingnagian mason's hand. Tottering piles of limestone, ready to collapse at the first touch of an alpenstock; chaos given temporal form was what faced the ambitious minds of the first geologists to explore the chinook belt of Alberta and Montana.

Emerging from the hill a few yards south of the Wheelhouse is an outcropping of fine-grained sandstone. Thanks to the work of the late R.J.W. Douglas of the Geological Survey of Canada, I know that this nondescript-looking stone is part of the Belly River formation, laid down in the Upper Cretaceous period of the Mesozoic era.

The stratigraphic maps in Douglas's *Memoir 402* show that the monstrous anticline (arch of rock) that forms the Livingstone Range, three miles west of here and 3,300 feet above our elevation, is composed of Paleozoic limestones and dolomites, some of them 400 million years old. This same Belly River sandstone behind the shack is only a teenage formation of the Upper Cretaceous by comparison, perhaps only 70 million years old, give or take a few million. Who's counting, really.

Douglas shows how that older Paleozoic rock, riding upward along the Livingstone fault, has been pushed over the top of the younger formations of the Mesozoic, causing Mesozoic strata to the east to be pressurized and warped. Down on the Oldman River bottom not far to the north, I have seen convoluted writhings and foldings in the canyon walls so intense that both syncline and anticline may ripple through the strata within the length of a yard. This type of chronological displacement is what led geologists to label our region "the disturbed belt."

Some of the rock is laminated. When I pick up a piece and tap it with a hammer, it will break into plates perhaps half an inch thick. The rock consists of non-marine sediments, but there are ripple marks on the rock in my hand. This sediment must have come from the still waters of a swamp, or the depths of a deep lake. That brief caress of the waters, a forgotten second among trillions of other happenings, so entangled in the creative chaos of life that it could never be retrieved, so it would seem, is brought into the light by the tap of a hammer, a blow as arbitrary as any other event leading to this moment.

The mute stone is warm in my hand; hard clay held by living clay. I hold what I know to be certain, what one day this body will become, and when I put it down, minute traces of my body (a few old epidermal cells, a little perspiration) stay on the rock, as if this mortal clay of mine were making overtures already to its own death. And so, in this minute at least, I imagine a fixed position where some mote of myself will abide eternally in this beloved landscape.

Not so fast, suggests Douglas. You forget that this topmost Belly River layer of surface rock was not even created at this longitude. In fact, it has been pushed by a cosmic hand at least four miles east whence its sands and silts were originally coalesced to rock.

The area within a few miles of our house is riddled with faults (zones of weakness in the rock), as many as six or seven per square mile. These are not discernible to the eye, under their coverings of forest and parkland prairie. My own house is a tiny black square on the map. My magnifying glass reveals a fault line drawn by Douglas right through the middle of that tiny square! Another runs through the rock on the west side of our hill. We are afloat on a raft of rock, at the shearing edge of two formations; we are at the mercy of the earthquake's faulty logic. So much for the notion of permanence.

The geologists may say that there is no longer any motion along the Lewis Overthrust or the Livingstone fault, but looking at waves in the rock that are folded back on each other, the layman can't help suspecting some unfinished agenda remains to be met. Yet how comforting to think that we, though we have managed to reduce a few smaller mountains into piles of Portland cement, are still mere insects on the geologic scale. Though we may very well destroy ourselves someday, we will not destroy this planet.

What will be, will be, sayeth the stone. The Livingstone formation, part of which fell on the town of Frank, is the same formation that hangs over our heads atop the Livingstone Range. There is a seismic survey crew working there this very week, setting off explosions in the rock. Be patient, Livingstone. Perhaps these rock fleas will soon fly away.

After the Rockies were formed, erosion by water, wind and frost riving (quarrying by ice), all directed by gravity, went to work to tear down what the earth had built up. West-flowing rivers deposited gravel and cobblestones far across the Alberta peneplain. This material, the Cypress Hills conglomerate, can be seen today in the top formation of those flat-topped eminences, which rise within sight of Montana's Bears Paw Mountains and Sweetgrass Hills.

The Alberta and Montana hills, uplifted by igneous activity in the earth's crust, were once connected by a drainage divide. Great rivers that eroded the surrounding plains left the Cypress Hills as a plateau on the eastern prairie. During the Wisconsinian glaciation, the Cypress Hills alone between the Rockies and Labrador showed their summits as a lonely nunatak above the vast ice-plain. The Creator Wind covered their cobbled summits with loess, a silt-like rockflour ground up by glaciers.

The story of how the Great Ice formed, advanced and retreated (at least four times over the last million years) is a theme familiar to most North Americans from school days. A decrease in overall temperature of only five or ten degrees may have caused it, but what caused the temperature drop, whether a shift in the earth's axis or a greenhouse effect fed by volcanic eruptions (to name two possible explanations), remains speculation.

I have only to look out my window to see the marks left by ice, the great shape-changer. The wall of the Livingstone Range is broken by a cirque, a roughly concave depression, riven into the mountain wall by the glacier it once gave birth to. At the foot of the cirque is a diminutive hanging valley, its terminus blocked by an end moraine now covered in spruce trees, its spring meltwaters drained by a brook. Small lateral moraines, now tree-covered, trail down the mountain on either side of the little valley. It was one of those glaciers that carved out and straightened the valley of the creek. Some 15,000 years B.P., the hill above our house was buried under a cordilleran glacier. As the ice receded, it gave rise to copious runoff waters and a glacial lake. "The lake," wrote Douglas, "may owe its origin to damming of the valley . . . by the southern main lobe of the continental ice-sheet." Our house sits at 4,700 feet, and Douglas placed the shoreline of this extinct lake at 4,650 feet. Call it Lake Livingstone. If it were still here today, I could cast a trout fly into it from the front step. But now it is merely a wide expanse of grassy lowland, a lake of buttercups in the spring. Dig deep into it and you will find lacustrine varves of clay, shining in their layers of centuries—the bed of the old lake. Several ponds and sloughs left along the channel of the creek are the last remnants of this body, which dried up with the glaciers. They are home to Canada geese now, to muskrats, beaver and hundreds of exultant chorus frogs. The rest of the old lakebed is given over to native grass and hay meadow. But in the middle of winter, when the chinook begins to blow, I have watched in disbelief as the snow turns to meltwater, the clock turns backwards, and an eerie version of Lake Livingstone returns, for a few days, to lap at the edge of our garden.

By 10,000 to 8,000 B.P., the Great Ice had receded out of memory. But its marks are everywhere in Chinook Country. On the plains, it is seen in endless fields of drumlins, small grass-covered mounds shaped like the bowls of elongated spoons. These mounds contain piles of glacial till that was dropped out of the continental ice as it receded. They show the direction of the ice as it advanced southward. Elsewhere, covered in grass now, there are end moraines, higher ranges of hills that marked the stages of its retreat, and great meltwater channels snaking across the prairie as broad, shallow valleys.

Whiskey Gap, a coulee near Cardston used for decades by smugglers hauling whiskey back and forth between Alberta and Montana, is one such channel. These broad, shallow valleys are far too large for the tiny streams they now contain. Such channels are found running across the slopes of the Porcupine Hills, at right angles to the direction of present-day drainage.

Closer to home, down on the Oldman River bottom, lies a block of limestone some hundred square feet in size. Greg Soule, a petroleum geologist, once pointed out to me the round circlets of chrinoids (stems of marine sea animals) visible to his trained eye in its surface. This rock had been carried six miles east from its original location, high on the Livingstone Range, probably during the Wisconsinian glaciation. It had been rafted down this river valley on an alpine glacier's tongue, to be set down here, very slowly and reverently, by the ice as it receded. It sits there now: a massive strangerstone, covered with red and grey lichens, among the crumbling golden shales of the younger Wapiabi formation.

The strangerstone tells us that the only constant is change. Nothing is fixed or permanent, not even what is written in stone. There were many interruptions in Pleistocene ice advances: the age we live in is merely one more such. Nobody knows how long it will last, but some scientists fear that our talent for creating carbon dioxide may precipitate climatic changes that will roust the polar ice into a premature encore.

Over the last 10,000 years, the cordilleran glaciers have retreated back to their protean den in the Columbia ice fields, but ice formed from frozen rain and snowmelt is still at work in these mountains, wedging into cracks to pry rocks loose every spring. Gravity loves a peneplain; the mountains are falling down and sometimes human eyes are there to see. The strangerstone's journey is not ended, but merely interrupted, until those Atlantean jaws lift it inexorably up once more when the Ice Age resumes.

The 570 million years of life from the dawn of the Paleozoic to the present is more than enough for me to muzz over. But I have seen, not far from where I live, the fossilized outline of a life even earlier than that.

This was during a fishing trip to Lineham Lakes, when Nathan was still a boy. The five Lineham Lakes are set in an alpine basin in Waterton National Park, Alberta, five miles north of the International Boundary. The basin, perhaps one mile long and less than a mile wide, is a hanging valley carved out of the living rock by an alpine glacier, which then retreated over millennia and disappeared, leaving the basin suspended nine hundred feet above the valley of Lineham Creek. Five hundred feet of this elevation form a sheer cliff between Mount Lineham and an unnamed peak to the north (lying between Mount Hawkins and Mount Blakiston). A small waterfall spouts over the middle of this precipice, emptying the basin above into Lineham Creek below, the waterfall being at the point of a V with a cliff face on either side. This is where mountain goats walk on spiderweb ledges to get a drink. A rainbow hangs there on sunny days, colouring the mist.

Nathan and I were hiking with a family friend, Charlie Russell. Charlie, a guide, former rancher and now photographer-turned-author, has an all-consuming interest in wildlife, especially black and grizzly bears. He has lived in these parts all his life.

The steep trail up Lineham Creek peters out below the Lineham cliffs, which are footed by talus slopes of fallen rock. It turns into a mere scratch over this mix of loose boulders and hardscrabble shales. Where enough earth has coalesced amid the rock, yellow hedysarium, a wild pea, grows. Grizzly bears love to eat its fibrous roots. Big holes were gouged out where some plants had disappeared, and boulders weighing hundreds of pounds had been rolled aside. Grizzly bear tracks, perhaps two days old, marked the torn earth.

The wildness of these mountains, which men first looked upon as a wasteland, has made it possible for the grizzly bear to continue living in a world that it has outgrown. The grizzly bear, known to Lewis and Clark as the White Bear, owing to its silver-tipped guard hairs, once roamed the plains and the Cypress Hills with the grey wolf. The last plains grizzly was shot in the Cypress Hills in 1906.

It was these rocks that saved the bear, back when men's eyes were always narrowing down a rifle barrel. Then, as our eyes opened a bit wider, and grew weary of the constant tameness of our creations, we saw the rocks were beautiful beneath their green mantle, and in our capacity for good, men and women worked to set some of them aside as national parks, which are now wildlife sanctuaries.

At length our thread of trail ended at the cliff, a puzzle to newcomers who may turn back in defeat at this point. But after a short pitch of rock climbing, one gains a goat trail, a slanting ledge wide enough for one person to walk along, angling upward, one hand always crabbing the rock for balance, since it bulges outward at times as if to push you off the edge. On this occasion I had the other hand firmly gripped on a length of climbing rope, its end rigged into a makeshift harness around Nathan, to keep him from running up the mountain and escaping all fatherly protection. On the opposite side of the V the cliff holds another goat trail, which we usually follow when coming back down. (Neither route should be tried by hikers without mountaineering experience, or who fear heights.)

A movement above us caught Nathan's quick eye. We looked up to see a mountain goat, stretched up on its hind feet, its front hooves braced against the rocks, busily chewing lichen from the cliff face about a hundred feet above us. When the ledges that goats follow peter out to a mention, and they can neither proceed nor retreat, they will walk their hindquarters backwards up the cliff and pivot on their front hooves to turn around. Their cupped hooves help them grip the rock.

While the aerialist in question fed, others lay on a ledge under a great concavity in the smooth mudstones higher up and peered down at us like bearded judges on a towering bench, the rock above them fading into the shadows of an overhang not even they could surmount. White goat fleece was snagged on the rock wall along the ledge, fluttering in the breeze like prayer flags.

In one spot, Charlie pointed out a few filaments of darker hair, faded to silver at the end.

"Grizzly."

Nathan wondered aloud what would happen if we met a grizzly on this ledge, or a mountain goat, for that matter.

"If it's a bear we meet," I told him, "we'll outclimb it." Of course, there was faint hope of moving fast enough on such steep rock. Our best hope would be that a bear, a sensible animal most days, might give us the road and retreat.

"What if we meet a goat, Dad?"

"It will probably turn and run the other way," I assured him, although I knew from past experience that a goat, particularly an ornery old billy, might also simply lower its head and run us right off the ledge.

Fortunately, we had no close encounters of the furred kind. The day passed all too quickly among the larches and alpine flower gardens of Lineham Lakes. We were inside a poem written by a Chinese water-colourist, we were meditating over Japanese rock gardens. Stepping stones were Zen koans to ponder in the lee of mossy cliffs. The trout sparkled by in emerald shoals, swirling out phrases of a haiku, making small whirlpools of interest around the dry flies we floated toward them over crystal water.

Fishing was an afterthought, but still our packs were heavier with bag limits of cutthroat trout when we came down to the lip of the waterfall. The afternoon was hot, and we lay on our bellies on the heated shelves of red mudstones by the creek, and drank deep from the sweet, shocking coldness.

There is a bad spot on the return trip that always gives me pause. One has to lean out over the abyss, step down onto a wedged chunk of fallen ledge, execute a pivot, and climb back up. It is a moment of existential ballet, with sheer rock above the step and sheer rock below. A hiker fell to his death there a few years ago, and that event, when you know about it, leaves a permanent cold shadow on that pitch that one feels no matter how hot the day.

Charlie, however, soon diverted me, as usual, with a piece of local lore. "Take a look at this," he said. A largish slab of mudstone lay by the side of the track. "This is the oldest form of life in Waterton Park," he said proudly, as if introducing an old friend.

We peered down at it, seeing only a brownish, flat rock. Then Charlie turned it over—he says he worries about some pilgrim removing it, so he keeps it face down (Charlie knows many rocks in these parts on a personal basis)—and there, etched into the surface, was something that looked like the outline of a big cabbage head. It was a Collenia, a fossil algae that grew here when the lip of this precipice, currently at 6,900 feet according to the topo map, was at sea level. It was then part of the shoreline of a vast embayment of the Pacific Ocean. "That was 1,100 million years ago," Charlie said in his quiet way. This man who loves bears is a bearish-looking fellow, dark, thick hair now tipped with silver. A square face corded with thoughts regarded, from his humorous dark eyes, the upturned face of my youngest.

Nathan's face, surmounted by a mop of sun-bleached brown hair, was a study. His mouth was one round O of astonishment.

He ran his fingers round the whorls of that petrified algae, while Charlie and I talked about a time when the atmosphere was mainly carbon dioxide, so no animals could exist. Algae like this one fed on the carbon dioxide, and released oxygen into the atmosphere. Bit by bit, molecule by molecule, the deadly atmosphere became friendlier to life.

"And back then the rivers flowed backwards, from east to west instead of west to east," I told Nathan.

"How come?"

"The old mountains rose in the east. They've been eroded away, and now what's left of them forms the Canadian Shield."

"Hmm," hummed Nathan dubiously. He had seen the Canadian Shield during two transcontinental trips. It was impressive, but he doubted that its stumpy old granite could ever have been mountains. "Bigger than these?" His small voice echoed across the canyon.

"Yep."

"But now they are gone?"

"Well, in one way they didn't really go," I told him, warming to my theme. "They were eroded away into gravels and silts, and the rivers deposited that across the plains thousands of feet deep." I pointed out a black formation high on the face of Mount Blakiston, a mile to the northeast. "That's volcanic rock. It poured over the ocean floor from undersea volcanoes, then it was covered by layers of mud. Later on the mud turned into stone."

Nathan grinned knowingly. It was one thing for Charlie to tell him wild tales, but he preferred that his father's stories make sense. He pounced: "So how did the ocean get up in the sky?"

It was my turn to gape. "Of course," I said, looking down at him with growing excitement. "That's the whole point . . ."

"Huh?"

"I'm glad you asked me that," I told him. "I have to think about it: it's a complicated business."

We gazed over the precipice for a minute, out onto the dun-coloured plains, out onto the upper deck of a small cloud filling the head of the valley, and beyond it saw the bottom of the ancient Bearpaw Sea, where now wheat was blowing in the wind, and men were working the thin soils with tractors, when only the grass could hold down the thin deposit of the last 10,000 years. Djinns of dust whirled and danced among those far-off, tiny machines. Yet, if you knew where to look, you would see the ruts left by Indian travois poles and by the wagons of the whiskey traders, where there was a bit of native grass that had not been broken by plows. It was a faint line that marked the journeys of men along these mountains for 11,000 years and probably much longer. It was a line that connected North America to Eurasia thousands of years before the natives discovered Christopher Columbus. It was a line that followed the ice-free corridor between the continents: a corridor that follows the contact point between the chinook wind and the land at the mountain foot.

We picked our way down through the rocks and clouds, until we came to the fallen ledge, where we danced in slow motion from age to age across the broken strata. The goats were ahead of us, behind us and above us, but we were not afraid:

To live here is to know
The jagged arcs of glory
are at war with gravity
That spent footfalls
of giant lives still echo
among earth's frozen blue
pavilions, the heaped up
sharpened bones of history
And blood, though petrified
is singing in the stone
Under our feet the raised beds
of ancient seas remind us
that we only came here yesterday
What gives us our dominion?
And yet we soar, and follow with the mind
anything the eye can cover
Until we think the eye can take in time
And the last thing we discover is humility
In the small, white-petalled anemone
below the swooning, ice-carved tower
Seeing in that green kiss, what power!
To take this mountain's measure
All that takes us
Everywhere

3

THE CREATOR WIND

~

Over the castellated crest of the Rocky Mountains, the sky is a blue ribbon, its bottom sawtoothed with limestone ridges and towers; its upper band formed of a bow in the clouds, the bow curved as the planet, stretching from Peace River in northern Alberta some 680 miles to Sun River, Montana, stretching on to Denver. The arch is so sharply delineated for miles at a time that it gives the cloud a solidity it cannot possibly possess, as if this curved border were carved out of ivory instead of vapour.

This is the Chinook Arch, the totem of a famous transformer, a warm Pacific wind that brings temporary spring in the midst of winter to the high border country of Alberta and Montana, the western edge of the ancient Buffalo Ground.

It is winter, and the peaks of the front ranges, from 8,000 to 10,000 feet in altitude, are corniced with snow that will endure, in the colder temperatures of those altitudes, until spring. The snow is carved by the wind's rough cat's tongue; burnished by the bronze-tongued sun. Today the peaks are backlit and bathed in sunlight, while clouds cast shadows over the Porcupine Hills, and over these lion-coloured hills of home.

Meteorologists classify this region as "part of the northern cool temperate belt," though there is nothing "temperate" about our climate that I can see. I was raised in Medicine Hat, where the temperature extremes can go from 108 degrees Fahrenheit in July to 51 degrees below zero in January. We south Albertans are not lulled to torpor by summer temperatures that could fry an egg on a human forehead, because it can snow in this country in every month except July. And I'm not ruling out July, either. Killing frosts in July and August along the foothills where I live stunt a gardening season that is only 100 days long to begin with.

The oldtimers described the Canadian climate as "eight months of winter and four months of rough sledding." But in Chinook Country, we don't have a climate—we have weather; a circus of weather, a Guinness record book of weather. The heaviest snowfall to hit Alberta in one day—44 inches—was recorded ten miles north of our house, at the Livingstone Fire Lookout Tower. And it did not fall in winter; it fell on June 29, 1963. Or consider that in 1992, Great Falls, Montana, proclaimed *August* to be the snowiest month of that year. More snow (eight inches) fell on August 23 than had fallen in the previous winter months of 1992. On the other hand, a record high was reached for winter, January 20, 1982, of 67°F. And sometimes the summer growing season will stretch out to 110 frost-free days, leaving disgruntled local gardeners wishing they had planted tomatoes or squash.

Craziness.

When it comes to weather here, the saying is, "If you don't like it, wait five minutes and it will change." The warm wind, in its gentler moods, brings us spring in the midst of winter, but King Winter rules the plains. We must be prepared for the frigid despot's return at any moment. Dark clouds will suddenly advance over the plains, as another arctic cold front pushes in from Lake Athabasca. The temperatures can seesaw with outrageous rapidity. Down in Havre, Montana, 225 miles southeast of us, the citizens once contended with four separate chinooks in five days, the temperature gyrating between –1 and 50°F as King Winter and Chinook battled for the field.

Cresting the mountains at 10,000 to 14,000 feet and higher, on average the wind strikes forty-five or more days each winter on the foothills and prairie that lie at the mountain foot from Pincher Creek, Alberta, south to Livingston, Montana, the area known to Montana meteorologists as the Northern Chinook Zone. The chinook zone stretches eastward from the mountain foot to an invisible boundary varying in width from approximately 180 to 240 miles. Where I live, we expect winds of 60 m.p.h. or higher at least once a month from November to February. And these winds mostly bring a whiteout of blowing, thawing snow, not a blackout of blowing dirt.

The Creator Wind begets many facts and as many fictions.

Fact: The most rapid temperature change in the United States—from –32°F to 15°F in seven minutes, in Great Falls, Montana, January 11, 1980—was caused by a warm chinook wind. Fiction: The fastest Montana wind speed, 82 m.p.h., was recorded at Great Falls, on December 10, 1956. This record has been broken many times in the Browning and Livingston vicinities, but there were no National Weather Service stations to officially measure it. Environment Canada has clocked the chinook at Pincher Creek, Alberta, at 84.9 m.p.h. and the maximum gust at 109.74 m.p.h. Nobody who has lived in the Pincher Creek area (including this writer) believes those records, either. They are too slow. The wind in the nearby Crowsnest Pass, the wind-tunnel of Canada, was once clocked at 135 m.p.h. by the staff of the old Saratoga gas plant.

"She's blowing a steady ninety," as one Montanan put it to me, "and she's whuppin' about one-twenty." Now that's more like it.

This Wheelhouse of mine is wired to the wind. I have an anemometer on the roof and a temperature sensor outside, both hooked up to a small Davis Weather Monitor on my desk, which records wind speed, temperatures and barometric pressure. It is blowing a "fresh gale" as I write this—according to the old Beaufort Scale, the equivalent of 39 to 46 m.p.h. It blew harder yesterday, gusting to 72 m.p.h. and raising the temperature, gradually this time, from –22 to 9°C. There were two feet of snow on the ground and on the roof of this shack yesterday morning, but by noon it was melting so rapidly that a spume of water blew in sheets from the trailing edge of my roof. Soon enough, water began dribbling through a crack in the ceiling right over "Alberta," which is the trade name embossed on the potbellied stove I use for heating. Water droplets hissed on the stove lid. The same old well-tarred leak had opened up again.

Out I went, down to the stable to fetch the ladder and the tar bucket. I had to walk backwards into the wind in order to carry the ladder back. It is long and heavy, but the wind carried part of it for me. I held one end, and the wind blowing under it lifted up the other. I might have been wise, and just put the bucket under that leak. Not me. I like to tar things—it's part of my naval heritage as a former Royal Canadian Sea Cadet. I clambered up, shovel in hand, and began to push the wet snow off the roof as fast as I could. But the wind came back, blew the ladder down, and knocked me to my knees. If I hadn't grabbed the chimney, it would have knocked me off the roof, too.

Sitting shivering in a puddle of slush, I contemplated the fifteen-foot drop into the mud and slush below. I knew that Frank Halek, the Local Oracle, would be passing by on the road any moment, heading home for his dinner, driving his battered green 4 x 4 half-ton one-quarter full of binder twine, old hay and cowshit. And Frank, hawk-eyed, would no doubt spot me perched on the roof, outlined against the clouds as some kind of gigantic, soggy raven: he would know immediately what had happened. Ignoring my frantic semaphore signs for him to piss off and mind his own business, he would back up at high speed to my driveway. And I would peer helplessly through the tops of the aspen trees, watching him roar up my drive. I would hear him cackling before he even got out of the truck. He would walk up through the trees laughing, fighting the wind, up through the slop and muck in his tall, insulated green rubber gumboots. And he would stand there in his tattered parka and coveralls, laughing and shaking his head in disbelief. He would savour the ridiculous spectacle for a few moments before he picked up the ladder for me.

I would never live it down.

Next to the alphabet, the parachute roll is the most useful thing a kid learns in the Royal Canadian Sea Cadets. I hit the muck, knees flexed, and immediately tucked my head in and rolled forward, taking the impact along right forearm and shoulder. I got a nice swath of slush and muck from head to toe, before I got to my feet again.

*   *   *

When I was a boy, a Montana uncle told me soberly that the wind was heated up by friction as it slid over the tops of the mountains. It seemed a reasonable explanation to my credulous ears back then. Now, however, I know that the chinook is a foehn-type wind, a moving mass of air whose temperature is warmed in passing over an incline, though not quite as described by my uncle. The foehn is a famous dry south wind of southern Germany and Switzerland. (The telltale cap cloud that forms over the mountain tops during such winds is known as the "Foehn Wall.") Such winds are found in many places in the world. The zonda of Argentina, the Mediterranean sirocco and the sharav wind of Israel are other examples. Another well-known foehn on this continent is the Santa Ana of California. This is the one that fans up brushfires and blows sand into the swimming pools down in Santa Barbara.

The physical descriptions of chinook wind creation and its effects become complicated: there is no room here to discuss the role of the jet stream (to give one example) in steering chinook direction. There are different degrees of chinooks, but I will aim for a more general explanation of what causes the major sustained chinook, when the whole troposphere begins to flow over the Rocky Mountains. That is the one that Westerners love to brag about.

Despite its tropical effect on the Chinook Country psyche, the wind owes its origin to a low-pressure system occurring off the Gulf of Alaska and a low-pressure zone east of the Rockies. A cyclonic (counterclockwise) motion of air around the Alaska low eventually drives the southwest wind into Montana and Alberta. The Montana chinook expert Warren Harding, a former weather observer in Alaska, once told me that the Alaska low "throws off wind like a big wheel throwing off mud." Eventually this moist Pacific air begins rising up the west slope of the Coast Ranges. "By definition," Harding explained, "when a surface and upper ridge of high pressure approaches a mountain range, the lee side trough will start to form—that is, the pressure starts to fall on the east slope."

Air flows from areas of high pressure to areas of low pressure. The air rises and partially subsides several times, lifted orographically by the interior mountain ranges of the northwest before it rises for the final time up the west slope of the Rockies. The cooling effect as it rises causes a loss of moisture (water vapour) to precipitation when the dew point is reached, and that is why most of the precipitation will fall on the west side of the Rocky Mountains. (This is also why the eastern plains, in the "rain shadow" of the mountains, are so arid.) The cooling effect of altitude rise is much greater in drier air, but in this wet air, the cooling is tempered by the principle of the latent heat of condensation. That is because energy from the sun (heat) was originally stored in the water vapour contained within that rising air. As this vapour condenses, it releases energy (heat) to the surrounding air. The air, drier now, sub-sides on the eastern side of the mountains, drawn into the trough of low pressure. As it plunges down, it is warmed further through compression, like the air in a bicycle pump. Since the air is drier, it gains heat at the dry adiabatic lapse rate of 5.5°F per 1,000 feet. There is a dramatic net gain in temperature from the windward to the leeward side of the Rockies.

Meanwhile, on the east side of the mountains, the snow-covered plains, all unsuspecting of these physical forces, may be gripped by tem-peratures that are well below zero, as in the case of Great Falls men-tioned above. So the warm air descends on this cold air mass like warm water on an ice cube. The variation between wind and surface tempera-tures accounts for the wild temperature swings during chinook condi-tions. There can be an eerie precision about the contact zone between chinook air and arctic air. I have driven to Pincher Creek at –30°F when, at a certain point on the prairie, the car enters the descending wave of chinook air. Instantly, the entire surface of the frozen vehicle, including every inch of glass, is covered with an impenetrable glaze, so that I have to roll a window down in order to see the white line. This can be a terrifying experience—especially if your last glimpse of the road contained an oncoming semitrailer truck.

Now take this winter. The weatherman may claim that five feet of snow have fallen so far this season, but why is there so little trace of it, save for a few white streaks in the creek bottoms and in the poplar forests along the Oldman River? Right now Alberta farmers in Pincher Creek and Fort Macleod, Montanans down in Havre and Cutbank, are staring glumly out of their picture windows at their fields. They are depressed, and it is not because of all the positive ions released by this witch's wind (a phenomenon I will deal with later).

There is no reserve of moisture in these dark brown and shallow black soils to germinate the spring grain crop. The snow, melting into the soil under the warm wind, might have provided enough reserve to at least get the crops started. So where *is* all this moisture? It has been "chinooked." This hound of a wind has not only melted the snow, it has lapped it up, and evaporated it not only from the surface but from deep within the topsoil.

When Chinook comes calling, it brings a desert thirst along. It could vacuum the milk from a cow's udder, drink the coffee from your cup, suck the alcohol out of your shoe polish. This is not only a winter phenomenon. Although it is also known as the Snow-Eater the chinook wind blows both winter and summer, and it dries up the soil in both seasons. Since the 1880s, its furnace breath has burned out many a grain farmer's green crops before they had a chance to ripen.

The medium that crops grow in is topsoil, the thinnest and most productive layer of the earth's skin, full of micro-organisms that make life possible. In southern Alberta, it has taken 10,000 years for this loam to attain depths of from one to 20 inches. In 1985–1986, the black blizzards carried off five million tons of this precious resource from 988,000 acres of farm land.

There have been many years in the history of the arid Palliser's Triangle when drought conditions were accompanied by dry west winds. In 1920, my grandparents' era, one million acres of topsoil was blown out by the wind, and, in 1934, so much soil blew off from the western states and provinces (300 million tons by one estimate) that clouds of dirt covered New York City. Dirt at 10,000 feet altitude forced aircraft to change course.

The irrigation skills that Mormon settlers brought with them to the Cardston area, along with modern dryland farming techniques and equipment invented by dryland farmers have helped to green in parts of the Triangle. In fact, it contains some of the finest grain-growing topsoils on the continent, and 40 percent of the region's arable land. It produces more wheat than any other region of Canada—75 percent—when enough rain fails to grow the crops, that is.

The story of the chinook began long before white contact, and the first European explorers noted the phenomenon long before the word chinook came into currency. Two early explorers, Peter Fidler of the Hudson's Bay Company, and his rival, Alexander Mackenzie of the North West Company, were embraced by the same warm chinook in 1793, though they could not have known it at the time. They were separated by five hundred miles of virgin wilderness, but thanks to their scrupulous journal-keeping, we are able to compare their experiences centuries later.

Mackenzie was embarked on the history-making journey that would make him the first white man to cross the continent and reach the

Pacific Ocean. Fidler had been sent south from Cumberland House on the North Saskatchewan River to explore the country and establish trade with the Blackfoot.

On December 7, 1792, Fidler encountered "Light Airs from the Westwards" and found the day "clear & hot at 2 1/2 PM," he wrote, "Thermometer 58 which at this season of the year is remarkably warm." The light airs soon turned into full gales that blew tents away and fanned campfires into prairie fires—wildfires in the wintertime!

Mackenzie meanwhile had embarked from Fort Chipewyan on Lake Athabasca bound for the headwaters of the Peace River, where he arrived in November, and went into winter quarters at Fort Fork. He found the weather so cold that axe blades shattered against the firewood. On December 28, five hundred miles south, Fidler noted gale conditions. On December 29, the chinook finally bulled its way through the arctic cold front surrounding Mackenzie. He notes, "the wind being at North-East, and the weather calm and cloudy, a rumbling noise was heard in the air like distant thunder, when the sky cleared away in the South-West; from whence there blew a perfect hurricane, which lasted till eight. Soon after it commenced, the atmosphere became so warm that it dissolved all the snow on the ground; even the ice was covered with water, and had the same appearance as when it is breaking up in the spring. From eight to nine the weather became calm, but immediately after a wind arose from the North-East with equal violence, with clouds, rain, and hail, which continued through the night and till the evening of the next day, when it turned to snow."

What Mackenzie and Fidler described in 1793 is the very same battle of winds, the same arid climatic conditions that Albertans are familiar with today. If not for the current controls we have over wildfires, if not for all the roads and summerfallow providing fire breaks and access for firefighters, I could look out my east windows on many a day and see the same clouds of smoke from distant prairie fires that Fidler saw two hundred years ago.

Fidler was a shrewd observer of natural history on the buffalo ground. "These fires burning off the old grass," he noted on January 15, 1793, "in the ensuing Spring and Summer makes excellent fine sweet food for the Horses & Buffalo, &c."

Fire, whether caused by men or by lightning, was driven by the Creator Wind to renew the grass, to keep down encroachment by willows and aspen trees. Aspens are shallow-rooted, easily damaged by fire. The roots of native grasses, however, go deep into the earth, making fine networks in the soil. Better yet for surviving droughts, the hair-like filaments of some native grasses, if unravelled, would stretch for miles. Fire, wind and rain nurtured the earth that fed the buffalo, whose flesh fed the people, and whose entire body, hide and skeleton furnished a hundred different objects of use, from bowstrings through to teepee covers, and from moccasins to natural glue.

Apparently it was a Euro-white who affixed an Indian name on this wind. The Chinook people, namesakes of the wind, dwelt in fur-trade days near the mouth of the Columbia River. The name was said to have originated as a joke made about 1840 by a Mr. Birnie, a Hudson's Bay factor in Oregon. A warm northwest wind used to blow toward his fort from the camps of the Chinook Indians between Fort Ellice and Cape Disappointment. He called this wind "the chinook," and it is possible that the name arose not only from the warmth of the wind, but from its perfume, because the Chinook villages were fishing villages.

The tribes living in Chinook Country had their own names for the wind. To the North Peigan, for example, it was `aisiksop`u, the oily wind, though according to two white authors who lived with the Peigan in early Montana, it was known there as the "Black Wind." Either description seems credible: the wind first turned the ground greasy with mud and slush, but might later turn the air black with dust. The Peigan or Piikani, my closest Indian neighbours, seemed to attribute the wind to the work of the Blackfoot trickster-creator figure Napi, or Old Man. The expression was "Napiua aisiksopumstau"—the Old Man makes the oily wind.

Everywhere you look in Chinook Country, you will see the marks of the wind upon the earth. It is there in the permanent lean of the aspen groves, those white tree trunks all leaning northward as living wind-vanes indicating the prevailing southwest winds. It is there as a current of energy wavering through the grain fields and through the sweep of remaining prairie grass. The wind keeps aspens, willows and rose bushes penned up in hollows behind the little drumlin hills left behind by the Great Ice. Those that try to root themselves in the open it attacks, blasting the leaves with flung dirt, tearing off the new leaves. It will thaw out the roots in midwinter so the sap begins to run. Then the frost comes back with an arctic cold front, freezing the tender buds, injuring the roots and sometimes killing the tree. Acres of conifers in Waterton National Park have had their green needles turned to a ruddy orange by this wind-burn. Trees killed by this process in winter are standing tinder for a summer lightning strike; the west wind waits to fan the strike into a forest fire.

What the wind likes is a clean slate of grass to slide over. What the wind hates is anything that obstructs its passage, anything that overturns the sod. So it is always at war with man's constructions, always testing these impertinent windbreaks.

The wind takes physical shape in a thousand hoodoos carved in the sandstone rimrock of the Porcupine Hills, and all the outlying ridges on the tops of the Rocky Mountain foothills. It is seen especially at that haunted, that joyful home of the First Nations, Writing On Stone, just north of Montana's Sweetgrass Hills. There the wind has made not only hoodoos but windows in the rimrocks, side streets, cliff dwellings for no one to inhabit but rattlers and coyotes above the Milk River.

By whatever name, this fierce wind is what keeps those wide open spaces open.

*   *   *

The Pleistocene, the Age of Ice, marks also the dawn of man. No one knows when the first people, those Paleo-Indians of unspecified Eurasian stock, made their way to the New World. That they followed an intermittently open ice-free corridor to reach the New World has long been an accepted theory of archeologists, though when the corridor was open for business and when it was plugged with ice remains a matter of debate.

The corridor stretched from Alaska, through the Liard River of the Yukon and down through Alberta to the Marias River of Montana, closely following the edge of the mountains, along the line where the continental glaciers and the cordilleran glaciers met, and later receded. This line would eventually be known to the oldtimers as the Old North Trail.

Across this land bridge came mastodons and mammoths, came members of the deer family. They shared the boggy wet grasslands at the margins of the ice sheets with New World animals, horses and camels. The horses and camels were slated for extinction here, and survival in the east. Horses would not return to this continent until the coming of the Spanish *conquistadores*.

No one knows how old the chinook is, but since it is a mountain wind, formed from air moving over an incline, it must have been conjured up inchoately from the sea when the mountains rose from the highlands. I have hinted at the creative power of this wind as a transformer of landscapes. A geographer, Ronald L. Ives, once went much further. Writing in *Annals of the Association of American Geographers* (1950), Ives suggested that the chinook wind, combined with the rain shadow effect of the mountains, created an ice-free corridor between the continental and cordilleran glaciers.

Looking at the distribution of loess (glacial silt) across the plains, and examining the fretting of rocks by the wind, Ives concluded, "Wind motion during much of the Pleistocene, was in the same general directions as wind motion today." He found further evidence of ancient chinook winds in the patterns of ancient glaciation on the windward and leeward side of the mountains, patterns still found today, and consistent with chinook wind and rain shadow effects.

Ives was writing about Colorado, but the thrust of his argument seems to apply to the entire range of the chinook wind. (I have but to climb the hill behind the Wheelhouse to see this same aeolian fretting in the sandstone outcrops there.) It seems likely that when the first people were ready to follow the corridor south into the unknown, the chinook was there to greet them.

The existing fauna of the Great Plains is only a shadow of what it was before white contact, and that richer fauna but a shadow of the species that roamed this country as recently as 15,000 years ago. As biologist Valerius Geist has pointed out, there was no historic grazer to compare to the prehistoric American mammoth, elephant or long-horned bison that were at home on these plains; no predator as fierce as the dire wolf, the sabre-toothed tiger or a sort of "running bear" large enough and fast enough to kill elephants. Only fossils remain to testify to that diversity, and one singular beast, the pronghorn antelope, which can reach a sprint of 65 m.p.h., hopelessly outgunning the poor little coyote, which alone remains to uphold wolfish tradition on the prairie.

Similarly, the history of Canada's first Paleo-Indian people may never be more than a fragmented record of artifacts discovered at widely dispersed sites throughout the continent. The precise cultural and racial linkages between those first-comers and those we think of as their descendants, who roamed the buffalo plains with only dogs as beasts of burden in the days before white contact, are open to debate. The stone age life was hand to mouth. But days of famine, or omnivorous days of snaring rabbits and digging out camass bulbs and bitterroot with a forked stick, suddenly turned to feasting when buffalo, run into box canyons or decoyed over a *piskun* (jump), were crippled or trapped, and could more easily be killed with stone-tipped spears or war clubs. They must have been a lean, athletic race, these hunters and gatherers, like the tribes who succeeded them. Their everyday life was a pentathlon.

When the first whites arrived in Chinook Country, they found that a vast expanse of territory, stretching south of the North Saskatchewan River to the Yellowstone, and from the Rocky Mountain foothills east to the Cypress Hills and the mouth of the Milk River, was controlled by the Blackfoot, a nation of fierce Algonquian-speaking nomads. The irresistible forces of British and American expansionism collided with the immovable object of Blackfoot territorial imperative; the white flood was pushed off course, forced to make historic detours. This equestrian, warrior nation would resist and redirect the thrust of settlement for fifty years, and many whites would leave their bones on the buffalo-ground for the sin of underestimating Blackfoot power.

4

THE VIEW FROM
MASSACRE BUTTE

~

Three miles north of Cowley, Alberta, standing above the historic confluence of the Oldman and Crowsnest rivers, a meeting point buried since 1991 under the waters of the Oldman River Reservoir, there stands a nondescript knoll, covered with native prairie—an outrider of the Porcupine Hills, whose timbered heights rise northward across the water.

The view from Massacre Butte takes in the distant plains southeastward, takes in the Rocky Mountains, takes in the welcoming notch at the head of Happy Valley, between the mountain foothills and the Porcupines.

The view goes backward in time.

The distant notch, beckoning horsemen and wagoneers to try their luck, marks one branch of the Old North Trail, which forked on either side of the Porcupine Hills but generally followed along the mountain edge, the old ice-free corridor, from Alaska south to New Mexico. This west branch was called the Stoney Trail by the pioneers, since it was used by that Siouan-speaking people whom the Blackfoot called the

Wapamathe or "Throat Cutters," who hunted along the mountains. Part of the Assiniboine nation, they pressed their ancient claim to take buffalo here, in the teeth of Blackfoot opposition, before white contact. The trail was used by Crow war parties travelling north on horse-stealing raids against the Blackfoot, and by obscure white trappers and prospectors in the early 1850s. Nobody knows how many white trappers, or marauding warriors, perished along its margins. The Blackfoot policy toward whites back then could be expressed as "Traders, when it pleases us; trappers, never."

A few hundred yards west of the butte, near a steep bank of the Crowsnest River on the Smyth farm, stands a small cairn. The lettering on it has been damaged, perhaps by cattle rubbing their haunches against the marker. It reads: *In 1867, an immigrant train consisting of about 12 men, women and children was massacred near this hill during the night by a war party of Blood Indians led by Medicine Calf. These immigrants were part of Captain Fiske's expedition from Minnesota, and had left the main party in Montana.*

The immigrants were believed to be a party of Germans led by a man named John Hoise, though even this is open to dispute. A "memorandum book" with his name on it and little else was found in the area by the Stoneys. Nothing is known about the other members, or their motives; all is speculation. Captain James L. Fiske had led several expeditions of argonauts and settlers, escorted by United States troops, from Minnesota to Montana mining camps between 1862 and 1866. The 1866 expedition, according to historian James McClellan Hamilton, "consisted of 160 wagons and 500 persons." Most of these were merchants with tools and supplies for the mines, but there were some gold-seekers among them. Another traveller of that era later told a U.S. Commissioner that the Hoise party arrived with the last expedition in Montana, and stopped at Sun River for a time. It appears they then decided to make their way to Fort Edmonton. In Montana, they likely heard rumours about a gold strike on the North Saskatchewan River. Whether the men were bent on merchandising or prospecting, bringing women and children along was the more foolhardy part of an already perilous venture. They knew better; the party had already experienced one Indian attack (near Fort Union) while still with Fiske's expedition. This was during an era known to Montanans as the Blackfoot War, and there was no cavalry to defend immigrants in Rupert's Land to the north.

Take a look at our great Canadian myth in the rosy light cascading westward onto Massacre Butte: it tells us that the Canadian West was a tame frontier; red-coated Mounties brought British ideals of peace, order and good government to our northwest. Only in America did gun law prevail, only in America were Indians massacred by whites, and only in America did the First Nations massacre the settlers.

That was news to the Hoise party, who crossed the Hudson Bay Divide into our peaceful land and were transformed into fragments. They were not only "rubbed out," as a Sioux would say; they disappeared from the white version of history. In 1870, Captain William F. Butler, sent west to gather intelligence for the Canadian government during the Red River Rebellion in Manitoba, compiled a list of recent murders as part of his report. The Hoise party was not even mentioned. No one ever came to look for them, as far as we know. And yet they managed to find the exact point at which to make a safe crossing of the Oldman River with wagons.

The first investigation, if one can call it that, into their disappearance was a hearing held, not in Canada, but by a U.S. Commissioner in far-off Fort Benton in 1870. It was there that Medicine Calf was identified as the leader of the war party. A few human skeletons among the wild roses and some charred timbers of wagon boxes were finally gazed upon by the Mounties about 1875.

When does the clock start ticking on a massacre? Could be 1806 on a branch of the Marias River, when Reuben Fields of the Lewis and Clark Corps of Discovery stabs a Peigan who is trying to steal his gun, and Lewis returns the fire of a Peigan horse thief, gut-shooting him— these actions supposedly precipitating fifty years of Blackfoot vengeance. Probably the starting gun was fired way back in 1670 by a Hudson's Bay Company trader. Geese fall out of the sky, and eyes are there among the stunted taiga spruce to see magic happen. The echoes of that shot will be heard everywhere in Rupert's Land, chartered to the fur-trading company by King Charles II, who had never set eyes on it, and who had no right to it, and whom the inhabitants had never heard of. The first massacre is the massacre of beaver to make hats for Englishmen. The next massacre will be the slaughter of the innocents, as thousands of native people succumb to the combined effects of trade whiskey and smallpox introduced by the whites. The final massacre will be the destruction of the buffalo, and with it the entire economy of the

Blackfoot and other plains people, an economy that has never been replaced to this day.

First among the tribes with guns were the Cree, pushing west for more beaver to get more guns and iron marvels. The Blackfoot were one of the tribes whose life was disrupted by the new weapon, to put fancy hats on European noggins. They called themselves the *Nitsitapii* (Real People) back then and traditionalists among them prefer that word. They consisted of, and remain today, the *Siksika* (Blackfoot proper), the *Piikani* (Peigan) and the *Kaina* (Many Chiefs), the latter known to us, incorrectly, as the Bloods.

The plains of Chinook Country was a land teeming with buffalo, which the Blackfoot called in their language "real food." Elk, deer, moose and bighorn sheep coursed outward on the plains following the stream valleys. The great plains grizzly and the plains wolf were in abundance. The river bottoms held poplar and willow groves and sheltered the people from the coursing wind. The cold winter was broken by the warm Black Wind at times, so the wintering bands could visit and trade with each other. It was a land worth fighting for, a land worth dying for.

Eventually, the Blackfoot forged transitory alliances with the Cree and Assiniboine interlopers. The fur traders and their *engagés* were fuelled with pemmican, a rich mixture of grease, dried buffalo meat and saskatoon berries preserved in rawhide containers. Blackfoot hunters had plenty of pemmican to trade. In return they received iron kettles, knives, hatchets, iron arrowheads and trinkets from the Cree. Most important, they obtained their first muskets, powder and shot. Eventually, the Blackfoot became traders dealing with the Kootenay and Flathead people across the mountains. As they moved southward, establishing control of Chinook Country, destiny, on four legs, was moving north to meet them.

The horse, long extinct in North America, had returned at last in the ships of the *conquistadores*. As time passed, surplus animals from settlements in New Mexico were traded to the Apache and Comanche, among others. The Blackfoot had heard about these horses long before they first set eyes on one. Most historians believe the Peigan first came into conflict with mounted tribesmen, namely the Snakes (Shoshone), around the year 1730. David Thompson, the great fur trade map-maker and surveyor, was a faithful recorder of First Nation history. In Thompson's *Narrative*, his informant Saukamappee relates how the Snake horsemen "dashed at the Peeagans, and with their stone Pukamoggin knocked them on the head." The Peigan's Cree allies gave the Snakes a taste of English powder and ball in return. The Real People admired both the gunplay of the Cree and the cavalry dash of their enemies. It would be their role to combine the two elements into an invincible whole, once they had obtained guns through trade, and horses through stealth.

They called the horse *ponokaumita*, which means "elk-dog," because the long-necked beast looked somewhat elk-like, but worked as a servant to man, like the dog.

Within the space of several decades, the Blackfoot left their pedestrian life behind. The horse extended both their range and speed of movement. A hunter could kill a dozen buffalo where once he killed one. Buffalo made the Nitsitapii rich. They became thorough equestrians; there were men among them, according to one account, who could tell a horse's age and health by the sound of its whinny; men who might possess a hundred head and yet know each one by its natural markings, or tell its name by feeling its body in the dark. Blackfoot culture reached its apex with the coming of the horse. Impossible the big painted teepees of buffalo leather, the willow backrests, the buffalo robe couches without horses to haul them. The savage cavalry had time now to indulge in the leisurely rituals of a warrior society, for gambling, horse races and counting coups around the fires greasy with feasting.

But horses inspired warlike ambitions, allowed scope for wandering and plundering. A warrior's wealth was measured in horses. For the buffalo Indians, stealing horses became a blood sport, an honourable profession. There were never enough horses. The Blackfoot raided far to the south, all the way to Mexico, according to Saukamappee, to obtain new mounts. They became the "Ishmaels of the prairie," with every man's hand raised against them—until they cut the hands off. The Hudson's Bay Company men heard how tough they were, but oh how rich, also! The problem was how to get by the pesky Cree intermediaries, cut out these middlemen, trade directly with the *Archithinue* (Cree for "stranger"), meaning the Blackfoot and their allies, the Gros Ventre (Big Bellies) and Sarcees.

One of the first whites to reach Chinook Country was Anthony Henday. He was prepared for these famous terrors but astounded to find them on horseback. A chief laconically declined his invitation to come east to trade. "Atticasish my Guide," writes Henday, "informed him I was sent by the Great Leader who lives down at the great waters to invite his young men down to see him and to bring with them Beaver skins, & Wolves skins; & they would get in return Powder, Shot, Guns, Cloth, Beads & etc. He made little answer; only said that it was far off; & they could not paddle."

Laughter at Napikwan's discomfiture (the word means "Whiteman") rumbled around the council fire, but the Indian sense of humour was wasted on Henday. This fierce cavalry preferred horses to canoes any day. They looked down on the bush Indians of the north. Rash young Henday was sticking his nose into a power arrangement between the Archithinue and the Cree. Lucky they didn't cut it off: but that would have caused interruptions in the flow of guns and trade beads.

Slightly peeved, Henday later adds: "They think nothing of my tobbacco; & I set as little value on theirs: which is dryed Horse-dung." Tobacco, in fact, was the only plant the Blackfoot cultivated, a plant of great spiritual significance.

The attitude of the Blackfoot toward the first white men ranged from hospitable to indifferent. Most historians have blamed Meriwether Lewis for the hardening of that attitude, and the fifty years of Blackfoot vengeance that followed the killings on the Marias. But Blackfoot hostility to white men was a strategic reaction to past experience. Their policy was, "Control any white traders who appear among us; prevent them from arming our enemies."

In Canada, only a handful of whites dared to explore Blackfoot country. With the help of the Peigan in 1793, Peter Fidler travelled farther south than any other Company trader and reached the Oldman River Gap within view of Massacre Butte. Fidler was a trained surveyor, come to map the country and to find more fur. He hunted buffalo with the Peigans, and left a vivid record in his journal of Blackfoot adapting to the iron age—and doing the first recycling. They were shooting arrows tipped, not with flint, but with "pieces of Iron hoop, old kettles, & old pieces of iron battered out betwixt 2 stones." He adds: "Men killed several Cows by running them upon Horseback & shooting them with arrows. . . . Sometimes when they happen to miss their proper aim (which is very seldom) they will ride close up to the Buffalo while at full Gallop [sic] & draw the arrow out & again shoot with it." Indian archers could draw and shoot again while the first arrow was still on the way. (25 December 1792).

The dangerous and more glamorous work of hunting and warfare fell to the men. A woman's life was more laborious. Fidler quickly adapted to the perquisites of the male Blackfoot. "The Indian Men generally goes first pitching along, the Women, children Horses & Dogs— all loaded more or less & by the time we think the Women have put up the Tent, Fire made &c, [*sic*] we contrive to arrive at that time & not before." (18 December 1792).

The Peigan liked young Fidler's pluck, and they treated David Thompson as a brother, but this greatest of all North American explorers had become Indian under the skin over time. James Carnegie, earl of Southesk, was the first tourist to visit Alberta. He travelled here for his health and pleasure in 1858, equipped with an indiarubber bathtub and volumes of Shakespeare. Camped on the winter prairies, he made notes on *Hamlet* while icicles ran down his nose. He was accompanied by twelve Canadian guides, and he says the Blackfoot liked Englishmen and disliked Yankees. (Most other writers agree. The Blackfoot called the British "Northern White Men" and the Americans "Big Knives.") Just the same, Southesk quickly changed his planned route to avoid Blackfoot war parties.

Colonel Robertson-Ross's attitude, expressed while he was reconnoitring southern Alberta for the Canadian government fourteen years later, suggests Southesk's opinion continued to hold true. Sighting some distant tribesmen, he and his men "all lay down with our arms loaded for altho the Blackfeet and Kootanies are friendly to the English we may be mistaken for Yankees (a horrible idea)."

The Peigan closely watched over Fidler's meeting with the Kootenay on the Oldman River. They pushed northern traders back to Rocky Mountain House and burned down their fort on the Bow River. Gold miners they simply shot like rabid dogs. So the traders had to cross the mountains via the difficult Athabaska Pass, now part of Jasper National Park, to trade on the Columbia. Rocky Mountain House, 150 miles from the American line, was effectively the southern limit of the Hudson's Bay Company influence in southern Alberta until the coming of the North West Mounted Police in 1874. The Company had a monopoly that encompassed what we call Chinook Country, but it was the Blackfoot who kept them from exercising it.

South of the border, the situation was much the same. Only with great difficulty, as Joel Overholster explains in *Fort Benton*, did the

Americans manage to establish the first fur trade forts in the Missouri Basin. Up to 1837, it was said that forty to fifty Big Knives died yearly at the hands of the Blackfoot—known as "Bug's Boys" (Bug being Beelzebub) to the Americans—while trying to penetrate into their heartland. One of the first Montana mountain men, John Coulter, discoverer of "Coulter's Hell" (the Yellowstone geysers and hot springs), barely escaped with his hide during four encounters with the tribe. On one occasion he survived a Blackfoot gauntlet and staggered three hundred miles stark naked to Fort Manuel Lisa on feet quilled with cactus spines. Coulter eventually quit the Blackfoot country in disgust.

Prior to 1831, the white fur forts were kept on the outer edges of Blackfoot domain. But in that year, the Peigan relented—perhaps they were short of Company ammunition—and allowed the construction of Fort Peigan on the Missouri at the mouth of the Marias. According to Joel Overholster's account, James Kipp, the founder, converted some alcohol into two hundred gallons of watered-down booze and five hundred lodges were drunk for three days at the grand opening. The rich trade, 6,500 beaver pelts that first year, ensured the whites would keep coming back. Other forts followed, and Fort Benton, destined to be the hub of trade for all of Chinook Country, was established as the head of navigation on the Missouri in 1860.

There were many massacres in Chinook Country, some of them small and intimate, some staged affairs with large casts, such as the killing of at least two hundred Crees and Assiniboines by Blood and Peigan warriors near present-day Lethbridge in 1870. The visiting Crees and Assiniboines attacked with muskets and bows; the locals responded with the latest in American rifles, obtained at a nearby fur trade post, Fort Whoop-Up. Jerry Potts, the son of a Peigan woman and a white trader and later the North West Mounted Police's most famous scout, led the charge. Of the battle, where he is reported to have taken sixteen Cree scalps, he once said, "You could shoot with your eyes closed and kill a Cree." Sometimes the celebrants were frustrated by a shortage of victims. In *The Blackfeet: Raiders on the Northwestern Plains*, John C. Ewers relates how the Crow carved up a captured Blackfoot warrior and scattered his parts around their camp.

Yet, taking a scalp was low on the scale of Blackfoot honours. To take an enemy's gun or his medicine bundle was a much greater honour. But mutilating the enemy dead was a way of telling their kinfolk what you thought of them, and also letting them know which tribe was responsible: a gashed throat meant Sioux; a gashed arm might mean Cheyenne. When it came to cutting up victims artistically, the Blackfoot bowed to none. A Blackfoot warrior told the artist Paul Kane of the time he skinned and stuffed a fallen Cree and left him where his tribesmen were sure to find him. Such tactics struck particular fear into white hearts, but white men collected Indian scalps for bounty in Texas, and stories were told of horse soldiers who collected Indian ears, and made tobacco pouches from women's breasts.

Rumours of gold in Montana and British Columbia brought a ragtag mob of whites through Fort Benton, the flood increasing with the end of the Civil War. The veterans were men steeped in violence, looking for their fortune. These "seizers," as the Peigan called them, piled off the steamers and scattered over the land like snowflakes—or dandruff. Some lingered in Benton's saloons, islands in the spring mud. A frontier street then was a meltwater pudding of mule dung and bull flop—its surface gay with a skiff of playing cards discarded from the gambling tables, its centre studded with drunks whom clouds of flies strove to lift into redemption.

In 1873, the Reverend John McDougall of Morleyville, Alberta, missionary to the Stoneys, travelling south for supplies with the Union Jack flying boldy from his wagon, arrived at Benton. He took a look at the inhabitants all armed to the teeth and full of a "revolting swagger" and said, "If these were the only products of our modern progress, then, for God's sake and humanity's also, give us barbarism." Though "Brother John" was no friend to the Blackfoot, he knew them well enough, and as far as he was concerned, "the wildest thing in this big country at this time was the ordinary whiteman."

Conflict between Blackfoot and increasing numbers of whites resulted in the Blackfoot War of 1863–1870. Fifty-six whites died in Choteau County in 1869 in scrapes with the tribesmen, and American conflict spilled over into Grandmother's Land. Natos-onistah (Medicine Calf), a.k.a. Button Chief, was a soldier against the whites in Montana, harassing the first crazy settlers, killing a party of woodcutters for destroying the poplar trees whose bark fed Indian ponies during winter camps. The U.S. Cavalry was soon hard on his trail, but he and other raiders dashed back into Grandmother's Land, a guerrilla tactic that was particularly galling to Americans. The Montana free traders were convinced that the evil HBC (they claim it stood for "Here Before Christ") had armed the Blackfoot and sent them to plunder horses and pelts in Montana Territory. In fact, the Hon. Company had been taking stolen American horses and other goods in trade for decades. The abuse was testified to by a number of witnesses before the U.S. Commissioner at Fort Benton in 1870. As a result, W.T. Christie, chief trader on the Saskatchewan, promised to "prevent as far as possible the trade of horses . . . suspected to have been stolen from the American Government or American Citizens." Meanwhile, American miners wanted to burn down Fort Benton for selling the Indians repeating rifles.

General Sully yearned to cross the Indians' magic Medicine Line after the Blackfoot, but cooler heads prevailed. A middle-aged Queen Victoria was sipping tea in England, but a hundred hotspurs milled restlessly around her petticoats, hungry for war. So Medicine Calf, not limited by boundaries, carried on the guerrilla war unopposed on Canadian soil.

To Medicine Calf, Hoise and his party were Americans, enemies and interlopers. They were also well equipped with horses, guns and other supplies the Bloods would have coveted. The party apparently camped for the night with the intention of fording the river, a few hundred yards to the north. When Medicine Calf and his warriors came upon these babes on the plains, their wagons were drawn up in a circle, but out in the open, when they might have availed themselves of safer ground nearer the ford.

American travellers who had heard Indians brag of the killings while at Rocky Mountain House in 1858 said the attack took place in darkness. A few of the whites escaped from the initial slaughter. They might have had a chance if they had taken to the riverine forest below the embankment. But, disoriented, wounded perhaps and mentally unhinged by the slaughter of friends and loved ones, they ran uphill to the bald summit of the butte, several hundred yards to the east. The Bloods followed at their leisure, surrounded them, and cut them down. The details of how the whites died, whether slowly or quickly, and whether they took some warriors with them, are not recorded. (The attackers very wisely kept their mouths shut in later years.) The Blackfoot and other tribes admired bravery in their enemies and detested cowards. A brave man might be dispatched promptly: it was an honour to count coup on a dangerous opponent. He went to the Sand Hills (the afterlife) ahead of you to tell the shades of your prowess, and to serve as a slave for ghostly kin. Cowards might be turned over to the women and children to meet a slower and much nastier end. Historian Hugh Dempsey, our foremost scholar of Blackfoot history, believes any women and children not killed by the initial shooting "would have been taken into the tribe and later turned over to local traders." As regards the Hoise party, there is no record of that having taken place.

*   *   *

As I stand on the summit of Massacre Butte, while cloud shadows coast for miles across the plain, I can't help staring at the earth, looking, I suppose, for some evidence of mayhem. But the remains of those hapless pilgrims were long ago collected for burial by the North West Mounted Police. The old marker below me, and the American depositions of 1870, condemn Natos-onistah as the leader of assassins. But his own people and some white traders, as well as the missionary John Maclean, thought very highly of him. Early in his career, he had adopted the enemy's Victorian habit of carrying letters of introduction around with him, some of which were noted by J. Ernest Nix in *Alberta History*. One dated at Rocky Mountain House in 1871 states in part: "Notose unistay, a Blood Indian Chief, wishes to inform the Public that in future he intends only trading at the Rocky Mountain House . . ." This seems a wise decision, given his likely reception had he returned to American territory.

Piqued to black humour, I picture him pulling one such missive from his shirt, and presenting it to the Hoise party at some point before the shooting started. It was written by an American Indian Agent, Gad. E. Upson, who had once described the Blackfoot as "degraded savages." Addressed "To the Miners and Explorers on the tributaries of the Saskatchewan, and other Whites at the North and in the Blackfoot Reservation," it reads, in part, "This will introduce one of the Medal Chiefs of the Blood Indians—he appears to be a good Indian and promises to aid and assist the whites rather than molest them." Upson requests that whites will "treat him and his people kindly . . . and report to me . . . the conduct of this chief." A venerable trader and contemporary of Upson's, William T. Hamilton, once said of Upson: "He knew as much about an Indian as I did about the inhabitants of Jupiter."

In 1877, Medicine Calf was the first of the minor chiefs to sign the Blackfoot Treaty, Treaty Number 7. In 1881, he showed his loyalty to a visiting Governor General by presenting him with the embroidered shirt off his back. John Maclean, who knew him well from 1880 to 1884, said of him: "Viewing this man's character after the lapse of years, I am compelled to say he was a noble man."

*   *   *

For many years the Blackfoot, refusing to be divided by the borderline, called the fur trade tune. They might trade robes at Fort Benton, Montana, and secure modern rifles from the Americans to use against the Cree and Assiniboine, or they might steal robes, peltries and horses on the American side and trade them to the British at Rocky Mountain House. But in 1869, a crushing blow was dealt the Blackfoot in Montana. The chinook blew rank with the smell of death that year. In Alberta alone, half the Indian population died of smallpox, including more than 2,500 Blackfoot.

At the same time, General Philip H. Sheridan decided to teach the Blackfoot raiders a lesson. He wrote to Colonel Philip R. De Trobriand at Fort Shaw, Montana: "If the lives and property of citizens of Montana can best be protected by striking Mountain Chief's band, I want them struck. Tell Baker to strike them hard."

Apparently Mountain Chief's band came up for punishment because one of his warriors, Owl Child, was implicated in the murder of a popular rancher and former trader in an affray involving Owl Child's wife. Mountain Chief was seething at this time over the cold-blooded murders of his brother and a small boy by toughs in Fort Benton. In 1870, people were fined in Montana for cruelty to animals, and for swearing in front of ladies. But although the white murderers of Mountain Chief's people were known by name, the authorities refused to arrest them on the grounds that no jury would ever convict them for shooting an Indian.

Baker had been ordered to avoid the camp of Heavy Runner, who was friendly to the whites. The band was camped on the Marias, thirty miles south of the Medicine Line. But on January 23, 1870, in temperatures of –20°F, Heavy Runner's people watched from their lodges as lines of ghostly bluecoats advanced through the blowing snow. Most of the fighting men were out hunting buffalo, and of those remaining, many were afflicted with smallpox. It made no difference. Baker told his men: "Open fire; continue as long as there is any resistance." His troops wiped out 173 Peigan, including 90 women and 50 children. One white soldier was killed, and one broke his leg.

Eugene Baker has a unique place in Chinook Country history; he has his very own massacre to commemorate his name. I can't help wondering how the fight would have gone if more warriors had been on hand, or if some of his victims had not been already half dead from disease.

One other footnote: Bear Head of the Peigan told author James Willard Schultz that as the shooting began, Heavy Runner ran, shouting, toward the soldiers "waving a paper writing that our agent had given him, a writing saying that he was a good and peaceful man, a friend of the whites." He was riddled with bullets and died with the note in his hand.

By world standards (though not from the perspective of its victims) the Baker Massacre was a modest affair. However, it marked a turning point in the fortunes of the Blackfoot. For generations they had successfully opposed white expansionism from the north and the south. Now many would flee into Canada to escape the Big Knives. Their power was broken, not by Baker, but by Baker combined with smallpox and whiskey. Revenge for the humiliation would now be exacted, symbolically at least, by the Sioux just six years later on the banks of the Little Bighorn. When the Sioux send the Northern Blackfoot a gift of tobacco and ask their help in the war against America, the Blackfoot will refuse to smoke it.

Canadians tend to believe such atrocities were typical only of the American West, the lawless West. But as Paul F. Sharp has shown in *Whoop-Up Country: The Canadian-American West, 1865–1885*, lawmen came to the American side of Chinook Country a decade before they arrived in Alberta. The law was upheld in Montana Territory by county sheriffs, federal marshalls and military force. But it was a law that protected only the whites. The Indians took revenge, according to their code, and Uncle Sam punished them.

"Tell Baker to strike them *hard.*"

Eastern Canadians, as well as eastern Americans, deplored the slaughter in letters to their newspapers and politicians. In the West, where atrocities like Massacre Butte were things that happened to relatives and friends, the whites were far more sanguine. The *Fort Benton Record*, 1875, relates how two white hunters were attacked at night by Indians near Carrol while sitting by their fire. One was killed, one escaped. The editor calls for the Army to retaliate. "An ounce of preventative is said to be better than a pound of cure. Let us have the ounce but let it be of the Baker kind."

Alberta in 1869 was more egalitarian than Montana: it was lawless for both races. Rupert's Land was about to be transferred to the new Canadian government in Ottawa; the Hudson's Bay Company monopoly on trade was finished. At the same time, American efforts to stamp out the whiskey trade in Montana Territory, personified by Deputy United States Marshall Charles D. Hard, were making business difficult in Montana. Alberta was a land of opportunity, by comparison. Looking north from Montana in 1869, wolfers, buffalo hunters and whiskey traders saw what we call now a power vacuum. No government authority whatsoever: no civilized white people, such as settlers or ranchers, to oppose the trade, and the several warrior nations much diminished by smallpox. But the survivors, God bless them, retained a powerful thirst for trade whiskey.

The whiskey trade had been outlawed in Montana since 1832, though the edict was seldom enforced. Trading booze to the Indians was profitable for the Yankee free traders because the liquor was so easy to transport by wagon or packhorse. It was watered down to make it go further; a thirty-five-gallon keg could make at least two hundred gallons of firewater, doctored with various condiments, such as red ink, chili peppers, chewing tobacco and bluestone to give it body, colour and kick. The Americans were not concerned about losing the clients: their experience in the States told them that their lawless trade could not last long. They had come to rip off the profits fast, and leave the mess behind them before civilization could catch them up.

Being enterprising gents, the free traders decided to take their products to the customer. In addition to whiskey and guns, the most sought-after items, the goods included many other items the Indians had grown fond of, such as salt, tea and sugar, as well as the usual assortment of hatchets, kettles, calico and trinkets. A.B. Hamilton and John Healy built the most famous whiskey post, Fort Hamilton, on Canadian soil in 1869. It was burned down by the customers upon completion, but Fort Whoop-Up rose like a Satanic phoenix from its ashes with the backing of the I.G. Baker firm of Fort Benton. While the Hudson's Bay Company fumed impotently, the profits of the trade ($50,000 U.S. in the first year) flowed south to Fort Benton, triggering a whiskey rush of traders heading north.

To protect themselves from their clients, the American-based traders built other barricaded cabins or crude forts in southern Alberta with names like Slide-Out, Robber's Roost and Stand-Off. Some of them were equipped with bastions and small brass cannons. The Indians were denied access to the trade goods except through a narrow, barred grille. The heavily armed traders lived like badgers in the interior rooms. Even the chimneys were barred to prevent entry. Proof that this protection was necessary at Whoop-Up is found in the *Helena Herald*, April 8, 1873. Whoop-Up was reputed to be "one of the toughest camps now existing in the Rocky Mountains [*sic*] . . . Ten days ago Kanouse, Latleur and Horness were in Abbott Saloon, when a band of Blackfeet walked in, shot them down and helped themselves to liquor. Abbott, in back room at the time, opened the door and with his Navy [*sic*] killed three in as many shots." The wounded whites survived the attack, though one of them, Kanouse, had part of his shoulder blown off.

The missionary John McDougall was one man who kept the federal government apprised of the goings-on in Chinook Country. This perambulating Methodist was a member of the first white family to take up residence in southern Alberta. He was a demon traveller, often carrying little more than a bible, and a Smith & Wesson .42-calibre revolver. His motto was to "trust in providence and keep your powder dry."

"Scores of thousands of buffalo robes," wrote McDougall, "and hundreds of thousands of wolf and fox skins and most of the best horses the indians had were taken south into Montana, and the chief article for barter for these was alcohol." To make matters worse, the Company (with whom McDougall's brother was in commercial cahoots) could not profit from the new eastern demand for buffalo hides, because the weight of the baled hides (around twenty-five pounds each) precluded their transport east by canoe. The enterprising Americans, however, could transport the hides south by wagon and load them on steamboats at Fort Benton, bound for St. Louis.

"There was no law but might," wrote McDougall. "Some terrible debauches occurred when whole camps went on the spree, as was frequently the case, shooting, stabbing, killing, freezing, dying. Thus these atrocious debauches were continuing all that winter not far from us. Mothers lost their children. These were either frozen to death or devoured by the myriad dogs of the camp. The birth-rate decreased and the poor red man was in a fair way towards extinction . . ."

Describing the same events at Fort Whoop-Up, John C. Ewers wrote: "Sometimes the Indians played a macabre joke on the traders by propping the frozen body of a dead comrade against the fort gate so that when the whites opened it in the morning, the stiffened corpse would fall on them." The Blackfoot heretofore had shown great respect for their own dead; booze was destroying their pride and self-esteem as well as their bodies.

Colonel P. Robertson-Ross, sent from Ottawa in 1872 to gather intelligence for the federal government on events in the North West, reported: "It is stated on good authority that last year eighty-eight of the Blackfeet Indians were murdered in drunken brawls among themselves. . . ." The traders told anyone who demurred that there was no force to prevent them doing as they saw fit. Captain Butler, in 1870, summed up the situation prevailing then with the comment "the wrong doer does not appear to violate any law, because there is no law to violate."

Contrary to another Canadian myth, it was not the Americans who first debauched the Indians with alcohol. In Rupert's Land, the Blackfoot probably acquired the taste by trading pemmican to the Hudson's Bay Company for watered down rum when other trade goods were in short supply. Canadian fur traders had long since become inured to the violence that characterized the drinking that went on around the forts. In 1814, Alexander Henry the Younger, a Nor'Wester, noted in his journal that the Indians asked for rum. "I gave them some. Grand Guele stabbed Capot Rouge, Le Boeuf stabbed his young wife in the arm, Little Shell almost beat his old mother's brains out with a club. I sowed garden seeds." By 1860, the practice was abolished. The product was killing off the clients.

The British regime was relatively tame compared to that of the Whoop-Up Americans. And yet Henry's suave detachment is as chilling as American ferocity. He plants his exotic garden of civilization in the wilderness, while his exotic booze waters seeds of destruction in its natural citizens. The American approach was more murderous and direct. But the two approaches had the same result for the Indians: annihilation.

In his memoir *From Home to Home*, Alexander Stavely Hill quotes a former whiskey trader: "If we had only been allowed to carry on the business in our own way for another two years, there would have been no trouble now as to feeding the Indians, for there would have been none left to feed: whisky, pistols, strychnine and other like processes would have effectively cleared away these wretched natives."

James G. MacGregor, commenting on this observation in *A History of Alberta*, maintains there was no deliberate plot by American traders to wipe out their own customers in this manner. Paul F. Sharp believes otherwise. "Ironically, many of the traders urged complete destruction of the Indians as the answer to the Indian problem." For their part, the Blackfoot certainly blamed the white man for introducing smallpox among them, as Sharp points out. "Blackfoot stories blamed the plague of 1869 upon the evil genius of an American trader who swore revenge for the loss of his horses to a raiding party. He allegedly purchased several bales of infected blankets in St. Louis and placed them on the banks of the Missouri River where innocent Indians filched them."

This story appears in different forms in western histories. L.V. Kelly, in *The Range Men*, even attributes a name, Evans, to the villain who spread the pox in revenge for his partner's murder. In fact, smallpox epidemics had been afflicting the Plains Indians since the early seventeenth century.

*   *   *

There is a throne—perhaps it was a million years in the making—carved out by the west wind from a sandstone outcropping on Massacre Butte. A passageway behind it is big enough for a buffalo cow to walk through, and the seat itself, a shapeless thing some six feet tall, must have been meant for a giant being like Napi the trickster/creator figure to recline on. I sit upon it, a mere pygmy, taking in the approaches to Massacre Butte. One could see a wagon train approaching for at least a day before it arrived. I ponder the message that Massacre Butte preserves: it was the Blackfoot, killing and being killed, who ultimately asserted sovereignty directly for themselves, and asserted the foreign policy, indirectly, by default, of the indifferent Canadian nation over these plains and mountains.

In the clinch, the British notion of the greatest good for the greatest number lies behind the Canadian spirit of compromise, a spirit at odds with the American cult of the individual. The Blackfoot discouraged American individualists from moving north. They discouraged settlers who would have disrupted Company business, and they discouraged competitors, free traders, which also suited the Hon. Company very well.

In 1867, the attention of Canadians was focused on Ottawa, where, on July 1, the new nation of Canada was born. No one noticed the death of twelve travellers in the far North West. Prime Minister John A. Macdonald claimed he would have been quite prepared to ignore the North West if the Americans would agree to stay out of it. But the American people, flowing like a tide under the aegis of Manifest Destiny, were moving into it for a good long time before he took steps to prevent their passage. It would take another kind of massacre, just six years later, to force the central government to "stable its elephant," the wild and woolly West.

As every Alberta school child should know, and as many of them do not know, Canadian destiny was shaped definitively by the actions of a party of Fort Benton wolfers in the Cypress Hills in 1873. The event was called the Cypress Hills Massacre, and it took place on Battle Creek in the shadow of Abel Farwell's American whiskey fort.

Once the Cypress Hills formed a nunatak above the Laurentide Ice; later they were colonized by plants of the montane life zone like the ones that grow around my home. To the people of the arid plains, the Cypress Hills have long been an enticing island of forest in a sea of grass. British explorer John Palliser wrote of them: "These hills are a perfect oasis in the desert we have travelled." By desert he meant the arid upland of the Missouri Couteau, the second great prairie steppe on which the hills form the divide between the South Saskatchewan and the Missouri drainages.

The Cypress Hills are a storied locale. Before the invasion of the free traders, they were a "neutral ground" used in common by tribes such as the Blackfoot, Assiniboine and Plains Cree. The Indian names, such as "Sweet Pine Hills," were ignored by the whites. French-speaking travellers, mistaking the lodgepole pines here for eastern jack pine or *cypres*, called the area *Montagne de Cypres*. This mistake, once anglicized, was enshrined in the atlas.

To the frontiersmen of 1873, horse stealing was a hanging offence, but among the Indians it was the equivalent, to paraphrase Sharp's analogy, of stealing home base. The whites of Alberta and Montana were of one mind on this offence, and that view hardened with time. It was summed up by the *Fort Macleod Gazette* in 1883 with the observation that "it would go hard on any Indian who attempts to hold down the opposite end of a rope over the limb of a tree." This conflict of values that Sharp alludes to—the white man's extreme sense of personal property, the aboriginal view of commonly owned resources—

remains unresolved to this day. On a day in 1873, it would lead to the deaths of many Assiniboines and one Ed Grace, a Canadian adventurer.

Earlier that spring, a party of wolfers, fresh from the Alberta plains and loaded with pelts of strychnine-killed wolves, had their horses stolen, possibly by Cree horse thieves, while camped on the Teton River near Fort Benton. Denied help by the authorities, they formed a vigilante posse, and tracked the thieves north into Canada. They lost the trail in the thick forest of the Cypress Hills.

Eventually, the party showed up at Farwell's post, looking for information and refreshments, and finding too much of the latter. According to Fort Walsh historians camped a hundred yards to the south were three hundred North Assiniboines under the leadership of Chief Inihan Kinyen, and Chief Manitupotis (Little Soldier), including some fifty warriors.

The timing of the Benton men was disastrous. The Indians were enraged at their treatment by the white traders. They had made numerous threats, particularly against Moses Solomon's post, and the whole community of Métis hunters, traders and Indians was in a state of "armed truce," as Sharp put it. Farwell himself had lost some horses to thieves, including one belonging to George Hammond, a friend of the Benton men. Farwell put up the posse the night before the massacre, and cracked open the whiskey supplies. Later that night, an Assiniboine brought in Hammond's stolen horse, and Farwell rewarded him with two gallons of "pop-skull" whiskey, which apparently wound up at Little Soldier's camp. But the horse went missing again the next day, a Sunday.

According to most accounts, both whites and Indians were drinking heavily on Sunday morning. Around noon, Hammond learned his horse was missing again. Enraged, he grabbed his rifle and vowed to get two horses from Little Soldier to replace his own. Farwell intervened, and went to the camp first to negotiate. Bad idea; according to Sharp, no one present trusted Farwell's facility in the Assiniboine language. Little Soldier himself was drunk and *hors de combat*. He insisted the horse was not stolen, but was merely grazing near by. He offered two Indian ponies as hostages for Hammond's, according to Sharp's account.

Meanwhile, Indian women, sensing a fight, were retreating from the area. The young men, fired up on bugjuice, had stripped themselves for war. Now they strutted in the clearing, taunting the nearby group of bleary-eyed whites, and brandishing their weapons. Little Soldier was in no shape to control these young warriors.

Hammond attempted to remove two horses from the back of a lodge, but was warned off by the warriors. The Benton party came to Hammond's aid, and all deployed themselves in an old stream channel fifty yards from the camp. Apparently they either refused Little Soldier's offer or didn't believe Farwell's interpretation of it. Fear and whiskey courage were driving events on both sides. Farwell blamed George Hammond for firing the first shot, but Métis witnesses said four braves, firing warning shots, were first. The result was a general firefight.

Each member of the posse was armed with a repeating rifle and two revolvers; the Indians had their old trade muskets. Three times the Assiniboines charged the Benton party, and three times they were repulsed. One party of whites eventually charged the camp and began shooting wounded men as they lay in the doorways of the lodges. In the Fort Walsh account, Little Soldier's mother-in-law relates how he was killed. She and her daughter were leading the intoxicated warrior from his lodge when he saw the dead body of his father. "He threw up his arms and . . . turning to them he said, 'White men, you will know what you have done today. You never knew a Woody Mountain Assiniboine Indian to harm a white man.' . . . at that moment he was shot through the heart by one of the party of Americans . . ."

Eventually, one Ed Grace, a Canadian, was shot to death by a warrior while coming to the aid of two other whites, and the invaders fell back to Farwell's and Solomon's posts, to continue showering the camp with bullets until nightfall, when the Indians fled.

In the morning, an unknown number of dead Assiniboines (anywhere from thirteen to sixty, according to different accounts I have read), including women and children, were sprawled in the clearing and willow bush. The atrocities included the rape of two women and the decapitation of Little Soldier. Farwell, whom Sharp portrayed as a dubious witness, pinned the decapitation on S. Vincent (whom Sharp has identified as a French-Canadian). Farwell and another witness claimed the chief's head was spiked upon a pole. It would not be the first time such a banner was set up on these plains—by Indians as well as whites. The other banners flying that day were the Stars and Stripes, hoisted illegally over illegal whiskey forts on Canadian soil. In the aftermath, the whites, sober now, buried some of their victims. Ed Grace's body they buried under Solomon's post to protect it from mutilation, then the traders burned the posts down. Farwell and Solomon loaded their pelts and goods and whipped up their teams for Benton, while the posse went on its way.

News of the massacre broke in eastern Canada in a wave of nationalism and anti-Americanism. The Benton men were described, among other things, as "American gangsters" and "American scum." The fiction that this outrage could be committed only by American frontiersmen has been maintained in every Canadian written history of the atrocity that I am aware of. But as Sharp pointed out back in 1955, the thirteen-man posse was, in fact, an "international brigade." Sharp wrote: "Of those whose nationalities can be ascertained, Ed Grace, George Hammond and Donald Graham were Anglo-Canadians while Jeff Devereaux, S. Vincent and Alexis Lebompard were among the several French-Canadians." One can quibble with Sharp on this issue. Farwell accused Hammond, a Canadian, of firing the first shot. However, Hammond did not ride with the posse. He seems to have been an associate of Farwell's at the time, and two other men may also fit this category. Hammond was known to the posse; he had trapped with Evans, the leader, the previous year. They were both members of the short-lived Spitzee Cavalry, a rascal brigade that coalesced out of a whiskey keg at High River with the object of trying to force rival trader Johnny Healy, at Fort Whoop-Up, out of business. (This band quickly evaporated again, legend has it, when Healy held a lighted cigar over a powder keg and threatened to blow it, and himself, to blazes.)

But although Canadians took part in the Cypress Hills Massacre, it remains an anomaly in western Canadian history. It took place under the Stars and Stripes, and represents a temporary extension of American frontier mentality into the Canadian North West, an ethos summed up most graphically by General Sheridan's infamous statement to Tosawi of the Comanche: "The only good Indians I ever saw were dead."

*   *   *

I have stood on the summit of the Cypress Hills, staring north beyond Medicine Hat where the prairie ends in a curved horizon like the ocean, and gazed south to where it washes against Montana's Bears Paw Mountains and her Sweetgrass Hills, and I have begun to grasp how 30 to 60 million bison might have been nourished on the Great Plains.

Travellers once stood on promontories like this and found the earth black with buffalo for miles in every direction. Captain Palliser, stalking a Canadian herd two miles distant in July 1858, says they "were in such large numbers that their peculiar grunt sounded like the roar of distant rapids in a large river, and [caused] a vibration also something like a trembling in the ground." The herd was always accompanied by hundreds of big, grey wolves, ready to pick off weaklings.

What is hard to understand is how the multitudes that had fed human hunters for millennia could be reduced to a few dozen survivors by 1879.

Coincident with the decline in Blackfoot fortunes, there arose a tremendous appetite in eastern North America for buffalo meat, especially tongues and smoked hams, and for buffalo hide. In 1880, the U.S. Army noted 5,000 professional buffalo hunters and skinners camped in northern Montana. Hide hunters were busy converting the Blackfoot "real food" into the raw material of furniture leather and machinery belts for eastern tycoons, leaving most of the carcasses to rot on the plains. In 1869, 15,000 hides went down the Missouri. In 1872, with four whiskey forts operating in the Cypress Hills alone, the figure jumped to 40,000. The year 1879 is usually given as the date of the extinction of the buffalo in Alberta, so it is interesting to note that in 1878, 75,000 hides were shipped out of Benton.

Some buffalo did survive to breed in captivity, thanks to Walking Coyote, a Pend D'Oreille Indian, who saved four calves, a gene pool for the future, during a hunt on Milk River, Montana, in 1874.

Along with the buffalo skinners came the most despised of all the white interlopers, the wolfers. They spread strychnine in buffalo carcasses and killed not only the plains wolves (now long extinct) but every other carnivore, including Indian dogs, golden eagles, foxes and, occasionally, starving natives. A hundred wolves might sometimes succumb to one carcass. In one season alone, 40,000 wolf pelts were shipped out of Fort Benton.

Looking back from 1911, L.V. Kelly recalled in *The Range Men*: "Across the boundary the slaughter of the penned-up herds of buffalo still continued, and the white and red hunters made huge kills. One hundred thousand buffalo robes were sold out of the Yellowstone valley from the winter hunt of 1880–81, but never again would there be such a shipment for the herds of millions had now dwindled to a few thousands, and the day of the buffalo was gone."

A poignant entry in the *Fort Macleod Gazette* for November 1882 adds an ironic counterpoint to Kelly's recollection: "There are from three to four hundred buffalo hunters between the Yellowstone and the Missouri rivers and the indications are that buffalo will be plenty this season." In fact, by then the hunters outnumbered the buffalo, and many would be ruined that season, having bought entire outfits and hired skinners to process buffalo that no longer existed. Time and again, the historical record reveals how limited is our species' powers of observation of even the most obvious facts about our environment.

In 1883, Indians on both sides of the Medicine Line were reduced to snaring gophers for food. In Montana, some six hundred Peigan are thought to have died of starvation that year, before the Indian Agents received supplies for them.

The white man is deservedly blamed for the extermination of the bison. But white observers, coming from Europe where game was in short supply, complained of wastage by the Indians also. It was noted at an Alberta buffalo pound by Peter Fidler in 1793, and commented on by George Catlin at Fort Pierre, South Dakota, in 1832. Hunters sometimes shot more buffalo than their women could butcher; at other times they took only the tongues or hides to trade for whiskey.

The recent fashion is to reinvent the First Nations as the noble savage *recherché*, the conservators of all wild game and the only American people morally qualified to speak about men living in harmony with the environment. They never killed an animal they didn't need, and never wasted its flesh, and so on. As a Westerner, I will not curtsy to this cant.

The historical evidence is clear that there came a turning point in history when the buffalo Indians lost some of the old respect for the game that sustained them.

We can certainly find many reasons for the breakdown of old values based on white influence, but to blame the white man entirely is to regard the Indians, paternalistically, as children incapable of reason, which is how the early whites regarded them. It denies them sovereignty not only retroactively but currently. It sounds like the "white man's burden" revisited.

I have stated my quibbles, but I know who was victimized, and there is the matter of proportion to remember. Getting back to the white wasters, the "seizers" as the Peigan called them, nobody knows how many thousands of buffalo were shot from the windows of passing trains for "sport" and left to rot. In some cases, nearly every male and many of the female passengers opened up on the herds for the sheer hell of it with everything they had, from derringers, through shotguns to Sharp's buffalo guns.

As Tom McHugh, pointed out in *The Time of the Buffalo*, General Sheridan believed that the buffalo hunters did nothing but good by destroying the Indians' food supply. "Send them powder and lead if you will; but for the sake of a lasting peace, let them kill, skin and sell until the buffaloes are exterminated. Then your prairies can be covered with speckled cattle and the festive cowboy, who follows the hunter as a second forerunner of an advanced civilization."

*   *   *

In order to build an advanced civilization, we have to understand what ground we are building on; we have to look at past mistakes, and stop repeating them.

The view from Massacre Butte takes in our advanced civilization. To the west, clouds spill eerily over the edge of Turtle Mountain and pour down over the scar of the Frank Slide. To the north, I behold the drowned extent of the Oldman River, beloved of the Peigan, sacred river of time. I hear the roar of two highways, see miles of barbed wire, see mile after mile of seismic lines scarring the mountains, dust cutting up from the naked fields to the east, two helicopters conducting seismic surveys for poisonous sour gas right over the place where I live, and a long string of logging trucks rolling down Highway 22, fully loaded with trees so thin they look more like corral bars than saw logs.

Let's not knock that barbed-wire fence, though. We need the fences, so we can keep the cattle out of the grain. We need the grain to feed the cattle; we need the cattle because we killed off the buffalo. We had to kill the buffalo: they would have wrecked all the fences.

I left Massacre Butte. Ultimately history merely annoys me, but modernity sometimes drives me to drink, so I stopped at the Falls View Bar in Lundbreck for a beer on the way home. There I ran into an Indian acquaintance. I told him how I felt the country was going to hell in a basket.

"We should have killed all of you when we had the chance," he said sympathetically.

"There were too many of us," I said.

"Still," he said, "We should have killed more of you . . ."

I shook my head. "No offence, but quite frankly, I don't think your hearts were really in it towards the end."

He nodded. "We sure let ourselves get distracted all right."

"The horses were okay though," I suggested.

"I liked the horses," he agreed.

We drank our beer. It wasn't bad, either. "Better luck next time," he said. We shook hands and I went back out under the fierce logic of the merciless Alberta sky.

5

HUNGRY MEN IN
STRANGE HATS

~

Three major factors slowed the advent of European settlement in Alberta's Chinook Country. One was the concept of the Great American Desert, promulgated by the earliest white explorers of the region. The second was the savage military prowess of the Blackfoot nation, and the third was the lack of efficient mass transportation over vast distances and rugged terrain, which the railroad would eventually overcome.

It is in the nature of arid lands to be visited by recurring drought. To describe our climate as temperate is to spin a lure for suckers, but "arid" or even "semi-arid" (the latter is technically correct in this case) are not popular words to use when you are trying to attract farmers to a region. In Chinook Country, all life must compete with the thirsty west wind for a share of whatever heaven bestows.

The Palliser Triangle, named for Captain John Palliser, was a zone notorious in the agricultural history of the Canadian West. "Triangle" is a bit of a misnomer. Imagine instead a whale-shaped area on the map of western Canada. Its belly lies on the 49th Parallel, its back is humped north to the head of the Battle River, then down between Saskatoon and Regina in Saskatchewan. The whale stretches, west to east, between the Rockies and Turtle Mountain, Manitoba, and its outline encompasses 51 million acres.

The Triangle contains sagebrush, cactus and sand dunes, and a big piece of short-grass prairie, but it also includes stretches of richer mixed-grass prairie, and even some inroads of the aspen poplar parkland that forms a fertile belt around its perimeter. In 1690, Henry Kelsey, the first white man to see our interior plains, called some parts of them "desert." David Thompson saw these plains in the eighteenth century. He said they were suited mainly for the "herdsman." "These great Plains," he wrote, "appear to be given by providence to the Red men for ever, as the wilds and sands of Africa are given to the Arabians."

My forebears, who broke their hearts trying to grow wheat in the middle of Palliser's Triangle, would have agreed. "They should give this country back to the Indians," was how they used to put it. It is a telling expression. Wasteland, desert, barren grounds—these were all terms commonly used to describe the high plains of Alberta and Saskatchewan before the advent of the Euro-white settlers. In their eyes, acculturated to European landscape, a land without gardens and orchards was barren ground, fit only for savages to inhabit. My own ancestors agreed completely with that outlook.

The American historian Walter Prescott Webb has shown how the concept of the Great American Desert as an uninhabitable region lying east of the Rocky Mountains and west of the 98th meridian can be traced back to the writings of Coronado, then forward in time, through the reports of Zebulon Pike, Lewis and Clark, Stephen Long and other American explorers. The term was applied to a region that extended from the Gulf of Mexico to the Parkland belt, north of the Great Plains. Influential explorers of the day declared it unfit for agriculture and virtually uninhabitable.

By 1850, the "Great Desert" was a term marked on the atlases available to Captain Palliser prior to his British North American exploring expedition of 1857–1860. Palliser himself called his triangle "a northern portion of the Great American Desert." Indeed, the land showed Palliser its desert heart. In July 1859, in the Middle Sand Hills, near modern Medicine Hat, his men and horses suffered intensely from the lack of water, and from the fiery touch of hot sand underfoot. Palliser reported that the whole region that we now call southern Alberta was not fit for agriculture. However, his estimation proved far too pessimistic; he visited the country during a drought, and after the herds of buffalo had passed through, denuding the land of the season's grasses. Palliser ran out of water within a day's ride of what would eventually become the Marty family homestead, now part of Canadian Forces Base Suffield, north of Medicine Hat.

Palliser's report was not the first negative appraisal of Chinook Country. The Hudson's Bay Company, anxious to protect its monopoly, doctored the reports of explorers such as Henry Kelsey, deleting his positive accounts about gardening potential in some areas of the west. Not everyone fell for the Company's ruse, or accepted Palliser's verdict, either. Minnesotans felt their westward progress blocked by the Great Desert. But looking north they saw not more desert, but rich lands in Manitoba controlled by a mere handful of Métis settlers and hunters. When Palliser passed through St. Paul in 1858, newspapers were urging the citizens to agitate for American annexation of the Canadian northwest.

Despite Minnesota's prescience of northwest potential, and despite the waning of Blackfoot power, this image of the Great Desert held sway in the public mind into the late nineteenth century.

*   *   *

I sit staring at an old map depicting the historic route followed by the North West Mounted Police along the International Boundary from Dufferin, Manitoba, to Fort Whoop-Up, and I hear my Aunt Sis telling me, emphatically, "They should never have put that line there in the first place." My Aunt Sis is American-born, pro-American still—but just don't meddle with her Canadian health care benefits! I have heard the same sentiments about the 49th Parallel expressed many times in Alberta. When I was a Calgary schoolboy in the 1950s, our teachers bragged that Calgary, Alberta (unofficial headquarters of Chinook Country), contained the largest concentration of American citizens to be found anywhere outside the United States. Most of those remaining are employed in keeping Alberta oil and gas flowing south. Americans have also been prominent in the ranching industry from the outset. As I write this, the last major Alberta packing plant has just been purchased by an

American corporation. An official with the cattlemen's association applauds the move: the corporation is large and offers access to the American market. It will be good for the cattle business. "Ranchers tend to ignore that boundary anyway," he says. The statement reflects the fact that since the days of the whiskey trade, economic gravity has pulled our raw resources relentlessly southward.

Southern Alberta, Chinook Country, is the most American of all our Canadian regions. My father's ancestors were American; my father-in-law's parents were American: the ancestors of many a south Albertan are American, and American expansionism has had a vital impact on the history of the West in general, and southern Alberta in particular. America has left its imprimatur on two key images that Canadians think of as typically Albertan: the cowboy and the oilman, both viewed in Alberta as rugged individualists.

Since the 1840s, America's expectation regarding Canada was that the Dominion would one day fall into her hands like a ripe plum, in accord with Manifest Destiny. (From an economic point of view, meaning the actual ownership of our resources, one must conclude that the plum fell long ago into the Yankee grip.) American expansionist sentiments increased with hostility to Britain and Canada after the Civil War. Anglo-Canadian capitalists and politicians, loyal to the British Crown, were well aware of American ambitions. They began to realize that Canadian settlement of the northwest was the key to financial success; they must win for the St. Lawrence Valley the commerce that was benefiting St. Paul and Fort Benton. Gold strikes in British Columbia in the 1850s had already drilled the British colonies there into Ontario's financial consciousness. British Columbia had been promised a railway link as the price of her entry into Confederation in 1871. She needed markets for her fisheries and lumber industries, and a continental railway would bring the settlers to the northwest to create a market for her, and for eastern capitalists.

Beginning with Manitoba in 1869, the Canadian government finally acted to impose its vision of the West's destiny, which was to be a dog wagged by its tail, the St. Lawrence Valley. But the Orangemen of Upper Canada didn't bother to communicate their plans for the northwest to the English settlers and the Métis buffalo hunters of Red River, who, like the colonists of Vancouver Island, had no particular love for "Canadians" in the first place.

The Métis people were descended from unions between Euro-whites (traders/voyageurs) and Indian women beginning, as some would express it, nine months after the fur trade first commenced. (The word Métis is derived from the Latin *miscere*, "to mix.") The federal government sent surveyors into the field to survey Métis lands near Fort Garry on the Red River without first guaranteeing these largely francophone Catholics any language, education or homestead rights under the new Dominion. Nor would they be allowed to control their own resources. This confrontation resulted in the Red River Rebellion of 1870, led by Louis Riel. Ottawa learned nothing from its high-handed treatment of Westerners, except that a railway was required to transport troops more efficiently into the West in order to put down the anti-Ottawa faction. Branded a criminal, Riel spent years in exile in Montana between rebellions, although he was twice elected as a member of Parliament for Red River, despite being unable to occupy the seat. Ottawa's indifference to the needs of the first Manitobans would result in Riel's return, and the much bloodier Riel Rebellion of 1885. The contemptuous attitude of the central government toward western aspirations in 1870 established a climate of distrust in east–west relations that has persisted ever since. Ottawa bashing, a tiresome but effective ploy still in use today by western politicians, feeds on this inbred attitude, especially in the un-Canadian, pro-American political climate of today's Alberta.

Eventually, the Canadian Pacific Railway would be Canada's answer, the Conservative Party's answer, to American ambition and the land-loving truculence of the Métis and their Cree allies, those first patriots of the West. Acceptance of the railway notion did not come easily, given the popular view of the northwest as a wasteland. Its main opponent, the Liberal politician Edward Blake, dismissed the railway as "two streaks of rust across the wilderness," and maintained, "It will never pay for its axlegrease." He would have been right, except for the government's generous subsidies and land grants, which would make the CPR the richest corporation in the land. Prime Minister Sir John A. Macdonald rammed bills through in order to zipper shut the young nation's overcoat from coast to coast, and exert sovereignty over endless miles of rock, bush and prairie, even though there were no markets, initially at least, to support it. The National Policy plank of the Conservative campaign of 1878 rested on three legs: settlement of the West, protective tariffs to shield eastern industries from American capitalists, and the railway as the great connector of east and west.

The North West Mounted Police, sent out to impose law and order on the West, were also the advance men for the great eastern capitalists, here to create a safe haven where they might operate, to drive the Yankee peddlers off the pitch, for the railway and settlers were soon to follow. As it happened, political scandals and economic recession delayed the coming of the rails until 1883. The railway czars would turn to the government for loans to complete the job, and Sir John A. had no choice but to oblige. "The day the Canadian Pacific busts," as one Tory politician put it, "the Conservative party busts the day after." The triumph of Canadian protectionist capitalism over Yankee free enterprise would have to wait for steel rails to ride in on.

The government had been dithering with the creation of a mounted police force for the West since 1869, but the news of the Cypress Hills Massacre was the spur that brought the North West Mounted Police into being. They wore the same red coats that had been favoured by the British military for generations. To the Indians, red meant British and a more honourable standard of justice than the brand dispensed by the bluecoats to the south.

But in September 1874, the police were a ragged force of hungry men in strange hats (pillbox forage caps or white pith helmets, to be exact). Their situation was parlous. They were a mounted force; their mounts were fuelled on grass, but prairie fires and buffalo had denuded the forage of the entire region. Scattered across the prairie in the trampled wake of the police were dead or abandoned horses and oxen. Many of the troopers were afoot, leading their weakened mounts. Their surviving saddle horses and oxen, the latter pulling supply wagons and artillery pieces, were gaunt and starving. They were under constant surveillance by Sioux and Blackfoot warriors, who bided their time, sizing up the new intruders.

The police had ridden and marched a thousand miles from the end of steel at Fargo, North Dakota. Their much-vaunted journey was indeed a great military feat. But it was nothing special compared to the mounted travelling done by vagabond Métis buffalo hunters of Red River and Fort Edmonton, who covered a thousand miles and more every year, hunting and trading. Few writers thought their journeys worth a paragraph.

The policemen, though strong and fit, were eastern greenhorns, not plainsmen. And they were afflicted with a guide, a Fort Benton man, whom they suspected of being a spy for the whiskey traders. Yet they were not exactly lost. The officers knew their latitude and longitude on the earth's surface, but Fort Whoop-Up, their destination, failed to materialize as planned thanks to a faulty map. Commissioner George A. French and Assistant Commissioner James F. Macleod detoured their hungry troopers and scrawny horses onto good foraging at the foot of the Sweetgrass Hills, where there was grass for the horses and buffalo for the men. The commanders rode south toward Fort Benton, into the very womb of the whiskeymen, to make a deal with Ontario's economic enemies. They left their men to shrug their shoulders and sing their favourite campfire song, to the tune of "God Save the Queen":

Confound their politics;
Frustrate their knavish tricks,
Get us out of this damn fix,
God save all here.

Eighteen seventy-three was a year of economic recession. The fortunes of the great Benton traders I.G. Baker and Brother and T.C. Powers were declining. Rather than being greeted as pariahs, the officers and their escort were the toast of Fort Benton. The hostesses of the town were delighted by the cultivated manners of these handsome redcoats. I.G. Baker, merchants and traders, and backers of Fort Whoop-Up in the first place, provided Commissioner French with the best guide his force could hope to find in Blackfoot country—Jerry Potts. His presence alone identified the redcoats as the friends of the Blackfoot in those days.

Macleod signed with the traders for purchase of 40,000 pounds of supplies, the first of many contracts with the Fort Benton traders. In that era, letters mailed in Alberta (known then as the North West Territory) had to bear American stamps: Fort Benton provided the only postal and banking service available to Canadians. It sold the police everything they needed, from bullets to bourbon. The Queen's police and Uncle Sam's bluecoats were the economic key to Fort Benton's success until the late 1880s. To Bentonites, NWMP represented New Wallets, More Profit. No doubt the traders appreciated the irony of acting as Ottawa's contracted paymasters to the police that had been sent west to put them out of business.

Most of the smaller whiskey traders had fled the Alberta scene well in advance of the police. Colonel Macleod and his men, guided by Potts, arrived at Whoop-Up on October 9, 1874, startled to observe the Stars and Stripes flying from the bastion. The fort was managed by D.W. Davis, who was conveniently away at the time. A few months earlier, Davis had told the Rev. John McDougall that "we will flood this country for one more year with whiskey," and that until the police did arrive "we will do as we **** please."

The gates of the fort stood wide open. The police had been warned to expect a pitched battle with five hundred hard-bitten whiskey traders. They drew up their two mortars and their brace of nine-pounder guns, ready for a fight. Colonel Macleod strode into the enclosure and rapped on the nearest door.

It creaked open, and one lonesome Dave Akers—a crippled Civil War veteran, and a former partner in crime to mountainman Liver Eating Johnson—greeted the new authority. He offered, not violence, but invitations to a meal of fresh vegetables and other luxuries; it was gladly accepted. For the travel-hardened troopers, the friendly reception was an anticlimax after three months in the saddle. They struck the Republic's flag and ran up the Union Jack in its place: Canada had arrived in Chinook Country to assert its sovereignty over 35,000 square miles of Blackfoot and Cree territory without firing one shot in anger.

Jerry Potts led the Mounties upstream to the site of today's Fort Macleod. There they built the first police fort on an island in the middle of the river. The founding of Fort Calgary, at the junction of the Bow and Elbow rivers, would follow in 1875. Overnight, Fort Macleod became the business capital of southern Alberta, just as Fort Benton was the nexus of northern Montana. But Fort Macleod was entirely dependent for its lifeline to the world on the Missouri steamboats and the efficiencies of Fort Benton's merchant princes. The Powers and Baker concerns ran the new town's biggest stores.

The vehicle of commerce on the Whoop-Up Trail between the two forts was the bull train. Each unit of several wagons, pulled by up to twelve yokes of oxen, was driven by a bullwhacker, who walked beside the oxen and kept them moving with a steady stream of creative obscenities and the pistol-like report of a fifteen-foot-long bullwhip. The long trains, richly loaded with supplies, were tempting targets for marauding warriors. But bullwhackers were a feisty lot, and came equipped with six-shooters, war knives with ten-inch blades and Spring-field rifles. Their tendency, when approached too closely by Indians, was to shoot first. At night they circled their high-wheeled wagons and threw down their bedrolls underneath them. They lived on coffee and chewing tobacco, and on bacon and bread cooked in Dutch ovens over a fire of buffalo chips. They raced along during the daylight hours at up to fourteen miles a day. The trains unloaded supplies for Macleod, and loaded buffalo robes and wolf pelts for the return trip.

Fort Macleod in the seventies was a town with the hide still on, but a place where some of the whiskey traders the police had subdued went on to become leading businessmen and politicians. The defiant booze peddler D.W. Davis, for example, was later elected in 1887 as the first member of Parliament for the North West Territories. But Harry "Kamoose" Taylor (Kamoose means "wife stealer"), who owned the Macleod House, was the most colourful inn-keeper. His hotel sported a signboard with some famous rules of conduct for frontier travellers. Some examples: "Spiked boots and spurs must be removed at night before retiring. . . . To attract attention of waiters or bell boys, shoot a hole through the door panel. Two shots for icewater, three for a deck of cards, &c."

One of the force's first investigations centred on the Cypress Hills Massacre. At a riotous hearing in Helena, the police failed in their attempt to extradite the accused whites. The entire State of Montana had come to the defence of these innocents. In the local press, they were portrayed as rugged, honest frontiersmen victimized by the British, hav-ing merely defended themselves from the unwarranted attack of depraved savages. The atrocities they were accused of, however, were not reported to the public. Eventually, the police did apprehend some of the posse then living in Canada, and they were tried for murder at Win-nipeg. The confused, contradictory testimony at both the hearing and the Canadian trial reflected the drunken state of mind of the partici-pants at the time of the atrocities. The men were acquitted: the event was seen by the judge as a frontier fight. "Whiskey was the real cul-prit," wrote Sharp, "and this fight was another of its fearful effects upon the western Indians."

A cynical response would be to observe that the law in this case did not serve the Indians much better in Canada than it did in Montana. That would be too harsh a judgment by far. In those early days, the

Plains Indians regarded the Mounted Police as friends and protectors. In *The Law Marches West,* Sir Cecil E. Denny remembers Indian hospitality. "We were always made welcome, the best they had was placed before us, shelter from frequent storms given us in their lodges." In Montana at the same time, Denny recalls, a state of warfare existed between the races. The soldiers travelled only in force into Indian camps, and "many a poor fellow caught alone was tortured and barbarously mutilated."

The arrival of a police force on the plains long before the railway was pushed through created an atmosphere of civility on the Canadian frontier after 1874 that was the mirror opposite of the American experience. But this legacy had been purchased at a terrible cost in Indian lives. In 1877, one thousand lodges of Blackfoot, Peigan, Bloods, Sarcees and Stoneys and 15,000 horses were camped at Blackfoot Crossing to hear the terms of Treaty Number 7, presented by Lieutenant Governor David Laird. They were offered one square mile of reservation land for each family of five persons, the right to hunt freely on any unoccupied Crown land, ammunition for hunting, breeding stock for cattle production, farm implements and seed. Twelve dollars in cash would be paid to each man, woman and child upon their chiefs' signing the treaty. The chiefs and minor chiefs (or councillors) would receive twenty-five dollars and fifteen dollars respectively per year, and each member of the tribe would receive five dollars per year.

The buffalo hunting was good that summer, and the tribesmen were happier, more prosperous and more peaceful than they had been for years—happier than they would ever be again. But the Blackfoot were no longer able to direct the course of Alberta history, a fact their wiser leaders clearly acknowledged. Some of the chiefs predicted that signing the treaty would bring them bad luck, that it would drive the buffalo away. But Crowfoot, their greatest leader, told them, "The Police have protected us as the feathers of the bird protect it from the frosts of winter." The actions of the police in ridding the country of whiskey peddlers profoundly influenced his decision to sign.

One dissident at this first, and last, love-in between the police and the Blackfoot was none other than the minor chief Medicine Calf, known to the whites in 1877 as Button Chief. Seen by some as a meddlesome interruptor of the proceedings, with hindsight, it is clear he had a better idea of what Indian resources were worth than the more illustrious leaders of his day. Medicine Calf wanted the police to pay for the wood they had consumed since 1874, suggesting a sum of fifty dollars to each chief and thirty dollars to each tribesman. But the principal chieftains demurred at this, and lost a chance to bargain for this scarce plains resource as a result. Lieutenant Governor Laird baldly suggested to the assembled chiefs that, in truth, the Indians should have paid the Great White Mother for sending the police into their country. This produced an outburst of laughter that must have been tinged with real bitterness. The Napikwan chose to hear it as Crowfoot's people appreciating Laird's witticism.

By 1878, when prairie fires set by the U.S. Army kept the buffalo from moving north into Alberta, the prophecy of the Blackfoot elders was proven correct. In 1882, the American Army closed the border permanently to Canadian Indian and Métis buffalo hunters. The *Apatohsipiikani* (North Peigan) were cut off from the *Aamsskaapipiikani* (South Peigan), and the Blackfoot of Alberta and Montana became a divided nation, while the buffalo economy that had sustained them was no more.

The railway reached Calgary in 1883. The locomotive's bell sounded the death knell for the golden age of Fort Benton, as Canadian goods flooded the market. By 1888, American railways would render steamboat traffic redundant in Montana. Railways in both countries had annexed the frontier into the domain of the "eastern Merchant Princes," as one western capitalist described them. Calgary, supplied by American bull teams before the advent of the rails, would soon supplant Fort Macleod as the economic capital of the region. Fittingly, the most important cargo the Canadian Pacific Railway carried back east that year was buffalo bones. They were ground up for fertilizer, or turned into charcoal for clarifying sugar. (In the U.S. they sometimes sold for eight dollars a ton.) The bones were gathered from the prairie by the pioneers and by destitute Indians and piled along the railroad right-of-way like stacks of cordwood, hundreds of yards in length.

Of course, the buffalo herds were long gone by then. What was left after their demise was a silence, a great absence of teeming life, in which nature held its breath, awaiting the next onslaught. What was left for the interlopers was grass that seemed limitless, free to the first rancher who threw his bedroll down in it.

The free-range ranching industry was founded in Alberta and Montana because public grassland was there for the taking, and because the chinook wind blows so often here that no hay crops were required to winter the stock—at least that's what the ranchers thought back before the turn of the century. Grass is the foundation of the ranching economy. These dun-coloured hills look unpromising indeed. But despite their shrivelled appearance, these mixed grasses, the rough fescue, needle and thread and wheat grass, are nature's finest hay: unlike domestic varieties, they cure on the stem, and store energy in the stem, where cattle can obtain it, rather than in the roots. But cattle will not paw through the snow to get food, or use their noses as snowplows, as buffalo do, so the snow clearing done by the chinook was absolutely essential to support free-range cattle ranching in the first place.

The first ranchers disdained to straddle the iron seat of a hay mower, staking all on the constancy of the chinook. They would have to learn the hard way not to take the wind for granted.

British and Anglo-Canadian financiers are often paid lip service as the founders of the cattle industry in Alberta in the early 1880s because they provided the cash that made ranching on a huge scale possible. Earlier, in fact, some of the same investors had played an important role in founding large ranches in Wyoming and Montana, but that was after migrating southern cattlemen had shown them the possibilities for investment. British speculators invested heavily in the ranches of Texas and Wyoming because they expected to realize profits of from 30 to 60 percent on each head of beef fattened at no cost to them on the public range. Thence comes the seed of the cattleman's attitude of noblesse oblige, suckled with his momma's milk, that he has a God-given right to pasture cattle on government land.

Despite the British involvement, the ranching industry in Alberta, like the oil industry, has southern, not eastern roots. American cattlemen were displaced northward then westward by the pressure of settlers encroaching from the east, and by Sioux and Blackfoot resistance to their advance in Wyoming and Montana. But gold strikes in Montana and British Columbia created a market for cattle, driven in from Oregon in the 1860s.

Few Albertans had heard the word "cowboy" until the first large Alberta cattle herd, seven hundred head, was driven east across the mountains from Columbia Lakes by a man named John Shaw in the autumn of 1875. In those days the pioneer rancher's main problem lay in keeping the buffalo from enveloping his stock and sweeping them off. His cows were courted by the buffalo sires, but his bulls might be trounced by rival behemoths or bloodied by enraged buffalo cows spurning unwanted romance.

By 1875, the free-range cattle industry in Montana was well advanced. There was a roundup of 23,000 cattle at Sun River that year.

As the Montana ranges gradually became stocked, more and more cattlemen crossed the Medicine Line to scout for ranches in Alberta where grazing was free—and free of sodbusters and hostile Sioux. However, bands of rustlers and starving Blackfoot tribesmen played hell with the free-ranging stock in 1877. The U.S. Army, destroying Blackfoot lodges and confiscating their goods, finally drove the Canadian Blackfoot north for keeps in 1882. With no game left in the country, they had no choice but to settle on their allotted lands. With the Blackfoot safely corralled, twelve hundred settlers established themselves in southern Alberta in 1883, and 25,000 head of cattle grazed between Calgary and the Medicine Line that year. By that time, the Montana ranges were heavily overstocked with cattle, all to be fattened on the free grass. This would soon result in large British-owned American ranches—such as the Powder River Cattle Company, a Wyoming concern—taking up big leases in Alberta, where the grass was still fat.

Alberta was still a district of the North West Territories when Senator Matthew Cochrane, a Montreal entrepreneur and cattle breeder, set up the first great Alberta "ranche" (as he styled it) in 1881. He used his political influence in Ottawa to lease grazing land, and together with associates obtained the rights to 190,000 acres of Alberta's best grazing land at a price of one cent per acre. The government also waived the tariff on American cattle to encourage the stocking of the range.

The newcomers to Chinook Country had not been around long enough to experience the freakishness of its weather. The Canadian prairie had not yet earned its well-deserved epithet as "Next Year Country." Instead, visiting journalists promoted the Alberta climate as a haven for the stockman, and called it "God's Country," an expression also used by the Métis to describe the Saskatchewan river valley. The Blackfoot had seen winters of arctic ferocity, but nobody asked for their opinion. In fact, the first two years of the Cochrane operation were an unmitigated disaster, as the chinook declined to clear the ranges of snow; thousands of head of cattle died. But years of milder winter weather dulled the lesson. The chinook was so frequent in winter that putting up hay was a waste of time. In 1886, and again in 1906, the petulant wind tired of being taken for granted, and turned the winter over to the blue Norther. In '86, when temperatures dropped to −54°F, even the antelope were dying, wandering into the prairie towns looking for grass. In the fierce winds and drifting snow that winter, 25 percent of the southern Alberta cattle died—50 percent at Medicine Hat. Steers were found with their throats and bellies punctured by the branches of trees they had tried to eat. Others choked to death on the hair they had chewed from the piled dead. Gaunt and desperate, they drifted through the streets of town by the hundreds, misery on hooves.

In the evil winter of 1906, the new barbed-wire fences across the range added to the carnage. Cattle drifted until they came to a fence: there they piled up and died by the hundreds. They wandered into outlying farms and into town, where they followed people into their houses in their desperation to find forage. The lesson of 1906, which wiped out many a rancher in Montana and Wyoming, hit home. The wind could not be trusted: hay must be put up every year for the stock; it must be purchased if enough could not be grown. The days of the great Cattle Kings of the open range were virtually over by then, though ranching, destined to grow into a multi-billion-dollar industry, was still in its infancy.

*   *   *

Along with squatting on an aristocratic scale, it was British ranchers who introduced the local cowboys to the elegant equestrian sport of polo. Cowboys in polo helmets: the image has been seized on by a number of writers to emphasize the difference between the Alberta Frontier and the American version, forgetting that the Americans had also taken to the sport. Along with polo and upper-crust ballroom attire there came a less harmless eccentricity. A polo match at Fort Macleod, *ca.* 1896, occasioned Abee Carter Goodloe, an English tenderfoot, to leave us with an insight into the origins of a uniquely Canadian brand of racism, which resides more in attitudes and words than in overt violence.

She described how the Union Jack flying over the fort, and some elegant English ranchers talking about their last visit to their clubs in

London, impressed her "with the feeling that this [is] England. In the morning there is polo, and one sees young English fellows in patent-leather boots and baggy khaki riding trousers, for which they have sent all the way to England, dashing up and down and 'running the whole show.' The Indians standing around look like aliens, like visiting strangers. The Englishman doesn't insult or bully the Indian. He simply ignores him, and by pursuing a life as nearly as possible like the one he would lead in England, and by appropriating whatever suits his interest or fancy, he makes the Indian understand that it is *his* country. He impressed the fact upon him even in his games."

And, as a result, learned nothing from the "alien" about the true nature of the earth these sophisticates had appropriated.

This Raj on the Range was short-lived. It was the Texans and Montanans (among others) who put their stamp on Alberta cowboy culture. One of the true originals of Alberta ranching was Frederick William Ings, a Charlottetown boy who came west in 1882. He would later write: "Most of our riders came from the States and they taught us all we knew of cattle lore. Over there cattle and roundups were an old story: to us they were a new game." One of the greatest bronc busters of the Alberta range, and one of the most liked and respected, was a black Texan named John Ware, who was never bucked off a horse until the day his pony tripped in a badger hole and killed him.

The Americans brought with them the skills of open-range ranching, and they brought the conservative attitudes of the Confederate south, which are still, in modified form, with us today. In Alberta ranching, as one observer put it, "The brain was British, but the heart was American."

So the cucumber sandwich set who remained on the range learned to slouch into California saddles on American quarterhorses, wearing Texan boots and hats and Spanish *chaparejos*. They learned to swing a Mexican rope and croon to the dogies with a Montana drawl. English equestrian habits made virtually no impression on the bronc busters. Instead of hacking with a polo mallet, Englishmen learned to "punch a hole in a rope" to "set a trap" and snare a calf by the hind feet: they learned to team rope a steer and "take a dally" (from *da la vuelta*—"to turn around") with the rope around the saddle horn without burning off a finger. One cannot rope a steer, or a black bear, or a coyote—all favourite cowboy sports, from an English saddle, sans saddle horn.

Cowboy culture flourished, yet the era of the great ranches was short-lived north of the Medicine Line. Ultimately, it was not in accord with eastern ideas of what the West must become. The Cattle Kingdom did not create the necessary markets that eastern manufacturers needed in order to expand their profits. What was needed were more settlers (more consumers in other words), one on every quarter section if possible—the eastern pattern, doomed to failure in the drylands from the outset.

As early as 1890, another short-lived boom began, as the first wheat crops began to flow in a golden stream into the CPR's grain cars. Most of the good land was already taken up in the United States, and European and eastern settlers were finally looking to western Canada. As the wheat began to flow east on the CPR mainline, a steadily increasing stream of settlers began moving west.

The men and women who would grow wheat in the Great Desert were on their way to the new Promised Land.

6

RAIN FOLLOWS THE PLOW

~

I was raised in a desert among the Philistines where there were no poets to people the landscape with heroes, where history waited to be discovered in a land where few people valued what had happened before their own arrival. In a land where they do not value that yet. They said the land was new, but they forgot the First Nations had peopled it for 11,000 years or more before the whiskey traders, gold miners and sodbusters fell upon it.

Medicine Hat in the summers of my childhood was a heaven few recognized. The sagebrush prairie began at our garden gate and stretched southward all the way to the Cypress Hills, and south again into Montana. Stray horses leaned over the fence; cowboys galloped by. Herds of deer came up from Seven Persons Creek to steal sweet corn from our garden, and jackrabbits jumped in alarm in the bunch grass every time a boy jumped the fence.

These Shortgrass Plains of southeastern Alberta, covering 12 million acres, are a singular intrusion of desert plants and exotic critters among the mixed-grass prairie and aspen parklands that prevail from Calgary to Edmonton. The lesser cacti, the prickly pear and pincushion, determine where boys can run without peril. Cowboy fantasies waned on the day I was bucked off a bareback pony into a bed of prickly pear cactus.

It was a wait-a-bit landscape of rose thorns, gooseberry thorns, buffalo-berry thorns, Russian thistle and cockleburs. I learned early that, from the point of view of the cocklebur and the beggar's-tick, the only thing useful about me were my woollen socks, which were velcroed into folds by their sticky seeds. I was not a boy; I was a vehicle by which plants propagated themselves.

Some of the desert beasts came with stingers too. There is a species of scorpion that lives on the sandstone cliffs above the South Saskatchewan. We used to take them to school in matchboxes for the edification of female classmates. Rattlesnakes rustled between the cucumber vines in our garden for my eyes only, politely vanishing when Jesse, my mother, came out to pick weeds. "Don't tell fibs," she said, but she kept a sharp eye out just the same.

Aridity, dust and wide open space are the prairie abundances. Average annual precipitation is eleven to fourteen inches. But when rain did fall, it tended to be a cloudburst, a lake emptied on our heads. Then the sun danced do-si-do with the hot-tempered west wind, and, working up a thirst, those two dried up the earth so fast that it was spider-webbed with mud cracks wide enough to trip a jackrabbit.

Picture a sky red with dust. Picture a flat, treeless expanse green in May and burnt to umber by August. This is why cowboy hats are so big: men have to live in their own shade to survive the sun. The heat had a way of immobilizing a child. You feel time slow down as a whirlwind dances forward out of the sagebrush, a moving container for oblivion. Your mother screams a warning from the garden and the wind hovers in front of you, darts sideways, dissipates. You want to ask why the sky is green. Then a ball of ice the size of a golf ball falls at your feet. You stoop to pick it up, and the next one hits the back of your neck so hard it knocks you to your knees. After the storm, the exhilarating perfume of wet sage drifts in through the blowing curtains, and I cannot tell where the prairie ends and my bed begins.

When I was a small, grubby boy, peering over the tops of plants, my view took in the table-like flatness of the near vista and the black outline of the Cypress Hills to the south. Gazing west, I could not see the Rocky Mountains, fabled place of snowy peaks my father, Orland, sometimes drove his truck among, himself a giant among giants to me.

In utter July the heat waved. Spoken words wilted out of the air. I stared westward through vast shimmerings toward the hamlet of Seven Persons, saw eerie snow-capped pyramids hovering above the earth in a desert mirage. The mountains were two hundred miles away.

I stared and licked my dry, chapped lips. Someday, I told myself, I will go there. The disloyalty made me feel guilty. Behind me I heard the rumble of the town, heard it sputtering and hissing like a stoked forge. In summer it was one vast furnace of brickyards, glass factories and steam engines, the latter huffing and wailing over a maze of hot steel in the CPR marshalling yard. Gas flares lit the sky at night: the whole city sits above a reservoir of natural gas that fuels its industries. Kipling immortalized it as "the city with all hell for a basement," and in summer, hell overflowed to the top storeys to wage heat wars with the sun. Out on the prairie, I felt the bronze tongue of that orb slowly eating me alive.

Sometimes the heat of summer was too much even for the rattlers. One breathless day, when she had left the door wide open to catch a breeze, my mother found a side-winder coiled around the cool base of the toilet bowl. And fled outside in magnificent hysterics until a neighbour had removed it.

There was no clear-cut distinction between urban street and wild country in those days such as we find today. Pavement and sidewalks were scarcer; shopping malls had not been invented. There was no television (at least in the Hat) keeping kids indoors. So the old world at times could flow into the new. The touch of a serpent is one of my earliest memories. As a child of three or four, I saw a length of dirty grey rope quiver in the heat on my uncle's front lawn at Redcliff. I stooped and picked it up, laughed to see it twist around my arm; felt the tickle of its scales and heard a humming in my ears. This was a gift of some God to a fool he had chosen, for a purpose not yet revealed, but my uncle snatched the gift away and hoed the rattler into bloody threads: I wept for what I would never touch again without fear, without danger.

I turned my back on the streetlights and sought refuge in the coulees of my second home, the prairie. Prairie kids back then ran through the summer half-naked, Coyote's children, brown as the wide South Saskatchewan River, in the days before the ozone hole, when the sun was the god of childhood. The big river held me in a fearful fascination.

My father claimed that my Uncle Sid once caught a sturgeon there so large he had to winch it ashore with his jeep. Such a fish might inhale a small boy by accident, or so I reasoned. I stuck to the pragmatic shallows and the sandy bottoms, hunting for basking "suckers" and freshwater clams. Sometimes my bare foot slipped into quicksand, but I was light and quick myself, and swam clear. The river washed me clean and the prairie wind was my towel. Yet I had a violent soul, waging war on creation with a BB gun and flung rocks. Once I went to pick up a mourning dove I had casually shot. The beautiful creature was still warm, and over its heart there was a perfect teardrop of blood. Out from the amber water of Seven Persons Creek, out from the riverine forest of willow and cottonwood, a love of wild creatures and wild places crept stealthily into my heart. I learned in childhood what every prairie creature knows: it is the coulee, the creek bottom, the river valley that offer the only shelter from the freezing winds of winter and the hot winds of summer. The coulees teemed with deer, pheasants, cottontails and grouse. In the coulees the birds sang defiance to the wind.

In those hungry winters, my father was often on the road. Often as not his earnings were eaten up on repairs to his battered gravel truck. Mom and I subsisted at times on her British pride, thrift and "bread and dripping." But in the summer coulees banquets of purple chokecherries hung from every bough: there were rose hips, saskatoons and gooseberries among the thorns. I came home with my mouth stained purple, and my stomach queasy with excess.

In school I was troubled by words: kept stringing them together into poems and essays. I won prizes at the Medicine Hat Exhibition and Stampede, the cultural highlight of the year. My father grinned at me and scratched his head. I was a kind of idiot savant to teachers who knew my background—the son of a truck driver with a grade school education and a feisty Limey war bride. "She's not a Limey," I told them stoutly, overhearing their gossip. "She's a Geordie." I knew the difference between a Londoner and a Northerner, even if they did not.

We all lived in "wartime houses," look-alike homes built for returning servicemen and their families. Conceived during war, we warred over turf in the alleys, grabbed garbage can lids for shields, and barraged each other with bricks and stones. We fought in the playing fields, we fought on the beaches and we never surrendered.

There were many lean days in Medicine Hat. It took all my parents' energy just to survive. At an early age I learned, watching my father sweat, that hard work alone was not enough to escape from the trap of poverty. When there was no work on road construction Orland would grab a scoop and shovel his three-ton truck full of gravel to service people's driveways, or load topsoil for their gardens.

He landed a contract once to cut up four war surplus aircraft for scrap. The only tool for cutting scrap he could afford in those days was a fireaxe that he found still strapped in position in one of the aircraft. There was no money left over to hire a welder: he was a desperate man. The temperature rose to 100°F in the shade of no shade, and a black cloud of mosquitoes rose to greet him as he started work. I remember him under the hard glare of the prairie sun, astride an arc of fiery aluminum—the fuselage of a derelict fighter. Returned from the war in Europe, shirtless and bronzed like a god, he lifts the axe over his head to destroy the very angel of death and destruction itself. He brings the axe down, and from the screeching metal, pink hydraulic fluid shoots forth like the bursting of a great shark's veins. I see him sliding, falling out of the sun, crashing down in the sagebrush. There is blood on his face as he gets up, shaking his head like an angry young bull. He paws at the dust to clear his boots of oil. He climbs back up on the beast to strike again. This is what he dared to do, to put bread on our table.

Loyalty to one's flesh and blood was engrained in me at an early age. But I watched the wealthier fathers of the town, listened to what they said, and I figured it out. What they had that my father lacked: only an education. The resolve to be educated formed in me like a great flint, goading me on.

All around me in those days, there was an extended family—aunts, uncles, cousins and grandparents, an element I never questioned, an order I could not imagine ever changing. I realize now that it would have been impossible to starve, or to go without a roof overhead, in the midst of that clan. It was only in my grandfather's house that I felt uncertain of my claim of kinship. I was oppressed by the silences that gripped the place when the old couple were alone. But family visits brought out the best in them. There was a dartboard on the porch that was the centre of any gathering. Aunts and uncles brought in cases of beer. On rare occasions, there was a huge wheel of white Ontario cheddar so sharp it bit back at every bite; there were piles of grandmother Ora's crusty baked bread and crackers, and thick, sweating coils of grandad's spicy homemade liverwurst that a small boy could never get enough of. The dart game was a boisterous, quarrelsome sport and my grandmother with her one good eye was an ace. As soon as I was old enough to hit the board, I was pressed into play, and roundly criticized for any lack of concentration as if I was a grownup.

"Stop mining the cheese, you little devil. Now make that deuce!"

I'm grateful for happy memories, because overall, in my memory of my grandfather, John Claude Marty, or J.C. as he preferred—his name was actually Claude John Marty—he seldom had a smile on his craggy face. In his seventieth year his face was often clouded beneath a shock of thick, black hair fading to grey. His tall, bony frame did not form a lap for a grandchild to sit on. During family visits, he usually retreated to sit, one arm propped on a big roll-top desk in his bedroom that I thought so grand, smoking his pipe like an office worker taking a break, not like an old sodbuster at all. He seemed to have a lot on his mind.

"The old man," said Orland one time, "made a big mistake when he moved out here. He regretted it all his days."

I think now J.C. must have been imagining himself a man of wealth and power surveying his estate in those pipe dreams. He didn't seem approachable to me: I had the notion that he didn't approve of my English mother, and perhaps not of myself, born in northern England when my dad was overseas with the Calgary Highlanders. There was not much love lost between father and son, either. The old man's rough and miserly attitude toward Orland had embittered my father at an early age.

My dad moved us to Calgary when I was thirteen. Years went by when I had no contact with J.C. whatsoever. It was my grandmother's death in 1970 that finally brought me back to Redcliff. I came as a stranger. The little boy was now a married man. I was the first of our family to attend a university and now I had a graduate fellowship in English literature. My warden service job in the summers saved me from turning into a total bookworm. I thought I was going to be a professor, but that was the cautious, conservative side of my nature asserting itself; the prairie side. The wild mountains were my real home.

Since the early sixties, I had been writing songs and performing in bars and coffeehouses on the folk music circuit, and that year of 1970 I had just learned that some of my poems were to be anthologized by

House of Anansi Press. I was flying high. Then came the news of my grandmother's death.

I drove down through the bleak, winter flatlands to Redcliff, and knocked on the door of my Aunt Dot's place. Suddenly after all those years during which I had seldom thought about my childhood, I was surrounded by the family again. They were a garrulous, inquisitive clan, all demanding an account of what I had accomplished and why had I stayed away so long, and why wasn't Myrna with me. Explaining my motives for all my esoteric pursuits to the family, I might have been speaking in Greek. They were more puzzled than impressed.

"How much do they pay you for teaching that English stuff?" demanded one uncle. And when I told him: "Christ, Sidney, you can make four times as much working in the brick factory."

"Maybe so. But I'm quite happy doing what I'm doing."

Which wasn't true. I had in fact already decided to drop out of graduate studies and join the warden service full time, but I kept that to myself.

It was a day in December, and thirty degrees below zero under a shocking north wind. I stood with my aunts and uncles, their faces streaked with frozen tears, watching Ora Belle's coffin lowered into earth as hard as iron. I was twenty-five years old, and as the clods of frozen earth drummed hollowly on the burnished wood, I realized with a shocked dismay that I had a hundred questions for her that she would never answer.

At the family gathering afterwards, J.C. seemed a bit friendlier. The loss of his wife had not really sunk in at that point. He addressed me in his gravelly, well-bottom voice: "You sure look like a Marty now." I had the wide shoulders by then, typical of the breed. I stared at the old man's high cheekbones, dark complexion and thick black hair. He looked more like a Sioux patriarch, in a certain light, than a white man. I wanted to ask him if there was some Indian blood in our family but decided he might resent the question. An aunt informed him that I played the guitar, that I performed for money in coffeehouses and bars. He didn't ask me to play for him when I went into his room, where he sat, as usual, pulling on his pipe. He had decided to give me some advice, for the first and only time.

"Son, don't be a musician," he said sternly. "I never met a good man who was a musician. Study the law, boy: become a lawyer." He stared at me keenly. "Forget about this music stuff," he said, and he waved his slab of a hand through the air, dismissing it.

J.C. looked far younger than his years. I thought of him as forever sixty-five. I would have been shocked if he had told me he was ninety-one years old. His hands were gnarled with arthritis, but at ninety-two he would complain about being cooped up in a nursing home with a bunch of depressing old fossils who wouldn't go to the Legion with him for a beer. But that day I looked at the old, gaunt man sitting there with his pipe and thought, "What would you know about music?" I thought myself unique, the only musician in the entire family. I was a proud, uptight kid and too easily offended. I could see that there wasn't much point in telling him about my literary pursuits. What should have been a new beginning between us was allowed to trail off into silence.

I was wrong about the music, too. It was much later that I learned that J.C., who dismissed music so disparagingly, had once played the pump organ, that he would play all night at country dances during the Dirty Thirties. They told me my late Uncle Allan, J.C.'s eldest, played fiddle back then, and accompanied his father. They were in demand. That was in the days when J.C. still had hope. The days he wanted to forget, to turn his back on. So he denied me his music, and his interest, and I returned the compliment.

Since then, experience has taught me not to wait for the elderly to break the ice, especially those who have been imprisoned in it for decades.

*   *   *

The Martys are a sociable but somewhat pugnacious bunch; some of us mellow with age, some grow decidedly waspish. My mother's family are Geordies, a race of Britons who hang around the border waiting for Scots to beat up—at least until the pubs in South Shields open for the day. The progenitor on that side was a crusty Norwegian sea captain, and my uncles were all merchant mariners.

When I started researching the Marty background, I discovered something significant right away: we seem to favour crime fighting as a trade. We seem inclined to try to right wrongs: we tend to be sheriffs. According to the American family, my great-grandfather Robert was a sheriff in either Minnesota or North Dakota. J.C. was likewise a sheriff (he may have been an under-sheriff or a mere town marshall) in North

Dakota, and later town constable in Redcliff. Great-Uncle Oscar was the most famous crime fighter. He served twelve years as the sheriff of Choteau County, Montana, once the den of Missouri border ruffians and whiskey traders. The county seat was, and is, none other than Fort Benton.

Nowadays it is a sleepy river town, but history clings to every meander of the fabled Missouri. My cousin Grace Nelson lives in a small house a stone's throw from the riverbank. Recently she sent me a picture of an old brick building built in 1881, bearing a door with a sign "Choteau County Sheriff Dept." Her note to me reads, "Sid—my home, 1931 to 1943—Choteau County Jail." The building was a duplex containing cells on one side and sheriff's residence on the other.

Oscar was known to his friends as "Kingfish." A lifelong Democrat, he was elected state representative for Choteau in 1945. His moment of hubris came when he was told by the party whip to vote a certain way on a bill. "Nobody tells me how to vote," declared Oscar. "If it's not good for Choteau I won't support it." His state career was brief: one term. He summed it up thus: "I went down to Helena to cut me a fat hog: but I found out that if I didn't vote for John Doe's bill, he wouldn't vote for mine." Oscar went back to Choteau and settled for being mayor and town marshall of Big Sandy, Montana.

Then there was yours truly, a former sheriff of bears and tourists. (A national park warden has full police powers—Smoky the Pig.) Ultimately, I don't like being told how to think, either. But it was comforting to know that I was not the first Marty to stand, and fall, on his principles.

What I have related about my great-uncle's career was unknown to me as a small boy in my grandparents' gloomy house in Redcliff. But I recall how the house suddenly filled with sunlight when my American great-uncles Oscar, Joe and Robert came to visit. They came with blankets, clothes and corn whiskey, with food and pipe tobacco, gifts to shower on their brother and sister-in-law and any other Canadian relative they knew to be in need. And suddenly the old man, J.C., had a grin on his face, and my fireplug of a grandmother moved around the place as skittish as a filly.

I remember them, hale and boisterous storytellers, men in stetson hats and big suspenders: big eaters, big drinkers at times, but, most importantly, big with laughter and life in what I thought of as repressive times. And now this crime-fighting clan is divided, like the Blackfoot nation that preceded them in Chinook Country, by the 49th Parallel.

Robert's and J.C.'s motives for moving west are a genuine mystery to my own father, who was born in the drylands near Suffield, Alberta, in the heart of Palliser's Triangle. He once said to me, "I don't understand why in hell they ever came out here in the first place. . . ."

It is a fraught question; the time-honoured family answer to it, "They were going to make a fortune growing wheat," explains nothing. Coming to grips with that question has led me through extensive readings of Alberta history. But the deeper I delved, the more my own people melted into the shadows of more famous people and bigger events. I was left with a childhood memory of my grandfather, a shadowy figure seated at a massive rolltop desk, smoking his pipe in the dim light of his bedroom.

Last year, my Aunt Dot, who had inherited the desk, decided to give it to me. It is ornate and very fine, but it is not a rolltop. The tiny writing table folds down on hinges. There is a small bevelled mirror on the top, and the left side consists of a small china cabinet. So much for childhood perspectives.

* * *

William Cornelius Van Horne, president of the Canadian Pacific Railway in 1888, had a problem: between Ontario and the Great Divide, and from the 49th Parallel to the Arctic Ocean, a mere 60,000 human beings provided traffic for his railroad. A goodly number of those people were Indian and Inuit, and had very little need of railway transportation. Even the more populated region, Ontario, was still half uncleared bush. In those days Ontario cities were heated with fuel logs rather than coal: conditions were primitive and eastern manufacturers were struggling for survival. The nation was poor, and to be fair, a great deal of its financial substance had been expended to finance the construction of the Great Railway. There is absolutely no doubt in my mind that without that railway, vast stretches of the western provinces would not now be Canadian, but part of the "Excited States" instead. But that expenditure, the price of entry into Canada, would have to be recouped: Westerners would have to pay it back—again and again.

What was needed, after the last spike was driven in 1885, was nothing less than the complete settlement and subjugation of the prairie wilderness by the agricultural *conquistadores*. What was needed, as years went by, to create traffic for the railway and markets for eastern factories, was farmers. Clifford Sifton, the minister of the interior noted for his immigration initiatives, stated his policy succinctly to the world: "Only farmers need apply." The Canadian Pacific Railway and the Canadian Interior Department embarked on a massive advertising program to lure farmers into the Canadian northwest. The agriculturalist would finish the conquest that the buffalo hunters, wolfers and rangemen had begun.

There was only one problem with this equation: most of the land in question lies west of the 98th meridian, which divides the humid lands of the east from the semi-arid plains. In *The Great Plains*, Walter Prescott Webb points out that west of that line, annual precipitation seldom exceeds twenty inches a year, the minimum amount necessary to grow crops successfully by the usual established methods, methods developed in more humid climates. The Canadian solution? Send out a scientist to prove that aridity is not a problem, that wheat can grow without rain. Then flood the market with a barrage of propaganda, a mixture of facts, half-truths and outright lies to attract the settlers to "The Last Best West."

In the year before the rails came to Calgary, Professor John Macoun, the Dominion botanist, had published a book, *Manitoba and the Great North-West*, which helped demolish the myth of the prairie desert and to replace it with another myth, the prairie as agricultural paradise.

Macoun was a self-taught botanist, an Ulster-bred Irishman with a tremendous faith in his own opinions. He was as simple an optimist about agriculture in the drylands as Palliser had been a pessimist. Neither man had the story completely right. In 1882, Macoun was sniping away at the prairie soil of the southern plains with a shovel. He was deeply impressed by what he discovered; one could sink a moldboard plow in the sod and turn a furrow all the way from Manitoba to the Great Divide. Then he chanced upon a homesteader who had raised a small wheat crop in a drought-stricken field near Maple Creek, Saskatchewan, surrounded by sun-baked clay and lifeless sagebrush. For Macoun it was an epiphany: he pole-vaulted to the conclusion that "sage-brush and cactus [are] no proof of aridity." He would report to the Dominion government, erroneously, that much of the West had the same agricultural potential as the more humid and productive parts of

Ontario. "The apparently arid lands were only so in appearance . . . all the land where not covered with sand or gravel would yet 'blossom like the rose.' "

Macoun didn't stick around long enough to get the point. The point was not that you couldn't grow wheat after the first plowing: chances were good that enough moisture might be already present in the soil to grow the initial crop. The trick was to receive enough Godwater to make it grow the next year, and the next. In Palliser's Triangle, annual precipitation might be twelve inches or less. Macoun discounted this scarcity, claiming that "aridity vanished before the first efforts of husbandry."

Paul F. Sharp has pointed out how this claim of Macoun's was a widely held belief on both sides of the border. The American general John Gibbon believed that the farmer, "by his labours, produces those climatic changes which are known to follow his footsteps." The agricultural sages of the day nodded in agreement and intoned solemnly, "Rain follows the plow." One eminent Canadian scientist, Henry Youle Hind, called Macoun a "charlatan" and predicted that sodbusters in Palliser's Triangle would lead lives of misery. But Macoun's view held sway: it, and other like opinions, would eventually be taken up by the Department of the Interior and by the publicity department of the CPR in a bid to attract settlers to the West. Palliser's judgment had been reversed. Instead of being regarded as a desert, the West was about to become the Promised Land.

As early as 1890, Canadian agents were touring North Dakota and Minnesota to persuade American farmers to move north. The railroad offered free passage to farmer "delegates" who would examine the Canadian potential and report back to their countrymen. A number of these farmers were originally Canadians who had been lured south in the first place by inflated propaganda bruited about by American railroads promoting the American West—railroads, it so happens, that had employed William Cornelius Van Horne as either superintendent or general manager prior to 1882.

Down in Underwood, North Dakota, my grandparents encountered Canadian Government Agent J.C. Koehn, who advised Americans looking for land to see him first, since he knew "the farmers who are anxious to sell, as they want to go to Western Canada."

DO YOU WANT A FREE HOMESTEAD?

Where you can raise crops which will make you comfortable and independently rich? If you do, you will find this opportunity in

WESTERN CANADA

Land can be obtained there for the asking. It will raise from 25 to 30 bushels of No. 1 Hard Wheat to the acre. The Canadian Government gives every man or every woman who is the head of a family 160 ACRES FREE. The energetic, industrious young man can make his fortune with this start in life. Thousands are doing it, so it is no experiment. There are railroad facilities making a market. There are schools for the children. There are churches. In fact, all the accessories of civilization with the land given as a bonus to those who will accept it. Railroad lands conveniently situated are also for sale at low prices and on long time. The climate of Western Canada is about like that of Minnesota, which means that it is the HEALTHIEST CLIMATE IN THE WORLD.

For further particulars, call on or write
J.C. KOEHN,
Canadian Government Agent,
MOUNTAIN LAKE,
MINNESOTA.

Canadian government blandishments, combined with CPR advertising, persuaded 600,000 Americans to settle in the Canadian West before World War I. My ancestors, great-grandfather Robert, grandfather J.C. and their families, were among them.

There used to be a saying in the Royal Canadian Navy when I was a sea cadet that summed up being taken for a sucker: "They sent for you."

They sent for American sodbusters to populate the drylands of Palliser's Triangle. The railway even paid their fare in many cases, because they were brought in to help the CPR make money; they were here to help pay down the national debt incurred to construct Canada's national dream, though no one ever stated the situation to them that baldly, of course.

If the American immigrants, some of them men of means, others with little more than the clothes on their back and a couple of work-horses, had ever heard of Manifest Destiny, they politely kept that to themselves. There were many other nationalities flooding into the West at that time, of course, each with its political and cultural singularities. But Ontario newspapers feared that the influx of Americans would lead to annexation of Canadian territory. In fact, many of those Americans would eventually be only too happy to exit Canada as abruptly as they had entered.

It was a land boom of unprecedented proportions, and it led to grandiose expectations and inflated "Boomer" rhetoric, as towns sprang up overnight, and vied with each other for settlers and industries. There wasn't a collection of shacks anywhere on the plains that did not see itself as a future Chicago as the settlers poured in. As a child, I knew one such place, where you could fire a cannon down mainstreet at noon and be lucky if you hit a stray cat. Redcliff was a small town that possessed a brick plant and a glass factory. In pioneer days, the village fathers pumped out a stream of bumf far and wide: "In Planning for the Making of a Manufacturing city." "We need merchants: we need factories; we need skilled tradesmen . . . join with us in the making of a SMOKELESS PITTSBURG—ALBERTA'S POWER CITY—PEERLESS REDCLIFF." Only in the last two decades has some of that hoped-for growth occurred, but at 3,000-plus souls in 1994, Redcliff is still a long way from city status.

The new settlers were in for some rude surprises. The CPR slogan "Come to Alberta, and go into partnership with the Canadian Pacific" acquired a different meaning when one discovered that the CPR controlled 25 million acres of land as part of a grant from the Dominion government. The railway would decide where new towns would be established, and where branch lines would run. The Hudson's Bay Company also controlled large areas (7 million acres) as part of the price for the sale of Rupert's Land to Canada. Eventually, a wall of tariffs was in place to protect eastern industry, so that the American settler found he could not afford to buy American machinery but must purchase the Canadian product at the going rate. This was basically a licence to print money at the settlers' expense.

Ontario set the template for our economic history that has rankled Westerners ever since: "They were forced to buy dear and sell cheap,"

as J.F. Conway puts it, in the absence of free trade with Uncle Sugar.
(Eventually, Westerners would repay the eastern investment many times
over, continuing to the present day. According to Robert L. Mansell, an
economist at the University of Calgary, from 1961 to 1992 Alberta contributed, in 1994 dollars, $138.8 billion more to Ottawa than it
received back in total spending and benefits, while Quebec received
$160.7 billion more than it contributed to the feds. Alberta, with one
tenth the national population, was the largest net contributor to the federal treasury. Mansell calls Alberta the "milch cow of confederation."
(It is a phrase that dates back to 1915.)

*   *   *

I doubt that my grandfather John Claude Marty would approve of my
hostility toward developmentalism and its cult of "progress," its notion
that the land was worthless on its own terms until humankind added
value to it. It was his belief in that philosophy that had brought him to
Alberta in the first place. It was his faith in that idea that brought his
family into hardship and poverty. But their sacrifice gave me a
birthright. I have no wish to condemn the nation's founding fathers, or
hack at the knees of statues. I only want to try to set the story straight,
to shine a light into the shadows where so many great hearts were
buried, unsung. Fortunately, there are some Martys left to talk about
those homesteading days in the British Block, a chunk of dryland north
of Medicine Hat that is now part of Canadian Forces Base Suffield.

Aunt Sylvia's memory goes back the furthest. She was born at the
first Marty farm near Underwood, North Dakota. She was eight years
old when the family moved to Alberta. Eventually, I was to make a trip
to Phoenix, Arizona, and to Fort Benton, where my American cousins
filled in some gaps in the history. To date, it remains a sketchy record.
There are few photographs of the homestead days, and very few docu-
ments, letters or diaries. Like the Blackfoot winter count, our family
seems to rely on the oral tradition to keep its memory of itself alive.
Until I came along, that is.

My great-great-grandfather Jacob Marty was born in Switzerland.
Given my love of the mountains, the Swiss connection appeals to me. It
probably also accounts for the family fixation on law and order, a notorious national characteristic of the Switzer.

Canadians tend to make a big thing out of their ethnic heritage: it is part of our multiculturalist mindset, a hangover of 1960s preoccupations. But the Marty family's collective memory trends against this tide of kitsch. In typical American fashion, our family memory begins not in the cantons of the Alps, but on the edge of the new frontier, in this case in Stillwater, eastern Minnesota.

According to family tradition, at the age of twenty-eight Jacob left Stillwater to fight in the Civil War, and never returned. He left behind a wife, Lisette, and three babies. I have confirmed only that he began his military career as a commissary sergeant and finished up as a first lieutenant, and that he was honourably discharged in 1864. After which he vanished. Lisette gave up on him and remarried in 1866.

It was not Jacob, but my great-grandfather Robert whom my Aunt Dot called "the Swiss man," even though he was born in Stillwater. He left Stillwater and, impelled by the same restlessness that led our progenitor to the New World, followed the Mississippi upstream and moved the family west to Sanborn, Minnesota, then farther west to Washburn, North Dakota. One wonders if he was running from something; the moves were made in middle age.

The Martys were part of a wave of American expansionism, ever westward. Father and sons took out homesteads near the shores of Lake Sakakawea, itself named for the Shoshone woman who helped guide Lewis and Clark to their western discoveries.

The Martys had moved west to the geographical centre of North America. They might have stayed, American and central; they might have gone west to Montana, or south to Texas. But Van Horne and Clifford Sifton sent for them, diverted them northward to Palliser's Triangle, the Bermuda Triangle of the prairie sodbuster. In 1908, great-uncles Jesse and Bob were the first to follow the Canadian propaganda stream to Alberta. There they sent back glowing reports about the money to be made growing wheat, though in fact they both worked on railway construction initially to raise money for farming. Robert Marty read the letters and testimonials and thought about moving north. He missed his eldest son, Jesse. The two of them shared a passion for fast horses and expensive sulkies.

Times were hard in North Dakota. The country was in recession and land was expensive and in short supply. Robert had either resigned from his sheriff position or simply lost an election. At fifty-five years of age, his future was looking bleak. It was late to start all over in a new country, especially with a wife who was prone to bronchial attacks. But Robert made the decision to go north, probably with Alice's blessing, since she was the driving force in the marriage. (Born Alice Fitzgibbons, she was descended from a southern family of planters whose fortunes were based on slave labour.)

Having made the move to join Bob and Jesse in Alberta, it seems that Robert and Alice then cajoled their other adult offspring, J.C., Lula and Joseph, with their families, to sell their holdings in North Dakota, which were too small anyway to support grain growing, and move to the land of milk and honey, southern Alberta.

According to Aunt Sis, J.C. lingered in Underwood (near Washburn), North Dakota, a while longer than the rest of his clan. Unlike his siblings, he had a lot to keep him there. For one thing, his wife Ora Belle did not want to leave. And by all accounts, J.C., still only thirty-three years of age, was well on his way to financial success at the time of his ill-fated decision. He was a law officer, but he also ran a real estate office. He owned a theatre in the area and a small farm. Raised in Minnesota, J.C. loved trees. He had lined the road to his small North Dakota farm with trees and watered them with a horse-drawn water wagon.

Aunt Sis remembers a piano in the house; she remembers comfort and security "and lots of grub, too," as she put it. Underwood, north of Bismarck "on the Soo Line," had potential. In 1908, it consisted of five hundred souls and boasted two hotels, a commercial club, grain elevators, five churches and a "graded school."

"We left all that for a new beginning," Aunt Sis grumbled. "It was the beginning, all right—it was the beginning of the end."

But Robert and Alice prevailed on their second-born to move west and join them—so our family maintains. "Best get a move on," they wrote. "The country is filling up fast, plenty Americans coming in. Land is being staked all around us. . . ." Their urging appealed to something that seems strange to us today but was a fact of life back then: an adult son's continuing duty to his parents, even after founding a family of his own. Robert's advancing age, his mother's frail health, the loss of his brothers' companionship—all this persuaded J.C. to make the move.

The real lure was land; 160 acres of Alberta homestead land, and the right to pre-empt another quarter at $2.50 an acre. The lure of 320 acres was enough, it seems, to make thousands of Americans forget national differences and leave America behind. They staked all they had on growing wheat in Alberta, where crops were said to be producing thirty-five bushels to the acre at minimum.

There was a plan afoot to irrigate the land in the British Block. For my ancestors, already experienced with farming in dry country, the promise of irrigation was the decisive factor. And indeed the hoped-for canals are all there—as wishful black lines on a map of the British Block drawn up before World War I. A railway is also shown there, with depots and branchlines all neatly plotted—but only on paper. Everything depended on British investors, and that money dried up with the advent of the war.

My people, travelling on immigrant trains from the east, their wagons and implements loaded on flatcars, arrived on the treeless flatlands at Redcliff between 1908 and 1912. Alberta had been created a province of the Dominion of Canada only in 1905. Yet when the Martys arrived in southern Alberta, they found that the Medicine Hat area was the most populous part of the province as a result of immigration, the white population having exploded from a handful of Anglo and American ranchers in 1880 to over 70,000 persons by 1911. Not only that, but most of those settlers had something directly in common with the Martys. According to historian D.G. Jones, "Seventy percent of the newcomers were from the States, Dakota and Minnesota particularly, where many had gathered from Europe shortly before." By 1915, 45 percent of all Alberta farms were in the drylands of the south.

Brother Oscar, my favourite great-uncle, moved his family to Alberta in 1911 just ahead of J.C. His brother Joe, his sister Lula and her husband, Fred Smith, moved around the same time. The newcomers arrived singing a popular song, "O Prairie Land":

We've reached the land of pleasant dreams,
Of level plains and deep ravines
Where flowers abound on every hand
In this our lovely prairie land.

They drove their wagons north, to some sections of land near the eastern edge of the Middle Sand Hills, and the song gradually died on their lips. They heard the wind moaning in the barbed-wire fences instead.

Some quarter sections near Robert and Alice were the only land that had not already been filed on, or that was not owned by the railway or the Hudson's Bay Company. They found Robert and Alice ensconced in a shack on top of the highest hill around. They called it the Box on the Buttes. The walls vibrated and creaked under the onslaught of the wind. As Alice prepared a meal, Robert's children and grandchildren gazed at him, and wondered. "Boys," he said, "we're going to make a fortune here." The door blew open and a tumbleweed rattled over the floor-boards. "Would you look at that view," he said. "Clear to the old U.S.A. Well, they can keep it. This is a brand-new country. We can start all over again." His eyes shone with a strange intensity they had not seen before.

I have a picture of Robert and Alice, standing next to this shack. There is a lonely aspen tree behind them, bent east by the wind. Alice's hair is blowing east, Robert's tie is blowing east like a windsock. They are gazing fondly at each other, as far as I can tell.

Robert's family looked about and saw rolling hills with a sandy sub-soil, but they found some quarter sections containing topsoil down on an old slough bottom, dried up now. The soil was about five inches thick over a clay-like base. They filed on it and set to work putting up shacks and barns. It was late in the season, but they were determined to break the sod that year, to let it rot over the winter.

But it was magic what the dry, west wind could do with exposed top-soil. You could see hardpan a few days after it was cultivated, and find your topsoil if you were of a mind to look for it, piled against the neigh-bour's barn.

It did not take the younger Martys and their spouses long to digest a bite of reality sandwich—laced with sand. Oscar's wife, Hilda, in partic-ular, was not seduced by the isolated life north of Medicine Hat. She stayed just six months, long enough to give birth to my second cousin, Lloyd. One morning she got up and stared out the window at the blankness of wind-blown sage. A few scrawny chickens stared back at her. There was a way out of this life, at least for the children. But not without good schooling, not without some amenities that would give them a glimpse of a wider world than this. She swept up the dust from the corners of the room, and put the broom carefully away behind the stove. Then she turned and stared at Oscar with a determined look. "Oscar; I am taking the children, and I am going down to my sister's place in Big Sandy. With you, or without you."

As he watched, open-mouthed, Hilda, with kids in tow, walked a mile to the nearest grid road. She hitched a ride eventually with a passing farmer to the railway depot at Redcliff where she would buy a ticket for Montana. Oscar fumed and brooded for a few days. Robert and Alice told him to sit tight. Give Hilda a few days to think things over, and she'd think twice about leaving a good man like him.

Oscar knew better. He loaded his wagon, hitched up the team and headed south on her trail. He was not about to let a good thing like Hilda get away from him. That was likely in September 1911.

Robert's sons Joe and Robert soon followed Hilda's lead. Lula and Fred stayed longer. Unwilling to face her parents with the news that she and Fred were going to leave, Lula helped Fred load the wagon in the middle of the night, and they beat it for the States.

J.C. and Ora, with children Sylvia and Allan, arrived in Alberta expecting a family reunion. There would be cousins for the children to play with; there would be a network of relatives, their own kin close at hand. "It won't be nearly as lonely as I thought," Ora must have told herself. So she tried to manage a smile as the wagon bounced over a sandy track north of the desolate village of Redcliff, where there was no Lake Sakakawea to soften the air, no groves of trees to breast the wind. But instead of a throng of excited relatives and children waiting to greet them, they found only J.C.'s parents at home. Bob and Jesse were away at work. Robert broke the bad news: the others had all decamped for the States.

"I don't understand it," he said helplessly, as Alice patted his shoulder in sympathy. Ora turned white with anger. It took a great deal of self-control to keep herself from screaming, so great was her anguish at what had been sacrificed for this brooding stretch of sandhills and cactus.

J.C. took over his younger brother Oscar's homestead claim. There was a barn, a chicken house and a rickety shack that the winds blew through at their leisure. J.C. took his workhorses and skidded in an empty granary that some other farmer had abandoned. He tacked that on for a master bedroom. Another bed folded down out of the kitchen wall, where Sis and Allan would sleep until they were gradually displaced by newborns. J.C. and Ora pulled a curtain when they wanted privacy.

So picture this shack on the lone prairie. There are no trees anywhere in sight; there is barely a bush anywhere in sight. Everything that represents shelter is man-made. Sitting on a rude foundation of stones gathered from the prairie, it has been plunked down in the middle of nowhere with no organic connection to the sweep of grass and sagebrush wherein it sits. There is no welcoming nook or cranny, not even that ravine so celebrated in song. Except for the buildings, the only place you can hide is inside your own head. The only shelter from the wind is in the lee of your own back. The land's face is implacable, unreadable. Except for the buildings, horses and a few cows, clouds alone form its shadows.

There was no well on J.C.'s Alberta homestead. The kids hauled water from a neighbour's well with a wooden yoke over their shoulders hooked to two buckets. It was a walk of several hundred yards. J.C. and Robert dug a well, with Allan helping as much as a small boy could. They dug it with pick and shovel. It was dangerous work; they risked cave-ins and pockets of methane gas. They went down as far as they dared to go, which was eighty feet in this case. It was a dry hole.

"What did Grandma think of the place?" I once asked Aunt Sis.

"She hated it. Hated every moment of it," was the reply. "And she had to go to work, and help break the land, don't forget."

Nowadays, prairie grain farmers tow fifty-foot-wide seeders with giant, four-wheel-drive tractors, and they might cultivate a thousand acres or more. My grandparents, by contrast, broke the sod with two moldboard walking plows, each pulled by a workhorse. He plowed one furrow, and she plowed the next; it was daunting, blistering work, unimaginable to us now. It was tedious, but dangerous. Should the plow hit a rock, the six-foot wooden handles could fly up and break a farmer's jaw. You had to be raised up to it, hardened to it like steel is hardened between the forge and the slaking trough.

At first, Ora took the move in her stride, and I think she kept her true feelings hidden. I have a picture of this stocky little woman, born Ora Belle Zook of Pennsylvania Dutch stock. J.C. is seated in front of their weathered shack, and she stands behind him with her hand placed, almost protectively, on his shoulder. She looked just as tough and testy in her matron years as I recall her looking in old age—blind in one eye by then—though she was always kind to us kids, in a brusque, matter-of-fact way. Having given birth to eight babies of her own, the novelty had sort of worn off.

Eight kids. Cousin Lloyd, himself raised in a tiny cabin on a Montana "Desert Claim," says, "They didn't have anything else to do out on the homestead on winter nights." Sis remembered her parents in their youth. "There were no two people more in love than them, when they were young," she recalled. "I remember how he'd take her on his knee and love her up, with us kids running up the walls of that little shack."

That love dried up in the years of drought, the poverty and the cabin fever of life out in the sage-covered hills. It was a love I had never witnessed, as a boy, when the old couple seemed to move through the shadows of their house in town like shades in different dreams, talking to themselves or to their company, to anyone except each other. That lost tenderness was the greatest of all their losses, the one thing they could never replace.

*   *   *

It was fire that delivered a crippling blow to the family when my father was ten years old. It started in the kitchen cupboard, probably as a spark from a loose chimney pipe.

Orland woke up first, smelling smoke, and he woke his father and the other kids. They lost nearly everything but their lives and had to hike four miles, wrapped in grain sacks and barefoot, to a neighbour's place. By that time, chronic illness had forced Robert and Alice to move to town. So the next day, J.C. borrowed a wagon and moved the family to the abandoned Box on the Buttes. He sent Orland and Walter back to the ruins, because Ora, who had gone to town for supplies, was due to arrive back later that day. "Listen here, you young lobsters," he told them sternly. "You watch for your mother. Soon as you see the wagon, you run out quick. You tell her everybody is okay, understand?"

Away they ran, barefoot and in their borrowed britches, down the buttes to the ruin of their former home. The scene of the disaster awed them to silence. The shack was a cinder pile, and not a very big cinder pile, either. They had had so little, and now they had nothing. They didn't linger long there as realization dawned; this must be what death looks like. But they were kids, and spring was on the land; chorus frogs were creaking and the gophers were up and about. The flies that could make life unbearable were not stirring yet, though the windflowers blazed purple glories through the green grass. Over it all there was the fecund odour of wet sage and wet earth, scents that make a young animal's blood race. One sight or sound led to another and they wandered off.

When they remembered at last, they were closer to the new place than the old one: they ran in and told the old man a fib: they had gone looking for their mother and sister, but had not seen them. J.C. was not fooled: he jumped on a horse and galloped back to the old place. Riding down the side of the butte, he caught sight of the wagon near the smouldering ruin and knew he was too late.

That wagon was loaded with supplies for the family. Everything had been purchased, in Redcliff, with an exacting economy by that pioneer matriarch who remembered what every child dared to hope for, and saved any cent she got to try to meet the demand. But now it was all worthless, forgotten. The horses wandered about, biting the grass, dragging the wagon in their wake. J.C. found his wife sobbing her eyes out. Ora was on her knees, black with soot, her hair streaked with ashes like Job's daughter—combing through the embers and ashes of the house with her bare hands, expecting to find nothing but the bones and skulls of her children and her husband.

Later Ora looked around the wind-blown shack that was to be her new home and looked at her husband, the sole inheritor of his father's visionary scheme, now come in to his final inheritance: his father's failed farm. And she wept. She wept, but she stuck to it, rock-solid to the end. God alone knows how J.C. and eight kids would have survived if she had quit on them.

"Why didn't they leave, get the hell out of there?" I once asked Aunt Sis.

She scoffed at the question. "They couldn't leave. They had no money, no place to go, and all those kids to feed. At least they could grow spuds out there. They had a roof, at least." Other families subsisted on jars of pickled gophers, on mule deer and jackrabbits. They used to say it wasn't a drought until your heart was broken.

J.C. was a stubborn man. The family would hang on through droughts, blowing soil, winter blizzards and plagues of hoppers and cutworms until 1929. He grew enough grain from time to time to keep some meagre income going. Allan and Sylvia contributed as much money from their earnings as they could spare. The old man seemed to think it was their duty, after all he had done for them.

Ora watched and waited as one neighbour after another loaded their wagons and drove away, part of the great stampede off the drylands between 1921 and 1926. This exodus was the last stage of what is known as the Prairie Dryland Disaster, which predated the better-known Great Depression of the thirties by a decade. The 1926 census revealed 10,000 abandoned farms in Alberta. Where J.C. lived, the population dropped by 30 percent in five years.

But J.C. hung grimly on. He was made for the bitter forge of Next Year Country. "It was always next year with him," recalls Sis bitterly. "Next year there would be a good crop. Grow wheat, grow wheat! He drilled the seed in all right, and then next year all he had to show for it was another baby."

In the end, the news that they would move to town was broken with no warning. J.C. had gone in to Redcliff—to see his folks, as far as the family knew. A few days later, Allan suddenly appeared at the homestead, having ridden out from Redcliff where he had a job.

Gazing out on the plains from the promontory where the shack squatted, the kids would have caught sight of the man on horseback when he was still several miles away. A rider headed their way was a very notable event, and they watched suspiciously, having been deluded by mirages of approaching horsemen more than once. They watched him coming on through the waves of heat lifting from the alkali sloughs, his body wavering in the haze, drawing closer, the saddle horse whinnying now to the workhorses in the corral, so they knew it was no figment of heat and dust. And then the visitor was revealed at last as that protective, bear-like eldest brother they all loved.

What news?

He dismounted, banging the dust off his coat, and hugged his mother affectionately. He beamed down at all the kids. "Dad says pack everything up. We're moving you into Tilley." The news was electrifying, like the gates of a jail sprung open.

J.C.'s decision sounds peremptory, but I doubt Ora much cared at the time. My father remembers how glad the family was to get out. They loaded everything they owned onto one wagon in a matter of an hour. I think they turned to look back, but for Ora it was mainly to say "good riddance" to eighteen years of hard labour, to failed crops and the few good harvests that had merely paid the debts and left them scrimping. My father got on a horse and drove their small herd, a couple of cows and several workhorses, ahead of him, following where the wagon led, to freedom. Freedom meant town, comfort, novelty and most importantly a job; a job that paid real money, not promises.

After the death of Robert and then Alice, J.C., Ora, my father Orland and the younger kids moved into the Redcliff house. The Great Depression was in full swing. Compared to the Dryland Disaster, the Dirty Thirties seemed like a cakewalk to the Martys, though Orland was the only one working for a long time, and turning over most of his earnings to his mother. J.C. finally found work fighting crime again—as town constable in Redcliff. He seemed to thrive on scraps. His favourite technique when provoked was an open-handed slap from hands the size of lunch plates and about as hard. "Hit 'em once with the open hand," he used to rumble, "and they seldom come back for more." Then there came a night, in his seventy-fifth year, when some cowboy laid a severe shit-kicking on him. Ora's tongue-lashing was probably salt on the wounds; J.C. turned in his badge and retired.

By current standards, one could say my grandparents died in poverty. They didn't see it that way. Ora could stretch a dollar until the King squealed for mercy. Frugality, perhaps, is what they died in.

Ora's end was sad. She had become a frenetic sports fan, the terror of the rink when the Medicine Hat Tigers were playing. "Kill him, kill him," was the favourite battle cry of this corsetted old woman with the severe bun and the one good eye. Confined by old age to television viewing, she became an authority on every sport from professional golf to badminton, though she had never held club or racquet in hand. Grandad used to hide in his room, embarrassed by her antics, as she squinted at the set and yelled advice and criticism.

That is where my American-born grandmother had the stroke, watching the ultimate Canadian event—Hockey Night in Canada. J.C. heard her moan, "Oh no . . ." but thought she was reacting to the game, as usual. After a while he wandered out and found her in a coma from which she never woke up. Ora Belle Zook, whom he had loved to distraction once, and whom he still loved in his moody, distracted fashion, was gone from him. His own heart stopped beating three years later. They lie beneath the prairie earth at Redcliff, Alberta.

7

WHERE THE DEER AND THE
ANTELOPE PLAY

~

They must have sown the drylands north of Redcliff with dragons' teeth, for eventually it sprouted with soldiers. The last of the settlers and ranchers who had entered the country now known as the British Block at the turn of the century were moved from the land when the military appropriated it in 1941. A stretch of short-grass prairie covering a thousand square miles was fenced off and patrolled by the army. It earned its nickname through being used as a joint Canadian–British army chemical warfare test site, and later a test site under Canada's Defence Research Board. In 1971, it was reorganized as Canadian Forces Base Suffield, one of the largest army training areas in the Western World. Currently it is used by British and Canadian forces for artillery, infantry and armoured training. The Defence Research Facility at Suffield, to state it officially, "carries on a full program of applied research in areas such as military mobility, rocketry, field demolitions, land-mine detection and countermeasures and nuclear, chemical and biological detection and defence measures."

I have driven by the base, which borders the Trans-Canada Highway, many times over the years. It used to give me the creeps, and in some ways it still does. To the passing eye, it is a stretch of prairie studded with sage and buckbrush rolling north to the foot of distant, impassive-looking buttes. Surrounded by barbed wire and No Trespassing signs, it gives no clues to whatever secrets it contains.

It is closed to the general public, and for long had a dark reputation with the uninformed masses, of which I was a member, as a place where mad scientists worked on doomsday devices. When I was a boy, and believed in UFOs, I knew deep in my heart that they all came from Suffield, and picked up their crew members behind local evangelical churches.

Jeeps loaded with white-coated eggheads and British tanks on training exercises rolled over my grandfather's land for decades. The fact that the majority of its first settlers had been Americans was lost to memory, and to name. The family did have one connection with the new order. My Uncle Walter worked there in a dangerous hush-hush job as a sapper. Walter had a slight stutter. "L-luh-loose lips sink ships," he once told me, lifting a finger up to hush my questions. His cover story was that he worked to detonate and destroy surplus explosives. It was dangerous work: there were fatal accidents at Suffield over the years, but Uncle Walter survived and retired with all his appendages in place.

He had another motto, which I took to heart: "T-t-take a chance."

My family history was nothing in the face of all that expenditure and activity. The base was not only secret but a state secret. The signs summed it up: No Trespassing. It seemed weirdly ironic that I, who was born in England during the last great war, would find my family's homestead to be a place warred over by British troops on exercises every summer.

In recent years, however, visitors have been allowed to tour the old homestead sites by appointment with Base Operations. My opportunity came in 1992.

March arrived with momentous news: the federal Department of Environment and the Department of National Defence had designated a 160-square-mile expanse of mixed grasslands, sand hills and riverbanks at CFB Suffield as a National Wildlife Area (NWA). At the same time, the army, acting on the advice of the Canadian Wildlife Service, announced plans to round up eight-hundred (later revised to fifteen hundred) head of feral horses, which, unbeknownst to most Canadians, had been roaming the base for years. They were a threat to the habitat of the new NWA, according to the Canadian Wildlife Service. Some 250 might remain to run free, the rest would be sold at auction. It seemed likely that those not purchased for rodeo stock, ranch or pleasure riding might wind up at the meatpacking plant.

Hooked on the notion that wild horses were about to be gunned down by crazed paratroopers, newspaper reporters rushed into print quoting animal rights activists who fired from the lip, denouncing the proposed cull as, for example, a "systematic round-up and slaughter of 500 horses that don't deserve this fate." So the welcome news about the new wildlife reserve was buried under a mudslide of criticism, and the military, instead of getting kudos for its conservation initiative, got a big black eye instead. Eventually, the military would act on the suggestion of a local horse lover and put the animals up for adoption. They would go to those who could guarantee a good home and freedom of movement for a horse.

It was July when I drove east on Highway 1, under a partially overcast sky. I was headed for a rendezvous with a photographer, Doug Leighton, a prairie bird nut from Banff. We would embark on a strange guided tour into the military version of ecological reality, and I would meet with a few of my own personal ghosts along the way.

The dryland prairie of Canadian Forces Base Suffield is a land where even the wind gets lonely. This rolling terrain was carved and shaped, mounded and flattened by the great glaciers thousands of years ago. Its sheltering coulees, spotted with white-rimmed alkali sloughs, began as drainage canals at the melting base of the Laurentide ice sheet. The wind has been polishing these rolling, sun-bronzed hills for aeons. It rides herd on sagebrush, wild horses, antelope and people, distributing rain clouds here, blowing them away elsewhere with a careless, unmeasured ease.

A flock of lark buntings sprayed up from the dust of the old Bingville Road, named for a place that no longer exists. It had been the social centre of the community at one time, where my father went for school picnics, where J.C. played at dances. It was originally named for a comic strip appearing in the *Spokane Herald*. Bingville, named after a fiction, was gone, and the fiction had also died. I thought that my father had imagined the place, until I found the name printed on an old Cummins Land Map at the Glenbow Archives in Calgary. On the map were hundreds of names. The original hand lettering was so small I could hardly decipher it. I stared at it for half an hour, my eyes blurring with strain, and then there it was, our family name on the Alberta earth. J.C Marty, Robert Marty, Joseph. I made a photocopy of the map to take to Suffield.

A prairie falcon wheeled overhead, and a meadowlark sang its defiance. The wind whipped through the open windows of the green Canadian Armed Forces truck. Major Brent McDonald, then Base Operations Officer, was at the wheel, and Doug Leighton was happily ensconced in the back seat, readying his equipment.

McDonald checked his map against the legal description I had provided. He is a whipcord-tough Calgary native, a conservationist and history buff, who was one of the main driving forces behind the formation of the Suffield NWA. "Major Mac," as he is known locally, did everything with an economy of motion, and spoke with the clipped, emphatic precision of a career officer. He slowed the truck at a lonely intersection about six miles west of the NWA boundary, and turned east. We bounced across the prairie on a cart track at the foot of a low range of hills. Here and there the white circlets of alkali rimmed the brackish sloughs. A sulphurous stink emanated from them. I suddenly realized these unprepossessing buttes were the same ones I had glimpsed from the highway. The gradual uplift northward gave them an elevation that one missed when close under the summits. Something about this drab scene was oddly familiar to me, though I had never seen it before in my life. It had the flavour of a dreamscape.

The dream shifted to nightmare as we rounded a corner and saw the stark outlines of entrenched soldiers, their weapons trained on us. The major laughed at my expression. They were only plywood silhouettes, guarding the approach to a wooden pretend-bridge spanning a pretend river of grass. It was all part of some old military exercise. "All this in defence of the Marty homestead," observed Leighton dryly.

We pulled up on a knoll above the plywood gunners. Below us was a broad bottomland that our map said was a lake: it was dry as a bone, despite recent rains. We could see that parts of the bottom had once been broken for farming, though it had not been tilled for fifty years. Crested wheat grass, a foreigner among the native blue grama and spear grass, formed a yellow rectangle marking the old farm. The wind boomed in my ear, as if boasting of the work it had done decades ago, blowing my grandfather's topsoil east into Saskatchewan.

McDonald glanced at his CFB Suffield map. "This is the spot," he said confidently.

We got out of the truck to look around. An odd shape stuck up from the grass near a patch of pasture sage. I walked over to it and was startled to find the wrought-iron headboard of a rusted double bed sticking up through the prairie sod. Nearby was an old cellar hole, like a sunken grave. Around it was a rectangle of stones. I stared at it, not comprehending its significance at first. It seemed impossibly small to mark what would have been home for my grandparents and their eight children.

"This is it!" said the major, jubilantly.

Dazed, I put my hand on the rusty metal wires of the old bedstead while Leighton looked on. "There are your roots, Sid," he quipped. "Literally." I stared at the headboard, and smiled, realizing the import of his words. This was the marriage bed, sunk now into rust and wheat grass, that my father had been conceived upon. For more than sixty years, it had been an abandoned harp for the wind to play upon, marking the place where love lay buried. I looked down at my photocopy of the Cummins Land Map, which showed the two tiny quarters of land worked by J.C. Marty back in 1918, and stared out at the space of cloud and sunburnt grass. I could not relate the draftsman's precise gridwork to this windswept immensity that had forgotten those who poured so much sweat and so many tears into its brown dirt. It would take a visit with my father and aunt to this spot, a few days later, to make it real for me.

Stirred to the quick, I gripped my hand hard on the old bedstead, the desert heart of my family's history; the only sign of their passage.

After a while, we moved on. I pulled my head together and listened as McDonald talked about the new NWA. Bounded on one side by the South Saskatchewan River, it has always been exempt from military training and marked and protected by the army as "Out of Bounds." It was part of the range's "ricochet template": in other words, without a soldier along to guide your steps, you might trip explosively over a live artillery round out there.

A limited amount of cattle grazing was allowed in the south part of the NWA. Oddly, for a firing range, there are natural gas wells scattered through part of the northern portion. Gas wells at CFB Suffield yield 3.5 percent of Canada's natural gas production. These uses are all part of CFB Suffield's efforts to be a "good corporate citizen." The idea of the army turning into a corporation was upsetting to me.

To the northwest we saw a pillar of smoke. The radio came alive. A prairie fire had been started by an artillery shell. The soldiers had dropped their weapons to fight fire, to keep it from running out on private land to the north.

Though cattle and gas wells have been permitted, hunting and farming are not. It may seem odd, but limited grazing as well as prairie fires can actually have a beneficial effect, since these events mimic the older regimen of pre-settlement days. Farming, the use most destructive to mixed grasslands, was eliminated at Suffield in 1941, along with hunting. As a result, the base contains magnificent stretches of wild prairie that had escaped cultivation. The rare prairie rattlesnake and the endangered upland plover share the coulees and grasslands of the base with 4,000 pronghorn antelope, 1,500 mule deer, 1,000 white-tailed deer and the feral horse herd. The NWA represents habitat for 173 animal species, 29 of which are of concern, rare, threatened or endangered. The area includes part of the Middle Sand Hills complex, tracts of wild prairie, and some of the South Saskatchewan river breaks. The horse herd, we learned, tends to frequent the northeast corner of the Middle Sand Hills.

Although the business of soldiers is to fight and to kill, the entire base at Suffield has long been a safe haven for wildlife. In fact the base had traditionally appointed one of its officers to act as conservation officer. The military was proud of the fact that, despite the planned violence practised here, only one big game animal, an antelope, had ever succumbed to a stray bullet. Base access roads, dirt tracks for the most part, are well named. There are mule deer on the Muledeer Road and coyotes haunt the Coyote Road. Rounding a curve on the Antelope Road we spotted the biggest antelope buck I have ever seen. He was standing next to a gas well site, flashing alarms to other antelope by erecting the white hairs on his rump rosette. I think he flashed out "Cheese it, da troops." Several distant antelope watched, but refused to flee.

Each gas well is buried ten feet under the ground, and protected by a steel grate that can take the weight of a sixty-ton tank. The high-tech nature of the wells did not impress the buck. As I watched from the army travelall, he showed just what he thought of gas wells by urinating, copiously, all over the installation.

He watched us through his large, wide-set eyes for a few seconds, then broke into a run and raced alongside for a moment at thirty-five miles an hour before suddenly breaking across in front of the truck and dashing off into the prairie. As a prairie boy raised in Medicine Hat, I am no stranger to this singular beast with its ornate colour and shape. But in one hour on the base I saw more pronghorn antelope than I have seen in my entire life.

I glanced over at Major McDonald. "They seem used to military vehicles."

McDonald nodded. He gave a guy that "on patrol, heads up" kind of feeling. Leadership was written all over the man, and I warned myself not to buy the military sales job wholesale. We had seen an area—though not in the NWA—where tank treads had chewed great swathes in the prairie earth far beyond the bite of horses' hooves. "I'll bet they run like hell when the guns open up."

McDonald, dressed in green battledress, grinned from behind his aviator sunglasses. "We were out here on a tank exercise one time," he told me. "Smoke and explosions all around. Right in the middle of it was an antelope doe and buck, busy mating. And they weren't about to stop and get out of the way just for a bunch of tanks. Had to split the battalion and drive around 'em—firing all the time. Of course, not one of us had a camera." I grinned wildly at this account. McDonald insisted it was true, and it sounded too crazy not to be.

The major is a dedicated conservationist despite his military mindset. The year I visited, his troops caught eight poachers trespassing on the base. He is the only game warden I've met whose office displays a collection of bombs, rockets and artillery shells. This hardware is situated quite near a sign that reads "Zone of Reception." As a former park warden, I was deeply impressed. I had fondled the weaponry, replaying a few old movies in my head, where a bazooka would have come in handy to ward off marauding skidoos and 4 x 4s. The collection is defused, of course. But there's plenty of real live firepower near by. He definitely had the poachers outgunned.

Over the next few days, Leighton and I wandered over the prairies and through the riverine forests. We were thrilled to hear a soldier had been bitten by a rattlesnake, and felt cheated when we could not find a rattler to bite us. Leighton told me fantastic tales of the loggerhead shrike, which will catch a mouse and impale it on a thorn. I told him he should wear a hat out in the midday sun. In lieu of shrikes we interviewed a colony of long-eared bats roosting in a dead cottonwood. We tracked the elusive Ord's kangaroo rat, which makes tiny runways among the spiny leaves of the prickly pear. We had a naturalist's fun holiday, playing tag with all creation.

One afternoon we lingered awhile at the nearby Ellis Medicine Wheel site, one of the hundreds of Indian archeological sites that dot the base. Here, under the bright glare of a prairie sun, ancient stone teepee rings are grouped around a mysterious, ceremonial circle. The windswept site sits on a bluff overlooking the river, where rock wrens call to each other over the mud-brown stream. One can see miles in any direction from this viewpoint. Five American pelicans lifted from the river far below us and flew directly overhead, like five souls giving us greetings, as we stood, meditating, among the white stones and cacti. Towering cumulus clouds to the north threatened a change in the weather.

Ironically, I had come back to the short grass country during one of its infrequent wet summers. The settlers who came out here in the late 1880s arrived in one of these wet cycles, finding the grass higher than they would ever see again in their lifetimes. They could not have imagined the frequent droughts that would return with the new century. I stared at the bare red earth and the cactus, knowing since boyhood that green years only last long enough to lull the unwary. Beauty in the drylands is brown, grey, tawny; is space, immense cloud-play, giant shadows and burning light. All life points down to the smallest leaf, but what we do not see are the fine, hairlike fibres of roots, millions of miles of subterranean cells: what feeds us all is under our feet.

The ranchers came closest to striking a deal with this world of grass and wind; theirs was the only culture that approached ecological balance in the most arid parts of the plains. But the settlers who followed stared into the heat waves and dust and saw not badland cliffs, alkali soils and cactus, but mirages of future wealth in spectral orchards and chimeras of wheat. A horned beast with eyes that could see for all the miles of miles stepped forward to offer itself to Napikwan as it had offered its flesh to the Nitsitapii before his coming. Napikwan learned little from the Afric look of this ancient plains creature. He shot it for its meat and in fact nearly drove it into extinction, without considering why its liver and kidneys were so large: that was to digest the poisonous plants that would kill the settlers' cattle and sheep. The antelope was a beast that could subsist on prickly pear—so long as there were prairie fires to scorch the thorns first, so long as there were men to set the fires. Man and antelope, man and buffalo had lives that converged, and which sustained each other.

But the settlers wired the fields together, and the wind in the wire sang a new song called "yours" and "mine." Man and antelope could no longer converge in their orbits around the seasons; the new fences stood in their way. The Indians, still roaming in starved, scattered bands looking for fugitive game, sat on their ponies and, in sign language, signalled "Wrong side up." But the whites only laughed and kept right on plowing. They knew that God, and Science, blessed the furrow.

Bombardier Michael Richards was our driver the next day. We travelled north through a cold rain, past a Canadian militia camp of soggy tents and rain-streaked tanks. The prairie suddenly looked like Rommel's North Africa—in a monsoon. A stretch of burnt-over prairie led north from the armour. Travelling east on the Kangaroo Rat Road, it took all of our driver's concentration to keep the 4 x 4 truck between the ditches of the muddy trail. At one point, we executed a complete 360 and resumed forward motion again without comment, as if it was merely routine. "Hey, what a day for photo opportunities," grumbled a voice from the back seat.

At last the black clouds parted, and there were the Middle Sand Hills, an endless corrugation of tawny whalebacks. Chokecherry bush and small, isolated aspen and cottonwood groves growing on their lee slopes offered shelter that horses love. There were freshwater springs near by to sustain the herds. We topped a rise, and beheld at last a herd of feral horses, the current kings and queens of the "charismatic megafauna." But these were not at all like the mustangs pictured by the public. There were horses in all directions, horses of all shapes, sizes and colours. We saw quarterhorse builds and workhorse builds and just about all types in between. Frisky colts followed their dams in small bands of mares, each band ruled over by a stallion. There was a band of bachelors, too, who nibbled each other's manes for want of mares to horse with. One of these stallions tried to run off a little black filly: she kicked him so hard in the side of the head that he staggered to his knees before running off, tossing his head at the smart.

The whole scene was like a gigantic cavvy of modern ranch horses, rather than a herd of "wildies." Major McDonald had objected to my use of that term. "They are not, I say again, not wild horses," he had insisted emphatically. "They are second and third generation illegal grazers!" In fact, although some of these horses could be traced back to stock turned loose by my grandfather's generation, most of them descend from trespass grazers left here by local ranchers between 1941 and 1982. That was the last time the horses were rounded up and culled by local riders. If they had been rounded up more frequently, they would not have grown to fifteen hundred head. According to Canadian Wildlife Service studies in '92, the horses could have doubled their numbers every five years. They had to be reduced because of the damage they were doing to the dunes and the springs, and the competition they offered to wildlife. But in honour of the homesteaders who had once lived there and depended on horses for traction, transport and just plain company, a small herd should have been allowed to run free, as recommended by CWS. Sadly, as I write this, they have all been rounded up and removed for adoption.

Time passed all too quickly for us in the desert solitudes along the South Saskatchewan. On the last day, we picked up my father, Orland, and my Aunt Dot, both retired Medicine Hat residents, and drove them out to the old homestead site, which they had not set eyes on since 1933.

My father put on a brave face when he finally saw the old bedstead, but I could tell that memories were overwhelming him. "Right about there," he said, pointing to the empty cellar hole, "would have been the clothes closet." Aunt Dot stood upon the stone threshold, and pointed out local landmarks.

"So was this land fertile?" I asked my father.

"Fertile? Never got enough rain to find out. By the time I came along we were farming on the hardpan. Where it piled up against the fences, it seemed to grow weeds and Russian thistle quite well. . . ."

What was left to commemorate all the blood, sweat and tears? Scraps of metal, coloured glass from the fire, a rusty spoon. But still there was the stone threshold of what had been a home, and the stone foundations. These were remnants from the Laurentide ice sheet, granitic rocks from the Canadian Shield. My grandparents had gathered them up off the prairie, loaded them into a wagon and brought them here with enormous labour.

Glancing down, I saw a glint in the dirt. I stooped and stared at some objects there. They were broken fragments of Delft china, and it came to me they were all that was left as reminders of my grandmother's vanished kitchen. I picked them up tenderly. I see them before me now, fragments of a dream, the only concrete memento I have of that woman who was the loving bedrock of a family.

Orland recalled the night this place burned to the ground. How do you get sleepy kids out of a burning shack? Grandfather picked up my Uncle Walter, then a toddler, wrapped him in a blanket, and simply threw him out through the front window, glass and all. As my father and Aunt Dot recalled that night, I looked down and saw, shining among the sage, pieces of broken, melted glass, coloured with time.

After a few moments, we got back in the truck. Following the long thread of homesteader's memory, we made our way up the hill until we came to another cellar hole. The building itself had been moved into town decades ago. This was it: Robert's Box on the Buttes, where J.C. moved his family after the fire. "You could see the old shack sitting here from miles away," mused Orland sadly. He turned away, wiped a tear from his eye.

I got out to look around. Two Blackhills cottontail rabbits, amazingly tame, had made a home in the thick sagebrush that had overgrown the cellar. My father said, "Just down that slope there, I was roping a calf; I was barefoot, as usual. And I cut my foot wide open, right to the bone, on an old mower blade."

"And I sewed it up," added Aunt Dot.

"Did a damn good job, too," affirmed my father.

I looked around, at the land unfolding everywhere like a rug rolled out to the horizons. Robert was no stranger to wind, yet he had built his home in the most unprotected spot he could find. It struck me that my great-grandfather was indeed a dreamer. Great-grandfather had built his home in the sky, and did it have a view! All the way to the Cypress Hills; all the way to Montana. And perhaps it was this "Swissman," as Aunt Dot called him, who had left me a gift. For when I looked down, there was a penny, a little green with age, lying at my feet, not even buried under the grass roots; a 1920 penny with the King's head on it. It seemed to me at that moment as glorious as a diamond; it was a miracle that I had even noticed such a small treasure in that immensity of sage and grass.

Far below on the plain, we could see a herd of antelope. We saw deer, we saw the dark apostrophes that marked a small band of wandering horses. I walked down the slope for some reason, clutching the penny in my hand. I should have been getting used to it, finding the hard evidence of every story my aunt and father told, stories that heretofore I had thought of as mostly myth. Perhaps it was just for doubting them that I nearly cut my own foot, or at least my shoe, on the old mower blade.

I picked it up and tested the edge with my thumb. It was still sharp, hardly eaten by rust, though it had lain in wait for me in the desert grass for over sixty years. I decided I would take it home; I don't know why. And I took one stone from the foundation, which the Great Ice once carried from the Canadian Shield to be a threshold for my great-grandparents' home, as it will be now, for mine.

THE SEASONS:
ASPEN VALLEY

8

A Dimple on the Lewis Overthrust

~

For a long time, I forgot about the wind because I forgot about the prairies, having spent most of my working life deep in the mountains where the wind is a less troublesome visitor. All that changed in 1981. A man who promised he would sell me a quarter section of mountainside for three times more than it was worth had a sudden greed attack and backed out of the deal. Myrna and I had sold our house in Canmore, and now we had no place to live; because of that failed transaction, I wound up back in school.

Myrna first heard about the Waterton School House from an old friend who lived near by. My spouse took her savings (this is not normally an impulsive woman) and bought the place and its two acres of land for about the price of a used car.

The Foolhouse, as Paul immediately dubbed it, was a used FORD (Fix Or Repair Daily) of a building. The big schoolhouse windows, the kind that my father's generation remembered, held 108 panes of glass;

two-thirds of them were broken either by flung stones, or, more ominously, by bullets—.30 calibre to be precise. There were bats in the belfry and bee hives in the walls, and when I bored a hole to check for insulation—ha!—honey leaked out in a golden trickle. At night, as we lay in bed staring up at the stars through holes in the roof, platoons of mice ran up and down the keyboard of Myrna's piano. But at dawn, rosy light poured in like wine. The sky was bigger than most minds I had encountered and some advantages were so peculiar they kept us awake, sheerly speculating. I mean the six inches of topsoil in the attic piled there in lieu of insulation. Later I would say I knew where the topsoil wound up that left Pincher Creek in the Dirty Thirties. Back then I said we could grow potatoes in the attic with enough light and rain coming through the shingles; if only we had planted it earlier.

Well, nephew, are you any wiser?

Oh believe me, Aunt Sis, we Martys have come up in the world since your day. Yes indeed. We made sure the place had a well this time before we signed the papers. Out of it, with a rusty long-armed bandit of a pump, we drew water the health inspector tested as "unfit for humans and baby pigs."

"He tells everybody that," said a neighbour. "Ain't no pigs died from that water yet." On the other hand, Sis, the place was heated with wood and there wasn't a tree in sight—I guess you'd call it a real Marty homestead after all.

I made some firewood in that school, though, while finishing my apprenticeship as a renovator. I would begin daily operations with a sledgehammer, and gradually work my way down through the lighter tools, the gravel bar, crowbar, nailpuller (this last being the veritable iron-beaked sceptre of the renovator), thence to framing hammer and finishing hammer. Building a home from a ruin, and all for naught. For like the other homesteads the Martys cobbled together on the prairies, the Foolhouse would not outlast our tenancy. We were to be its last pupils, and the new owner would convert it into a garage.

Any wiser? Well, we learned we had been living without sunsets and sunrises for two decades. Mountaineers are the last ones at the banquet of the sun, hidden behind towering furniture in the corners waiting for the main course, while the prairie guests are already eating dessert.

One July night the moon flooded light over the red earth of the Belly Buttes eastward where the warrior dead of long ago were laid to rest along the Belly River. We woke up to the sound of drums beating like a heart in the night.

It was a sun dance, the old religion rooted here centuries before the white man arrived with ten commandments and a gibbet. The Indian Agents, the missionaries and the police had tried to stamp out the old religion. But it only smouldered under the prairie wool, to burst out every summer with increasing energy.

Later, as we were going to bed, sheet lightning flashed for miles across the eastern horizon. The thunderbird was walking across the sky. Brilliant flashes of light shot through our big windows and lit up the dim corners of the room with surreal brilliance. History was alive, dancing on the stubble fields of all disclaimers.

We woke up, that winter, to bulldozers of wind, Concorde jets of wind and a legion of all the hurricanes. Which had been pounding on the Waterton School House for around seventy years. The corners of the building were rounded off as if they had been sandpapered by God with flying dirt and flying snow. There were evil nights when I woke up choking; the wind had pushed smoke back down our chimney pipe, and we had to crawl out into the snow on our hands and knees. Paul said we must be crazy. It blew the outhouse over; I set it back up. It blew the outhouse over and buried it in a snowdrift; I dug it out, set it up, cabled it to an old wrecked truck. There was a surfeit of those about the place.

It blew the outhouse to pieces. And then it began to blow seriously.

We learned what shelter means in a treeless land of blizzard white-outs, and why neighbours keep an eye on you; it's because they want you to keep an eye out for them, also. We learned how little you need to be comfortable: a roof, fire, food, water and companionship.

Myrna and I learned about romance in the days of the pioneers. At night she donned her sleeping costume: wool long johns, wool knee-length socks, cotton turtleneck T-shirt and her favourite leopard skin patterned flannel nightie. She liked to top this off with an Irish knit cardigan sweater. I myself simply put on a set of wool combinations and a ski mask and left it at that. Still, our attire was not conducive to romance: there was a woman under all that material, warm, vibrant and gorgeous—but somewhat hard to locate, and more interested in staying warm than dealing with her ardent husband. She said I looked like an IRA terrorist in heat. I thought about my grandparents, who had begotten eight kids under even colder conditions than this. Inspired, I wrote:

I slipped my fingers neath her hem
she shivered and she shook
"Your hands are cold, as cold as ice
Please wait for the chinook
The temperature is 28
I do not mean above
We need our clothes on to survive
It is too cold for love"
At night beneath piled sleeping bags
We dare not make a shift
Jack Frost waits for an opening
To freeze us, hip to hip
How did the sons of the pioneers
ever come to be?
The prairie mating season seems
a trifle short, to me.

But we also learned about hate, the hatred between whites and native people that had its origins at Fort Whoop-Up in the horse and buggy days, and had flourished ever since, like the sun dance, right into the space age.

In Fort Macleod, we were known as the Hippies in the Schoolhouse. They don't know from hippies, in Fort Macleod.

The trouble with the schoolhouse, despite all its primitive advantages, was that it was just not far enough away from syphilization. In fact, a meatmaker (highway) went right by the front door. Before we came along, some local Kaina people were wont to pull into the yard and party a bit before driving on to the reserve. The place had a bad reputation in the white community as a result, and there were some ignorant souls who tarred us with that brush. We found ourselves right at the crossroads of hostilities.

One day Paul, wearing his Walkman, saw a white trucker pull over on the meatmaker to adjust his tie-downs. Milo, a visiting red setter, shuffled out to greet him, wagging his tail. Paul heard him yelping in great pain a bit later. Milo was bleeding profusely but we could not find a wound. The vet discovered he had been stabbed in the shoulder, probably with a screwdriver.

Our presence annoyed some of the old party crowd, also. One night as we were sleeping, drunken voices woke me. A rock the size of a baseball crashed through the window, missed Paul's head by a fraction, and rolled around on the floor. Energized into a killing rage, I charged outside, buck naked and barefoot, and chased the tail lights of a car down the highway for several hundred yards. I felt like I could run for twenty miles and snap human necks like toothpicks. The car slowed down for a minute. They could not believe their eyes, I guess. I could not read the plate number, but I got just close enough to scoop up a rock from the shoulder and bounce it off the car's trunk lid. That ended the hilarity; they sped off. I stood in the middle of the road, the fight gone out of me, trembling like an aspen leaf in the cold air. Napikwan, the pink, angry bear.

I found Myrna sweeping up the glass, looking pale and worried. Our boys slept through the whole thing. "Have we learned enough?" I asked.

"I think so," she said. "I think it's graduation day."

We looked west to the mountains, and thought of being in the lee of that barrier, safe from the brunt of the tyrant wind, and well away from the populated precincts of enmity. But there was no land for sale anywhere within a two-hundred-mile radius that we could afford.

Kismet alone accounts for the way I found the place at Aspen Valley back in 1982. It had been for sale for some time but was not advertised in any local papers. The local realtor had an obscure office in the Cowley sawmill. I had driven out there to pick up scrapwood for fuel, and I noticed his sign.

He had one listing of interest to me, a small holding owned by an elderly Scots couple. "He keeps driving the buyers away," he said ruefully. "Say anything critical about the place, he'll tell you, 'I'll nae sell to you for twice the money. Goodday. . . .' It's been listed for months."

"Where is it located?"

He gestured vaguely northwestward. "Wanna take a look at it some time?"

I felt the hair on my neck stand up. There were mountains in that direction. With hopes raised, and afraid of being disappointed, I couldn't bear to ask any more questions. "Sure."

"When would you like to go?"

"Well . . . how would right now be?"

He grinned and reached for his coat.

All the details of that drive stand out clearly in my mind. The day was cool and blustery, the ground bare, the grass and trees all stripped and withered for the season. We drove north in the agent's deluxe Detroit iron, through rolling prairie between the Porcupine Hills and the Livingstone Range.

Not too bad, I told myself. Mountains only six miles west now. Porcupine Hills very close. Not bad at all. Be prepared to compromise, I warned myself. Impossible to find a place in the mountains that you could afford.

Then the agent turned west, heading right for the Rockies.

"Hey."

"Something wrong?"

"Not at all. I just really love this direction."

"West?"

"Yeah. It's my favourite."

He chuckled nervously and gave me a sidelong glance. After a few miles, we came to the top of a low rise of ground. Straight ahead was the main wall of the Livingstone Range, seen through an opening in a long ridge of tawny hills.

"See that stand of poplars? Sun's just coming on it."

"Yes."

"Little house to the right there, below the big hill?"

I swallowed hard. "That's it?"

"Yep."

"Somebody is actually selling that?"

"You bet."

"You're sure?"

"Positive."

"I'll take it."

"Ha ha. Better have a look first. Place needs some work."

"I'll take it."

"Oh, ha ha. Let's go have a look at it, anyway," he drawled. "Before we draw up the offer."

We turned off the main road, down the long driveway past the trees that were to be so beloved, looking up at the hill that would guard our sleep for always, or so I thought, so I hoped back then. I loved the grey log barn crumbling into the earth, the stable roof leaning northeast like a sail. Don't think about the renovations, I told myself. Don't allow logic to get in your way.

I shook hands with shrewd old "Sandy" and his jolly wife "Betsy," who lived here then with two German shepherds and seven of the largest cats I have ever seen. Then, on Sandy's direction, I found the north fence and followed it west up the hill to learn the limits of the future demesne. Straight up, almost hand over hand on the steep part, I went through outcrops of rock and through bullpine, steeply down, picking holds on some low cliffs, round the other side through grass, back to the road, then east back through the aspen woods. I lingered for a while, staring at the trees; wondering why they were all leaning to the southeast instead of growing straight up. I shrugged off the question; the trees looked strong and healthy, that was the main thing.

The old house was full of antiques. The linoleum was shot, the kitchen floor was a ramp uphill to the back porch, the bathroom cried out for sledge and crowbar. "Roof me, roof me," moaned the attic. The sink drainpipe was plugged with frost and would remain plugged until April. I toured the basement, and peered into the crawlspace, over the body of a desiccated mouse, beneath the old part of the house. Two fiery eyes glared back: a stink of tomcat greeted me. But it was the sight of blocks of wood and stone holding up the floor joists, of iron pipes drifting free of rusted straps that made the interior voice say: Don't linger. Don't hesitate. Don't think.

I sat in the kitchen drinking tea, stunned. It seemed I had been climbing half my life to reach this dimple on the Lewis Overthrust. I had barely arrived, yet I already felt like I had lived there for years. If Myrna feels like I do right now, I told myself, this will be our new life.

Betsy, tall and silver-haired, glanced silently at my face as she poured more tea, and read my expression like a book. In the living room she told Sandy with complete certainty, "He's going to buy it."

Myrna always tells everyone how nonchalant I was about the whole thing. No excitement, no big pressure. I wanted to be sure that she felt the same as I did. "I think you should go and look at this place right away," was all I really said. I showed her a few pictures Betsy had sent with me, of the house, the aspen grove with hills and mountains, the summer garden rich with peonies.

"My God!" gasped Myrna. She went the next day with her friend Donna, and when she came back home that evening her face was shining with excitement.

"I can't understand why you aren't climbing the walls and whooping," she told me.

"I know, I know. If I wasn't in a trance I probably would be." We made an offer the next day, and it was accepted. Sandy said he knew I was the guy for the place when I went charging up that hill. He said I was the only buyer who had shown the slightest interest in the land itself; Betsy said Myrna was the only one who asked what perennials were in the garden. The others had all complained about the work the house would need. The statement amazed me. Any fool can fix a house. Only God can create heaven on a hillside.

*   *   *

Our south Macleod neighbours, with trucks and horsetrailers, helped move us to Aspen Valley. It was a cold day late in February. Nathan and Paul had already claimed their rooms in advance. Nathan, aged six, settled in over the furnace vent in his. He was delighted: "Look, Dad, heat comes out of the floor." I didn't have the heart to tell him that it would soon be turned off, and the wood-burning heater fired up instead. Paul, eleven years old, had snuck off into the snow towing his toboggan, only appearing again when the smell of a hot dinner wafted up the hill.

Late that night Myrna and I bundled up and went out to stand in the yard and gaze at the house. Warm yellow light from its lamps glowed against the dark woods.

"Look," she said. "Trees." The sky above them was studded with white fires. We saw the brilliant cluster of the Pleiades and Myrna pointed out the constellations with a surety I have always envied. There were forest sounds that night that startled our prairified ears: a saw-whet owl scraped a song across the snow-covered valley, and frost cracked a protest from the frozen aspen trunks. "So this is it," said Myrna. "My God, it is beautiful."

And in the morning there was still a big sunrise, for the valley opened outward to the east on that stretch of distant prairie. We stepped out-side to test the air, clutching our cups of coffee.

Days went by, and one morning the sublime quiet was shattered by the excited roaring of Lion, our golden retriever. I peered uphill: a frightening sight. The boys were already up at that ungodly hour, tobogganing. "You'll miss the schoolbus!" I yelled up at them.

Whoops of delight greeted the thought of it. (The bus, we soon discovered, was a boxing ring on wheels. They fought their way to school, fought at school and fought all the way home. It was an average boy's education in southern Alberta. I was not comforted by the continuing tradition.) They had packed a run two hundred yards long through the snowdrifts on the steep hill. It looked like a chute for a luge. Here they came, huddled together, rocketing straight down the hill, through a narrow gate in the barbed-wire fence that made me gasp. Between the truck and Myrna's station wagon they went streaking, their faces plastered with snow. They shot up over a ramp of snow they had built, "catching big air" as Paul termed it. A crazed yell and—crash! Onto the thin snow there, rolling end over end, the toboggan careering on without them, its sprung boards rattling on the hardpan. And they lay there laughing and moaning by turns, at the end of a trail of lost mitts, toques and scarves.

"Don't look, in future," advised Myrna.

I stared at her, at a loss. "Why are they so damned reckless?" I demanded.

"Why are you so damned surprised?" she countered.

A nightmare starring barbed wire tuned up in my head. As soon as they left for school, I took the entire section of fence down, put old tires and some old hay bales around all other obstacles, and said a prayer. The toboggan run turned out to be the cheapest entertainment imaginable, with lots of extra kids coming home with ours to try it out.

Late morning brought its monarch to honour us, a golden eagle circling over the ridge behind our house. To our delight, we found that we had bought a house that sits right on the annual migration route of both the golden and the bald eagle. The morning light etched the eagle's shoulders with gold, and the dark outline on its wings looked like a smaller eagle tucked against its breast. It coasted down over the yard, as if in greeting, for this bird had been watching me for some time before I started watching it. Locally, it is surpassed in wingspread only by the trumpeter swan and the bald eagle. According to legend, this great raptor, with its six-foot-plus wingspread, can lift lambs from the earth. Just then, it seemed willing to settle for Sasha the black-and-white cat, busy exploring her new boundaries. It swooped down so close to her that I could see the fierce beak open as if in anticipation, or else to silently coax, "Here kitty kitty." The intuitive beast glanced up, growled defiance, then turned and vanished through a hole in the barnboards.

Myrna and I went for what she calls a "trudgercize," which is what you do in country where the snow is too thick for jogging, but too thin for skiing. We were followed by the dog who was followed by the cat. The eagle followed her and some magpies followed the eagle, amusing themselves by dive-bombing the noble bird, which twittered furiously with an incongruous, sparrow-like voice. Eagles don't always enjoy the results of cat grabbing. An old tomcat will just about eviscerate an eagle if the bird's big talons happen to miss the vitals. But Sasha was a small, rabbity looking thing. I picked her up and wrapped her around my neck like a scarf, where she promptly fell asleep. It was a trick she had. The eagle spiralled up higher to hide in the sun.

The air had a completely different smell in Aspen Valley. The sun-bleached odour of prairie grass was replaced by the perfume of pine boughs and juniper. There were groves of Douglas fir so dark green they looked black. The mountain, great dictator, set the theme for weather, controlled the sunset, dominated the skyline. It held the sky up, the pillar of a house of cloud. Returning home, we watched its moods from our west window. Snow blew in manes from cornices overhanging the east face of Cirque Peak. "So much wind up there, and yet it's dead calm here," I mused, happy to be back in the arms of the mountains.

We both knew the windless idyll could not last. "But there's no way it can blow here like it does on the prairie," we told each other. And yet we could see how the aspens grew with a permanent northeast lean, which was echoed in the slant of our ancient log barn and stable. Men lean into the wind and forge blindly on. Everything else gives way and rolls with the punch of the ineffable.

The first heating bill arrived, and we turned off the furnace. I went into the woods with the chainsaw and a snow shovel to fell some dead aspen trees. After dropping a dozen or so, I became aware of something very odd: the tree stumps were not round. They were actually oval, like the cross section of a modern sailing mast. And glancing around, I saw that the ovals were all lined up in the same direction—southwest to northeast. There is a purpose to this adaptation, I thought uneasily. Which is no doubt to offer as little resistance to the prevailing wind as possible. Fascinating aspen clones. A forest of you was shown to be the biggest living organism on earth. All springing up from a single mother tree, from common suckers underground. In the fall, all the clones from one particular mother tree turn yellow on the same day. Men on the other hand are all so singular; each one must rediscover the wheel, each one must teach himself how to be. How to live with others or live apart, and how to die, alone.

I filed away the thought of oval tree trunks under O for "Oh-oh."

*   *   *

Pincher Creek, a town named after a pair of pliers, was forty-five rattle-trap minutes away. (The pliers were in fact a pair of lost hoof nippers later found by the first Mounted Police detachment. Apparently not much was going on back then.) We were now living in the premier ranching country of Alberta. The first calves of the year were already dropping with a steamy hiss into the snowdrifts, as we rattled and back-fired in to the Pincher Creek Co-op. A bumper sticker on the truck in front of us read "Please don't tell my mother I'm working in the oil-patch; she thinks I'm playing piano in a whorehouse." This led us to believe that "Pincher" must be a pretty humorous place. (It is, but it doesn't mean to be.)

Meat was amazingly expensive there, considering you could rope a steer from the back door of the butcher shop. We were fairly carnivo-rous at that time, but our budget demanded that meat rations be pared to the bone, so to speak. We opted for oatmeal breakfasts and vegetar-ian dinners—lots of rice and beans. It would prove a wholesome, if bland diet. Unfortunately, the boys were not fond of oatmeal porridge, charmingly referring to it as "swill."

After two weeks of this fare, the boys reported that they were dream-ing about prime rib, served rare. They seemed pale and dispirited, and blamed their inability to do homework on a lack of red meat.

"They need iron pills," suggested Myrna.

"We need blood," moaned Nathan melodramatically.

"Look, too much red meat is not good for you anyway," I told them.

"Tell it to the marines," suggested Paul. "Now the cowgirls on the bus are starting to beat us up, too."

"And that's because they eat too much red meat, also."

"I don't care. I'm startin' to feel like a damned bunny rabbit."

"No need for that kind of language."

"Dad. You are so out of it, I just can't believe it."

"Believe it."

And Nathan made a face, lifting his spoon to show me: "There's a dead beetle in my swill, Dad!"

"That's a raisin. I picked out the beetles; there weren't enough to go round."

"I hate raisins in my swill," muttered Nathan.

Every night the neighbourhood coyotes rendezvoused for the evening hunt a few hundred yards north of us, and serenaded us with howls, yodels and hysterical piccolo playing, which is the Coyote Way. After a few nights, Lion began joining in. She hadn't had a bone to chew on for a month. The boys lay in their bunks, harking to the predators' serenade. Their eyes shone in the dark.

Paul suggested that I should "take the .270 and go waste a deer."

This is where Scruples raised its angelic head. I explained that the hunting season was over until next fall. "I spent twelve years enforcing the game laws, capiche? I'm not going to start breaking them now."

Apparently, word of my resolve spread far and wide. At night, as the northern lights danced to the music of the spheres, resident mule deer gathered in our vegetable garden. They pawed up the snow, revealing discarded potatoes and other treats. When I went outdoors to enjoy one of the male privileges of country living—writing one's name in the snow—these overfed deer stepped back into the shadows to watch my performance. One of them actually farted in disdain. Yet another literary critic. From under the porch, a soft growl and anxious whine. This was Lion, the watchdog, who watched deer very carefully. She had been traumatized by this species as a pup, when an expensively protected national park doe had punted her into a wire fence like a furred soccer ball.

"Ooo, there's a big fat doe," said Nathan, shining his flashlight out the window. "Yummy."

"Sit down and eat your turnips," suggested Myrna.

A gang of fat American elk invaded our neighbour's hay supplies that March, knocking down the fence, scattering bales and fouling with their urine what they didn't eat. Come sunup on frosty March mornings, these aristocratic beasts, proud noses held high, trooped through our yard on their way home from work. One day we woke up to find deer tracks on our front steps. There was a large dark form lying prone in the corral, licking at the remains of an old salt block. It stood up to stretch when I opened the front door: it was a cow moose, sighting back along her flanks at me like an old brown mare.

"She's doing a B.M.," commented Nathan. "Gross." When I closed the door, she lay back down again. Myrna and I were thrilled to have a moose in our corral, something we had last experienced at Maligne Lake in Jasper, during park warden days. But Paul and Nathan's reaction was more pragmatic. "Why don't we take this damned oatmeal and make a trail of it?" suggested Paul. "Lead her down to the basement. I'll bet she would walk right into the coldroom."

"Yeah, Dad," chirped the youngest. "You could bean her with your typewriter."

"Just kidding, Dad," said Paul, with a predatory grin.

When I wasn't chopping wood, renovating or hacking out prose on the Remington, Myrna and I discussed provisions. We might be meatless, but we had wonderful fresh, unpasteurized milk and fresh eggs from two neighbours, Amy Halek and Tammy Broda. Tammy was scandalized that we wanted only skim milk. She refused all payment. "I can't take good money for something that I usually feed to the chickens," she said primly. To our rancher neighbours, who used to sell their extra milk to a dairy, milk prices, and hence milk's virtue, was tied to butterfat content.

Myrna thought we had enough grass on the place to support a steer or two. Maybe we should go to the neighbours and see about buying a calf. Myrna wanted her own chickens and a milk cow; there would be times when the neighbours' chickens were not laying, times when the milk cows were dried up or with calf. We had outbuildings that could be fixed up for livestock.

Enter Amy Halek, agricultural consultant. She rattled into the yard in a low-slung Ford landship one morning. She was wearing her winter rancher ensemble: overshoes, nondescript slacks, a shapeless parka, mitts and, for headgear, the winter liner out of a hardhat. Watching her walk was painful. She had a touch of something chronic in her legs. The Haleks, as we would learn, lived to work. Amy loved the morning routine of feeding cows, but she also ran the household for her husband and two grownup sons.

"We done feeding for this morning," she said. "I come to borrow your wife. To show her the ranching business."

Myrna was game, and donned her coat. "We lost a calf, Myrna," said Amy. "Stillborn. So we have to go and buy one."

"Oh, really?"

"Fifty dollars the man wants. And if no one buys it, he just knocks it on the head anyway. Now I ask you," she finished indignantly.

Amy has a strong, beautiful face full of light. She takes no guff from man or beast. She is built generously compared to her husband, Frank, dubbed by me the Local Oracle, who is tough, slight and given to puckish pronouncements. Once he drove up while my friend, poet Andrew Suknaski, was visiting. Andy had the pipe-smoking habit bad. He used to keep one in his mouth, and two others loaded and ready to go in either pocket. His hair needed hedging, and his black beard was of a Tolstoyan luxuriance and length. I told Frank that Andy was a Russian Orthodox priest who had come to hear my confessions.

Suknaski held up a freshly loaded pipe, and muttering poetically in Ukrainian, gestured a blessing on the Local Oracle. "Careful with that incense burner, Father," said Frank, as Suknaski held a match to his pipe bowl, "or we're gonna hear another voice from the burning bush."

Aspen Valley was mainly settled by coal miners overflowing from the Crowsnest Pass. Many of them were eastern Europeans originally. Frank's father worked underground at the turn of the century. Frank Sr. established the ranch around 1910 and worked on it on his days off. Every Friday he would hike from the mine and follow an old Indian trail that climbed over the Livingstone Range to reach his ranch. It was fourteen miles one way. The entire valley was one big forest in those days. He would clear bush for two days, then take off and run all the way back to work on Sunday in time for the late shift. His wife stayed on the place full time, guarding their one milk cow. There was an ongoing feud with some nearby ranchers who had been running cattle in the valley before these settlers showed up. Cowboys used to roam the hills by night, rounding up any newcomer's stock they could slip a rope on. The coyotes ran in big packs, and when they came into the yard, Frank Jr.'s mother would throw open the window and blaze away at them with a pistol. News of this tactic kept the cowboys at bay also.

Frank followed his father into the mine for a few years. That was after World War II, and the coal cars were still hauled underground by workhorses. "And you better believe, they were in a lather," he said, when I asked him about it. "They sweated buckets, and so did we. We worked on slopes of forty-five degrees, following the seams. Two men put up sixty tons of coal per day." Frank had enjoyed the underground, the whiff of danger, the hardcore toughness and skill of the miner's trade. "But it's not the kind of job you want to do for long," he admits.

Amy and Myrna came back to pick me up later that day. I pulled a toque over my ears and buttoned my coat against the cold. Crossing behind the car I jumped when I heard a loud bellow—"*MU-WAH.*" The trunk lid was propped slightly open and tied down with rope. Two white eyes stared out at me from the darkness. The little calf, curled up on an old blanket, looked small even in that space.

It was a short drive to the Halek ranch, where Amy showed me how to pick up the brown-and-white calf. I carried it into the cow shelter. The little calf's warm body smelled sweet and milky; the place smelled of fresh hay and fresh manure, and it was warmed by the animal heat of several cows. Seeing them, the little beast struggled and bawled as I set him down. He headed for the nearest udder as Myrna and Amy discoursed. "Milk cow?" snorted Amy. "Nothing but trouble, Myrna. Why, I've got all the milk you need from mine, if you can't get enough from Tammy's. Beef is hard enough to deal with, but once you get one of them Swiss beasts you may as well be married to the darn thing."

"Hey! You stop that, you mean beggar!" she suddenly cried. A heifer had struck out viciously at the little orphan with one big hoof as it tried to suck, sending it flying arsy-versy. Now the heifer in turn dodged a kick from Amy's manure-splattered boot. "You've got such ugly tits anyway," she scolded, "it's a wonder the calf will even try to suck them. Poor little thing," she added mournfully. "He can't even find them, for cryin' out loud."

"That ain't gonna help matters," said a patient voice in the dimlit recesses. I had not noticed Frank, who I now discovered was busily skinning out a stillborn calf with his stock knife. It had belonged to the mean heifer. Frank explained that he planned to tie the dead calf's hide on the new orphan to mask its alien scent from the heifer. "You don't have to do that," urged Amy.

"Yes I do."

"You do not," she protested, affectionately.

"I do, I do," crooned Frank, affectionately, in return. "Or that young cow there will just keep playing feetsball with his head. Until she kicks it right off."

"Oh she will not!" protested Amy, delighted, inviting us to enjoy this caution of a man.

"Will too, will too," crooned Frank, preoccupied with his task.

"Just rub some of the cleanings on it," she insisted. She stooped painfully, grabbed a mittful of afterbirth from the straw and held the raw, purplish mass up to the light. "That's what we call the cleanings, Myrna," she explained. And she gave Myrna a short lecture on the attributes of the discarded organ.

"Grab ahold, kiddo," Frank commanded. "If you're not too busy being entertained. . . ."

"Oh, sure."

I felt the sticky wetness of the dead calf's hide. This lag end of winter is a hard season for a calf to be born into. Imagine dropping out of a nice warm womb into a snowdrift. Branding and castration are just around the corner, and after eighteen months of fattening, the male beast is off to the abattoir. The females may be kept on as breeding stock. For a bull calf, dying seemed like a shrewd way out. Ranchers spread lots of straw around for bedding on the calving grounds, but cows often sneak off on their own to give birth. We learned that cowsheds were not necessarily preferable. A herd needs lots of fresh air around them, or any infection harboured in one beast will quickly spread to the others. I pulled hard on the hide as Frank trimmed it off at the knee joints. Amy grabbed the naked beast by the hocks and dragged it unceremoniously to one side. Over the years, I have watched ranchers deal with life and death on a daily basis. It is not that they don't feel for animal suffering, it is just that feeling bad doesn't help the animal; one must act, quickly and decisively.

Frank, moving with a perfect economy of motion, cornered the little orphan and nipped him up off the ground in one scoop so he could not kick. He offered the little beast his thumb to suckle, and deftly eased a dose of scours powder into the calf's mouth before he could spit the thumb out. Scours is a form of bovine diarrhea, not uncommon in newborns during cold weather. We worked the raw hide over the calf like a bloody coat, while he bawled piteously, partly from being man-handled, but mostly from sheer hunger. Frank gently rubbed the afterbirth from the dead calf on the orphan's head. The cow banged its side into the shed and rolled its eyes at this small Lazarus, while Frank pushed the calf toward her udder through the bars of the holding pen. The cow looked slowly down. She lowered her big wet muzzle and sniffed at the bloody head of the little animal. She bawled out an earsplitting greeting. The calf darted forward and leeched on to a teat, butting into the udder so hard the young cow flinched. He began to draw the milk. Relieved as the pressure subsided, the cow relaxed. She began licking at the bloody hide over his back as he nursed. "She wants to clean him up," said Amy approvingly. His first meal would be rich in colostrum that would help to immunize him against infections.

"She thinks it's hers," said Amy. "Thatta girl."

"And I think it's coffee time," said Frank.

And over coffee Frank wondered aloud why we would want to raise beef for the table, when there were all those wild cattle standing around in our garden eating "spudadoes." "Why hell," he added, "you could probably carve a roast off that cow moose you're salting in your corral. She wouldn't even miss it." I could see that not much missed the Local Oracle's hawk-like eye.

"Don't you like eating beef, Frank?" I inquired.

"Look here, young fella. I can't afford to eat beef. It takes everything I got just to raise it. Beef is for rich people."

I grinned into my cup.

"Think I'm kidding? Take a look in the freezer. There's elk, moose and deer meat in there. All legal, by the way. . . ."

"And chicken," put in Amy.

"But no beef. Costs eighty cents a pound to raise beef and they're offering seventy cents a pound to buy it from me. And what do you know about diseases?"

"Diseases?"

"You said it," he cried, slapping his cap on the table for emphasis.

"I did?"

"You said a mouthful there. First they get pneumonia," he said, counting off his fingers. "Then they get the sore feet walking through drifts. Or after a chinook, you get that icy crust? That'll cut hell out of their fetlocks. Then the sun comes out and sunburns their udders. So then next you got mastitis, infection in the tits. Then the wind gets up and blows dirt in their eyes. They get sore eye. Or pink eye—that's caused by a kind of worm they figger. Got to put 'em in a squeeze chute, put a needle in under the eyelid . . ."

"Oh, I hate that one," cried Amy, squirming at the thought.

"Go blind if you don't treat it," insisted Frank. "Got to glue an eye patch over the medicine afterwards. Seen any of them pirate cows in yer travels?"

"Come to think of it . . ."

"Then you got yer coxciddyosis. It's in the brain. Ear droops on one side, next thing you know, they are following it around in ever diminishing circles; the balance is shot. Wire cuts, bot flies, colic, black leg, broken leg, no leg, sonofa—"

"Don't get him started," cautioned Amy.

But it was too late. After he had wound down slightly, Myrna blurted out, "What about chickens?"

"Chickens?" asked Amy doubtfully. "Well now, you can always get eggs here, you know." A pause as she frowned. "They're okay, aren't they?"

"They are absolutely wonderful," said Myrna hastily.

"Best we ever ate," I affirmed.

"Oh, for Pete's sake!" Amy smiled helplessly and slapped at her temple: "But you was wantin' to get some of your own, you mean? Oh well," she said, one hand waving the idea to fly on in, "I'll sure help you get started with that. You're just in time to order the chicks if you do it this week." And in the meantime, Amy dove into her deep freeze and loaded us down with cuts of packaged venison and a chicken or two. "Just call it the welcome wagon," she said, waving off all our protests, and she slipped a box of eggs under my arm as I went out the door. "In case Missus wants to bake you a cake," and gave me a knowing swat on the shoulder that nearly knocked me off the step.

Frank drove us home. He had plenty of aspens on his land, but the cattle knocked down and broke a lot of young saplings. "Lots of deadfall there if you ever need more firewood," he offered. I could see big snowdrifts in the lee of his aspen groves.

"So I guess you get a lot of wind here, eh, Frank?"

"Wind? Oh I wouldn't say that. Hurricanes, now. We get lots of those. But not much wind."

"Uh huh." I thought about the big drifts in the lee of our own woods. Those woods were obviously a very important windbreak. An animal that destroyed the trees would destroy the very thing that protected us. I expounded a bit about my theory of aspen trees adapting to the wind.

Frank put a finger to his lips. "No need to keep mentioning the wind over and over," he said. "Especially when it's lyin' doggo. No need to roust it out, you know."

"Frank! Are you superstitious?"

"I know what I know," said Frank mysteriously. "And I know I ain't seen any oval aspen trees, by the by."

"So your tree trunks aren't oval shaped, in cross section?"

"No, and neither is a can of Ovaltine. Boy, I can see why they get you to write them tall tales. Ha ha ha!"

That night our cubs tore into their first feast of Amy's free-range chicken. Our plan to raise chickens was heartily approved. The boys entertained us with many lies about the hours they would put in feeding and watering the new chicks Myrna had ordered.

As for raising cattle, I suggested to Myrna that perhaps one of us should qualify as a veterinarian first. Chickens were easier to raise, we assured each other. Chickens probably delivered more value in protein, per pound of feed consumed, than did cattle, and a chicken contained far less cholesterol than did beef. (Elk meat, however, contains even less cholesterol than chicken—but set that aside for now.) Also, most importantly, chickens did not knock down trees. Actually, Amy's directions notwithstanding, what we knew about chickens at that point would not fill the back of a penny matchbook. We didn't know, for example, what Gail Damerow, author of *The Chicken Health Handbook*, knows—that chickens are subject to at least thirty-six bacterial diseases, eleven viral diseases, five fungal diseases and six diseases of unknown causes. Let me not dwell on their parasites overlong, except to note there are nine varieties of lice alone that love this toe-picking, vent-picking, feather-picking, head-picking species, and also there are twelve chicken-hating toxic plants waiting to poison chickens at every opportunity.

Such knowledge would probably have put us off ever getting into the poultry business in the first place. Blissfully ignorant, I cleaned out an old garden shed, windproofed the walls, and made incubators from two old washtubs rigged with heat lamps. I drove into town and picked up a load of woodchips at the local mill for bedding, and some bags of "starter" feed from the co-op.

Later that day, standing quietly in the brooder house, which was in fact a mere garden shed, I heard a whir of many wings followed by the scratching of bird feet upon the roof.

I crept outside and beheld an entire covey of ruffed grouse sunning themselves up there. Wild chickens come home to roost. The grouse ignored me. They clucked and muttered *sotto voce*; they jerked their heads from side to side nervously, staring westward as if a predator was on their trail. Gazing that way, I saw an awe-inspiring sight: a dark layer of cloud overhanging the mountain front. This was the Foehn Wall or cap cloud of the chinook, stretching north and south as far as the eye could see. The actual arch of the chinook wind was not yet in evidence. I had never seen the Foehn Wall at such close range before. As I stared at it, wondering, some dead leaves on the trembling aspen began to quiver and rattle a warning against their frozen branches, though there was only the merest suggestion of a breeze. In the darkening woods, a great horned owl called twice, and on the grace note, I felt the first temperate fingers of the oncoming wind ruffle through my hair and pass overhead.

I went in and tapped the glass on the barometer; the pressure was falling, though not rapidly. Some kind of change was inevitable at this time of year, and I thought little more about it.

Late that night I awoke to hear what sounded like a flute being played down our chimney pipe. The ghostly music made my hair rise "like quills upon the fretful Porpentine." Then came a roaring to the west like an oncoming freight train, and a "boom" as the wind returned to Aspen Valley and broke full upon the balsam trees above the house. A dead branch thudded down on the roof. Suddenly, three doors slammed in the dark house, one after the other. I jumped out of bed to investigate. The boys slept on, oblivious. I found the wind had sucked open the hinged windows in our bedrooms and slammed all our doors shut as the pressure changed.

The entire house trembled like an old man with palsy, then quieted again, steadying to meet the strain. I lay awake for a while until I convinced myself that if the roof had managed to stay on since 1939, it probably would not blow off that night either, and I fell into a fitful sleep.

9

IN BIRD-BRAINED SPRING

~

Over the years we have learned that if a chinook blows in around March 1, it seems at first to break the winter's back. Snow turns into a flood of meltwater; the roads are running freshets. But March is just a battleground between Pacific and northern fronts. The ground may quake underfoot as the warm wind blows. But during the night, the wind backs up as the cold arctic air pours south like water. Warm and cold air mix up a low fog that oozes west toward us off the prairie, a grey blanket being drawn upslope. In the morning there is a fairytale landscape of lacy hoar frost on every twig and stem. Underfoot, the frost has tightened yesterday's quaking pudding into a drumhead again.

More than snow and cold, winter (between chinooks at least) is a silence, and the night is the heart of it. There are long intervals when the only sound you hear is your own pulse. This is the night that the first homesteaders knew, the night of forgotten centuries. In the daylight hours what is most noticeable by its absence is birdsong. All winter we have had no avian company on the ranchette except for rascally magpies stealing the dog's food, and faithful chickadees around the feeder, cracking sunflower seeds and singing "Here, pretty" to each other. These little grey-and-black birds have to feed constantly to keep their metabolic fires burning. They fluff out their feathers and hole up in old woodpecker nests at night, surviving temperatures of –40°F with ease.

But then comes a March morning when our front deck is a tussle of chattering slate-coloured juncos, usually duelling with an irate downy woodpecker who ruled the roosts all winter. They seem to squabble as much as they eat. This is promising, but a true Frostback (what Montanans call us Canadians) stays sceptical. I have looked up through driving snow on March 5 and heard the wild cries of returning Canada geese that I could not see though they were flying at treetop height. Unearthly voices, they speak of the annual wedding of heaven and earth. I almost believe their boasts of an early spring. See them next morning, though, waddling clownishly over the frozen surface of a pond where they expected open water. Soon they take wing again, headed east for the Oldman River, where they can find a pool to swim in until the ice goes out on our creek.

By the middle of the month a few impatient crocuses may stick their purple heads up on the hillside above the house. Comes the vernal equinox and covers them with snow again. It was still March when I heard the song of a meadowlark from the caragana hedge behind the house. Impossible, this early in the season. And there was no lark in sight when I looked, only some beady-eyed starlings shining like blue-black streaks of coal in the hedge. Cheeky little imitators, birds of false hope. Not even the robins can persuade me, because often as not they spend their first week huddled in the treetops like small, orange baseballs, embarrassed to silence by a spring snowstorm. Watching as I shovel runways in the snow for them so the sun can thaw out a worm or two. I am waiting for something much more tangible even than robins, a song that will finally shatter the brooding incubus of winter.

Over the years, I have come to expect the song in early April. But that first year it came to my astonished ears on March 31, when the chinook had melted all the snow in the wetlands below the house. I thought I was hearing crickets, and then realized it was dozens of tiny chorus frogs creaking out their mating song. The wind was breezy and mild, and the night was a black, shining pool smeared with stars, filled with their cricketing exultation. A little bit of last year's summer had sprung loose from the frozen muck.

*   *   *

On April Fools' day I was sent for: "Your chicks are in." I picked them up at the Cowley Co-op, two cardboard boxes full of animated yellow fluff. They would grow into large white adult birds in only six weeks. This variety was a meat producer, with a preponderance of cockerels. But the hens, when mature, would produce large, tasty eggs. Back home, the chicks crowded together under our heat lamps, peering out at the universe of the garden shed. Soon they scattered out to line up at their tiny feeder, made from a length of eavestrough. They played the anvil chorus on the tin trough with their bills. The boys were thrilled with the cute things, glad to feed them and change their woodchip bedding. But after a few weeks, the teenaged chicks had a gangly, reptilian look as they shed their down and started fledging. The boys' interest began to wane.

As spring descended, the aurora borealis made its last appearance of the season in a fiery band of ghostly dancers. Gazing north we observed a symptom of progress that the pioneers never bargained for: the toxic-pink glow of light pollution from the distant city. A shimmering airborne oilslick in the heavens, it was a tawdry imitation of the glorious aurora.

On April 15, the ice went out on Livingstone Creek. Valley nights were slap-happy with beaver tails echoing across the flats. Ducks came whirling in landing cycles over our yard and geese gabbled and honked in cacophony. This constant singing by night and by day—this is spring at the mountain foot. It woke us from the sleepy ennui of the cold days. We hurried around the place tending to chores, sung to, squawked at, our lives registering on all those others. One evening we stood on either side of the creek, watching a beaver repairing a dam. "Don't move," hissed Myrna. A shadow came in over the treetops and a great blue heron wafted down over the creek, its pterodactylian wings whoofing the air in such regular beats, they might have been drawn up and down on puppet strings. "It's that damn herring!" I said, delighted. This is a joke we had, occasioned when a neighbour said to us, "Used to be plenty of trout in the crik, but them damn herrings ate 'em all."

Back home, a murder of crows threatened the aspen trees like a black net thrown down. They lifted in a quarrelsome mesh after a red-tailed hawk, like fishwives nagging the butcher's boy. The first yellow tulips, planted by our predecessors along the south wall of the house, had long since bloomed. The red curls of the rhubarb poked up through the thawing earth. The first mountain bluebird made a brilliant exclamation point on a fence post. There came a flight of swallows, in and out of the workshop, furiously gluing mud to the sides of the house and barn, starting three nests for every one they finished. There was at last an exaltation of larks to claim the east fence line, and the red-winged blackbirds flashed their red chevrons over a meltwater pond.

All the wild birds sang of new life in the land, and as they sang, the chickens began to die.

Lefty, who dragged his right leg awkwardly behind him, was the first. We discovered him one morning, unable to stand, but fighting gamely for a space at the feeder while stronger birds employed him to their advantage as a stepping stool. It seemed to us that Lefty's leg must be broken. At the Pincher Creek library, Myrna got a book on how to care for our feathered friends. Equipped with this, we took the game little fellow into the house, and cleaned him up, then set him on some newspaper on the kitchen table, and opened the book. There was a diagram showing how to splint the broken leg of a budgie with toothpicks. This inspired us to make a larger version for Lefty's leg out of popsicle sticks. Lefty seemed to resent our attention, however, and refused to try out the leg. Sated with food and drink in his infirmary box, he preferred to crawl on his belly like a reptile.

I hiked upstream to visit my agricultural consultants. Over coffee, I described Lefty's problem and our first-aid efforts. Frank suddenly convulsed, and expelled a sip of coffee halfway across his kitchen table. "Splinted his leg! You never did."

"I did. I felt I owed it to Lefty. He's a trooper."

Amy handed Frank the dish cloth, giggling wildly.

"What's next, you figger?" demanded Frank after a moment of hilarity that left him gasping for breath. "Crutches?"

"Well, I thought I'd ask you guys."

"Well, now you finally done the right thing. Got a hatchet?"

"Of course, but—"

"Well, if you bring the pointy end down on that chicken's neck with sufficient force, that'd be the best first aid you could give it. Just don't cut your thumb off while you're at it."

"There's no hope for him, then?"

Frank blinked owlishly at me. "Know what, kiddo? It ain't really the chicken that I am worried about."

We sipped our coffee. "It's the feed, Sid," said Amy sympathetically. "It's too hot. They grow too fast, and the leg can't support the weight of the body, so it gets all bent. It's called slipped tendon. They're not really bred for people like us, for free-range use. It's kinda the fast-food market they aim the damn things for. . . ."

People like us. I grinned, pleased that Amy had included me in the description. "Maybe you could whittle him a cane," suggested Frank. "Use one of them twigs from them oval poplar trees of yours. Keep him aerodynamic."

We changed to a feed mixture Amy recommended to try to subvert the madcap speed of growth programmed into the chicks. Later we would learn that one must control the postmodern chicken environment and feed quantity in a more scientific manner, so that the skeletal development stays in balance with the body growth. But it was too late for Lefty. He sulked in his cardboard box in the kitchen while I broke the sad news around the supper table. "Boys, I'm afraid that Lefty must be terminated—with extreme prejudice."

"All right!"

"Outstanding."

They took the news a little too well, I felt. The noble bird was given a final meal before the sentence was carried out. The grim task fell to me. I elected to dispatch him with the same small-calibre weapon I had previously used to finish off scores of crippled big game animals—deer, elk, moose and bighorn sheep—mangled by cars, trucks and trains, when I worked in Banff National Car Park, protecting the wildlife from poachers. (For every deer killed by a poacher, we probably lost about fifty to the internal-combustion engine.)

Lefty declined the blindfold; he died like a real chicken. Unfortunately, we could not dine on his undersized carcass, because he was too recently on the medicated feed. We gave him a tree burial like a true warrior instead; we fed him to the sky. In due course, several more birds were found dead whose legs had suddenly given out under the strain. Their bodies were pounded into the woodchips by their voracious fellows. Learning how to raise chickens was obviously more complicated than greenhorns might assume. But even among experts, losses will occur. Chickens, we would discover, are extremely inventive when it comes to dying.

We cleaned out the ancient log chickenhouse, repaired the dilapidated wire pen and moved the newly fledged chickens into their new home. During the day, they were left out to range around the premises. They were fat and healthy, and already bigger than the chickens one usually sees in the market. They were about as happy as a chicken ever gets. Some juvenile crowing identified potential roosters. But as butchering day approached, they began to drop dead again, sometimes singly, sometimes in pairs. We would find them lying on the ground, feet in the air, wings outspread, grinning. The district agriculturalist had a look at our facilities, but found nothing amiss. He sent two victims in to the lab. The report that came back was enigmatic: "Specimens died of rollover or SDS." It sounded more like a traffic accident than an avian disorder.

"What is rollover or SDS?" I asked the Local Oracle, when we chanced to meet on the road one day.

"Ha! Sent some chickens to the lab, didja?"

"Yes."

"I figured. Well now—S-D-S; that stands for Sudden Death Syndrome. Not even them eggheads in Edmonton know what causes it."

"In other words, these chickens died of death."

"That's about the size of it. And take my advice, kiddo. Hurry up and kill those chickens, before they all die."

"Kill them before they die?"

"You said it, kiddo. You said a mouthful there."

We weren't looking forward to butchering day, however, so we tended to find reasons to postpone it. I had a good excuse. May found me back in Banff after a long absence from the place. Instead of riding the trails, however, I rode herd as resident editor to a group of writers at the Banff Centre for the Arts. I tried to get home every weekend to get some work done, but had no time for the great chicken kill.

As May came on, hearty with sun, Myrna switched to gardening mode. The chickens took to digging her garden seed faster than she could plant it. The garden contained earthworms, which they loved. The robins were very miffed and took to dive-bombing them. Myrna was opposed to fencing the garden with chickenwire. She loved the log fence that the old couple had left us.

"Those birds are looking good," I said one Saturday morning, as she returned yet again from shooing them out of her seed beds.

"Yes," she said plaintively. "Gee, I sure wish they were dead."

"Hush," I cautioned. But it was too late. Another one rolled over within the hour.

The Great Chicken Massacre finally took place. It was a stinky, gory day of wet feathers and tubs of guts that had the boys reconsidering a vegetarian diet. For a week afterward I could not close my eyes without picturing, as if on a screen, the puckered-up anus of a chicken. Our rate of loss had been high. We started out with seventy-five chicks. In the end, we wound up with one rooster and twelve laying hens in the chickenhouse, and fifty birds, each weighing from six to eight pounds, stashed in our freezer. Our family got a lot of value out of one chicken, however. Each one represented three meals, such as roast chicken, chicken casserole and chicken soup.

Over the years, I have learned that chickens, despite their tendency to drop dead if looked at crosswise, are very popular creatures. Hawks love them, coyotes love them, mink love them. The least weasel will drink their blood like wine. Coons very wisely wash them in the watertrough before partaking. Coyotes, however, are too clever to get caught stealing a chicken. It will have to stray quite a ways from home before the little wolf will nab it. Skunks are reasonable though dedicated killers. A mother skunk will whack out one free-range chicken per day. Like a burglar with a sack, she throws the booty over one shoulder and carries it back to her kits.

The predators that first season robbed us blind. Lion, the beloved mountain hound who had practically raised Paul as one of her pups, was old and ailing, and unable to attend to business. Her life would soon be over. The solution was to purchase another dog. This was Mojo. Colour her ink blot. Billed as a pure bred labrador before purchase, Mojo developed, after the cheque was cashed, the head shape of a golden retriever and the body of a Newfoundland water dog. Nature had apparently designed her for retrieving lobster traps. I built her a beautiful dog house, which she never entered.

Her assignment, as she saw it, was to avoid conflict. When threatened by the least weasel on its commutes to the henhouse, she would whine anxiously, and later moan sadly, deploring the carnage. Her main interest, when young, was barn cats. She collected them—sometimes going so far as to cat-nap kittens from god knows which empty culvert—and carry them home, in her mouth, for us to feed. The cats aroused her maternal instincts, and she soon learned to steal eggs from the henhouse to share with her little ones. The cats slept on top of Mojo, under the porch. By all appearances, she was a very comfortable cat mattress.

Mojo despised mink, and kept well clear of them when they visited, though she would quietly moan or groan an alert whenever she glimpsed one approaching. Hence the mink that hiked over from Livingstone Creek one night was the most extravagant assassin. It managed to burrow under the chickenwire while Mojo was cuddled up with her barn cats. Once inside, it killed seven chickens and our new additions that season—two beautiful white ducks of great size and impeccable dignity.

I had loved those ducks. They'd ridden herd on the entire flock, including the rooster. We had only a child's plastic wading pool, dug into the ground, for a duckpond back then. But every day, those ducks had herded the little flock to the pool and, quacking hysterically, tried to teach those chickens to swim—to no avail, alas.

The mink had munched its victims' heads to get at the blood, and ate a few mouthfuls of breast meat. The chickenhouse looked like a slaughterhouse the next morning; the rooster refused to come down from his roost until well after lunch, and the laying hens went on strike for two weeks.

This same rooster became psychotic as a result of the mink incident. Roosters are probably a bit crazy to begin with, it's true. They make interesting alarm clocks, but unless one wants the hens to go broody and raise chicks, the only other use a rooster has is to die on the job, if necessary, protecting his hens from predators. This one was too clever for the job, wise enough to hide from mink and skunks while they were murdering our hens, but happy to fly at us when we went out to feed him and his wives.

One night during that same year of the predators, Nathan, aged eight, went out to pick eggs. In the dim light of the chickenhouse, the rooster flew at our little one. It lit on his head, sinking one of its ugly yellow talons right inside his mouth, and just missing one eye with the other set of meathooks. Beating its wings around his ears, it drummed its beak on his head like a woodpecker from hell. The pain was terrific; he groped upward at the thing, felt a talon nail scrape at the roots of his front teeth, tasted blood and acrid chickenshit, his terrified scream choked in his throat. He pulled the bird off, pushed, punched it away from him, made for the door, tripped over the feed bucket and went down, while the rooster circled the place squawking his fury. Nathan got to his feet as it came running back and launched up at him again, outlined against the moonlight pouring through the chickenhouse door. With a frenzied yell, Nathan delivered a roundhouse kick in midair that accelerated the bird's flight, and sent it crashing through the window out into the pen. Nathan rushed into the house and scared hell out of us; his mouth poured blood, and he had a bloody cut over one eye. The cut in his mouth was deep and nasty. Thank heavens, the talon had not come back out through the lip. But the mouth is wonderful at cleaning and healing such wounds. Nathan soon recovered. The rooster was not injured; he wound up in the stewpot.

*   *   *

It takes an optimist to plant a garden at 4,700 foot altitude, which may be hit by frost, as we discovered, at least three times before the end of August. But by the last weekend in May of our first year in the valley, the aspen trees were leafing out and winter had begun to fade in memory as we planted the last row of potatoes.

Now the days came on with serious heat, and a dark green tinge stained the skin of earth under the old autumn colour of the desiccated grass. Then a sudden storm dumped eight inches of snow on the green grass. Snow caught in the new leaves bowed the aspen saplings and the willow boughs right down to the ground. But such a snow makes the farmer smile as it melts into the cultivated fields. As it melted in these southern foothills that first season, we saw something new to us.

The high slopes and ridges blazed with big yellow flowers of the balsam root. These plants are beloved by the Stoney and Blackfoot people, who still dig the gnarled roots and use them for cold medicine. Now the montane flowers burst forth in all their extravagance. The meadow turned to bright yellow as buttercups erupted. On the hillsides were scarlet clouds of three-flowered avens and scattered along the deer paths were fiery shooting stars.

Our boys made the best of the warm days and cool nights. They pitched our old canvas tourist tent deep in the woods. I went to wake them for breakfast. The trembling aspen had covered their tent with catkins. They smelled of canvas and sunlight as they tumbled out into the green grass, and jumped on my back, wrestling me to earth. I remembered my own father, who could not remember J.C. offering a fatherly embrace, and I hugged them to me, fiercely.

"What's for breakfast?" asked Paul.

"Eggs. Poached, boiled or scrambled."

"Yech. We had eggs three days in a row now."

"You got a better idea?"

"I do," said Nathan.

"Yes?"

"A nice, piping hot bowl of lovely swill."

"Swill, swill," I chanted, "beautiful swill. If we don't eat it the chickens will. . . ."

10
BACK IN THE SADDLE AGAIN
~

As I drove into our place one June morning after two more weeks in the neurasthenic hothouses of the Banff Centre, a bronzed goddess, rising amid a palette of glorious pink columbine, red poppies and white peonies, waved a welcome from her garden. I got out of the car, my ears still ringing from the tumult of metro Banff. The summer had come on like gangbusters and the garden sprouted with lettuce, carrot tops and the first potato leaves. Alberta homesteaders say that even at the worst of times, one would have to work at it to starve to death on a farm. Myrna, wearing shorts and some outrageous tube top under a big straw hat, hoed and delved with gusto. Starvation was not an option. From morning to evening, one mainly saw only the derrière of this earth mother as she bent over her seed beds. I once saw a "folk sculpture" modelled on that view of a lady gardener: it was a brilliant take on this domestic image; sensuous, comic and touching all at once.

I had several renovation projects under way, and the inside of the house looked like a construction project most of the time. Come summer and I took a break from renovating. There was basically nothing wrong with the house that $100,000 and a crew of twelve tradesmen couldn't set to rights. We lived out of doors much of the time, and sat late around a campfire pit at night. The boys had adapted to a summer life under canvas. Sometimes they loaded their backpacks and vanished into the hills for several days at a time.

On a warm morning in mid-June, local ranchers were moving a lot of cattle west on our road for some reason. The valley echoed with the sound of barking stock dogs and shouting riders. The phone rang; it was the Local Oracle. "Say, are you folks going to keep us waiting all day or what?"

"Pardon?"

"You already missed the spring branding party, you know."

"When was that?"

"Last week."

I explained that I had been away, and Myrna and the boys had gone to visit her mother. "Besides, you didn't invite us anyway."

"Ha!" he pounced. "How the hell can we invite you if you ain't there? Anyway, we gotta get these cattle on the reserve today. Got two horses saddled and ready to go. So get on over here. G'bye." And he hung up. Puzzled, but extremely pleased to be included in the goings-on, I called Myrna up to the house. We had no horses of our own yet, and every time our neighbours rode by, Myrna would wave wistfully at them and watch them pass. As a Girl of the Golden West, she had coveted a horse of her own from childhood days—a palomino stallion, of course. We pulled our riding boots on and hurried over to the Haleks'.

We found their yard busy with horses and stock dogs. The Halek boys were already pushing the family's Hereford herd out onto the road, as we drove over the cattleguard and pulled up to the house.

"What's going on?" I asked.

"Hey? Well hell, kiddo," said Frank. "It's June 15th. That's when we put our cattle out on the government grass. Everybody knows that. Don't you know nothin'?"

"Frank, as I get older, I know less and less."

"Do you remember how to ride, at least?"

"Sure."

"Well, step aboard that white nag over there, and learn something new. It thinks it's a cutting horse, that damn little bug—so watch your seat. Name's Candy. Myrna, take that pie-eyed summabitch yonder, the brown gelding. . . ."

"This one?"

"Nope. The 'I-wanna-be-a-pinto' brown. That's him."

"Oof," said Myrna, swinging up to the saddle. "It's been a while."

Frank chuckled. "Don't worry. He won't do much until you wake him up."

"What's his name?" she asked, patting his shoulder.

"Hey? Well hell, call him anything you want. Ha!" Frank slapped his leg. "You'll find a name soon enough."

Amy rolled her eyes at Frank's jest. "His name is Dimples, Myrna."

"He's beautiful."

"Wal . . . if you say so. . . ."

I glanced at the gelding. I didn't see any dimples. He was hammer-headed, rafter-backed and witherless. One eye was white and crazy looking. And there was too much white in other places that reminded me of the old horseman's saying:

One white foot, buy me
Two white feet, try me
Three white feet, deny me
Four white feet and white on the nose
Knock me on the head and feed me to the crows

But then the horse I was on was white from top to bottom. We rode out of the yard and soon caught up to the cattle. The whole valley was on horseback. Some riders wore stetsons on their heads, some wore ball caps. There were men, women, oldtimers and lots of kids. The more energetic riders rode "swing" on either side of the herd, cutting off calves that tried to crawl under the fences. Others rode "point" at the front to keep the cattle aimed in the right direction.

Frank explained that every year at this time, the locals took some of their cattle up into the provincial forest reserve on the slopes of the mountain for the summer grazing season. A few miles ahead was the Harris ranch. There we would take half of the combined herds west up the mountainside, while the other half would be thrown out to graze farther north. The idea was to spread the cattle out and graze the entire reserve efficiently. All along the East Slope, other ranchers would be doing the same on this day. They would leave the cattle in the grazing allotments until the fall roundup.

These grazing allotments are the tag ends of those public grasslands where pioneer ranchers once grazed their cattle at a cost of a few pennies an acre. (There are currently 35,000 cattle producers in Alberta. This includes people raising a few head, and 23,700 who produce mainly cattle—ranchers, in other words. Cash receipts for cattle and calves in 1994 were estimated at $2.1 billion.) Native grasses are still an important factor in the profit margin of this agri-business. Since public land is so limited now, grazing permits to it are jealously guarded and passed on when a ranch changes hands. The cost per cow in the allotment was eight cents per month back in 1918. Now the rancher pays a fee that is tied to the market value of his cattle. In more recent years, it was 13 cents per cow (with calf at heel) per day.

Myrna was radiant as she turned to grin at me. "This is what we came here for."

"You bet."

Everything started off pleasantly. Both of us love the smell of horse-flesh, the stretch of the wide back that makes your legs bow and stretch with it; the intelligence shown in the perk of those big ears cocking backward to your voice; the slight turn and nod of the head as the wide brown eye looks you over. You can feel the power of those great muscles collected by the reins into your hands. Unfortunately, Dimples spoiled the idyll when he started popping his head up and down like a chicken, a dangerous habit. On the first jerk, he nearly struck Myrna in the face.

Myrna lowered her hands to get some leverage on the bit and Dimples pranced with a bow in his neck that I didn't like. "Thatta girl, Myrna," said Frank. "Watch him. He wouldn't hurt a fly, but he would knock you cuckoo with the best intentions in the world."

I looked an incongruous sight riding Candy with my feet dangling close to the ground. Advanced in years even then, she was a stocky little beast. Not much to look at compared to the powerful, expensive quarter-horses that the ranchers rode. I doubted her ability to carry me comfortably at first. But she soon put that doubt to rest. She seemed to float forward, but she hated being in the drag, not giving a damn for the pedigree of the nags that led the procession. She was born to lead, and she had a ribald streak. When an old cow lagged behind the herd, she suddenly nipped it on the buttock, sending it loping to catch up. When another one, a dry cow inclined to wander, came trotting back along the ditch, Candy startled me. With no direction from me, she darted after the cow, and I had to grab the saddlehorn to keep my seat. The cow tried to feint its way around her and the old white mare spun on her hind legs and cut her off. Baffled, the cow ran back after the herd again.

The Harris ranch is a beautiful spread; its sprawling ranch house overhangs a sparkling mountain stream. The rugged face of the mountain towers up behind it. The first Harris had ridden into the country from the U.S.A.—on the back of a mule.

Soon we were hazing the cows up a steep bank through a wide park of big aspen trees and scattered Douglas fir. Now the fun began, as cows and calves tried to turn back to the pleasanter meadows on the valley bottom. If given her head, Candy would take the straightest line through the bush to cut them off. Her attitude toward me was cool and catlike, as if to say, "I chase cows. If you want to come with me, that's your problem." She seemed to know the difference between green limbs and dead ones, however. Green ones she would duck, and I would flatten myself along her neck or fend them from my face as best I could when I saw them coming. Dead ones of a certain thickness she would simply break off with her head. Myrna had no chaps, vital in the bush to avoid spearing your legs on branches. She stuck to the trail while Candy and I siwashed through the bush. From somewhere in the forest, above the bawl of the cattle, came loud yells from Frank and his sons. "Comin' your way. Head it off, head it off!"

Candy froze on the edge of a small clearing, ears pricked forward, trained on something I had not heard. A crackle of twigs; a brown shadow between the pines. I touched Candy with my boot-heels, which was a mistake. We were across the clearing and into the trees before I could check her. Something lay across our path, which was only a deer trail: a fallen tree. I leaned forward as she gathered her short legs and jumped it. There was the target, fifty yards ahead of us, branches swaying in its path: strange-looking silvery hair outlining the hindquarters. Those legs were long and horsey for a cow, but it was a cow all right—a cow moose, that is. Candy tried to follow her into a thicket of close-set pines that the moose shouldered apart, and which sprang back behind her like a gate closing—but I pulled on the binders: "WHOA!"

We worked our way through the woods back to the main trail. Up ahead I glimpsed the reserve fence, the cattle all safely on the other side of it now. The two Halek boys, Donnie and Randy, sat their horses with Frank and Myrna watching me coming up, grinning.

"Well, where is it?" demanded Frank. "Don't tell me you let that valuable government cow get away?"

"I had to," I said. "I don't have a rope."

"Now what the hell you gonna do with a rope in that bush, hang yourself?"

"That's why I didn't bring it."

"We were hoping to find you a black bear," rumbled Donnie Halek, who towers over his father. "Maybe next time."

We reined around to push the cattle on up the slope.

"How long have you had these horses, Frank?"

"Hey? Who said they were my horses? Do they look like my horses? Those are Hank's. He's lent 'em to ya."

"Hank Broda?"

"Yep. And don't fall in love with that white mare, because she's gonna be gone pretty soon."

"Where's she going?"

"Goin' to gay Paree. To choke a Frenchman."

The notion startled me. "You mean they're going to can this horse?"

"They don't do that any more, kiddo. They send a planeload of horse-meat to France every week. That's a gourmet delicacy you are sitting on."

They eat horses, don't they? But they love baby seals. We forged on up the mountain and Candy was in continuous passing gear. I had to keep pulling her up to let the other riders catch up to me. I had never been on a horse that could walk like this one. The idea of turning such a horse into hamburger and steaks for humans to munch on appalled my western roots. I decided right then that I would ask Hank about buying her.

Back home Myrna and I discussed the idea over bottles of cold, homemade beer. Myrna said she wanted a younger horse for herself and was content to wait until we could get one. Candy would be an all-round family horse, we decided. "I'm so happy here," she said. "These people around here just take you right in, don't they?"

"They sure do."

There are 30,000-plus horses in Alberta, and what sets the bottom-line price for horses in this part of the country, setting all other mea-sures of value aside, is the price per pound at the packing plant in Fort

Macleod. I went to see Hank one morning. He was a tall, affable man, good-natured and fair-minded, a long-time member of the Baptist Church and the local school board.

"So you want to buy Candy? Isn't that funny? You know I've been planning to send her off to the plant. You know how old she is?"

"No."

"Well, if I was a crook, I wouldn't tell ya. She's twenty-two."

"You're kidding."

"Boys oh boys, I wish I was. Do you know that I saved her from the plant once myself? I bought her from a horse dealer in Lethbridge who was going to fox her. They used to use the horsemeat on fur farms in those days, feeding mink and foxes. She had that Indian brand on her, so I guess she's two-thirds Blackfoot cayuse and one-third something else."

"Well, whatever she is, Hank, she's sure got twinkle in her toes." I paused. "So, why do you want to get rid of her? What's wrong with her?"

Hank tilted his head back and guffawed. "Well, what's the fun of horse tradin' if I list you her faults? You rode her; you tell me."

"Well, I guess I should come up with something, so as to try and knock your price down."

Hank shook his head. "No need. Tell you what. I have no use for her here any more at her age, but I hate to see her finish at the plant. They're paying forty cents a pound at the plant. Now she's probably about a thousand pounds, so I'll sell her to you for four hundred dollars and that is cheap, let me tell you."

"Sold."

"Not so fast," said Hank, whose grin was now a bit crooked. "I do have one condition."

"Yes?"

"Take that Dimples and put some miles on him. One horse is no good to you folks, you know, unless you like riding alone all the time. And you'll never keep Candy behind a fence if she's alone. A horse needs company, or it goes crazy. If you decide to keep him, we can make a deal on him next year. Whaddya say?"

Hank was right, of course. It would have been churlish to refuse. "I say never look a gift horse in the mouth."

"Haw haw," laughed Hank. "I'll tell you one thing about Dimples.

Ain't nothing wrong with his teeth. Or his stomach, either."

And so I left his place riding the white cayuse and leading, or rather towing, Dimples.

Candy was a huge hit chez Marty from day one. Myrna's nephew and a friend from the city were visiting. Every time we looked up, Candy was going in a different direction with four kids on her back, facing backwards as likely as not, and the dog barking at her heels. Dimples was a different kind of fish, despite Frank's belief about his gentleness. He was too wise to buck kids off, but he had a sly way of stopping suddenly and letting them fly forward over his ears.

You had to watch him in the bush. He had the habit of giving you the brush-off on the first tree he could find. He was particularly hard on greenhorns, sensing their fear and their lack of control. After he tried to kneecap me a couple of times, I put on the roweliest spurs I could find, put on some old hockey shin pads, and let him squeeze me against some aspens until he got tired of poking himself with the spurs. But Dimples was not stupid. He would go for a tree again the first time you forgot to strap your hooks on.

Dimples became my horse by default. I did not trust him with the kids after he ran away one day on a dangerous sidehill with the youngest. I heard Paul yelling and stared down the valley, seeing the whole thing unfolding: I watched Paul kick Candy into a gallop and take off at breakneck speed, trying to catch the runaway fool of a gelding. I knew he would not make it in time and ran after them on foot, feeling as if I was made of lead. Riding bareback, Nathan had hung on for dear life as long as he could, but eventually fell off and tumbled forty yards down the hillside like a ball.

Dimples did have one habit I found endearing, though annoying. If the wind was blowing hard, he would refuse to face it, and tried instead to travel in reverse, backing into it. So you would have to keep turning him around with the reins, and could only progress in a series of dizzy circles against the wind.

Both Dimples and Candy were inclined to roam that first year. They would head for their old home at the first sign of a downed fence wire or a gate left open. But the sight of them cropping the buttercups in front of the house gave us a feeling of having truly arrived, of being part of the life of the valley.

*   *   *

It is strange how it sometimes takes the comment of a friend to point out a fact so obvious that one practically trips over it every morning. Tim and Sherry, old friends from warden service days in Banff, came to visit one day. Getting out of their car, they stared around at the hills and mountain backdrop, smiling their approval.

"You've even got the bell mare!" cried Tim, pointing out Candy with his thumb as we went out to welcome them. In the mountains, when horses are hobbled and put out to graze after a day's travel, one horse, preferably a white mare, carries a Swiss bell around her neck on a strap. It echoes through the valley as the horses wander, grazing, though a smart old mare learns to move so smoothly that the clapper hardly jangles. The geldings will stay with the white mare, but even with hobbles horses can wander far from camp. Going out to jingle them in the morning, your legs wet with the dew on the dwarf birch, you can see the distant blaze of the white mare, shining among the trees where the darker horses are camouflaged in shadows.

"Got the bell mare, cabin, barn, stable, woodshed," said Tim, amused. "All you need is the flagpole. Better get that maple leaf up, Sid, and make all this legal."

Understanding dawned; I broke out laughing.

"You realize what you've done, don't you?" he demanded.

"What?" asked Myrna, coming in late.

"You've bought your own warden station!"

11
THE YEAR OF KNIVES

~

In those first autumns of pooled gold days and cold clear nights, the weeks went by like wild horses running. The isolated valley was a world of its own, and the migrating flocks of geese and ducks, with soaring specks of eagles higher up, circled over the house and abandoned us at last to the coming winter. Great silences enfolded the hills, but we were never lonely. Yet there was a price to pay in isolation, far from the cities; the price of being out of circulation and forgotten by those who might offer me work. Nowadays, bucolic word slingers have fax machines and modems to feed copy into the city word-mills, but in the eighties, all I had was the rural party line, which frequently broke down under the strain of wind and snow.

As the roads drifted over and shut down for days at a time, as the economy drifted on in recession, the ugly financial realities of freelancing in the boonies began to overwhelm me. I had reached a point in my career where time was no longer on my side. I knew that I would have to go to the city and pound on some doors, stick my face out, get some magazine work, write a radio play, write advertising bumf if I had to, let's face it, if anybody would give me a chance to do it. But my ambition seemed to have frozen up like the landscape outside the window. Over the years I have learned that it takes the stamina of an ox to live by your wits.

One day, replacing shingles that the chinook had torn off our roof, I slipped on some ice and fell off the roof onto a pile of lumber. A patch of flesh on my leg, as big as my palm, was nerve damaged—permanently as it turned out. I found myself walking with a cane for a while. It was just one of the many knocks of country living on the cusp of the poverty line, but it made me think. We had no margin for error, no disability insurance, hospital plan, dental plan or plans of any kind. The pressure in my skull mounted to produce something that would earn money, but then I would hit a patch where instead of writing an article, I spent days working, totally obsessed, on a single poem, which would not earn us one nickel. I felt powerless in the grip of crazy inspiration.

"What would you do if you won the lottery?" Myrna asked me one day. And paraphrasing an old farming joke I replied, "Just keep on writing poems until it was all used up."

We could survive on the root vegetables and chickens we had put up for winter, but we could do little else, and life for the kids was particularly straitened. Thank God that patched blue jeans were all the rage back then.

Consumed by worry, I was becoming as approachable as a porcupine most of the time, and as self-absorbed as a black bear pondering an ant colony, as far as my family was concerned. Myrna said, "You are so heavy, so bleak these days. The kids are afraid to go near you. For God's sake, lighten up already."

It was around this time that Myrna decided to show some leadership, since I was floundering badly and in fact feeling like a complete failure as a provider, husband and father. I said I would give up writing and find a real job of some kind. But my spouse would not hear of it. She found a job instead, slinging hash at a local ski-hill some thirty miles away, brushing aside all my objections. This was not the bargain we had made as a couple. We had always scraped by on one income up until then, because the most important thing for her was to be at home for the children.

"They're big enough now," she said, "to pitch in around here. It's time for me to take some of the money load off you." Frankly, if not for her fierce and unwavering belief in my talents, I would have thrown in the towel years ago. Behind many a struggling creator type let there always be some strong, loving soul—kicking butt when it's needed.

Frustrated at the typewriter at times, I would rush out of the Wheelhouse, strap on a tool belt and resume the endless renovations of the old house, or make repairs to fences and outbuildings.

Myrna has a favourite story about me in those days: "One day," she says, "I turned the hot-water tap on in the bathtub, and went to the bedroom to get my bathrobe. So I heard this terrible muffled yelling coming from under the floor. I ran downstairs looking for him. He was in the crawlspace, under the old part of the house, yelling, 'Turn it off, turn it off!' I guess he went under there to jack the floor joists up again. I don't know why he bothers—I swear he turns into an absolute Nazi when he picks up a carpenter's level. Anyway; somehow he got astride of the hot-water pipe while he was working, and got jammed in there and couldn't get out. He claims the pipe got scalding hot when I turned the water on. He says I did it on purpose! His shirt was way up around his head, and he had hooked his sweat pants on something and pulled them partway down, so there he was with his bare belly and whatever on the pipe, and he had his legs and feet kicking all over the place. He looked like a stranded lobster. Laugh? I thought I'd die."

I am always glad to provide my spouse with amusement; God knows I have given her enough to frown about.

Snow lingered on the ground at times while the wind hibernated. I came to and found myself scritting along on my cross-country skis, breaking through some abominable crust, and clattering over windswept prairie part of the time. It was as if my body had a mind of its own, and was trying to save itself from being absorbed into the fabric of my office chair.

The seasons whirled by me in a daze, into another spring, and then something happened, something that would make all those anxious months of self-doubt and self-loathing fade into a great distance, as if seen from the wrong end of a telescope.

*   *   *

The year of the knives began one day when Paul was stricken at school with a severe migraine headache. This was the first of that season of pain that was finally terminated by the blade of a surgeon's scalpel. The attacks kept recurring, always ending with a heavy bout of vomiting; and they were, we soon noted, always followed by the onset of a chinook wind. Our doctor had no magic bullet available. While talking to Charlie Russell on the telephone, I mentioned Paul's problem.

"Sounds like Foehn sickness," suggested Charlie.

"Phone sickness?" I pictured a telephone handset taking root in the kid's ear. Paul had discovered girls that year—and vice versa. "What causes that—too many busy signals or what?"

Charlie laughed and spelled the term out for me. "It can cause headaches and depression, all kinds of things. Watch the barometer. It's sometimes the falling pressure that triggers the headache."

Sure enough, as barometric pressure began to fall several hours before the onset of a chinook, Paul would experience the migraine "aura." The intense headache soon followed. He could not move without jolting pain; he could not see straight. We tried several medications, to no avail. It was maddening, watching him suffer, and having no help to offer him. After a while, he began to fear the onset of the wind; he was anxious about it most of the time. He had hollows under his eyes, and had trouble sleeping at night.

An entire discipline, biometeorology, is devoted to studying the influence of atmospheric forces on living things. Scientific interest in that subject is as old as medicine. Hippocrates summed up biometeorology in 400 B.C. His *Airs, Waters, Places* (Chadwick and Mann's translation of 1950) reads: "Whoever would study medicine aright must learn of the following subjects. First he must consider the effect of the seasons of the year and the difference between them. Secondly he must study the warm and the cold winds, both those which are common to every country and those peculiar to a particular locality. . . ."

About 30 percent of the population are said to be weather sensitive. We all know someone who can, for example, predict a storm by the ache in an arthritic joint. In Chinook Country, some people can predict the arrival of the wind strictly by emotional reactions. Sandra, a friend of ours, can predict the onset of the chinook a day before it arrives. "I get apprehensive, confused, unable to think straight," she says, "unable to concentrate. And I say to myself—chinook on the way." We know of people in our area who suffer complete, immobilizing depressions at the onset of these pressure drops. Such changes in emotional states have long been attributed to the positive ions released by foehn-type winds in many countries of the world. The changes can be dangerously negative. Some researchers have found that suicide and crime rates increase with the onset of these winds.

One wind of this type is the Santa Ana of California. The belief in its negative effects on people's moods has long been a part of popular culture. In an article "Ill Winds That Can Make You Sick," journalist Eric Schwartz quotes from Raymond Chandler's story "Red Wind" to support the connection between "ill winds and crime in southern California." Chandler starts the story: "There was a desert wind blowing that night. It was one of those hot dry Santa Anas that come down through the mountain passes and curl your hair and make your nerves jump and your skin itch. On nights like that, every booze party ends in a fight. Meek little wives feel the edge of the carving knife and study their husband's necks. Anything can happen." Reading Chandler's description one winter day before I had my morning java made me even edgier. I was definitely ruling out an evening booze party. I thought of Paul, and hoped he would escape another attack that day. Myrna, dressing for work, eyed me suspiciously, wondering when I was going to get to work myself. Should I hide the carving knives? No need. This woman, once trained in self-defence by her big brother known as Biff, might biff or bop me one if she caught me moping but would not meekly resort to cold steel. I decided to climb the hill and get some exercise; it is the best way I know to calm the nerves and focus the worried mind.

I could see ragged drifts of dark cap clouds peering over the mountain peaks. The Foehn Wall of the chinook is a zone of turbulence overridden by the prevailing wind. The folks over those mountains were probably breathing in coal dust and sawmill smoke in a temperature inversion of cold, heavy air, capped by the cleaner, warmer air aloft. Sometimes this polluted air will burst through the opening of the Crowsnest Pass or the Waterton Lakes as an outflow wind, in a vast, dirty exhaust plume that dissipates over the plains. Not surprisingly, asthma attacks increase markedly during dusty chinook conditions. Alberta has the highest incidence of deaths from asthma attacks in Canada, but at the time of writing, the role of the chinook in such attacks has not been scientifically established.

The chinook is a shape changer, pushing its arch slowly east, building its immense, vaulted roof of cloud over our home. The edge of the arch cloud forms when moisture condenses from air in the form of a standing wave, at the point where it crosses the mountain crest and then descends onto the foothills and plains. This standing wave is like the crest of an invisible surf line miles in length, which may rise to the lower limits of the atmosphere in height. I stared up at the arch, which had always seemed so beautiful, but which for us had become a harbinger of misery.

In Europe, foehn winds are known as witches' winds; they are associated with forest fires, with suicides and criminal acts. European judges have considered the influence of the foehn on criminal behaviour when passing judgment.

Some researchers suspect that an errant molecule, the positive ion, may be at the root of Foehn sickness. Ions are particles of matter that, among other things, help us absorb oxygen in the lungs. In the nucleus of the atom are found positively charged protons. Orbiting around them are negatively charged electrons. Stable molecules contain an equal number of positive and negative charges. But electrons, which are lighter than protons, can be easily lost as a result of atmospheric disturbances, pollution, and a host of other reasons. This gives the molecule a positive charge—hence, positive ion.

Foehn-type winds in Europe, Israel and elsewhere are tremendous generators of positive ions, producing, for example, 4,000 ions per cubic centimetre where the normal rate is around 1,100. Researchers have found that high doses of positive ions have a physiological effect on weather-sensitive people. The ions apparently increase the level of serotonin, a stress response hormone. This leads to some of the typical reactions, which can range from exhilaration and high spirits all the way through to migraine headaches, joint pain, insomnia and severe depression.

Although some European researchers have linked foehn-type winds with increased suicide rates, others doubt that such a link exists. Alberta is notorious for its high suicide rate, but so far there is no scientific basis for blaming the wind here, either. In the folklore of southern Alberta, the chinook is sometimes blamed for driving people to suicide. Lethbridge is the windiest city in Alberta. Professor Roy J. Fletcher (retired) of the University of Lethbridge studied the occurrence of positive ions there during chinooks, but he was unable to detect significant increases in positive ions during chinook conditions, except under rare instances of severe high winds accompanied by dust storms. The winds also have

to be sustained, he found, not just gusty, as is often the case with chinooks, to produce maximum amounts of positive ions. Severe, dusty
conditions, however, registered a strikingly high positive ion count—
15,000 per cubic centimetre. It seems to me that blowing dust and wind
are not a rare occurrence in these parts.

Paul's attacks continued through the winter and on into summer, a
fierce summer of drought and searing winds. The migraines and heat
drove him downstairs, where he would lie down on a thin blanket
spread on the cool cement of the basement floor. He would curl up in a
fetal position there, marooned inside a red, splintered star. As the wind
began to roar through the trees, the nausea would overwhelm him.
After this purging, I would carry him up to bed, and he would fall into
an exhausted sleep.

The cure for Paul's migraine attacks came as a longshot when my
mother read an article about magnesium as a cure for migraine
headaches. We put him on a daily dose of dolomite, and to our everlast-
ing relief, the attacks stopped. As the weeks went by without a recur-
rence Paul was his old self again, which means he was hilarious and fun
to be around on some days, and infuriating on others—a normal thir-
teen-year-old boy.

The summer of 1984 began a return of the cycle of drought that
would last until 1988. On August 9, I wrote in my diary, "The drought
continues, no end in sight. Money runs down to a trickle and dries up."
A day of 85°F ended with a clear evening, then a severe frost before
dawn killed Myrna's sunflowers and turned the potato vines and the
other vegetables from green to black.

That summer, which farmers described as the driest growing season
in sixty-five years, was so hot that it actually kept the boys indoors at
times, dodging the sun. The Oldman River became our oasis; swimming
in the rocky potholes of that blue-eyed mountain stream was a daily
ritual.

We came back home one evening at the end of August. Paul had been
complaining of stomach cramps. Night came in a fever, and by morning, Paul's rigid abdomen had him writhing and moaning. We rushed
him in to the nearest hospital, an hour's drive away. Fearing a burst
appendix, we approved an operation. The appendix was not involved,
as it turned out. There was a minor problem with the large intestine,
which the surgeon set to rights, or so we were told.

In a few days I brought the patient home. The hollow-eyed look had returned; Paul moved with a caution that we had never seen before. Myrna watched him, instinctively knowing that something else was amiss, despite the doctor's reassurances.

Late that autumn he was suddenly stricken with exactly the same symptoms we had seen in August. Our isolated little valley seemed like an ominous place, far from the specialized care Paul now needed. We packed an overnight bag, picked up Nathan at his school and drove Paul into Lethbridge. It was a long, agonizing ride for Paul; every bump in the road made him cry out with pain.

The specialist was very busy and unable to treat him for several days. The staff were wary of giving him painkillers, not wanting to mask the symptoms. "And we don't want to turn him into a drug addict, do we?" said the head nurse, primly.

We were living out of a local motel, one of us commuting back and forth so Nathan would not miss school, and meeting up in the hospital each morning. Being at home, a hundred miles away from the hospital where the boy was suffering, was the hardest part of the ordeal for the one left behind. Snow fell, and the roads were slippery and dangerous, adding to our anxieties.

Bathing Paul one night, I was shocked at his yellowish pallor, his frailty. Every motion was agony. "I wish I was dead," said my first-born son in the voice of a tired old man, and I felt the teeth of a great disaster hinging down on my brain. A knife turned in one child cuts the entire family: its whole existence is in peril.

The next morning we watched, both terrified and relieved, as the grim-faced victim was wheeled into the operating room.

The surgeon slouched in afterwards, munching from a bag of chips, and greeted us in the hallway. "He's doing fine," he said. "It's a good thing I got in there though. Two more hours and gangrene would have set in. No wonder he was hurting."

Myrna and I hugged each other, shaken but relieved. There had been a congenital obstruction, not found by the first surgeon. Paul had had it all his life.

I went home and tried to work, but wound up wandering aimlessly around the empty house. Two hours short of the end of a life, or of a crushing ordeal at the best. It could have been closer, but it was close enough.

The house, silent and empty, full of family pictures, rebuked me. Every hard word I had ever said to my sons came back into my ears. On a shelf was a picture that Myrna called "Moses in the bullrushes." The two boys, aged four and seven, had on their swimsuits, sitting in a rowboat surrounded by bullrushes, mugging for the camera. Paul had turned to his little brother and said, "Let's be partners." I had my hands on the oars, intent on steering the boat. I am the father; I'm supposed to know where I'm going; I'm supposed to ward off the knives, but I am helpless, a hostage to my love for these ones, though in the hands of fate I keep up the fiction of strength, and must go on making my little plans.

I climbed the ridge above the house to stand staring south into Montana, and west back toward Lethbridge, where the patient still remained, recuperating. On the ridge the west wind combed through my beard and I stood there thinking, let it blow these ashes and cinders out of my mind. I can see a long way, but I cannot see tomorrow. Snow drifted down as I stood there, and I let it melt on my face. My father had called that day to check on Paul. "Put up everything you can this summer; it's going to be a hard winter."

There was barely enough money left to put gas in the car and get Myrna and Paul back home from the hospital. "My God," I said aloud. "What am I going to do?" A wave of self-hatred, disgust and desperation surged through my brain, that I should have to even think about money at a moment like this. Who was that young fool back then who would put his family's security at risk on behalf of a *principle*, on behalf of what he saw then as his *integrity*? My God, I could puke on those words, while those bureaucrats I contended with laughed up their sleeves, took their pay cheques, took their retirement or sat back down to update their frigging résumés. For the next promotion into their well-earned oblivion.

Yes, yes. But you wanted more than that; you wanted your work to matter. You wanted to protect the national parks; *you wanted to save the earth.*

I gripped hard on the bough of an old bullpine, shook it like an enraged ape and yelled my impotent fury out over the valley. But as I gripped the gnarled bough, helpless, shaking, I felt at last the power of its life surging out of the rock it was rooted in; I felt its strength subduing my rage. The fit subsided; I sank down, leaned against its trunk, breathing in the sharp October air.

Count your gifts, and count your blessings, fool. It is the earth that will save you. These valleys and forests have fed generations before you; some had nothing but skin tents to keep out the wind; this will surely sustain you and yours also. It's a surety, far beyond the paltry ambitions of those pencil-necks who go to bed each night with a balance sheet for a pillowslip. It's not supposed to be easy. William Blake, Dylan Thomas and Theodore Roethke never found it easy. Easy learns nothing, and knows nothing. Easy is not even an option, considering your genes. You were programmed at birth to kick against the pricks; you can't whine every time you stub your toe.

The family believes in you. The family, threatened, tested, is still intact. Out there beyond the horizon, so many are being destroyed.

The human family is all there is.

"I'll be ready," I said, though only the great gnarled bullpine, its trunk deformed by the wind, its branches imploring the sky to send on more wind, was there to hear me.

*   *   *

Like Old Mother Hubbard I went to the cupboard on the day Myrna brought Paul home. There was not much there and in the fridge there was less. Paul was a white shade in the shadows of his room. The boy needed nourishing; chicken was too chicken for what ailed him. After the year of the knives, he needed powerful food, medicine food to grow sinew and put the colour back in his cheeks. It was up to me to go and get it. It was something real that I could do; something I knew how to do. I would go after an elk because an elk meant perhaps four hundred pounds of venison for the winter, while the little mule deer might only provide a hundred. If you are going to eat meat, might as well eat the best. There are no growth hormones, fly sprays, antibiotics or other chemical residues in God's cattle.

For several days the cap cloud had clung to the summit of the Livingstone, towering upward for a thousand feet, its top surface surprisingly smooth, curved away south and north from the high point of Cirque Peak. The Chinook Arch, which most Albertans see to the westward, was actually just east of us. The effect was to create a great round opening to the sky, ringed all around by cloud, into which the wind rushed as if dropping into a pool, a pool in which we humans, horses, cattle and elk all swam.

At night the moon quartered over this great pillowy circle of cloud, picked out the white slopes of the mountain, and glistened on the ice of the yard and fields. And above the rim of the cloud bowl, in the clear night sky, I saw the brave belt of Orion glittering—the hunter.

During the night a cold front pushed up the valley. I got up in the pre-dawn darkness to find the stars blacked out by unseen cloud. It was still breezy, however, and that was not good. It meant the elk would be even more skittish than usual and hard to stalk. The tracking would be poor with so much interruption in the snow surface from recent chinooks. In the woods the snowpack might be uninterrupted, but it is old, rotten snow, noisy to walk on.

At daylight, the elk will go into the thickest timber they can find and not come out of cover until it is nearly dark. But the Local Oracle had predicted departure of all visiting hunters by lunchtime. Disgruntled hunters are spreading the word: there are no elk in Aspen Valley; the elk have all pulled out of here.

This is what I love to hear. When the going gets tough, the tough get going. For home. And leave us local yokels room to move. You cannot hunt your own way when the hills are full of humans: if there are twelve men ahead of you, you have to hunt twelve different ways, and you spend most of your time detouring around humans, trying to find where men are not, which is where the elk are.

It will take a few days for the elk to settle down, but there are only four days left in the season, so I must make the effort at least to locate the herd. First I will find them, then I will hunt seriously.

The American elk, or wapiti (a Shawnee word meaning white-rump), is the second-largest of the North American deer after the moose and is cousin to the Old World red deer. The stags or bulls weigh up to 1,100 pounds and stand 55 inches at the shoulder; the hinds or cows reach 1,090 pounds and a shoulder height of 51 inches. The thick antler beams of a trophy bull may reach 63 inches in length and as much in breadth. The animals are noted for their camel-like necks; they are big-bodied deer with long, powerful legs. Elk once ranged over much of North America. In *Big Game Hunting in Alberta*, Jack Ondrack explains that early American settlers called them by the European word for the moose (also an Old World deer) after the German *elch* or Danish *elg*, which led to confusion, but the name persisted over time, although many prefer the Shawnee name.

Some explorers knew the difference between moose (*Alces alces*) and red deer (*Cervus elaphus*). Ondrack notes that red deer stags and hinds were reported along the St. Lawrence River by Jacques Cartier in 1535, and were observed by the Spaniards in the American Southwest. On the Great Plains, they were second only to the buffalo as the hunting choice of the Plains Indians. Some 10 million of them are thought to have inhabited the continent before the coming of the whites. John C. Ewers noted that their tusks (canine teeth) were a prized possession of both men and women and they are still highly valued today. During the buffalo era, a woman's dress decorated with elk teeth was worth two good horses among the Blackfeet. Here and there on the plains, there were pyramidical towers of piled elk horns to testify to their abundance. David Thompson hunted "the Red Deer" on the North Saskatchewan, and Lewis and Clark sustained themselves on elk on the banks of the Missouri.

After sodbusting, roadbuilding and other development, their range today is a fraction of what it was, and by 1901 the animals were over-hunted and in danger of extirpation in Alberta. Elk hunting was closed here from 1907 to 1933. Thanks to the work of federal conservationists in founding Elk Island National Park, and in protecting and reintroducing elk in the mountain national parks, a sufficient gene pool of elk was preserved, the elk multiplied accordingly and surplus animals were transplanted to colonize their former range. According to Ondrack, in 1983, the Alberta elk population was between 15,000 and 25,000, not including the national park populations. There were 34,000 elk hunters that year, and between 1,500 and 2,500 head of elk were killed by hunters. Many more are killed annually by predators (wolves, bears, lynxes, cougars and coyotes) and run-ins with vehicles and trains, or die of natural causes, than are "harvested" by hunters.

I dislike that term "harvested," which implies that these animals were sprouted from seeds by some wise government husbandmen. The fact that we managed to curb our greed and pull back just short of pushing them into extinction does not mean that we somehow created these animals. When the meek have finally inherited the earth and all hunting and wildlife management is outlawed, the elk will still be here—punting, forking and spearing the meek off their front lawns until the local wolfdog pack catches up and guts some old bull on the patio. I am a great supporter of animal rights, by the way. By which I mean that humans are animals, like the wolf, like the elk. I support the wolf's right to hunt elk, and only ask for the same right for myself.

The windchill felt like −20°F when I went out into the darkness with the rifle slung on my shoulder, wearing packboots and three pairs of knee socks, war-surplus wool pants, wool shirt, wool sweater and a balaclava to protect my face. No jacket, because in this hill country I would soon be warm from the exercise of hiking. I carried Frank's old jacket in my pack for extra warmth and also for luck. A hunter had given it to him, but it was ridiculously large for him. "Give it to me," I had suggested. "It doesn't fit you."

"Judas Priest," he had protested. "You'd take the shirt right off a man's back." But he stripped it off and handed it to me forthwith. I had been fortunate enough to get an elk the first day I wore it, and have worn it hunting ever since.

I moved quietly above the willows, talking a little bit in a soft voice as I went along, hearing a rattle of horn on the snow. That was the family of mule deer that hangs out in our garden, moving uphill away from me. Although we are always hard up and much in need of meat, we would have to be literally starving to death before I would be so uncharitable as to slaughter a beast claiming asylum this close to the house. I also don't wish to spook the old cow moose, which appeared this fall with a calf at heel, from her hideout in our willows. I don't want some hunter to claim her as she tries to cross the road to the willows along the creek. Once it was common to encounter several moose in every fold of the hills that held an aspen grove. But now their numbers have been decimated because the greedy Fish and Wildlife Department issued too many moose tags in 1984 to gain more revenue for the Tory government. It would take years for the population to recover. I heard the willows scrape together below me in the darkness, but I knew the moose was not moving away from me with undue haste, though she had the wind off me.

So I went on through the night, moving quickly uphill to the head of the valley as a faint glow grew in the eastern sky. I heard our neighbour Peterson's yearling cattle bawling ahead of me, and edged to the left around them. The hill rose under my feet and the forest edge drew near, a brooding shadow in the dark. The wind is going the wrong way for me, but if I gain the ridge quickly, my scent will probably dissipate upward. Now I went straight up, slipping at times on patches of ice, clinging to the saskatoon bush and the willows that came to hand. The snow would not bear me up but broke and crunched underfoot. I must have sounded like an oncoming bear to any deer bedded down near the forest edge.

When the sun came up I was on top of the ridge at 5,700 feet, with forest dropping away on either side. The ridge was bare of snow in places, covered with age-hardened drifts in others. In some places small cornices overhung the slope of this mini-mountain, their windward slopes carved into wave-like sastrugi by the wind. Sastrugi resemble the whipped crests of meringue on a pie. The wall of the Livingstone to the west turned salmon-pink as the sun rose over the Porcupine Hills. I moved slowly along the ridge, stopping to glass for elk but seeing only small bands of scattered mule deer.

The ridge I followed and the ridge across the valley to the east make a great U-shape, the bottom of the U being to the north, and are covered in forests of aspen and Douglas fir. I would walk this U, keeping always to the higher slopes since this was more of a looking trip than a hunting trip. My only company were occasional whiskey jacks, scolding me for trespassing as they hunted for cones among the limber pine. Once I heard the startling *whup whup whup* of wings and a raven circled me hopefully. "Ka-wonk, wonk," it cried hungrily. Kill something already. It dangled one leg at times, talons extended, as if testing the air currents for some warm uplift. I stopped and let it move away: I didn't want any heralds announcing my approach.

I dropped down from the ridge out of the wind, and nooned in a circlet of Peterson's massive Douglas fir trees that are some four to five feet in diameter. There is a spring that runs by the spot year round. I took the small primus stove out of my pack, set a billy tin full of water on the stove and threw in a tea bag and some sugar. Boiled together, it makes a pungent, strengthening brew trapper style, Indian style. A few fir needles fell into it for spice as I watched it boil.

I wouldn't say I know every big fir tree in this valley well, but I am acquainted with a good many of them that have given rest to my back while I waited for a deer, or sat happily watching a grouse or a mourning dove just being itself. I was sitting here one time when a bobcat came popping along through the woods with two kittens bouncing along behind her. She froze when she drew abreast of me, looking suddenly embarrassed, and turned to stare at me with her wild, lantern eyes. The two kittens peered around her lanky hindquarters at me, and blinked. Then she turned in a flash and faded into the woods, galloping comically away, her kittens echoing her every motion as they bobbed at her heels. Somewhere a ruffed grouse clucked its scandalized protest. The woods were gayer from that feline visit, the shadows were animate with possibilities.

After drinking the tea I went on through the silent woods, thinking of what those trees could tell of the people who had come this way over the centuries of their tenure. Some feasting, some trysting and some sad or violent endings had occurred beneath their long, equivocating boughs.

Elk hunting is a long walk with all senses fully engaged; one eye on the ground, one eye on the ridgeline; an ear to the sky, a nose to the wind. It is running a mitten over elk pellets, sniffing like a hound for their freshness; pondering a sapling barked by antlers, or a tuft of long grey-and-tan hairs caught in the barb on a wire fence. Sometimes the hair on the back of your neck tells you the elk have outflanked you. When you find a place where elk have bedded down, marked by cavities in the snow lined with ice, you remember the place for a future ambush. But I would not go there with a camera and disturb the elk for any trivial purpose.

After a while I could almost smell the recent presence of men in those woods and was not surprised to cut their trails where they had plowed uphill through the woods. Or find the places, sometimes hundreds of yards farther on, where the long-toed elk had stood and watched their approach, then scattered through the firs with winged pasterns.

Elk hunting in this country is a hard workout. It is harder on the Livingstone Range where the elk will go right up to the treeline to browse and avoid us humans. These foothills are rugged enough, and the day is a series of stiff climbs and rapid descents from one ridge top to another. I have tried hunting them on horseback, but ultimately one is tied to the habits of the wrong animal. Elk compete with mountain sheep for the upper limits of the range, and compete with the snowshoe hare for thickets. There are places where elk can go where it would be foolish to take a horse. One such is a stand of second-growth spruce of the kind where elk like to bed down by day when they are hunted. All morning I had been thinking of this place, a forest of poles, branches tightly woven together with barbicans of pointed snags angling in all directions. It runs up to the summit of the ridge, and bottoms out in a stand of aspen. There is no chance of stalking the beasts upslope, while going downslope might at least afford a shot at them going away.

I came to the place about 2:00 p.m. and found a veritable elk high-way plowed into the drifts, coming up from the west to join the ridge. I checked the safety on the .270 and moved quietly along the ridge fol-lowing the trail until I found a tunnel-like opening among the trunks where the elk had gone downhill. I had to sit down in the snow to enter where the elk had kneeled down and shrugged their way through.

There was no place to stand up comfortably for the first twenty yards. I inched my way down on my seat through the deathly quiet of the gloomy spruce, stopping frequently to listen. I came at length to a short cliff. The elk had jumped down single-file to a narrow ledge, mountain-goat fashion, then jumped from there to the base of the cliff. I sat and stared down among the spruce boles of a small plateau formed by an ancient slippage in the hillside. The wind was upslope, in my favour, and on the wind was a musky odour that told me I was very close to the bedding ground. I sat there for perhaps half an hour, watch-ing and listening. There was nothing I could see or hear in the shadows under an overcast sky. It was when I found the first foothold above the ledge, and was stepping quietly down with one hand on a tree and one hand on the rifle, that I heard the whistling bark of a watchful cow elk. Dark shadows bolted up among the dark trees as I jumped down to the ledge and raised the rifle. Branches snapped and hooves thudded on deadfalls. But there was nothing to shoot at, only shadows moving among shadows. I knew they would run for a long time this late in the season before they stopped to check the back-trail.

I went back up to the ridge top, not at all disappointed. Despite the hunting pressure they had been subjected to, there were elk in the valley and my chances of collecting one looked good if I persevered.

The deer family tends to avoid people when in its natural state, but they are capable of injuring or even killing us when cornered or pro-voked into defending their young. A cow moose with calf, when harassed by humans, has been known to turn on the nearest assailant and trample him to death. Over the years, people in national parks who insist on the idiotic habit of feeding the animals are occasionally wounded by the sharp front hooves of the smaller deer. An acquain-tance of mine was in Waterton Park when a yappy poodle went after a mule deer buck near the townsite. The buck lowered its head, speared the dog deftly on one of its tines, then ran off into the forest cradling the unfortunate mutt in its antlers and disappeared. End of dog. I know a rancher who was pinned to the ground by the antlers of a wounded white-tail buck one time. It gave him a good raking with its front feet before he managed to kill it with his hunting knife.

When a grizzly bear sow chases you up a tree, it tends to get bored fairly quickly, especially if it can't knock the tree over. Bears are the politicians of the animal world; they have a short attention span, and their brain is mainly focused on filling their stomachs. They are always dreaming about finding a dead moose around the next bend and they usually beetle off eventually to look for it. But when an elk or a moose with calf at heel chases you up a tree, things can get miserable. They may hang around for a long time, grazing, waiting. Perhaps they will lie down nearby to chew the cud and watch with great interest, as you slowly lose your grip and start wishing an elk poacher would wander by.

In my Banff warden days I was stationed at Bryant Creek one summer, near the foot of Assiniboine Pass. We worked ten-day shifts in there, and the warden I relieved passed on a report of a cow elk treeing backpackers on the Assiniboine Pass trail. The trail was ordered closed as long as the elk was raising hell there, and it fell to me to ride up and see if said elk and calf were still in residence. One day I saddled up Monte, a wall-eyed government bronc, but very smart. I knew he was smart because he was so lazy. Except when he got a chance to jump out of a corral, which he did on a daily basis unless I kept him hobbled. We should have entered Monte at the Spruce Meadows equestrian trials. At any rate, we left the cabin behind us and trotted west, heading for the Assiniboine Pass trail.

It was a hot day, and a steep climb. I was somewhat tired, because as local police chief and health inspector, I had worked undercover at a nearby outfitter's camp the night before. I had gone there to inspect the food and beverage service at their weekly hoedown, and I'd had to play the guitar all night as part of my disguise.

So you have a tired warden on a lazy horse going slowly up a steep mountain trail. At a point about a mile below the summit of the pass, Monte became semi-alert; that is, he raised his head and stared meaningfully into the forest. I looked down and saw fresh cow-elk tracks printed in a wet spot on the trail, and kicked Monte into motion again. My plan was to follow the elk tracks until I found an elk standing in them. I'd encountered cow elk on horseback many times and never had any problems with them before.

The tracks left the trail a few yards farther on in a small clearing and I reined up. What happened next was a bit too fast for both of us. I heard an elk calf bleat, which caught my attention, but before I had a chance to locate it, a cow elk came out of the forest at a dead run, ears back and neck stretched out, coming straight at us. It seems to me this elk was making an angry, hissing noise like air leaking out of a tire—but I may have imagined that.

With a speed never shown before, Monte had swapped ends and lunged forward, heading back down the trail. I glanced back and caught a glimpse of the cow in mid-air, her front legs spearing out for us, and her cloven hooves spread like two pairs of pruning shears. Something hit the saddle behind me as I ducked forward on Monte's neck. We went down the steep trail at a hard run, which I reined back from an outright gallop, all the while talking to the horse, trying to keep us both collected. I heard the clink of his shoes on the rocky trail; I had seen that horse trip before. I didn't glance back for perhaps a hundred yards, and when I did, I wished I hadn't. The cow was close behind, ears back, lip curled up and showing her teeth. We took two sets of switchbacks at breakneck speed, and when I looked again the elk was some yards back. But the story doesn't end quite there. Because what really inspired Monte was when we both looked to our right uphill, and saw the cow shortcutting the switchbacks, coming straight down the mountainside through the trees to try to cut us off. This is an animal that can move at twenty-nine miles an hour and weighs up to six hundred pounds. To us, she looked as big as a rhino. Finally, the elk slowed down a bit, keeping us in sight, and keeping us moving for a bit longer before breaking off the chase.

I decided to keep the trail closed. When I finally got off to inspect Monte for damage, I found him lathered up but unwounded. A divot of thick saddle leather was missing out of the cantle where the old cow had struck with her hoof, missing my back by a few inches. That was close enough for me. Monte got a double helping of oats next day. It was not the first time a horse had saved my life. I suppose the moral of the story is, don't play the guitar all night if you're going elk hunting in the morning.

As the autumn rut winds down each year, the bulls, exhausted from the season of mating and mayhem, no longer exert control over their harems. The matriarchal structure of the herd reasserts itself, and one cow, the most observant one, becomes the herd leader. She is joined by females, either dry or with a calf at heel, and by some juvenile bulls or "spikers." Sometimes a more mature bull tags along with the rest. At other times, the bulls form wary bachelor bands and browse away from the main herd of females.

The big bulls were few, and of little interest to me. I have never been a trophy hunter, having been turned off from that sport years ago when I spent my time on boundary patrol in the national parks, playing cat and mouse games with outfitters. Trophy hunting is big business and foreign headhunters will pay thousands of dollars to obtain a mention in the Boone and Crocket record book. (Ty Lund, the current Alberta environment minister, set a new standard for catering to trophy hunter insanity in 1995. During the annual convention of the Foundation for North American Wild Sheep in Phoenix, he auctioned off a permit to hunt a bighorn ram, out of season, for $315,000.)

I am only a humble meat hunter and I have turned down the chance to pot a bull elk more than once because it looked thin and worn out, or just too tough to chew. The survival rate for cows is higher than for bulls, because the bulls go into the winter in poor condition after the rut. That year I had drawn an "anterless" tag, and I hoped to find a fat one.

Now that I had jumped the cow herd right on its bedding ground, the boss cow would be watching for me. The Plains Indians felt the elk were imbued with supernatural powers because of their habit of disappearing from one valley and suddenly turning up in another one overnight, unlike the deer, which will circle repeatedly through a range of a few acres and seldom leave their home grounds. I expected the elk to pull out of the valley and draw back deeper into the hills, and they did not disappoint me. It snowed several inches that night, and when I took to the hills the next day, I found the old tracks were covered. I hunted hard again on the third day without luck, and when the last day of the season dawned, I began to question my own optimism.

A promontory at the end of the valley offered a commanding view of several drainages. I climbed up through sugary snow to its summit in the darkness on that last day, praying for luck. The breeze was slight and fitful, and the sky overcast. Slowly the sun lightened the hills to the east until there were telltale streaks of red in the sky. I stared through my glasses at the neighbouring ridges, hoping to find the elk skylined crossing a ridge.

From my aerie I could see one light shining in the dark valley a mile south that marked my home. It meant that Myrna and the boys were at breakfast. Far to the north, the light of another ranch house gleamed in another darkened valley. All else was a vast shadow of quiet expectation.

While I waited for more light, I indulged in an old ritual. I gathered some stalks of pasture sage from around my lookout, then rubbed them into a moist ball with my bare hands. This I rubbed over my head and wrists, hoping to mask my human scent with the aromatic herb.

The light touched the treetops of some distant whaleback ridges and swept inexorably south toward my lookout. It fell upon a range of hills two miles to the west. I followed the descending line of light. I was staring at the elk for half a minute before I realized it: mere specks of glowing reddish-gold on the tawny upslope below the trees, two miles north. I counted thirty head. I glassed around the ridges nearer at hand hoping to find a gang closer to me. There was nothing. That distant herd of elk represented my only chance for the winter's supply of venison. My bare wrist revealed the wind was blowing from the southwest. It could very well give me away, but it might be less active down in the valley. Even with the naked eye I could see the herd was feeding on the move, working its way up the slope to the safety of the trees. In thirty minutes it would reach the top of the hill. The elk might feed for another fifteen minutes close to the safety of the trees, or they might enter the woods and keep moving. If I came straight at them from below they would see me or wind me long before I reached the bottom of the hill. My only chance was to approach obliquely, to round that hill, climb it, and come out in front of them. I had thirty minutes to cover two miles of snow covered ground, and climb a steep 600-foot hill without being seen or heard.

Something in me said I could not do it that fast, and something else, a fiercer voice, said stop stalling and start moving. I stared at the ridges and forest edge for a moment nonetheless, planning the route while I stuffed my jacket into the pack. I tightened my bootlaces, shouldered the pack and tightened the bellystrap. The chamber of my bolt-action .270 was empty. I never run with a loaded rifle in my hands, safety catch be damned. You cannot shoot yourself when the chamber's empty. Then I took off down through the forest.

It was a 600-foot loss of altitude in a few minutes. I descended in big strides through the sugary snow, dodging among the second growth spruce. Once I caught my foot under a hidden root, described a complete somersault with the rifle clutched to my stomach, rolled back to my feet and just kept going without missing a stride. It is the sort of recovery that exhilarates you when you are forty years of age, but who's counting.

Then the work began. On the level, the snow was my enemy. There was a thin sun crust, which would bear my weight just long enough to throw me off balance when it collapsed. Under the crust was depth hoar (sugar snow), which rolled under my boot soles like ball bearings. I hugged the forest edge and kept going, running until my ribs were cramped and sore, running until the soreness went away. There were patches of ice here and there where springs had flooded across the valley. I ran with my knees well bent, feet wide apart, concentrating on keeping my footing, and keeping my breathing under control. The hill crept closer. I came to a stream bed, the one spot where I was in plain view for a moment. My back and chest were soaked with sweat. A beast would smell me a mile away. I put my glasses on the distant gang of elk. They were perhaps a hundred yards below the summit of the hill. I kept the glasses on them, watching for a head to come up and look my way, stepped into the open, crouched, moved quickly across to the trees, and ran on through the snow.

I hammered away at it, my face flushed with heat. At length I rounded the corner of the hill, following an old logging road. Now the aspen gave way to firs once again. My mouth was parched. I scooped up a mittful of snow and crammed it into my mouth. I went up, hand over hand on the branches at times. The packboots were good in the snow, but lousy on ice and rock. I slipped on a patch of ice and slid twenty yards backwards, banging my knee on a rock, stifling the urge to yell, and hobbled back up again. I felt blood running down my leg from a cut, but decided not to look at it for now. The leg would be stiff the next day; it would be stiff today if I thought about it too much. I stopped below the rocky crest of the ridge. On the other side of that were the elk—if I was lucky. But the wind, which had forced me to run so wide around the goal, had dropped when it might have helped me.

An upslope breeze fanned my face, the wind doubling the hill and playing tricks again. It looked like my effort would be for naught. If the elk
had not already winded me, they would as soon as I topped the ridgeline. I sank to my knees, dizzy and starved for air. A light mist whorled
through the trees and I felt a puff of air on my face. I looked up, hearing
a rush of wind, and saw the fir tops tremble.

The warm west wind had surfaced again. It was tentative, but it was
there, and in my favour.

My heart was pounding, and I forced myself to wait until the racket
of blood in my ears grew quiet. I eased a bullet into the chamber and
moved slowly over the ridge top with the rifle raised to shoot. This was
the moment that would take all my willpower, when the warrior must
come to the fore and all doubts be stilled, or there would be cowardice,
ineptness, a mess and terrible pain for the beast and pain in the soul for
me. And there were the elk, sixty yards below me, their white rumps
toward me as they fed into the wind. They were grouped close together,
with several spikers bunched up among the cows and young of the year.
Farther down the slope was the boss cow. I stopped as her head came
up, but she was looking the wrong way, and soon resumed feeding. I
moved in silence, humped over, as close to a beast on all fours as I could
get, in my drab-brown jacket and tan pants, from one tree to the next,
stopping when an elk lifted its head, moving as it went down again, to
fifty yards, forty yards, when all the heads swung up at once and turned
on me, and their manes went up as the hair on my neck went up with
them. The old cow barked a shrill warning, a fat cow stepped nervously
out from the others on the very edge of the hill, craning its neck out in
the clear, and I held on its heart, exhaled slowly, and squeezed off the
shot. The crack of the rifle was deafening, a sudden thunder rebounding
from hill to hill. The herd broke on either side of me into the enveloping
trees and were gone from sight in the space of two heartbeats. The sacrifice fell, stone dead, slid over the edge of the hill, disappeared from
sight. I went tearing down after the carcass, sure of the accuracy but
bound to make sure anyway. Slipped and fell on the hard crust, scraped
my hand on a protruding rock, and braking as best I could with my
boot-heels slid all the way to the bottom in a wild slide for two hundred
yards.

There was blood on the knee of my pants and blood on the hillside;
some of it was mine. Fair enough. I knelt by the dead elk, unable to

move, fighting for breath, and I felt the sorrow of killing the beast and the relief that it had died so quickly.

I drew the knife from its scabbard to set about the gory business. I knew what I had always known, in the old days in that paradise for the middle class, when I had seen so many beasts die, beasts whose flesh had been thrown on the rubbish tip and whose substance had been wasted, whose energy had been denied to the forest and the mountains that had given them life and sustenance, and denied to the hungry people who could have been fed. I knew that there was a spirit gone out of it, and I felt it going, though not far, not lost. And never as lonely as man's must be, at least in the going out. I believe what the Blackfoot of old believed, that though I had earned the right to that final shot, it was the elk that had allowed itself to be taken. Like the hunters of the ages before me in these hills, I raised my face to the sky and gave thanks to the Creator and to the spirit of the elk, and praised its flesh, and praised its kindness to me and mine to nourish us through the winter. When the work of dressing the carcass was done, I wiped the blade clean in the snow. The year of pain was nearly over, as I put the knife back in its scabbard.

Voices on the Wind

12
The Train That Flew
~

Medicine food makes for strong young men. They shoot up like weeds in the freedom of the country. I don't know if you can ever put a finger on the moment when you realize that your children are grown up. It is a very particular epiphany, like most other human moments, hard indeed to explain to anyone outside its intimacy. I think it happened to me one night as we were gathered around the cowboy television (campfire) next to the house, the night before I was to leave for Montana to do some research on the Snow Eater.

The legendary wind in question, still anxious to serve as a muse, sighed through the aspen trees. By the quarter moon, the mountain shone ghostly white with new snow. The night was radiant; an unearthly stillness was broken only by the creak of aspen tree trunks swaying in the breeze. I looked up and suddenly discovered once again (this had been happening a lot lately) two strong young men, both over six feet tall, sitting across from me where two tow-headed boys had sat only a week before, or so it seemed. But there was some kind of final realization this time. "The days run away like wild horses over the hills," I said. It was the title of a book of poems by Charles Bukowski. I felt as if time, like a fullblown chinook wind, had caught me up and hurtled me through a wormhole in space into the future. Myrna caught my eye and smiled, guessing my thoughts.

After a while they went inside and we soon heard them kicking up a hideous charivari, pounding away on Paul's drum kit down in the coldroom with a ghetto blaster turned up full. Out in the hills, a coyote howled in protest at the racket.

"I heard them shouting to each other across the valley today," I told her. "It was like hearing my own voice, broken up by the wind. They're here, but they're already so far away. . . ."

"Big or little," she said firmly, "boys or men, they'll always be our kids." The wind whirled leaves in a spray around us, the fire leapt up to greet it.

It was one of those moments that had us thinking about family, about relatives we had lost track of, and some we had never met. Montana was on my mind. I had been calling up cousins, introducing myself at last; piecing together the story of my great-grandparents.

Montana, happy name that rolls from the tongue, was derived from the Spanish word for mountainous country. Alberta was named in honour of Queen Victoria's niece. It is a hard-sounding word, and like many such British place names, it recalls mainly an imperial mindset; it is an imposition, a whalebone corset of a word that will not fit our rolling plains and exuberant mountains, one that has no inherent connection with the place it is supposed to describe. "Montana," a happy name that rolls from the tongue, was derived from the Spanish word for mountainous country. So Montana was the name I conjured with when I was a boy, back when I was taught so little about the history of my own country. Americans, weaned on the saga of Lewis and Clark, or Pickett's charge, must shake their heads at this in puzzlement. My own peers well know where my historifying tendencies arise: they are the stories my teachers never told me about the land where I was raised. But imagination writes its own history; in my mind there was no fence between the nations. It was always a tentative boundary, to our family.

As a child, I thought my Uncle Oscar was the sheriff of all Montana, and I was disappointed when he showed up in Redcliff driving a car, instead of on horseback. I could not comprehend how a man who wore a hat as big as his, a man who lived in a fort on the Missouri River, had ever learned how to drive an automobile. He never seemed to stay in Redcliff very long. There were road agents and train robbers all over Montana that required his attention. Uncle Oscar would drive away, laughing, down the gravel road headed toward the Cypress Hills where the edge of the Montana sky began. My friends said they were damn Yankees down there; they were not like us. But I could not tell the difference. To me he was just Uncle Oscar, one of many men visiting town wearing stetson hats and suspenders, though always bigger than the rest, even the suspenders, and happier than most.

Montana eluded me for a long time after that. Not until I finally started chasing the daemon Chinook, and began to realize the glory of the big wind's reach into the States, did my lack of knowledge about Montana begin to really bother me. At last there came a chance to follow the Chinook Arch south, to make a circle through the state and back into Canada, gathering some chinook stories from both Montanans and Albertans along the way.

It was a pretty simplistic idea, I see now: Montana is just too big and raunchy to be grasped by one little toe that-a-way; but it was the beginning of a one-sided love affair I am still conducting with that state.

The geography of Montana is a puzzle to Albertans. Our own mountains form our western horizon; eastward the only real uplift is the Cypress Hills. Farther west lie the ranges of the British Columbia cordillera. There is nothing in Alberta like the Flathead Valley of western Montana. It's a state of great breadth, lying south of three Canadian provinces—British Columbia, Alberta and Saskatchewan. Driving east into Saskatchewan, one encounters only rolling prairie. But to drive eastward in central Montana is to encounter a constellation of mountain ranges, formed by igneous activity originally, unlike the sedimentary formations of the Rockies. So above the prairies, for example, rise the Adell Mountains, Highwood Mountains and Little Rocky Mountains. North are the Bears Paw and beyond them the Sweetgrass Hills of the Medicine Line; southward lie the Little Belt Mountains, the Castle Mountains and the Crazy Mountains; the list goes on.

Mountains are likewise encountered in every direction when you travel south along the Front (the east slope of the Rockies) to Choteau, Helena and Butte, then east to Livingston. The other thing you notice about Montana (though this is beginning to change rapidly now as yuppy trendoids move in) are all the places where nobody lives.

Most Americans, if they think of Canada at all, picture us as a frozen wilderness, dotted here and there with the scarlet tunics of the Royal Canadian Mounted Police. Each Mountie, mounted on a pair of snow-shoes, is trunching across the frozen waste in pursuit of a cruel and insane trapper. Sometimes he stops in at isolated trading posts, where wild beavers roam the street by day, and gnaw their way through the walls of log cabins by night.

America seems hopelessly cosmopolitan by comparison. So I owe it to my countrymen to try to burst this bubble by pointing out that there are 2.7 million people in Alberta. There are nearly as many people in Calgary (717,000), as there are in the entire state of Montana (800,000). Calgary, Alberta, Canada, is the largest urban centre in Chinook Country.

Speaking of frozen wastes, Montana holds a national record for low temperature, and the coldest temperature record for Chinook Country: –70°F, recorded at Rogers Pass, January 20, 1954.

Except for the built-up urban areas of the Flathead Valley, Montana in the mid-nineties feels like Alberta in the sixties. Visiting the ruined glories of Butte, hanging out in a Livingston saloon or roaming in the great wilderness of Glacier National Park, one feels close to the life described in Norman Maclean's magnificent book *A River Runs Through It*. God help Alberta, and God save Montana from the curse of popularity.

My favourite entrance to Montana is the Chief Mountain Highway south from Waterton, Alberta. The road climbs up to the flanks of the sacred mountain between Glacier National Park and Montana's Blackfeet Reservation. To the left is rolling prairie. Downhill to the west, out of sight to me, is the Belly River, which rises in Glacier National Park, Montana, and flows northeast into Alberta. Down there is a hiking trail that leads to Elizabeth Lakes in Glacier Park, U.S.A. Charlie Russell, who lives near Waterton, knows the American park well. He and I backpacked into the valley one time, taking a bottle of Glenfiddich single malt as a gift to an acquaintance at the Belly River Ranger Station. Work was done for the day when we arrived. Our man packed a .45 on his hip, unlike Canadian park wardens, who don't carry pistols (yet). Part of his task was to protect the Land of the Eagle from backpacking dope smugglers trying to bypass U.S. ports of entry. "Scotch whisky!" Dave had cried, his eyes lighting up. "And you know, boys, are we ever in luck."

"Why is that, Dave?"

"Because I have been saving three cans of Coke for an occasion like this. . . ."

Charlie and I had exchanged a look: these Americans! Might as well spit in the communion cup as put Coke in that elixir. "Dave, with all due respect to the badge and this great nation you are sworn to protect, if you put Coke in our whisky, we might have an international incident right here."

I chuckled at the memory and continued on south and downhill to Babb, a town you can miss if you happen to blink while driving through it. The Stars and Stripes flew proudly over a weathered-looking school-house. Generally speaking, parts of northern Montana look a bit run-down compared to the wealthier-looking farms of southern Alberta.

The Montana section of the historic Old North Trail is now called Highway 89. Its northern section can be a lonely road. I have driven in it one March with big snowdrifts towering over the car, and had to get out at Kiowa and use my boot toes to nudge two dogs that would not get out of a patch of sunlight and let me by.

For me, Montana's different faces are associated with faces of people I have met. East Glacier calls another park ranger to mind—Dick Matt-son, a Vietnam vet and a parksman to the core. Montana that night was a meal of elk steaks and the shelter of a log house in deep snow; the warmth of a wood heater and talk about a black wolf seen way out on the prairie where Route 89 crosses Badger Creek. Wolves in Montana were shot out of existence years ago, as they were in southern Alberta. But there was always a small population in Banff National Park that had survived the slaughter and were too wise, when leaving federal land, to take poisoned bait set out by Alberta government hunters. In recent years, Canadian wolves have expanded their holdings, and made their way to Glacier Park and the Flathead Valley, delighting conserva-tionists and infuriating some ranchers. They are travellers par excel-lence. A wolf collared in Glacier National Park was shot six months later north of Dawson Creek, well over five hundred air miles away.

I collected some yarns of Montana blizzards from Mattson's friends. I heard of trains derailed by snowdrifts, and semitrailers buried so that only a small round hole in the snow, puffing diesel smoke, marked their location. "How did the engine get air under all that snow?" I demanded to know.

My informant never missed a beat. "Oxygen," he said. "They carry oxygen for backup. For when the snorkel gets drifted over and plugged."

"The snorkel, eh?"

"The snorkel, uh huh."

Next morning Dick Greenshields, a merchant in East Glacier, Montana, showed me windows pocked by wind-blown gravel. His anemometer was homelier than most. "We know when the wind is gusting at 100 m.p.h.," he says, "because at that speed the upstairs toilet flushes of its own accord." I went down to the Burlington Northern depot and tried to find out about the difficulties of railroading in Montana's winters, but the station agent just smiled faintly and said, "You'll have to talk to public relations in Havre about that."

The Old North Trail led on along the Front to Choteau and past the flat-topped rimrock of Priest Butte. Louis Riel, Métis patriot, spent five years in exile at a Jesuit mission on the Sun River near here, in the 1880s. He was brought to bay, that plainsman, on American soil with the mountains at his back, driven into exile with the timber wolf and the grizzly bear on the edge of the frontier. When I asked the curator of a local museum about Riel's sojourn, she said, "Louis who?"

Riel worked as a school teacher at St. Peter's Mission. He met with couriers from Manitoba by candlelight and plotted his eventual return to his beloved country, thereby ensuring an appointment with the hangman's noose.

I turned off the highway and rolled down a big hill and over the Sun River to the hamlet of Simms. This is the home of chinook guru Warren Harding, who is a rancher and a retired meteorologist. The wind rolled me in on him in the middle of calving season. This meant he was busier than a cat on a hot stove, yet I found this senior citizen jumping up and down with excitement about the glorious Chinook Arch that day. By way of an omen, the arch that day stretched almost exactly from Cirque Peak above my house to Shaw Butte just west of his—a distance of approximately two hundred air miles.

Warren began his career as a weather observer on the Gulf of Alaska, where the chinook has its beginnings. (His explanations found their way into the earlier part of this book.) I made notes while he talked non-stop about zones of divergence, the venturi effect and high-level jet streams.

Warren, unlike most Americans, thinks about Canada a great deal. He is always looking north to watch our weather. "If I can predict the wind in Lethbridge," he told me, "I can predict the weather for northern Montana." He has scientific knowledge and instruments to do that, but Warren's a rancher now. So he knows when a cold front has reached Cutbank, three hours north, because his cattle start to bellow and look for their calves. He can tell when a chinook is coming by watching the pressure falls between Lethbridge and Great Falls. But his wife, Grace, is a better indicator. The pressure fall associated with a chinook gives her a headache. Predicting the weather is otherwise a complicated process. As Warren puts it, "Imagine a leaf falling from a forty-foot-high branch in a breeze; now write an equation that will describe the path that leaf takes; you will start then to get into weather." On the way out the door he caught my questioning glance and laughed: "Hey, pardon this stain on my slicker. Picked up this newborn calf this morning, an' he shat right down my sleeve 'n' filled my pocket while he was at it. You know what it's like with some of these births where the calf gets turned and comes out backwards."

I left Simms and drove on to Helena, the state capital. I played the tourist and did some shopping. In the "Excited States," pipe tobacco and rye whiskey cost a fraction of their cost in Canada. For example, a pouch of tobacco that costs me $13 Canadian in Alberta sells for $1.50 in Montana. Shop around and you can buy a six-pack of beer for $2.99 or less that would cost $8.00 in Canada. A person could really injure their health down here, I thought. The difference in prices lies in our government tax grabs, both federal and provincial. American government knows better than to punish the working man for his simple pleasures. If they tried those kinds of taxes in America, I think there would be riots in the streets. Canadians bitch about it, but since the only credential Canadians require of their politicians is that they be wealthy, we keep on voting in oilmen, lawyers and millionaires—rich people who subsidize their cronies at the taxpayer's expense.

Later that night, I checked into the King Henry room of the Knight's Rest Motel in Helena. I sat brooding about national identity and cheap pipe tobacco, looking for common cause with American ancestors, I suppose. I grabbed the remote at last and flipped on the stunner, seeking mindless entertainment, and found something that made me yelp with astonishment. It was a machine-gun festival, unhallowed notion, where families bring their own machine guns to shoot at exploding targets for one dollar a round. The pipe fell out of my mouth as I watched red-blooded American women firing fifty-calibre tracer bullets at old cars loaded with barrels of diesel fuel and explosives. Cars began exploding; everybody hugged each other and cheered. Prizes were awarded. A gun-happy dentist talked with perfect lucidity about the "machine-gun smile," brought on by the enjoyment of handling a well-greased, heavy-duty weapon. Cut to the Mr. Ken doll host, who declaimed, "Only in America do we enjoy the kind of liberty that makes a festival like this possible."

Badly shaken, I changed the channel and found myself gazing in horror at the real-life shootout between federal officers and religious nuts down in Waco, Texas. CNN said the movie script was already being written. And now I felt like a complete alien in this land: America had me surrounded. Nervously I peered out through a crack in the drapes. It was quiet, no traffic in sight. I wondered who was out in the woods, drawing a bead on me with an infrared scope. But it looked like suburban Lethbridge, Alberta, on a Sunday night: go figger.

Thank God for gun control in Canada, flawed as it is. (In 1994, 34,000 Americans died as a result of gunshots, compared to 1,400 Canadians.) We have had some atrocities up here, also. The Montreal massacre of 1989, where a lunatic chauvinist shot fourteen female engineering students to death, still gives us a national nightmare. It resulted in demands for stricter gun laws. But Canadians have long been prohibited by law from purchasing working machine guns. Few of us own pistols. It is difficult to obtain a permit for a handgun, and most of us like it that way.

Helena is a hilly town with a busy and collegiate feel to it due to the presence of the legislature and the many rambling old houses on shady streets. The handsome brownstone buildings of Last Chance Gulch speak of a place that knows its origins. Up and down the streets of Helena, I walked where my Uncle Oscar had walked so long ago. Thinking about Kingfish, I went to the capitol building that houses the state archives. I stood for a while in the handsome assembly room with its dark woodwork. There was a time when the wealthy traders of Fort Benton in Choteau County directed the fortunes of this state. Under the glorious murals painted by western artist Charlie Russell, under the watchful eyes of his immortal Blackfoot warriors and cowboys, my

Uncle Oscar had once risen in defiance to speak out for Choteau against the upstart power brokers of the new day. In the empty chamber, I imagined him rising again, a farmer-sheriff in a store-bought suit, speaking his mind. He told his family and friends, "I had my say." But I wish I could have asked him if he had ever had second thoughts about that moment when he rose and fell on the rock of principle.

The entrance to the state archives is guarded by a stuffed albino buffalo. The living version was a sacred animal to the plains tribes. I spent the day researching Montana weather.

The weather in Montana is notorious in the U.S. It is famed for both chinooks and arctic temperatures. In the archives I discovered, among many things, a *New York Times* piece by A.B. Guthrie Jr.: "How to Live at 58 Below." An old rancher says he has to "get home and unfreeze the lantern." "It was an old gag," wrote Guthrie, "and none of us told him kerosene didn't freeze. If we had, he'd have answered, 'It isn't the coal oil but the blaze. It froze, and I got to thaw it out before I can blow it.' "

An elderly lady sat near by and we chatted a bit about Fort Benton and the history of southern Alberta. "We're the same people, you know," she said at one point. She meant Canadians and Americans, and she meant it as a compliment. But I came of age in the sixties, and one of my best friends is an American draft dodger who left the United States and never returned. I thought about Vietnam, and I thought about the events of the night before: I could not imagine a Canadian foreign policy that would embrace the Domino Theory; I could not imagine a machine-gun festival taking place on Canadian soil. "There are some pretty major differences between us," I said.

"Oh I don't think so. Aside from that free medicare you have. I grant you that. But I've been up there many times, and it sure looks a lot like the U.S.A. to me."

Her idea was suddenly appalling to me in the light of those televised images, and in the light of what history had spelled out for me. I was startled by my emotional reaction to it, when I thought of my own family origins in America. She was a kindly soul, and I declined to argue the matter further just then—a typically Canadian reaction, I might add. At the surface there are so many similarities between the nations. Montanans and Albertans do share that strange mixture of western exuberance and taciturnity that manifest themselves by turns, as well as a common distrust of eastern politicians. But the differences in national character and outlook on the world are pronounced. Philosophically, we are poles apart.

Take the gun-control issue again, for example. Though Albertans own the highest number of guns per capita in Canada, there is a point on the gun issue where they diverge radically from their Montana neighbours. There is no such thing as a "right to bear arms" in the Canadian Charter of Rights. Recent court cases in America have thrown that notion for a loop in the republic also, though gun advocates refuse to bite that particular reality sandwich. There is no corresponding popular belief in Alberta, or in Canada, that having an armed population is somehow an admirable achievement. Actually, the thought of it frightens a lot of us to death, myself included, and I speak as a rural type who owns four firearms, and as one who flatly opposes our government's intention to register every firearm in Canada. My distrust of big government on that and other scores, however, is typical of a south Albertan. It sets me apart from other Canadians, who believe the government is supposed to solve all our social problems, and it is more in accord with American attitudes. But in their hearts, most Albertans, like most other Canadians, don't believe that much can be achieved through the use of direct force by the lone individual. This faith in law and order, and in the greatest good for the greatest number, is something we absorbed with our mother's milk.

*   *   *

I followed the Big Belt Mountains down to Livingston, a beautiful old city on the Yellowstone River, and one of the windiest places in North America. It reminded me of Pincher Creek, where I do my shopping, but Livingston's old stone buildings make it more picturesque by far. The trees grow into a permanent northeast lean, as if coyly trying to escape the wind's passionate embrace. The Yellowstone River, swollen by spring rains, had turned an ugly brown. It lapped hungrily near the top of the pylons on the railroad bridge, but the local people remained unconcerned. Under the heading "Chinook Challenge" in the local paper, a reporter droned on about a broken water main on Chinook Street.

I went to Dan Bailey's world-famous fishing store and soaked up the ambience. There was a row of women working in the back room hand-tying trout flies with quick, deft fingers. Among all the fishing hardware was a strange little object with a plastic catheter and squeeze bulb. It was a stomach pump for trout. You caught a trout, one inclined to experiment with its food, and you pumped its stomach to see what the main course fly was that trout were feeding on that day. Then you released the victim, and tied on the appropriate fly or nymph to catch more trout.

Over a bottle of Miller's in the Mint Bar, I wondered aloud how the trout felt about having their stomachs pumped.

"Hungry, probly," suggested the barkeep. There was no talk of the wind after a blustery day that made the weatherman a liar. Grass was in motion, whole trees were moving, and the clouds were walloping along like white sailboats on a blue bay. Such zephyrs do not impress Livingstonians, who save their bragging for the real thing. "When highway signs read 'Chain Up Here,'" they will tell you, "it means chain your truck to a tree so's it won't blow away." Truckers fear this area because a few semitrailer trucks can be blown over in this vicinity each year. On Highway 90, they have an innovation that we could use in southern Alberta. Signs reading "Danger, Cross Winds" are equipped with wind socks. I met a trucker in the Mint who told me, "When you look in the rearview and see your trailer wheels starting to lift off the ground, it's time to pull over. I can't believe the wind in this country. Montana blows, and North Dakota sucks."

I went over to a restaurant in a cool, sandstone building for a meal of chicken fried steak, swimming in savoury brown gravy, topped with a dollop of white milk gravy, and with a small dish of golden gravy on the side. "Does it always blow like this?" I asked my waitress.

"Always," she replied, in a slow Montana drawl. "Since the day I was born."

Later I checked with Bill Evans, a local air traffic controller, who told me that wind gusts in excess of 100 knots (115 m.p.h.) have been recorded in this area. There is no doubt the wind speed has been much higher, but the anemometer only went up to 115. After that, centrifugal force has been known to blow the instrument to pieces. It is not unusual to have winds of 55 m.p.h. gusting to 100 m.p.h. in this region. During the windiest months from October to April, the wind can blow at 45 m.p.h. for two to three weeks at a time. It is not surprising that people think the wind never stops.

It is also not surprising that entrepreneurs of a decade ago should select this windy city as a test site for wind-powered generators. They discovered a startling fact: Livingston was too windy for most wind machines of that era to operate safely. On a high plateau near the airport, the blades of two high-tech windmills, looking like big aircraft propellers, turned brilliant circles in the afternoon sun. Each produced twenty-five kilowatts of power.

Steve Hicks, a local wind power expert, told me, "It's like the Good Housekeeping Seal of Approval, if you can keep a wind machine operating here." Hicks recalled two machines that were set up some years ago. "The wind destroyed them both in twenty-four hours. In one case the nacelle—that's the generating part—jumped right off a tower. In another the machine threw a blade. A blade weighs four hundred pounds. So the whole thing got out of balance and self-destructed. That one took the tower down with it."

Abrupt temperature changes and high winds that suddenly shift direction had damaged or destroyed thirteen of the fifteen machines set up here. The metal bases of old towers poked up like steel tree stumps through the prairie grass. (Four machines were in operation here in 1995.) Major players, such as U.S. Windpower Inc. have bypassed turbulent Livingston for California, and more recently, for Pincher Creek.

Highway 2 west of Shelby, Montana, curves and dips through rolling prairie hills. I felt the wind tugging at my steering wheel. Tumbleweeds were piled against the barbed-wire fences in ominous, dark hedges. A solitary antelope posed by the side of the road, but ran off at high speed when I stopped for a picture. Looking north, I got a typical Montana view: the towering clouds of a cold front moving down from the Great White North. The sight made me grin patriotically.

In the ranching town of Cutbank, I interviewed two Highway Patrolmen, Bob Paul and Jim Vollrath. They were part of a seven-man detachment that patrols five counties lying just south of the Canadian border. Vollrath is a trim-looking ten-year veteran of the force; Bob Paul is a husky former Marine officer with a military bearing.

Severe winter weather makes their work challenging. The early promoters of Montana talked of chinook winds as "the warm breath of spring." But sometimes it is a polar bear's bellow from Canada that Montanans call a "Klondike Chinook." Dragged by a southbound jet stream, it roars down from Canada then swaps ends to veer out of the southwest, bringing only trouble. Blowing snow and a windchill factor that has gone as low as −70°F make for treacherous winter driving. Called out to emergencies, the officers must deal with "whiteouts," blowing snow that inhibits depth perception. "You're blind as a bat at times," said Vollrath, "but there's still some clowns out there driving around. The audio tone on my radar set has warned me of oncoming cars more than once."

Vollrath remembered driving slowly up behind a car that was stopped in the middle of the road during a whiteout. He pulled over, flipped on his blue lights, got out of the cruiser and walked up beside the driver's window. The driver, strapped into the winter hell of Glacier County driving, sat rigidly staring into the storm, turning the wheel cautiously and convinced his car was still moving forward. "I rapped on the window with my flashlight. He just about jumped right out of his skin when he saw me standing there!"

The chinook is a mixed blessing. It blows the highways bare of snow one day, and coats them with black ice another day. Officer Paul recalled a wind storm on January 30, 1989. "The wind blew a schoolhouse roof off at Velour. It blew several semitrailer trucks over on the interstate." He paused to let the next line sink in. "It blew a train off the tracks at the S curve just west of Browning. Now that is wind," he said, banging down his coffee cup for emphasis.

Sunday, January 29, 1989. All day the warm wind blows snow across Highway 2 between Browning and Cutbank, coating it with slush. At sunset the slush turns to black ice thick enough to skate on. Truckers wrestle with 80 m.p.h. wind gusts that send them skidding across the highway, out of control.

January 30. Paul is dispatched to Browning to deal with two "rollovers." Faced with 102 m.p.h. gusts as he heads west on Highway 2, he must keep his speed to 45 m.p.h.; Paul feels the front end of his Chevy Caprice cruiser lifting from the ground. On the radio, he hears reports of 110 m.p.h. gusts farther west.

At the accident scene, Paul struggles against the windblast to open the door of his cruiser. The wind rips his expensive sunglasses off and blows them right out of sight. He sees two trucks lying in the ditch: a potato chip van, and a twenty-four-foot Mercedes U-Haul. The chip man's cargo has spilled out and left for North Dakota. The

U-Haul driver's cargo, pottery, is still there but he wishes it wasn't. The drivers are shaken up, but not badly injured.

"The pottery driver was funny," said Paul. "The wind blew his rig across the road, but he got it stopped. He could feel the wind lift the truck up, and then just hold it in the air a minute. He had this powerful urge to stick his arm out there and push that truck back! So he rolled the window down, then all of a sudden it hit him: 'Now boy, that's stupid. I mean I got 26,000 pounds here. There is no way I'm gonna stick my arm out there.' "

As the warm wind tears across the foothills of Alberta and Montana the morning of January 30, it melts the ice and dries the pavement again. It happened that two acquaintances of my friend Charlie Russell, Alf and Ella Baker of Waterton, Alberta, left home that morning, in a steady 40 m.p.h. breeze, headed south for Kalispell.

They are grateful that the roads are not icy. But at Browning, Alf and the chinook are wrestling for control of his '82 Chevy in severe wind gusts. As the Bakers near the railroad overpass two miles west of Browning on U.S. 2, they notice a freight train approaching from the north. Topping the overpass, the road curves directly into the wind. Alf and Ella glance down on the railway just as the Burlington Northern freight train enters the infamous Browning S curve. One of those 100 m.p.h. plus gusts strikes the car violently like a bulldog shaking a rabbit. It strikes the freight train broadside on.

Ten empty cars, each weighing up to thirty tons, suddenly topple off the rails and fall into the ditch where clouds of snow blast into the air with the impact. Stunned at the sight, the Bakers pull over for a few minutes to get control of their jangled nerves before driving on. Below them the freight train slows to a stop. There is nothing the Bakers can do to help; as it turns out, nobody was injured that day. Back toward Browning, the lights of emergency vehicles flicker through the blowing snow. The wind bellows its triumph all around them. This is not the first time that the Black Wind has taught a freight train how to fly.

Wayne Dusterhoff, a tall, rangy Glacier County deputy sheriff, stopped by as I talked with the officers. I asked him if there is an increase in violent crime during the chinook, as there is when the foehn wind blows in Germany.

Dusterhoff was wary of me at first. "Who is this for?" he asked. "The last time I was quoted, I wound up in court." Reassured, he explained how "disturbances," including family violence, occur three times as often during the winter as they do in the warm months.

"Rapes increase in the summer though," put in Paul.

"That's about what you'd expect," drawled Vollrath.

The officers felt that the wind was just one factor causing people problems. Shut in by severe winter weather, people may suffer from "cabin fever," and unstable personalities can crack under the strain.

I asked how they chase speeders in such severe wind conditions. Vollrath told me, "In this wind, you work speeders with the wind, 'cause they can't speed against it, and comin' with it they're doin' 70 m.p.h. ridin' the brakes. It's hard writing tickets though. Every time you open a door, all your paperwork blows to North Dakota."

"How does the wind affect you?" I asked Paul.

"It just makes me want to write more tickets." Officer Paul's grin showed how that made him feel much better.

*   *   *

Leaving Cutbank, I drove west on U.S. 2 headed for Browning, headquarters for Montana's Blackfoot Nation. Bands of snow, shot through with afternoon sun, fell on distant alpine meadows. The Lewis and Clark memorial marker stands alone in ranching country not far from the main road. It marks the expedition's farthest point of northern advance in the lands then known as the Louisiana Purchase. It also marks the beginning of conflict with the Blackfoot Nation. On the reservation, stretches of "prairie wool" brightened by blue silky lupines and yellow balsalm root have never been broken by the plow. Except for the occasional barbed-wire fence, the land looks much as it did when the buffalo roamed these hills, and the Blackfoot were the lords of creation.

I have not heard many Blackfoot stories about the origin of the chinook. One informant told me that the wind represents the ghosts of the buffalo returning from their hiding place in the west to run out over the prairie once again. The oldtimers believed that when a mist formed at the foot of Chief Mountain in winter, the snow eater would soon appear. In *Stalking the Mountain Wave*, Ursula Wiese records two stories she found in her researches, attributed to the Northern Blackfoot people. One of them is as follows:

One day the West Wind looked down on the earth and saw that it was covered with snow and it was so cold. He felt sorry for the people and the animals, so he asked Old Man Winter to make it warm so everyone wouldn't be so cold. But Old Man Winter refused and they started fighting.

West Wind started shooting arrows into the sky and was winning, so then it warmed up on earth and everything started melting. Old Man Winter then tried harder and he would start to win, and everything would turn cold and freeze again.

This kept on for some time, then West Wind finally won and that is when spring came. So from that time on every year during the winter we always have Chinooks.

But this account of the wind's origins, describing the war between warm and cold fronts, is not necessarily accepted by the other tribes of the Nitsitapii. The man I wanted to see lived in the South Peigan, the Aamsskaapipiikani culture. I had been warned that he could be a hard man to find. My first stop was Browning's famous Museum of the Plains Indian. "Where might I find Curly Bear Wagner?" I asked the attractive young lady at the front desk.

"About five feet to your right," came her calm reply.

Curly Bear is a powerfully built man with a handshake to match. He wears his hair in braids decorated with red cloth, and he is proud of his heritage.

"Our people were always prepared for the wind," he said, as we sat on the museum steps. He gestured to the west. "They camped along the river bottoms to get out of the wind. They stacked winter wood in a tepee shape to shed the snow."

I told Curly Bear how I had been reading George Bird Grinnell's *Blackfoot Lodge Tales*. Grinnell had alluded to the Windmaker. Curly Bear nodded. "But you know, there's a lot of b.s. in that book." I learned that the southern Peigan are quite certain of where the wind rises. According to tradition, the wind originates some nineteen miles northwest of Browning, in Glacier National Park.

"A long time ago," said Curly Bear, "a warrior wanted to find out where the wind begins. Travelling alone, he made his way into the mountains to what the whites call St. Mary's Lake. As he gazed upon the waters, they began to move. Then he saw something slowly rising from the lake. This was the Windmaker. Now this was a gigantic elk, who lived on the bottom of the lake. When he emerged from the water, his ears began to move. As they moved, they began to fan up the wind and make it blow towards the prairies."

Curly Bear looked at me, defying me to doubt the story. The comic picture he had painted made me smile. But I had heard the story before. A version of it occurs in Walter McClintock's *Old North Trail* (1910), where the eyes of the Medicine Elk are red, and flame pours from his nostrils. As he subsides below the waves, the wind dies out. McClintock's record compared with the version told by Curly Bear shows how the oral tradition changes over time, and yet stays true to its origin. But to Napikwan's ears, it seemed like a story for children, because the context of the old Blackfoot spirituality that gave rise to the legend is not available to a paleface. Also, the Blackfoot were not averse to pulling the leg of their white interlocutors. According to Hugh Dempsey, one of them once told the Rev. George Maclean that the chinook was caused by the farting of the bullmoose. A fabulous natural phenomenon like the chinook deserves fabulous explanations.

We gazed out toward the great semicircle of mountains west of Browning. "I love the beauty of this place," said Curly Bear quietly. "The wind made this country for grazing animals. It's the richest grassland in the United States. Our people always welcomed the chinook wind. It cleared the snow and allowed us to get out, move around, go hunting.

"I like to sit in the hills and meditate when the wind is blowing through the trees. If you listen long enough, the wind will talk to you," he assured me. "You should try it some time."

"I will," I told him. "But it must be tough to meditate when the wind is blowing trains off the tracks."

Curly Bear laughed. "That's good for 'em. Teach 'em a little respect when they come into Blackfeet country."

*   *   *

I left Browning and retraced my route to Waterton. The Prince of Wales Hotel, a gracious Swiss-style chalet from another era, sits on a bluff above Upper Waterton Lake. The view of high mountains and emerald water takes in both American and Canadian mountains in one brilliant panorama. The resort village of Waterton, its streets shaded with pines and aspens, sits below the hotel, on Cameron Creek. Here I stopped in to visit Alf Baker, lean and wiry at sixty-two, and his petite wife, Ella, long-time residents of the park, who confirmed their experience at the Browning S curve. For forty-six years, Alf skippered a barge on Waterton Lake that was the main source of supplies for the Glacier National Park rangers stationed at Goat Haunt, Montana. Americans dread the fierce north winds that blow down from Canada. But Alf learned to respect the fierce warm wind that the Windmaker sends out of Montana's Rockies to howl down Waterton Lake into Alberta.

Windy days meant a rough time on the lake for Alf Baker. One morning in particular stands out. At 8:00 a.m. one day in early May, the Bakers left for Goat Haunt. They were freighting a twelve-ton fuel truck up the lake on Alf's sixteen-ton powered barge. The day looked promising enough, but partway up the lake the chinook came calling. Waves broke over the bow, enveloping the pilot house and the entire truck with freezing spray. Icy water foamed around the truck tires, swept across the deck and spilled back into the lake as the wind raged. The truck, chained down fore and aft, strained against its ties.

"The waves are only about six feet high," said Alf. "But there's no swells to ride"—Alf made a gentle rocking motion with one hand— "like you get during storms at sea. This lake just gets plain bloody rough. Every wave hits you, and every fifth wave is a bad one. Now I had twenty-eight tons there. But those waves hit the front of the barge, and the whole thing would just shudder."

"It got so bad," said Alf, "that Ella had to get in the truck, and start the motor to run the power brakes, to keep that truck from rollin' back and forth and breakin' the chains." Ella is a wee slip of a woman. An unpleasant image of the huge fuel truck disappearing into the 460-foot depths of the lake came to mind.

Ella kept her foot on the brake all the way to Goat Haunt. "I had one leg longer than the other," she said grimly. "I was scared to death. When I got to Goat Haunt, I could have kissed the ground."

Not surprisingly, they are happy to be retired from the freighting business. Alf knows too well that not all encounters with the wind have happy endings. He remembers the day the wind blew a note of tragedy. The Windflower Motel was under construction across from Alf's garage some years ago. A young tradesman from Cardston had come across the street to chat with Alf. "The wind was severe that day. He had just left, and I went inside. I heard a terrible crash. I ran out, and the whole roof of the motel had blown off. He was under it. I dug through the wreckage until I found him."

Alf stopped, still affected by the memory of that day. "He died in my arms. Just a young guy. He had a wife and kids, too."

We were silent for a moment, listening to the mournful sighing of the wind in the evergreens near the house. It was time to go.

"Did you hear about the dog that blew away?" asked Alf, a glint of mischief in his eye. "A dog blew off of Main Street one day, blew across the lake, lit against the front of the Prince of Wales Hotel, and before the wind subsided, he starved to death."

"No kidding," I said, playing the tourist.

"Oh Alf," Ella scolded. "That's a joke."

But there is an underlying truth nearly as bizarre, I think, as I drive past the great hotel heading north. During construction in 1927, the wind pushed the eighty-foot-high frame, weighing hundreds of tons, three inches off its footing. Teams of horses and winches were employed to heave the building back into position, but the wind struck again, moving it back out. It was impossible to get it square, and to this day it remains out of plumb, a witness to the Windmaker's power.

*   *   *

Montanans had favoured me with modern-day anecdotes about the wind. But the chinook had engendered many stories among the pioneers as well. What is surprising is how interrelated the stories are, how they so often seem to be variations on a few protean, seminal tales. In one strain of the yarns, the wind comes on so suddenly, and melts the snow so quickly, that it leaves the winter traveller stranded in the mud. In another version, the traveller, benighted in a chinook wind, ties his horse to a tree and makes camp, oblivious to the depth of snow beneath him. In the morning, he wakes up on bare ground, and finds his horse hanging from the top of a telegraph pole—or a church steeple.

What is interesting is how the elements in a chinook story are tied to real-life experience. These are not fairy tales, they are more Bunyanesque in nature. The wind is the giant in the yarn, but as a real-life force to those of us who know it, it is obviously gigantic even beyond fiction. Any prolonged account of the wind's antics winds up sounding like magic realism after a while.

Country people often watch the wildlife for signs that indicate a change in the weather. Crows going to roost early in the day, or elk changing cover for no apparent reason may mean a storm on the way. I passed the Wellman ranch, remembering what Cal Wellman told me once about a flock of ravens who weren't that weather wise. Every night, he watched them fly over his ranch, flying west to roost on the mountain side. Ravens are most accomplished aerialists who play tag in mid-air for sheer fun. But one evening, during a wild southwest gale, he saw the birds on the ground. They were in flying formation, but they were walking west to roost that night.

A grounded raven waddles like a drunken sailor. Every once in a while, one of them would get impatient and take to the air. The wind would cuff it backwards end over end and knock it out of the sky. The others stopped, and craned their necks backwards, looking irritated, and waited for the dazed show-off to catch up. Cal watched in disbelief as the birds waddled out of sight into the forest. He went home knowing he had seen something new.

In *Folklore of Canada*, author Edith Fowke's researches seem to point to the pioneer McDougall brothers as the originators of chinook tales. There used to be a saying in Alberta that there were just three liars in the province: the trader Dave McDougall was one of them, and his reverend brother John was the other two. The saying came about because of the great delight the McDougalls took in stringing along the greenhorns with tales of the Wild West. But John McDougall was also a capable writer and historian. I think he knew the difference between fiction and non-fiction—most of the time.

Nowadays, most people prefer to watch their liars on television. "Watching the little people," as an Irish friend of mine puts it. Walk down a suburban street in North America, and the weird blue light from many a window marks the worshippers of the cathode tube. In some houses the stunner is never turned off; apparently they use it for central heating. The TV set is the postmodern equivalent of the fireplace. But in the country, there is still a chance to stare into a fire while the coyotes are howling just outside the yard fence. There is still time to let the ancient, dancing figures of flame light a spark in the imagination. So, particularly in the rural areas of the provinces, a few authentic old-

time storytellers, men like rancher James Riviere, live on in defiance of
the satellite dish.

James and his wife, Gay, live a few miles north of my friend Charlie
Russell's place, near the hamlet of Twin Butte and in the shadow of
Shell Canada's Waterton Gas Plant. An old trail used by the Stoney people as they travelled south, hugging the mountains, passes through the
ranch, which sits at the foot of Spread Eagle Mountain. I went to see
them on my way back from Montana.

James Riviere's gravelly voice reveals traces of his French and Cree
background. He is a big, rawboned old man, lean and strong. He wears
the sun on his face; his leathery features are seamed by time and sudden
laughter lines. Gay is a smiling sprite of a woman, but with an edge of
cowgirl toughness still evident in her small frame.

The Rivieres have lived here going on four generations now. At one
time, James made his living from outfitting and guiding. Then along
came the oil company, pushing seismic roads up every mountain valley
and drilling scores of gas wells all along the front range. That was the
end of the outfitting business, but James did not want to move from the
place where he was raised. So he went to work for Shell Oil and wound
up running a contracting business maintaining the very roads that had
put him out of business.

The house's big windows overlook a creek and forested slopes. On
the high, panelled walls, the heads of hunting trophies, mountain goat,
grizzly bear and cougar, overlook the guest. The Rivieres have interrupted cougars that were trying to kill a colt within sight of the house.
Cougars have long had a sweet tooth for colt flesh. The wilderness
comes right into the Rivieres' back yard. The Flathead Valley of British
Columbia and Montana, home of wolves and grizzly bears, lies just a
few miles to the west of their ranch. The bears that range between the
Flathead Valley and the backcountry of Waterton National Park may
still venture out on the east slope, especially in the spring. At one time,
they would have been looking for the remains of winter-killed buffalo.
Now it is winter-killed beef, deer, elk and moose that lures them eastward. James and Gay have seen a grizzly, lethargic after cleaning up
such a carcass, come walking down among a herd of their bedded cattle. The bovines never even bothered to get up; they could sense that
the bear was not a threat at that moment. Some ranchers, like James,
will tolerate the big bear, but others in the Waterton vicinity do not.

Occasionally, a grizzly turns into a cattle killer, preying on yearlings, which are stupid and easy to capture. This gives all bears a bad reputation, in some eyes. A number of bears who wander out of Montana into the grazing reserve at Poll Haven, next to Waterton, have died of "lead poisoning" over the years.

James's father, Frenchy Riviere, was a mountainman, guide and forest ranger who was once hired as a professional yarn teller by the Prince of Wales Hotel. He came into the country as a bullwhacker, freighting supplies for the I.G. Baker outfit between Fort Benton and Fort Macleod. James's mother was part Cree. His aunt, also part Cree, was the wife of the famous mountainman Kootenay Brown, one of the founders of Waterton National Park. James learned to speak Cree at an early age, and he learned about his Cree heritage at this woman's knee. The Plains Indian culture was an oral tradition. Their history was handed down around the campfire, and James was steeped in the lore of that race; he was the son of storytellers, both white and Indian. For the First Nations, all parts of the creation have a spiritual presence. When he went to dig red clay for his mother for ceremonial paint, Mrs. Kootenay Brown would give him some tobacco to leave as an offering. "Make sure you thank the spirit of that clay," she cautioned him. "Leave this tobacco as a gift."

"We used to thank the clay all right," he told me, settling into his favourite chair in his panelled living room, "but we was kids, you know. Sometimes we'd smoke the tobacco 'stead of leaving it."

Prompted by James, I explained my search for stories about the chinook. He listened patiently to my example of such a story, the one about the stranded dog team, attributed to the McDougalls. James was annoyed at the imputation.

"That story was invented by old Windy Paul," he said vehemently, "old Paul Le Buck."

"Paul Le Buck?"

"Yep, or Lyin' Paul. Paul Cyr was his name, but he had several names, that old feller. Now I'm eighty-eight years old, and Windy Paul was here long before I was. He was an old man when I was a kid, and he would come round to sell hay to the mines and logging camps. They used horses in the mines back then. Horses did everything back then. Built the whole damn country. Anyway, this here Windy Paul, after supper in the cookshack, he would start to tellin' stories. And he told that one you mentioned, often." James leans forward a bit, remembering. He is suddenly more animated; the pleasure he takes in having an audience to hear the tale is touching to me. He reminds me of someone familiar to me; I try to think of whom, as he launches into the story.

"He said he went to town with a load of hay, with a team of horses and a big sled. 'By God,' he said, 'it was forty below when he left.' So he had on his big buffalo coat, but even so, he was pretty near freezin'. Now on the way back home, a big chinook blew in. Well pretty soon, he was a sweatin' settin' up on that wagon. Windy Paul had to take that big coat off. He's settin' there in his shirtsleeves.

"Now the wind was at his back, and even though it was comin' from the northwest, it was hotter than hell. The snow was piled deep, but it started to meltin'. It melted so fast that he had to whip that team up into a trot, and even at that, the front runners was on snow, but the rear runners was draggin' in mud. He said, 'When I got to my gate, that's where the chinook caught up and passed me by; it left me stuck in the mud.' "

James straightens and catches my eye before he delivers the last line: "He said, 'I stood up, and looked back; and here come my poor dog, a swimmin' up the road behind me.' " And James's dog paddled with one big paw on the tail end of his story in a way that made me picture the poor dog desperately following Windy Paul, as if it was real water and not just a river of fibs.

Gay is laughing in the kitchen; it seems I'm to stay for dinner; it's expected. James is on a roll now. He tells me how we youngsters know nothing of cold weather these days. How once, at a hunting cabin, he threw out a bucket of water, which froze in mid-air, struck his partner and knocked him unconscious. "Had to drag him into the shack by his heels." When telling a story, he will pause at times as if to let you absorb the information, or factual portions of the yarn. If you don't get it, he will back up and run over it again, because the stories depend on an understood experience.

A local cowboy, Mac Main, spent a fair bit of time helping James out when he was younger. "I used to tell him a story one week," said James. "The next week I'd tell him the same story again. And the same again the next week. He musta figured I was gettin' senile. But you see, I wanted him to get the story right," concluded James with a smile.

"I see."

"There's not many of us old buggers left, Marty." He begins to name a few people I should go and talk to, but his voice trails off when he realizes they are all gone. He has straddled the decades between pack-horse and space shuttle, and outlived most of his generation. As he turns his angular face toward the light to glance outdoors, the light plays across his high cheekbones. His Indian blood has stamped its blueprint on his features, and now I realize why he seems so familiar: he bears an uncanny resemblance to my American grandfather, J.C. Marty: the same angular, Amerindian features, the same tall, sinewy build. The realization of this resemblance is a cloud over my thoughts. There was so much my grandfather could have told me; not knowing more about his history has been a continuing handicap to my sense of my own origins.

"Well, you must have seen a few chinooks up your way," suggested James politely. I told him about February 1986. "We had a foot of snow on the ground. Three feet more fell in nine hours."

"I remember that day," said James. "A big chinook came in."

I nodded. "The wind reached seventy-one miles per hour, and the temperature climbed to fifty-three degrees. The snow melted in a matter of hours, and water poured down our hillside. The whole valley turned into a lake. We had waves, like a surf, breaking over the barbed-wire fence, crashing on the driveway."

"You don't say so?" said James politely.

"I opened the hatch on the root cellar to get some spuds . . ."

"Oh oh . . ."

"Had four hundred gallons of ice-cold vegetable borscht in there. Whole basement floor was flooded . . ."

James laughed good-naturedly and flicked his hand at the story like a man shooing flies. He has forgotten worse chinook floods.

"Didja hear the one about the rancher who kept his branding iron hanging from his main gate?" he demanded. He is readying me for a knockout. "Fellah asked him, 'What the hell's that there for?' 'Well,' he says, 'that there's my wind gauge. Tells me when I can go out and feed stock and when I can't. When it's stickin' out a quarter, I can still go and feed. When it's sticking straight out, I don't go outside.'" James pauses for a few seconds to set his hook. "He said, 'I used to hang a logging chain up there, but I don't use it no more. When the wind really gets up, it pops all the damned links off.'"

The laughter this fable arouses in me has something to do with the memory of the weight of a logging chain hung over my shoulders on a cold, wet morning in October in Jasper National Park. The firewood logs I was skidding behind Rusty, alias Seldom Swift, a government skid horse, kept snagging in the bush, and I wound up shifting them clear with my own back and that length of wet, slippery chain. I revenged myself with laughter on the greasy iron snake there in James's living room, picturing the half-inch-thick steel links snapping with a satisfying "ping." I realize now why some stories do not translate very well. The stories arise out of the common experience of a community, and without the community to supply the context in which the stories occur—what the writer calls explication—the stories lose their dramatic or comedic force. As in the case of Blackfoot legends, without the cultural context, they sound like simplistic yarns or like fairy tales to our ears.

A tantalizing smell of home cooking wafted out of Gay's kitchen. "I'll tell ya," she says proudly, "if you want to hear stories, you've come to the right place. Now come and eat, you two."

We went into the big kitchen with its million-dollar view looking south toward Waterton. On a ranch, the noon meal is often referred to as "dinner," and this meal is a far cry from the light lunches now popular in the city. Still I was overwhelmed by this ranch woman's hospitality. Gay presented us with a roast of ham and a roast of beef. The beef was prime and marbled lightly with an edge of fat; the ham was crusted with a glaze of honey. There were whipped potatoes and half a gallon of delicious, dark gravy. There were two fragrant bowls of steaming vegetables wafting an odour of gardens in August sun; and on a sideboard sat a freshly baked pie, adding fruity bouquet to the atmosphere. The meal was a feast, a privilege.

Between bites, I told James and Gay how neighbours of mine that past week had the entire roof of their brand-new, two-storey log house lifted up and pushed out of position by the wind. At the same time, the picture window, which should not have been installed in the windward wall in the first place, imploded into fragments leaving daggers of glass stuck in the living room wall. Fortunately, the couple and their three small children were all downstairs at the time; nobody was injured. James nodded sympathetically at my attempts to impress him; he had a roof story of his own—also a factual one.

"Years ago, Ralph Vroom, a local rancher, and another oldtimer were building a log cabin on their homestead. Ralph said, 'Lord the wind was blowin' and it really got up in the night.' Marty, have some more of that ham. A young feller like you should eat more. . . .

"Anyway, they'd just finished the cabin. They had banked up straw and snow all around it to keep out the drafts, and they slept in it that first night after that. Then Ralph woke up suddenly. He opens his eyes, lyin' there on his back. He thought, 'Gee, that's a pretty ceiling with all them stars up there. . . .' Well it took a while before it dawned on him that there was no ceiling, 'cept the sky. The roof was gone. He never even heard it go. The wind picked it up, and they found it lying down in the flat next morning."

Gay says, "When the wind gets going, nothin' is protected. You have to build things strong. You know those satellite television dishes?"

I nodded yes. The television dish, looking like a flying saucer crash-landed in the sticks, is a fixture on many farms and ranches in Alberta.

"Well around here, when the chinook starts really cutting up, it will take those things and turn them into pretzels."

"Praise God!" I exclaimed.

"Amen," seconded James. "It's the worse damn thing they ever invented," he declared. "Before that thing come along, the kids learned local history by listening to the oldtimers. 'Tell us about the olden days, Grandad,' they'd say. Now they're not innarested. Now," he added gloomily, "they just want to sit in front of that box. They don't know the history of this little old part of the world, this part where they live. It's a damn shame, to know nothin' about your home."

I stared at James a moment, and decided not to depress him, at his advanced age, with my own dark forebodings about the truth of his statement. It is very much in the interests of the developmentalists and their political accomplices to keep young minds buttoned to the stunner, and to discourage, via their cuts to the school curriculum, the prolifera-tion of knowledge about local history, local culture, local ecosystems. The ignorant, rootless and uninformed are meat for the multinational grinder.

People who see the land as a living entity with a past, and a future that is a natural continuum rather than a temporary stasis between "improvements," get attached to a locality. They are rusty cogs in the rolling wheels of the multinational money machine. They are the Indi-ans in the rainforest. They distrust the mitigation voodoo of your hired environmentalist. They come to believe that we can't really improve on nature's sublime landscapes, these heretics.

We cleared away our plates. Gay was up and serving the pie. The sweet taste of huckleberries, picked last season on the nearby mountains, freshened our palates. As we gazed out the window, James said it was a tough country to make a living in, and the wind was a hard thing to put up with. But without it, ranching would be impossible.

Until the Alberta Forest Service set up a weather station near by, James and Gay used to think their snowfall amounted to five feet in a winter. James was astounded to learn that his ranch gets ten feet of snow in an average season. Moose can trample such snow into yards and survive browsing on bark and twigs; cattle would perish. "By God, if it wasn't for the wind blowin' that snow off down to the grass, no cows or elk could live here. Even the coyotes would starve to death," James declared.

"It blows the greenhorns away, too," he added, grimly. "That's another good thing about it."

I took my leave of the old couple reluctantly. "Don't be a stranger," James called after me, and I promised not to be.

*   *   *

In the country, the oldtimers' eccentricities and their stories are treasured topics, are shared memories of place and particularity. Their stories, and stories about them, survive in bunkhouses and kitchens. The truth of their experiences, or of observations about them, are kept in mind to tell off the years, to give meaning to an old ruined barn, to explain the names of the creeks or the mountains. It is a kind of white man's version of the Blackfoot "winter count." A Blackfoot elder recorded the years by means of a symbol that stood for a striking event, such as "the year all the horses died." And he would tell you the story of that year, the oral history of events. Windy Paul lives on through James Riviere and other oldtimers, and James and Windy depend on another storyteller to remember them, as their yarns are embroidered into another cowpuncher's saga.

The cowboys down at Twin Butte tell a story about James that illustrates how hard this country can be on cattle. They say a young rancher was helping James doctor some stock at calving time, which can take place from late February on into May. Spring blizzards are a real risk to the stock at this time. A terrific blizzard had hit, and the temperature was well below zero; the snow was deep. James and the neighbour were laying down straw for the cows to deliver their calves on. One old ornery cow snuck away into the teeth of the storm, to find her own secret place to give birth, a common enough instinct of pregnant mammals. After the storm, they trailed her through the snow, down along the creek. The pale boles of the poplar trees looked green enough, the hidden colour brought out by the wet snow, but their branches were still bare. There was no place, no shelter for a pregnant beast to hole up in; no cave or roof to escape the wind. The creek was running open, this being spring, at least theoretically. Contrasted with the deep snows that surmounted it, the blue water looked as black as obsidian.

At length they came to a place where a shelf of ice protruded over the shoreline and the stream. This was a surviving remnant of an ice dam created by water backing up during a previous cold snap. That is where James found his cow. She had gone down under this shelf of ice to hide, slipped into the creek, and drowned. They sat their horses, the breath of men and animals steaming in the cold air, their hands numb on the reins, and they contemplated this grim tableau for a moment without comment.

"James," said the younger man at last. "What the hell did she go and do that for?"

James stared at him for a moment, considering the question. Turning in the saddle, he waved one arm around, indicating the snow, the wind-blasted bare spots on the brown hills above the creek bottom, the saw-toothed mountains on the frozen horizon and replied, "Take a look at this country. It makes me wonder how in hell anything survives out here in the first place. Ain't it obvious? She committed suicide."

13
THE LIVINGSTONE WAVE

~

"Take it," says the voice behind me in the cockpit. "Go ahead."

The left wing of the ship known as the Plastic Pig drops as we bank into another lazy turn into the ascending air, and my eyes slide down its slick surface 8,000 feet into the silver meander of the Oldman River. My stomach tries to jump out of my mouth and slide down the wing after my eyes; I hold it back as the wing floats back up to horizontal.

"It's all right," he says. "Take it."

It occurs to me that my pilot is crazy. And Rob, let me remind you, you're not really a pilot . . . you're an architect, for Pete's sake! And this is not a real plane: real planes have engines. I cannot move my hands to the control stick because I am flying this damn thing already. It is only my willpower that is keeping us under control as it is. If I keep my hands in this exact position on my lap and keep smiling rigidly like this, Oldman, invisible trickster of the Blackfoot nation, may decide it's not worth the trouble of smiting us down out of the sky. . . .

*   *   *

North of the village of Cowley, at the foot of the Porcupine Hills, there is an old emergency landing strip for airliners (where none ever had to land). Every summer it blossoms with a colourful array of sailplanes as the pilots of Alberta's Cu-Nim Glider Club rendezvous for the July soaring camp. Cu-Nim is short for cumulo-nimbus, a cloud formation that signifies what glider pilots love—thermals. (Glider and the newer term, sailplane, tend to be used interchangeably these days.) They call the strip the Cowley Glider Strip, and it is the home of the Livingstone Wave, a natural phenomenon that is world famous in the annals of sailplane pilots.

The Livingstone Wave, which runs parallel with the Livingstone Range (hence the name), is yet another aspect of the chinook.

Earlier, I explained how the mountain crest forces moist coastal air upwards to create the chinook effect. During wave conditions, the crest of this rising air may peak anywhere from 6,000 to 38,000 ASL. The long wave of air so formed consists of stable air, which is denser and cooler than the air around it. Gravity will return this layer to its initial level, downwind of the mountain front. But this wave then oscillates up and down, deflected by the layer of air beneath it, to form a series of standing waves, also known as atmospheric gravity waves, or as mountain lee waves.

These waves, gradually decreasing in height, can extend from 100 to 200 miles east of the Rocky Mountains. The first three waves of the series are the most important to sailplane pilots. This trio consists of a primary wave over the Livingstone Range, a secondary wave over Highway 22, and a tertiary wave over the Porcupine Hills. A primary wave of this type can create stratospheric ripples of energy extending to 60,000 feet ASL.

When I try to imagine what visual form this could take, I picture a ghostly waterfall from six to ten miles high pouring over the ridgepole of the continent for hundreds of miles in length to form into standing waves that are several miles apart. The crests of these waves are often marked by parallel ranks of lenticular (lens-shaped) clouds—when the air is moist enough. The first of these wave clouds is often the classic Chinook Arch itself.

Some decades ago, a generation of Canadian sailplane pilots learned how to ride these waves of energy. They began to look upon the lee wave as a free ride up to the lower stratosphere at speeds of (initially),

3,000 feet per minute or higher. But where there is rising air on the front of the wave, there is a tremendous sink of equal power on its lee side. And as water breaks over boulders in a stream and forms ripples behind them, so this fall of air, this half-an-atmosphere in motion, forms pockets of turbulence in the lee of hills and forests, or where there are breaks in the great mountain wall.

Pioneer sailplane pilots learned to avoid such low level turbulence, as well as the dangerous "rotors" that accompany lee waves in southern Alberta. Rotors, typically found in the troughs of the lee waves, are often marked by roll clouds that can be seen to boil with the energy of huge volumes of air being turned inside out. A sailplane in one of these rotors bounces around like a hanky in a clothes drier. Aspen Valley is notorious for such rotors, and for horrible sinks of descending air. Rotors have destroyed many airplanes over the years.

The lee waves themselves can offer a fearful insult to airliners and their passengers. Liner pilots are always wary of the chinook and its lee wave manifestations. In *Turbulence: A New Perspective for Pilots*, Peter F. Lester cites a flight over the Great Divide in 1965, which illustrates the problem: "Two severe jolts were experienced. 'The pilot estimates that the aircraft descended 800 feet in 3 to 5 seconds, followed by a choppy interval, then a second violent descent. Three seats were pulled loose in the cabin. Passengers with unfastened seat belts were injured. Roof panels were bent and displaced when passengers were thrown upwards. Some seat mountings were broken. . . .'"

Not only do soaring pilots "surf the big one," they set records doing it. In 1981, Calgarian Bruce Hea, flying a fifteen-metre Libelle sailplane, set a Canadian altitude record when he rode the Livingstone Wave to an altitude of 34,400 feet. Equally fascinating was a flight described to me by Calgarian Dick Mamini, who once had a cabin at Lee Lake near Pincher Creek. After being towed aloft courtesy of his wife ("Former wife," he had added ruefully) and the family Chevrolet, he had sailed at 150 m.p.h. along the front of the Chinook Arch all the way from Lee Lake to Exshaw, Alberta, 120 air miles north. Riding the wave southward at speeds peaking at 250 m.p.h., he returned to Lee Lake, and after fooling around for a while at 18,000 feet, he landed in the same cow pasture he had taken off from six to eight hours earlier.

Both these famous flights took place right over our ranchette.

According to Frank Halek, one of these pretty planes landed in his brother's bull pasture one time. The pilot, sitting close to the ground in his space-age bubble, was immediately surrounded by bulls, whose testicles were about level with his head, and he had to be rescued by men on horseback. "They never landed there again after that," said Frank with grim satisfaction. "They must be crazy," he added.

"They have to be," I said.

But the trouble is, they aren't. They're on to something, in fact, that most of us experienced only briefly in childhood dreams, where we sailed like runaway kites tucked in the arms of the wind. Nevertheless, when I called Cu-Nim's Tony Burton to find out more about his club and the lee wave, he scared the bejesus out of me. Now, I am not a big fan of flying. I'd rather jump into a pork barrel with a live Tory than strap myself into an airplane. But Tony told me that the only way I would understand anything about lee waves was to go for a ride in a sailplane, and he invited me to come to the July camp. "Bring your wife along," he suggested. And that was the problem, because unlike me, Myrna loves flying. I suppose that is what compelled me to blab the news to her.

"It's the chance of a lifetime," she enthused. "You said yes, right?"

I only hesitated for half a second. "Absolutely," I said.

"Aren't you excited!"

"I am thrilled," I said. "To the depths of my being." And we both pretended that I wasn't lying through my teeth.

*   *   *

I skipped breakfast that morning, just to be on the safe side. Myrna and I drove out to the strip with completely different expectations. Myrna was elated at the chance to go up in a sailplane. She expected to soar like an eagle, get some pictures, have the trip of a lifetime. My outlook was basically bleak. When I think of flying, my heart soars like a golf ball. Then it bounces through the rough and sinks into the swamp.

At the airstrip the pilots were busy hauling the fuselages of planes out of their trailers and locking the wings into position for flight. We walked around, admiring the various ships. Sailplanes at rest are futuristic sculptures of fibreglass and plexiglass, giant dragonflies, resting with one long wing tip on the ground and the other angled skyward. They seem to shiver gently along their whole length at every touch of the breeze; they resonate with something that is as close to life as an inanimate object can get. Perhaps it is all the human handiwork and love that went into their construction and maintenance that has animated them at last. Sailplane cockpits are streamlined and narrow, and the slim tube of the fuselage, devoid of cargo space, is an elegant bridge between cockpit and tailplane.

Their message is cool, their performance is hot. White is the safest colour, a thin outer skin or gel coat of white paint or epoxy. It reflects the heat: it keeps these fibreglass and composite ships from melting in the desert sun of western North America. Red is favoured for trim stripes on nose and wing tips. An exception was the cheerfully ugly Blanik trainer, a two-seater aluminum ship the colour of tinfoil.

The planes, with gear down, were nestled into the grass on their low front wheels, tails strapped temporarily onto a set of tail wheel dollies to save wear and tear on the tiny tail wheel employed on sailplanes. Thick steel cables lie in the grass at Cowley, permanently anchored in place, and the planes are bridled to these cables. A chinook wind could easily flip them over otherwise: it has happened before, and resulted in the total destruction of planes.

The pilots were huddled here and there, talking in subdued tones. This looked bad. Sure enough, there had been an accident. The pessimist in me was not surprised.

"He turned the ship into a ball . . . ," said one pilot. (This turned out to be an exaggeration.)

"How the hell did he land on a gas well site anyway?"

"With great difficulty," came the reply.

It seems that two fliers, new to the area, had "landed out," way out in Mamini Country, which means the west side of the Livingstone Range. Aside from being mountainous and therefore rugged, the valleys between the Livingstone and the Great Divide are either timbered, or covered with stumps left by clear-cut logging. It is not a happy place to encounter turbulence, or sink, and mountain terrain is the very cradle of both. The pilot went over the top too low to begin with, I learned. He and his cohort had sunk out of the sky like an expired clay pigeon. On the way down, he had apparently spotted one of the gas well clearings that are scattered through this part of the Forest Reserve: it was the only clearing he could reach. He had managed to pull off a landing—of sorts. The Lark trainer, a $40,000 Romanian-built ship, was seriously damaged. Everyone was amazed that there had been no injuries.

It had been raining off and on for days in this land of drought, the continuation of a wet cycle as it turned out, and the hills of home, seen from this vantage, were monsoon green. We met with Ursula Wiese, camp co-ordinator. The author of *Stalking the Mountain Wave* is an athletic-looking woman and the spirit of efficiency. She explained that those western pockets of cumulus were caused by moisture condensing above the sodden fields. I could see a rather large cloud that would have been right over Myrna's garden. Above Cowley, however, the sky was Alberta blue. The wave was breaking elsewhere. Maybe it had turned into water and was working the off season at Waikiki. Ursula's face showed concern. "I'm afraid it's going to be a day for thermal flying only," she said.

I was cheered, but only slightly.

"You'll still have a good time, but it's not a wave day. That's confirmed by the high altitude forecast."

"Hell. That's too bad," I said sadly. A happier thought occurred: rain might ground all the planes. "Any chance it will rain?"

"Thirty percent chance," replied Ursula.

"Only thirty, eh?" I said. And this time the apprehension was starting to show. Myrna elbowed me in the ribs.

The camp would end the next day. Ursula said I might have to come back in October to ride the big one. I fought off a relieved grin and sighed heavily to show my fake disappointment. We took a walk. There seemed to be an epidemic of Tilley hats among the pilots. They showed off their sailplanes and I showed off Myrna. "They look so distinguished," she said—meaning all the grey hair.

I scoffed at the thought. "These guys are only half as old as they look. They're all prematurely grey from scaring the shit out of themselves."

"Bulltweet," said Myrna.

Here and there, some craggy figure was seen gazing up at the heavens. Clear skies are tolerated in the morning, but toward noon, glider pilots want to see some clouds.

Sailplanes fly on solar energy. Even I have to admire that. Imagine it: up to the lower stratosphere, riding on a sunbeam—or air heated by sunbeams, to be more precise. The sun, by heating the earth unequally, energizes the atmospheric engine. Unequal heating causes pressure imbalances on the earth's surface. Air flows from areas of high pressure to areas of low pressure, and there is a persistent trough of low pressure along the east slope of these mountains. The vast motion of the air is what we call wind. Gravity causes oscillations in lee waves, but the waves ultimately owe their origin to the sun.

Of course not all soaring is done on lee waves. So consider this sun action on a somewhat smaller scale, the creation of thermals. The sun, by radiation, heats the earth: the earth heats the parcel of air above it, mostly by convection, and this warm parcel (which seems to have the shape of an elongated bubble) rises because it is warmer than the surrounding air. This air is termed "unstable" and may rise indefinitely—except in the case of a temperature inversion, where the air is trapped by a warmer layer above it. Thermal lift, however, is not completely predictable, nor is it always of great extent. The lift may occur in scattered parcels, several miles apart. Skillful pilots, towed aloft either by vehicles or by power aircraft, learn how to read the sky, and where to look for lift—even the tiniest lift—to keep going. Sailplanes have even hitchhiked a ride on the hot air rising from an ashpalt parking lot to gain some meagre altitude, and escape to some better spot of lift. That kind of low-altitude self-rescue is known as a "save." The idea, the challenge, is to stay aloft, cover some ground, and either return to home base or get to your objective—a safe landing strip—and not "land out."

Over the strip the air was relatively clear. The temperature was climbing to 70°F. I took off my shirt for the first time that summer. But around eleven, Ursula pointed out some puffy cumulus centred over the Porcupine Hills. "Looks like lift," she said. A murmur of excitement swept through camp. Reluctantly, I bought two tow tickets, each good for 2,000 feet of altitude. Rob Young, dashing young pilot, and a Calgary architect, had volunteered to take us up. He soon appeared, riding a mountain bike though he wore a walking cast on one leg from a spring skiing accident, which made me grin in a scary way. "Okay," he said, "you're both down on the manifest. Sid, you and I go first, then I'll take Myrna up." And Rob was off to prepare the ship.

Myrna was elated, but my downcast looks were a pain. "Try to have a good time," she urged me.

I found Rob out on the strip where the Grob trainer rested on one wing, number four in the lineup. "Sid, meet the Plastic Pig."

"Howdy, Pig."

The Pig was named for its weight, but even at eight hundred pounds the ship looked far from corpulent. It was slick and fast looking to my eye, with red trim and a jaunty high stabilizer on the tail fin. Still, its nickname did not inspire confidence in me.

Despite my dislike of flying, necessity has forced me aloft many times. In fact, as a park warden I'd even had occasion to fly into the site of climbing accidents hooked to the end of a climbing rope attached to a Jet Ranger helicopter. I was forced to become a willpower pilot, in self-defence. Willpower fliers are finicky about names. I like the name "Jet Ranger"—get the hell in there and get it over with, quick. I like planes named for projectiles, birds or even flying insects: like Avro Arrow, Grumman Goose, Mosquito Dive Bomber. This also has to do with my belief, as a writer, in the power of words. I need a word I can chant over and over again under my breath like a mantra—I need magic, and a good, firm set of armrests to grip. It is hard to fly a badly named aircraft on willpower. I once flew, with great difficulty, something called a Beaver floatplane. Landing had been sheer hell. For one thing, that was my first floatplane landing, and to top it off, the seats were made of nylon mesh, and there were no armrests.

The sight of me gripping my knees and feverishly chanting "Beaver, Beaver, Beaver" under my breath while the guy up in the cockpit fiddled with the controls had caused the passengers to doubt my abilities to get us down safely. Everyone knows a beaver is an amphibious rodent, not a bird. Everyone had felt my lack of faith in that name. So back at Cowley I thought, I must get a grip on myself, try to hide my hysterical reaction to this Plastic Pig.

Okay, I told myself. I can do this. I stroked the smooth wing surface, trying to make contact with the animus of the machine. Inspired, I began to softly chant the old Arkansas hog call: "Pig pig, pig-eeee; pig pig . . ."

"Pardon me?" It was Rob, wondering what the hell I was up to.

"Oh, there you are, Rob," I said sheepishly. He was in the rear seat, checking his instruments. "Just clearing my throat."

Rob glanced over at me. "I hope you're not uncomfortable with this?"

Rob was a nice guy. I confided that flying made me a bit nervous, and explained how the Helicopter Sling Rescue Technique still gave me bad dreams. Rob fed me some reassuring bumf on how safe soaring is to cheer me up. "Besides," he added, "this time you get to ride inside."

Darwin Roberts, a Cu-Nim instructor, showed me how to get into the cockpit without breaking something expensive. This is like trying to put on a kayak for the first time without capsizing it. The Pig is a trainer; both the front and rear positions have controls. The cockpit seemed spartan and cramped. Gripping both sides of the fuselage, I gingerly levered my svelte 220-pound frame into the tiny opening. There was an inch of clearance on either side for my shoulders, and I found myself in a partially supine position, like a motorist with a broken seat-back.

From the sidelines, some snide fellow shouted, "You guys are gonna have great penetration." This was followed by hearty guffaws. It was a comment on our weight—about four hundred pounds—added to the Pig's eight hundred. It meant that we could accelerate like mad, that the entire force of gravity was at our personal disposal. I was thrilled by the implications of that.

An array of instruments was before me; Darwin pointed them out: altimeter, variometer (more about that later), air speed, clock and compass were fitted into a tiny black console. Darwin explained how the controls worked. The control stick was in easy reach. I could feel the rudder answer to the touch of my feet, could see the ailerons, which roll the aircraft into a turn, responding to my hand moving left or right on the stick. The elevators, located on the stabilizer (part of the tail plane) controlled our pitch, our nose up, nose down movement. It was fun to play with the controls on the ground: I promised myself not to touch them once we were airborne.

Two shoulder straps and a seat belt anchored me firmly into position. They are kept almost painfully tight. "Never undo your straps," ordered Darwin sternly, as he snapped me in.

Rob lowered the canopy and locked it up. The effect was claustrophobic. Glancing up through the plexiglass, I saw Myrna smiling down at me. I felt trapped, and stifled a desire to unhook and jump hysterically out of the plane. Instead I gave her a sickly grin and the old RAF thumbs-up sign. "That's the spirit," she said, her voice muffled and faint. The sun was out in the clear and burning down on us: I was soon bathed in sweat. The canopy cover might as well have been the door on a microwave oven.

At last the ship in front of us was off and gone. We were next on the tow. Darwin Roberts approached our torpedo-shaped nose holding what appeared to be a waterski rope that was attached to the tow plane. He held up the "weak link," a loop of rope designed to break and separate tow plane from glider in an emergency. It terminated in a steel coupling that looks like a piece of chain. I've seen bigger chain on a watch fob. Darwin snapped it home in our nose. Rob would release the rope at the appropriate time by means of a lever. Darwin trotted to one side, talking into a hand-held radio. There was a tentative roar from the tow plane.

"Comfortable?" came Rob's disembodied voice. His position was behind, and also higher than mine. I couldn't see him without cranking my head around like a barn owl.

"Yep," I yelped.

"Okay," he said cheerfully. "Just keep clear of the controls for now. You can put your feet on the pedals, but don't bear down on them."

"No problem," I said fervently. I kept my feet as far from the pedals as possible.

*   *   *

The tow plane's engine rumbles and we begin to move forward. The undercarriage seems to make a lot of noise, rumbling and thumping. The grass runway is surprisingly rough. They were filling gopher holes earlier. God, I hope they found them all. I can feel every bump right on my tailbone. Our wings wigwag and steady out. There is also some arthritic squealing from the Pig's joints, which I try to ignore. But in a moment, the rumbling noise fades. We are rolling faster now, and are actually airborne a few seconds before the tow plane leaves the earth. Faces looking up fall back and disappear. Cars and trailers shrink away: we are rising with the mountains and the hills. Two hundred feet in front is the rear silhouette of the tow plane. The roar of its engine rings in my ears. We are undulating up and down in its wake, synchronized to the tow plane's motion. Now the Pig is in level flying attitude with its streamlined snout lowered. Rob cranks the gear up noisily. I feel better sitting up properly; staring around with a hundred-mile gaze; I'm the boy in the bubble. The stick weaves around in front of me. Rob is keeping the ship in correct position, just a little lower than the tow plane so as not to get too high and pull its tail up with the rope, which would break the weak link. The tow plane's left wing dips into a turn and we follow, choreographed. We are shaking now, hitting some rumble strips of air. I'm slammed back in the seat, hard. The altimeter needle winds up, slowly approaching 6,000 feet. Off to the right and down I glimpse the dirty blue waters of the reservoir. The wind has kicked up some waves down there that look like the ripples on a slop pail.

Rob says something that I don't quite get.

Clank. The noise of the coupling popping free makes me jump. What the hell . . . a yellow thread of rope snakes away in front of our nose . . . I get it. Rob has punched off the tow. Now he cranks us over into a forty-degree right bank—to avoid flying into the tow rope (but I don't know that till later). "Fly Piggy fly," I mutter under my breath, seeing the left wing go up, up, the right wing go down. I grab the flesh above my knees in lieu of armrests and concentrate on the turn as the angle increases. I'm going to fall out of the cockpit! Relax, I tell myself; let your body hang against the harness. Fatalistically, I let the straps do their thing.

Halfway through the turn I realize something. It has become quiet, eerily quiet. The clamouring tow plane is gone. All I hear now is the whisper and hiss of air over our wings and fuselage. I am seduced by my ears; I become so enamoured with this sound, which must be what flight sounds like to eagles and Canada geese, that I forget my mantra, forget to concentrate; Rob is forced to complete the turn without my willpower.

Niggling doubts afflict me. Is it possible that what the scientists say is true? Perhaps there really is this force, called lift, as air moves over the curved surface of a wing. Perhaps this is Venturi's rhapsody, this soft singing. Maybe synergies, other than willpower, keep planes aloft.

Heresy! Plug your ears, willpower pilots—like Ulysses did to keep from succumbing to the charming songs of the sirens.

It is so quiet in the cockpit that Rob's voice startles me. "We'll head for the Porkies," he says. They rise near at hand. As we glide that way, Rob is looking for signs of lift, a ripple in the dirty water that is once again off to our right: a tidal surge of wind through the yellow grain fields bordering the reservoir. I notice now that somebody has taped a piece of red string in the middle of our windshield. "Believe it or not," says Rob, "that is our wind direction instrument."

This is a day to believe anything. As usual, the wind is WSW. Looking over the top of this string, I can see the course of the Oldman River and the Castle River west of their confluence. The bongo drum inside my chest beats less wildly now. I start to notice details on the earth.

We are sailing now, quartering the wind toward the Porcupines. Up ahead there is a kind of amphitheatre in the hills, formed around Olin Creek. This is a natural suntrap, and over it, at about 10,000 feet— there's our ride, that cumulus cloud, marking the top of a thermal. The airspeed indicator winds up to 70 knots. Down below a tiny pickup truck pokes around a farmyard. I can see a tiny figure moving toward an outbuilding. I've glimpsed people's movements before, on aircraft landing approach, but it was always accompanied by the scream of engines. There was always the need to absorb the glimpse in a hurry. But now the view unrolls in quietude, in bird's eye time. A wheeling around to go back and look down again: to see it completely; to watch life unfold. If we wanted to, we could spiral down and stop for a cup of coffee. We are superior by point of view: we are powered by powerlessness.

"Feel the lift?"

"Yeah." But Rob immediately shoots us into a turn, looking for the sweet spot at the core of the thermal. When he finds it, we are bumped down in our seats as the ship shoots upwards. The spiralling turn continues, endlessly. We are carving up through cloud wisps.

"Tell me if this makes you uncomfortable," says Rob.

We are leaning over hard at forty degrees again as the Pig gobbles into the core. The variometer, measuring our ascent in feet-per-minute, begins to sound its electric tremolo, the pitch ascending as we keep in the sweet spot of lift. It will decrease in pitch if we sink. The vario audio tune allows a pilot to fly without constantly watching his altimeter. In this case there is a bit of up and down—"Eee, ooo." When it lengthens out to a shrill scream, we are flung up on the whale's back, burning around in the corkscrew turn—"E-E-E-E-E"—and now I'm letting out a whoop with the vario. What is this? Some idiot joy has whelmed me over.

We're going round and round endlessly, spiralling up at three hundred feet per minute. The earth is falling away below us. We're lying sideways in the sky, leaning on the wind as we circle up. How long can this go on? I remember reading how these thermals bend downwind. They don't always rise like pillars; they are like smoke rings, whose core goes upward as the sides spill down. Sure enough, a few minutes later we slip out of the core of lift and fall like a rock, caught in sinking air spilling down from cloud shadow. The vario moans. My Adam's apple turns into a tennis ball—"Yuhhh!" The altimeter needle can't catch up to the fall until it ends several hundred feet lower. My body bangs against the straps: I'm glad they are tight. Even an inch of slack would be unbearable. And I'm glad my stomach is empty.

Encounters with turbulence put instant positive or negative pressures of several G's on sailplane pilots. A flight of four hours in rough going will beat the hell out of a pilot, as if he had gone several rounds in the boxing ring. I inched one hand over and tugged at the tightener on my seat harness. I was remembering a story they'd told me about an unfortunate pilot. He had discovered a loose screw on his console and thought—"I'll just undo for a second and tighten that." He had released his belt, and a few seconds later he'd encountered some hellish turbulence. He was ejected out of his seat with such force that he'd smashed right through the canopy and exited the plane. There was a happy ending: he was wearing a parachute.

"Feel okay?" asks Rob.

"Fine."

"I forgot to bring an airsick bag," says Rob.

"I got one if you need it."

There is a silence. Incredible. Did I really say that?

Rob laughs wildly, the voice of an unseen *deus ex machina* somewhere above and behind me. I am totally in his power and he warns that if it gets rough, even the toughest of the tough guys get sick. Meaning I can get sick too. I think to myself, nice going. Now you have your pilot/god thinking you're playing tough guy—you mad fool! I'm being taken over by elation. This aerial merry-go-round is making me dizzy: I'm turning megalomaniacal.

"Seriously, let me know if you feel sick," says Rob.

"Will do." And around and around, up and down goes the aerial rollercoaster on rails of air until we come up under the cloud around 10,000 feet, and Rob says, "Okay. Like to try and fly it?"

The tough guy veneer instantly shatters. The inner wuss takes over. "I wouldn't feel comfortable doing that." I try to make a joke out of being a chickenshit. "Hey, you're doing a good job without me." And the old scary notions come rushing back. But Rob is such a confident, patient instructor that after some discussion and delay, I find myself talked into reaching for the control stick "just to see what it feels like." I slowly close my hand on it: a shock of incredible elation courses through my whole body.

"You've got it," he says.

"Huh?"

"I'm off the controls, you've got it."

It's too late now to go back. In a trice my brain connects with steel cables and pivot points, with ailerons, elevators and wind in the pinions of the glass bird. Prayer and desperation elude my faltering resolve. My soul teeters on the brink of compromise with the technovoodoo of lift and drag.

"You okay, Sid?"

"Oh. Yeah, but I'm not really in control here, Rob. . . ." In fact I am weirdly elated: an adrenalin high.

"You're doing fine. . . . A little left rudder . . . that's right. Now easy, pull up easy on the stick, watch the wind. . . ."

I can feel the whole flying machine trembling under my touch. I swim through the wind with my feet, feeling it as a sea, ruddering against it, curving into it with an eye on the little red string. And the wind exults. It whispers through the vent in the cockpit and sighs, lifting us, lifting us up to cloud base, higher than the mountains now. The wind calls me *mastah*.

Then it backs up and vanishes—gone. We fly like an anvil back to reality. Rob's hand is on the stick, his feet are on the pedals. And he turns us back into the lift.

The flight continues and I've lost track of time. The sky is a lonely place and there is no fixed measure in a cloud. But now I start to talk that talk. This wave flying—it sounds like it might be a lot of fun. This thermal flying is great, but it is a little tame, isn't it? Rob humours me along, chortling inwardly at a joke he has in mind. There is no warning as he drops the nose and whips us into a steeply banked turn: the wings whirl, the mountains seem upside down. I see stars in front of my eyes: the altimeter needle is spinning like a top: blood rushes to my brain.

My gorge isn't rising, it is going to fall right out of me. I clamp my mouth shut on it as we whip around right side up and level out.

"Stomach okay?" inquires Rob kindly.

The old thumbs-up sign is my reply. Can't risk opening my mouth. Just as well: mustn't provoke further acrobatics. Swallow hard now, force the bile back down. But my stomach soon settles down. Inside I am calm, and deeply pleased at being calm.

Rob cranks the gear noisily down as he flies his down-wind leg. We turn on our base leg and then come in on final approach. Now we are gliding steeply down and the spoilers lift from the wing, our angle of approach increases, the strip comes up to meet us, the grass softly rises: the sudden noise of the earth, the roughness and the short roll ending as the handbrake is applied. The sweet smell of green cut hay wafts in through the vents.

We open the canopy and earth sights and sounds flood in. Myrna is there to help us; she is startled by my cheerful greeting, my sudden enthusiasm for the whole sport of soaring.

"Is this the same guy who took off two hours ago?"

"Two hours?" I glance at my watch: I'm puzzled as hell. "Twenty minutes, I would have said. I can't believe it. It's like the Twilight Zone up there. . . . Wow."

Rob just shrugs and says, "Hey, time flies when you're having fun." He's off to stretch his injured leg and rest a moment.

Strapping my wife into her seat gives me sober second thoughts. But look at her: she's beaming. She wouldn't miss this adventure for the world. When I had been bouncing around the mountains in a helicopter, or on skis, or horseback—being at one with a national park—she had mostly stayed home with the kids. It was what she wanted back then. And when I had jetted around the country on the lecture circuit, she had not complained because we couldn't afford a ticket for her to accompany me. Now there is this day of sun and adventure: it's her chance to fly.

I smile down at her. "You're gonna have a blast, honey."

"You betcha!" She grins at me. She reads me like a book, but she appreciates my attempt to show some class.

I glance back. Rob looks cool, in control, in good spirits. Everything will be fine. The cockpit cover closes. I take a picture and step aside. The hookup is made; she waves and they are off. There goes my whole life. . . .

*   *   *

Near by was a craft I had not inspected yet. A Ventus, West German make, fifty-foot wingspan looking sleek and hungry. I walked over to have a look. "Glide ratio of 45 to 1," said a voice. The speaker had the build for that ship. He was a trim-looking retiree in the inevitable white hat, in his late sixties. "It means that when descending, you sink one foot for every forty-five feet of forward momentum."

"Impressive," I said. "Your ship?"

"Yeah," he said, the friendly grin reasserting itself. "I'm Bruce Hea [pronounced "hay"] and you must be the writer we heard about."

Bruce Hea: This lean-looking senior citizen was the man who had taken a sailplane up to 34,400 feet from this very field. He had set the Canadian absolute altitude record with that flight (which he still holds), and also the altitude gain record—26,000 feet (since broken).

He is about five feet ten inches tall, his auburn hair turning to grey. He looks pretty mild for a hotshot pilot. In fact he looks like a retired accountant. As it turns out, my first impression is about right. He had been a self-employed executive most of his working life. But like many enthusiasts, he was happy to talk about his obsession. He had, I learned, logged over 1,850 flights in sailplanes "the last time I bothered to count," as he put it modestly.

Though an elder in this sport, Bruce is slim and agile. (Most of the pilots work at keeping fit, so they can wrestle thermals and rotors more efficiently.) "Try out the cockpit," he offered. I climbed in carefully; it was hotter and more cramped than the trainer.

Bruce said that during the October camps, the cockpit can turn into a deep freeze. You can start out on the ground at 4,000 feet altitude and 40°F, ascend to 18,000 feet (a not uncommon flight) and encounter temperatures of –20°F. There is no heater in a sailplane. Pilots wear insulated flight suits and warm boots. Oxygen masks and helmet further cramp their bodies.

"Bruce, how cold was it up there, during your record flight?"

"Minus 57 Celsius at 35,000 feet."

I could hardly believe my ears. Minus 57, or –70 on the Fahrenheit scale: impossible to conceive of flying an unheated plane at such a temperature. I had to shake my head. "What do you remember about that day?" I asked him.

"Everything," he said simply.

The bedroom window in Bruce and Sheila Hea's Calgary residence faces west. When Hea woke up on the morning of October 31, 1981, his first thought was that the sun was rising in the west. A ruddy light dyed the bedroom curtains pink and flooded across its walls. Looking out, he saw a brilliant Chinook Arch stained with sunrise orange that extended beyond the horizon to the north and the south.

Bruce Hea had been preparing for a day like this for many years.

There would be ten other pilots, all friends, heading for Cowley that morning. They all knew that an altitude record might be set that weekend and Bruce, aged fifty-six, hoped to be the man who would set it. His old 1968 Chrysler was gassed up and the 440-cubic-inch motor purred as he pulled away from the curb, towing the homemade trailer that cradled his Libelle sailplane inside. Driving south, he glanced occasionally at the sky. The wave clouds that day looked to be at 25,000 feet. As the day wore on, they would move upward to around 30,000 feet.

At Cowley, the pilots wasted no time in unloading and rigging their ships. "I remember that the winds were blowing at 80 knots [92 m.p.h.] at 25,000 feet," recalled Bruce. "We could see the rotors under the primary wave at about 14,000 feet. We could literally self-destruct in the forces that were operating there. We decided to find our lift in the secondary wave, then transfer to the primary far above the rotors."

The Bellanca tow plane pulled Bruce and his 450-pound Libelle aloft and the pilot turned to the north. Eight minutes later, Bruce punched off the tow rope.

The sudden "bump" of lift in the secondary wave came very quickly; he headed into the wind to hold his position, and the earth began to recede below him. He reached 20,000 feet, and eyed the Livingstone Range a few miles to the west; rotor clouds marked the trough below the primary wave. "It looked like a popcorn field from that height. Mine field," he added dryly, "would be more accurate."

He had to cross from the secondary to the primary wave to gain more height. He dropped the ship's nose and heard the variometer moan as he stripped off altitude at 100 miles per hour. The popcorn clouds began to swell upward under his wing as he eyed the altimeter; suddenly the variometer changed pitch and began to sing as the lift of the primary wave registered on his wings. The altimeter needle began to spin like a sweep second hand as the Libelle sailed upward. "You feel just on top of the world," he said, remembering the sensation. "The lift is so huge, you just can't miss."

Accompanying him on that trip, flying an RS-15, was Tony Burton, whose barograph stylus would run right off the chart at 33,000 feet. At 29,000, a jet liner closed on them at high speed; but it was 3,000 feet higher. Bruce was on the radio to Air Traffic Control, getting clearance for the level 3-7-0 flyway at 37,000 feet.

"At 30,000 feet," said Bruce slowly, choosing his words, "you are seeing the earth curve away from you: you have the feeling of being on the edge of space."

For a moment, I could see, Bruce was back out there. "And you got that far up without an engine," I marvelled aloud. "You just sailed up on the wind—to the edge of space."

"Right. On solar power. It's exhilarating going up at four hundred feet per minute. It's a smooth, laminar flow of air when you get up there. So smooth, you could set a coin on edge in the cockpit, and it would stand up—if your hands were not too cold to handle it; if you could find a place to stand it. Picture this canopy, this whole cockpit, covered inside with ice," he said. "That's what it was like."

And there was no sunlight to afford solar heat, owing to a cloud layer at 40,000 feet. Bruce wore nylon snowboots with felt liners and a war-surplus flight suit; wool toque, war-surplus flying helmet and two pairs of gloves. "I remember the rabbit fur hood on the suit, how glad I was to have that," he recalled. "I had a few inches of visibility through a frost shield on the right side. On the left, I opened a vent about two inches."

"You were flying blind."

"That's right," Bruce agreed. "I wasn't worried about running into anybody else at that altitude; but I could only turn to the right; that's the only direction where I had some visibility."

I stared out the front of the Ventus at a blue patch of sky over the Livingstone, pictured the cockpit covered in ice, tried to imagine the controls freezing up, getting stiffer and more sluggish by the minute. Of course, gliders employ gravity as well as lift to fly; you could always get down again—eventually—but you could run out of oxygen or start to freeze to death on the way, if you hung around up there too long.

"When you have lift like you get in a lee wave," explained Bruce, "you are going to have a sink on the back side that is just as strong. After going up to 35,000—that's what I personally pegged it at—anyway, after that I was looking to get out of that cold. I was still going up, you see. But since I was slowly freezing to death I thought I'd better quit." Bruce paused and looked at me intently. "You see, at that altitude, once you say to yourself, that's high enough, there is no point hanging around. It's imperative you get down at once."

"It's a fine line, and once you lose your edge . . ."

Bruce nodded uncertainly, not sure if he could really explain just what he meant to a non-pilot. I recalled reading in *Stalking the Mountain Wave* that Tony Burton, who landed just ahead of Bruce, was beginning to experience two dangers of lingering: hypoxia and hypothermia.

I stared at this slightly built, quiet, even ingenuous man. He had spent most of his working life in an office, but his real life was pushing the envelope of Canadian soaring out to the edge of the atmosphere, protected only by a plexiglass bubble and his innate wits and courage. He had gone surfing with the wind gods up in heaven.

I thanked Bruce for the story, and took my leave. I was vaguely worried about Myrna. She had been gone now for several hours. I scanned the sky: the Pig was up there, lost among a gaggle of other ships, white dragonflies against the blue.

Fortunately for me, I was unaware of what's being said in the Plastic Pig, as Rob glides back toward the strip.

"Well, what do you think of soaring, Myrna?"

"It's just great," she answers. "It's sure given me an eyeful."

"Hey," says Rob. "You ain't seen nothin' yet."

"I don't know what he did," she would say later, "but the mountains were spinning and I just about lost my breakfast." But Myrna said it was very exciting—maybe too exciting.

And now suddenly there was the Grob, the Piggy, on landing approach, looking fast and hot, with the green hills rising behind its gleaming red-and-white colours. The beauty of the thing lay in the quiet of its approach. I went running up to the strip for a better look. The air tingled with a low whistle from overhead: I saw the dive brakes clearly now. The ship swooped steeply down: the whistle increased somewhat in intensity, then the ship levelled out in a landing flare over the field. The small wheel reached down, the shining wings flexed reluctantly in the wind of coming down to humdrum earth again. I was close enough to see the smile on Myrna's face now; she was enjoying every second of the ride.

I wondered at that moment, seeing her looking so at home in that beautiful machine, and knowing her love of flight, what other career might have been hers if she had not thrown in her lot so totally with my own.

With a clunk, the gear touched down on the grass runway. Now the wings waggled up and down; the graceful plane, suddenly a bit maudlin, rumbled along; the handbrake was engaged, and one wing finally heeled over to touch the earth.

"How was it?" I shouted, as she climbed out of the cockpit a few moments later.

"Like riding on an eagle's back!" she cried.

That summed it up for me, too. And so we said goodbye and thank you, thank you for the ride of a lifetime; come and see us, and see you again soon, maybe in October we'll ride the big one, who knows—and rode off into the sunset on and above and behind the Livingstone, and the Livingstone Wave.

14

FOOLING WITH THE BULL

~

"Never complain about the wind," a cowboy friend once told me. "Without the wind, there would be no prairie. And without the prairie there would be no cattle ranching."

"And no cowboys," I said.

"Don't be foolish," he said. "There would have to be cowboys. If not for cowboys, there would be no blue jeans."

"You're right," I said. "What would we wear?"

"Suits. Think of the dry cleaning bills. Besides, what would rodeo be without cowboys in it?"

"Probably a bit dull," I said. "And the bone-doctors would all be on welfare."

"Damn straight," he agreed, with a nod of his big hat. He tucked a pinch of Copenhagen behind his bottom lip and added: "So just let her blow. Let her rip."

And she had certainly obliged. For hadn't she that very winter blown Mojo's dog house away—Mojo was not in it at the time—blowing it right through a barbed-wire fence, and breaking several fence posts along with the wire? Yes indeed. The dog house, spurned by Mojo, was my pride and joy. It weighed some four hundred pounds. But it had lifted off the ground as if powered by jets. And when it hit the fence, it had exploded, showering pink insulation and barn cats all over my neighbour's duck pasture.

I believe that was the winter Chinook blew another neighbour's round bales several miles cross country and deposited them in the Old-man River. Each one of those bales weighed 1,000 pounds. The sight of them tumbling across the highway, flattening fences and chicken coops hither and yon with a random and arbitrary insouciance, gave Hank Broda quite a start on his way home from church. It was a hayseed apocalypse. "He should have picked those bales months ago," Hank had said primly. "Now the wind has picked them instead."

It was spring again, when a young cowboy's fancy turns from thoughts of indoor rodeo to thoughts of outdoor rodeo. It was a rodeo event that had brought me to the Girletz Arena north of Calgary at Balzac one blustery March day. I was to learn about bullriders and rodeo bullfighters.

To the west, the massive dark grey of a roll cloud denoted chinook conditions. The under edge of the cloud, at some 10,000 feet in altitude, was lined with a pearly down. White lenticulars (lens-shaped clouds) sailed here and there below the frowning alto-cumulus of the arch. A smaller cap cloud clung to the mountains. The sky ranged in colour from a silvery blue above the cap cloud, to a cobalt blue near the edge of the arch. Gazing south, I could see that Chinook was treating the poor city folks to one of its tricks for a change.

The distant temples of commerce protruded through a yellow-brown dermis of polluted air, the exhaust of 309,000 cars, trucks and buses combined with the usual smokestack emissions. At a distance the towers, clustered in the valley of the Bow River, looked like the papillae of a gigantic wart—or a child's Lego set abandoned in a mud puddle. I call that brown layer "schmog" because it is smog kept in position by the chinook air overhead.

The city was locked in one of its far too typical temperature inversions. The air at ground level was just below freezing. Chinook, instead of blowing the smog away, was rolling over the top of it. It was squeezing that layer of cold schmog down over the city like a suffocating pillow. The hospitals were being deluged with asthma sufferers even as I stood there, serenely breathing in the clean country air. Then I got a whiff of something pungent, something fecundly, joyfully unpleasant: it was, I soon discovered, the piggy essence of a boar named Albert.

Albert, the Girletzes' nine-year-old pet pig, had rooted up the sun-warmed earth from one end of the arena to the other with his calloused snout.

"Howdy," I said.

"Oink," replied Albert, ambiguously. He was a truculent swine and he hated bulls and journalists.

The tentative sun played over the yellow hills north of the ranch and over a grey hump that was the back of the General, a Brahma bull about the size of a small elephant, who was soaking up some rays in a nearby pen. My first eyeful of the General gave me a jolt. I knew right then there was going to be a lot of bull in this story, a formidable pile, and the General, who weighs 2,200 pounds, would be only a small part of it.

The sun had melted the frost out of the ground beneath the outer walls of the Girletz Arena. The arena was surrounded by pickup trucks and horse trailers. Thirty-three young Canadian, American and New Zealand bullriders (average age nineteen) had come here for four days of bruising lessons in the dangerous sport of bullriding, taught by Alberta's Johansen brothers. I had come specifically to watch Saskatchewan's Ryan Byrne, professional rodeo bullfighter, as he tutored five young men in his arcane art.

The cowboys were there to test themselves on the bulls, and rodeo contractors were there to try out their bulls on the cowboys. The bulls were there to beat up some cowboys and earn a chance at siring more bulls just like themselves. Both man and beast must become great stylists to succeed in rodeo, where performance is everything. The cowboys wanted to learn to ride with good form—up straight on the bull and anticipating his every move; extra points if you are insane enough to spur the bull with your big, dull rowels (it doesn't hurt him, it just tickles his quarter-inch thick hide and pisses him off). But ultimately, 50 percent of a bullrider's score on each ride, 50 percent of a bullfighter's score during competition, is based on how well his bull performed. Fortunately, the bulls don't know that.

The pig ignored the General and me. He had his own ideas about bullfighting. He paused in his labours, raised his snout, and grunted interrogatively. Albert smelled bullstink, more bullstink than even the General could emit. With an angry squeal, he trotted off to a nearby corral and confronted the trespassers: some ninety head of feisty rodeo bulls, each patiently awaiting its chance to destroy a bullrider.

Grunting a challenge, Albert charged into the herd. He drove his snout into several prostrate behemoths, forcing them to get up and fight. Several younger bulls ran at him, bellowing their annoyance. He was too quick for them. Albert darted under their loins, bunting their massive dangling scrotums out of his way with his snout like a prizefighter striking a punching bag. Albert finally trotted off with a glint in his eye. He left the bulls moaning angrily, pendulous *huevos* swinging in the cool breeze.

Glancing suspiciously at an ambulance parked near the entrance, I entered the arena. The light inside seemed very dim. I heard some bull-riders whooping and shouting down at the far end. They seemed all to be looking my way. Something big and humpy stood in the shadow of the fence a foot in front of me. I felt its hoodoo eyeballs gunning me. A glimmer in the shadows came into focus: horns—big horns. A wild bull, separated from me by a two-inch-thick plank, stared fiercely into my eyes: I blinked.

I first learned about bulls and bullriding while working the chutes as a volunteer at an amateur rodeo. In the rural west of North America, the desire to ride on the pro rodeo circuit has the same appeal that professional hockey holds in the rest of Canada. Considering the risks they take, the financial rewards for Canadian riders are relatively modest. (Wayde Joyal, the 1994 Canadian champion, earned less than $37,000 for the year.) But there is glory, evident in the flash of a championship silver belt buckle, or a profile in the sporting pages. And beckoning behind the Canadian finals held in Edmonton is the superbowl of rodeo, the national finals in Las Vegas, "the World," where the big championship is decided and the big money is awarded.

But first comes the pain.

Rodeo bulls are bred to buck hard, to provide eight-second rides into hell or glory. Famous bulls (worth five to twenty thousand dollars) are given names that reflect the cowboy sense of humour—names like Jig-saw, Rest-In-Peace and Body Bag. These are characters whose quirks and foibles are mentioned with real admiration wherever bullriders gather: "Back Alley Brown [a well-known bull] came down along the fence and just picked a cowboy right off the top rail. Man, he was slick!" But unlike broncos, who have no real desire to injure humans, rodeo bulls will turn on a fallen rider, to hook, trample and gore. Fortunately, bull horns are "capped," their working ends cut back to the diameter of a twenty-five-cent piece. But the bulls don't care. As we say in Alberta, "Fool with the bull and you'll get the horn"—capped or uncapped. The only thing that stands between a fallen rider and a serious shit-kicking is the rodeo bullfighter.

It is the job of the bullfighter to draw the bull away while the fallen rider runs, or crawls, to the safety of the arena fence. Mounted pickup men, who work the bucking horse events, are of little use to bullriders because of the objective violence of the bull; he would just as soon gut a horse as he would a human. Like the Spanish torero, the rodeo bullfighter is a pedestrian. But in this case, he has no mounted picadors to tire the bull, no sword to deal death to his opponent, no intention to harm the bull whatsoever. All he has is a pair of cleated baseball shoes, good reflexes and an attitude—which last is a mixture of bravado and foolery. He wears the traditional face paint of the rodeo clown; he dresses in the clothes of a jester, as if he meant to make the bull die of laughter.

Although the crowd may think of any rodeo performer dressed in baggy pants, false nose and face paint as a rodeo clown, the cowboys themselves recognize a real difference. The traditional rodeo clown or "barrelman" is a comedian who jokes with the announcer and the crowd. He uses an aluminum barrel as a prop and escape-house to dodge charging bulls or broncos. On the other hand, the bullfighter, dressed traditionally in cut-off jeans known as "baggies," seldom has time for comedy. If a cowboy gets hung up in the bull rope (a rope that passes around the bull's brisket and is then wrapped around the rider's hand), the bullfighter must free him. If the bull tries to gore the fallen rider, the bullfighter must lure the bull away.

The numero uno fighter in Canada in 1991 was Ryan Byrne, a twenty-nine-year-old rancher from Prince Albert, Saskatchewan, with thirteen years of experience on the rodeo trail. He had appeared eight times at the Canadian finals, and he was the only Canadian bullfighter to have worked at the World. But the cowboys themselves were the best judges of Ryan's ability. Guy Johansen, a former Canadian Bull Riding Champion, said, "Ryan's there to take the shot from the bull for us. That's what he's paid to do, and he knows it. When you come off a bull, you can be stunned and disoriented, and yet you only have split seconds to move. Ryan is always there. He's the best bullfighter in Canada, one of the best in the world. Other guys can fight bulls, but Ryan's got cattle sense. He only takes a few steps, but they are the right ones. He seems just to be walkin' round the bull: he hardly seems to be movin'."

I found Byrne and his students gathered around a television monitor, watching a bullfighting competition taped at the world finals. Tiny bulls chase tiny clowns around a miniature arena. One of them is caught by a horn and flung through the air like a toy. Ryan froze the action, and tugged thoughtfully at his moustache. "He made his move too soon," he said critically. "Let the bull get closer," he told them. "Let him think he's got you, then you make your move," and he did a smooth "stepthrough," bullfighter ballet, to illustrate his point. At six foot two and two hundred pounds, Ryan was in his prime, and he moved with a cougar-like efficiency. He was out of costume just then, in jeans, vest and yellow sweatshirt, but the cool aura of leadership rested lightly in every gesture he made. If he had doubts about the student fighters gathered around him, it didn't show in his genial grin.

The five students were a ragtag bunch at first glance, but not without courage, as they would soon show. Their motives were mixed. Miles Tornberg, a musician, was one of three students present who had fought bulls before; he was building a career in rodeo. Charlie Stefan, a shop clerk, and Darcy Olesky, Coca-Cola deliveryman, were looking mainly for adventure. Byrne sized them all up. He approved of their gaudy shirts, the fringes on their baggies, the several bright bandanas trailing from their belt loops. The baggies would come off easily should the bull hook them: that's good.

Byrne doesn't waste a lot of words when instructing, which is the usual Cowboy Way. (This is an old-fashioned method in the current age of bafflegab and doublespeak. The speaker thinks about what he is going to say before he opens his mouth. In turn, he expects you to consider what he said before you open yours.) "Anything that flashes," he told us, "will make a bull throw his head up. When he throws his head up, he slows down." I concluded that a slowed-down bull is probably a less dangerous bull. The bullfighter uses his colours, his hands, his bandanas, even his hat to make the bull focus on him, to turn himself into a target at the crucial moment. "Keep your eye on the bull," said Byrne, "always. And whatever happens, keep thinkin'. Don't let the bull trap you against the fence. If he hits you, keep rollin' and scramblin'."

The students are not wearing face paint. Paint is for performances, and some of these young fighters have not yet "found their face." They have not yet created the painted mask that marks a seasoned fighter. This cannot be rushed: once a clown finds his face, one that brings him luck, he will stick with that mask for a long time, superstitious about changing it.

Inside the shadowy arena, stock contractors herded several bulls into the steel chutes. The bulls are crossbreds; Brahma blood is the constant factor, crossed with Charolais, Hereford and other breeds. A big-humped, tan-coloured bull weighing perhaps 1,600 pounds charges forward into a chute door, and the metal pipes ring like a requiem bell—or a dinner gong. He looked like a meat-eater to me. There was something sanguine in the toss of his horns, in the baleful looks he gave the cowboys who lined the top of the chute, as they gingerly worked a bull rope up around his sides.

The ranker the bull, the more the cowboys like him. (The tamer the bull, the more he is disdained.) "He's a pointy looking sonofabitch," said a cowboy admiring the tan brute, and he spat a dark spot of Copenhagen into the wood shavings of the arena floor for emphasis.

Back in the chutes, the steely-eyed and intense Dale Johansen showed the boys how to survive the hazards of mounting the bull, how to think out the next move. "You got yer motor runnin', and you want to ride that bull, but whoa—hold on: your rope is twisted . . ." In the neighbouring chute, the tan bull let out a whoof and tried to climb straight up the chute wall.

I had to gape when Byrne led in the General on the end of a halter rope. A cowboy clambered up on his back, and sat with one hand twisted in the bull rope while the General stood there quietly, a visual aid. "Think of his horns as handlebars," said Byrne. With his back to the General, he reached out with one hand, touched a horn, then pivoted into the "pocket," the safety zone behind the bull's shoulder, where he can't reach you with his "clown stickers." Byrne boosted himself up to the bull's shoulders in one springy jump, and yanked up on the rope tail, releasing the rider's hand from the twisted rope. During a ride, of course, the wild bull will be moving like a hurricane on a dime, not standing still like the amiable General. "Stay close to him," said Byrne. "Keep steppin' through into that pocket.

"You're here for just one thing—cowboy protection," he reminded them, gazing around the circle to make sure each man got the message. "You've got to get to a wreck before it happens. When the rider's feet start poppin'" (flying up and away from the bull's sides) "you know he's gonna come off. That's when you start moving in closer. Remember, the first guy in, go to the bull's head, get his attention."

The bullfighters exchanged glances. They knew it wasn't quite that simple, but Byrne was with them in the arena, and they were anxious to fight the bulls.

The General was led out. "Well boys, are we ready to buck?" shouted Don Johansen to the riders gathered behind the chutes. The boys whooped and whistled, and it occurred to me that some of those present might be several hay bales short of a stack.

A young Indian cowboy tucked his fringed chaps up behind him and gingerly lowered himself onto the bull. He slipped his low-heeled boots into the "sweet spot" in front of the bull's hips. These kind of boots are less likely to hang up on the fence rails. He must have tickled the young, inexperienced animal with his blunted spurs, because it suddenly went straight up the front of the chute, whoofing and moaning. The spotters lifted the young man bodily off the bull's back by the strap of his chaps, and he vaulted off the rails like a cat as the bull swapped ends and thumped down on all fours, facing the wrong way round.

Men pulled a gate open, and a bull was out, bellowing and spinning, his hind feet kicking high. A heavy bell attached to the bull rope added to the commotion. The rider sat a few jumps, one hand gripping the rope— and he was gone, sent flying and rolling in the dirt. The weight of the bell pulled the rope off, and the bull punted it several yards for a field goal.

One after another the bulls came out, and mostly the riders lasted only a few jumps before they were thrown. The bullfighters would try to lure the bull out into the open, away from the chutes and barrier fence. They couldn't always succeed in this, and then the riders would be scraped off along the fence; they'd scramble underneath the catwalk that runs along the wall, hiding from the bull's fury. There is a ladder up one wall of the arena, and riders thrown on that side scuttled up it like squirrels. As the day dragged on, several gimpy riders were helped out to the lobby to be checked out by Aaron Paramedical Services.

When I think of bullriding, I think of that Friday afternoon and Eric Delude, a siding applicator from Lethbridge who would dearly love to be a rancher. He was sitting hunched under his black hat on a bench watching the other riders at the time. He had taken a bad fall and been shaken up—or so I thought.

"How long have you been riding bulls?" I asked.

"What time is it?" he replied, wincing at his own joke.

"That long, eh? Tell me, what's it like to ride a rodeo bull?"

"It's hard to explain," he said. "It's like a zone that you and the bull go into by yourselves; it's like nothing else on earth," he said, clearly dazzled by the experience. But as he talked, I suddenly realized that Eric was holding a bag of ice cubes against the fly of his jeans. The bull had grazed him with its horn, wounding him in the groin. In this most macho of rodeo's testosterone-charged events, Eric had come close (about half an inch, as I recall) to emasculating himself. It would have been unfriendly to point out the irony of that just then, and that isn't the point anyway. The risks are high, and the rewards more intangible than real. But young men need adventure like bulls need grass. Eric followed the Cowboy Way. He had wanted to try bullriding; he had paid $350 for his tuition, and his only regret was that he couldn't ride any more that day.

I was sitting with the bullfighters on the narrow catwalk three feet above ground level, and starting to take things too much for granted. A black bull came bucking down along the walk, bear-like and vast, his hump erect in anger, raking the wood with one horn a few inches from my feet. I shrank back against the wall. It occurred to me that sitting with the clowns at this event is like sitting with the clay ducks in a shooting gallery.

If you ask a bullrider, "Why do you do it?" he will probably say something like "I got in it for the excitement, but I stay in for the people." Rodeo people really are a family, standing up for each other in the arena, and backing each other in the alien streets of town. Miles Tornberg, a local musician, fights bulls for similar reasons; for a challenge, for excitement, for the male love of adventure. "It's an addictive sport, rodeo," he said thoughtfully. "You get addicted to the adrenalin, I think."

The afternoon became a blur of bucking, twisting beasts. There was an acrid, gamy scent in the air, a mixture of bull urine, sawdust and male hormones. I sensed an increasing tension in the air as the afternoon progressed. The bullfighters were nervous about being hit. They knew it would happen, and they wondered who it would happen to first today. At one point, a violent retching sound was heard throughout the arena. One of the riders, overcome by nervousness, had the dry heaves behind the chutes.

Tornberg, who has fought bulls before, was pushing hard, staying close to the bulls, working on developing his own style. Byrne complimented him on his footwork. "He fought that Hereford cross in just twenty steps," he said enthusiastically. "Didn't waste a move. That's good work."

Tornberg moved up to the chutes. Byrne moved out into the arena, ready to back up his student. A brown bull with stubby horns explodes out of the gate, blowing steam. He ignores Tornberg's waving arms and turns, bucking and spinning, toward the fence. The rider is there for three seconds, and then falls between the bull and the steel fence; dragged by one arm, then crumpled on the ground under the bull's feet. Tornberg darts in and catches the bull's eye.

The brown bull rounds on him with startling speed, and he turns, running for the chute bars. A stubby horn hooks him behind one knee and the bull lifts him slightly with a frightful ease. His butt is square on the bull's head, and its neck snaps up: Tornberg flys straight up as if vaulting from a trampoline. He goes up above the chutes, and comes down, hits hard, rolls and scrambles as Byrne shouts encouragement. Byrne is there, whistling shrilly, and the bull turns on him: he offers his profile, keeping his eye always on the bull, and does a "stepthrough" as the bull sweeps past behind his back, hooking at empty air.

Tornberg makes his way over to us, grinning. He is shaken but unhurt.

"You took a helluva hit," somebody says.

"The cowboy's all right," says Tornberg. "That's the main thing." Tornberg told me afterwards that he knew there would be no escape for him. "You have to be willing to do the suicide charge, without hesitation," he said, "or the cowboys won't respect you."

As if inspired by Tornberg's example, the bullfighters worked closer to each bull that came out. One after another they were hit, and sent rolling through the dirt. The glaring grins on their smeared faces were the looks of initiates: they had felt the bull's power, they had touched the horns and lived. Perhaps today, one of them would "find his face"—or have it ground into the dirt.

Ryan Byrne told me that he spent nine months of the year on the rodeo trail and three months at home working on the family ranch. He earned about $60,000 a year from bullfighting, but the life was hard on mind and body. His schedule that week: teach at Balzac during the day, perform at the Medicine Hat Spring Rodeo every night. This meant a 400-mile return trip every day. He put 50,000 miles on his truck in eighteen months that way.

At 4:30 p.m., we were in Byrne's '91 Dodge "dually" truck near Brooks, Alberta, rolling east on Highway 1 through the flatlands, talking about the hazards of bullfighting. The wild wind rode on our tailgate, pushing us east, ramming the fumes from the diesel engine back up the exhaust pipes. Go east young man, said the wind. And stay there. I watched pensively as the water tanks that mark Canadian Forces Base Suffield came into view. The low range of hills that marked the old homestead was hardly visible. I would stay with my parents in Medicine Hat that night. The bull of a truck shook the wind off into the ditch where it rolled through the sage in a fierce eddy to pick up speed and counterattack. I was back in the antelope country. A small band looked up from a circle of dark slough water, streaked with whitecaps, as we sped past. Could those be the same tumbleweeds I saw at Cutbank, blowing across the highway in front of us; drab ghosts of the summer before, catching up with me again?

"I guess I can literally say I have a hole in my head," chuckled Byrne at one point.

I turned back from the window and saw his grin. He tapped the small scar between his eyebrows with one finger. "It was in Morrin, Manitoba. Glad my wife didn't see it. She'd been videotaping me, but she'd left on an errand. The rider had been knocked out, and I went in to help. I ducked a kick: the bull turned as I was getting up, and me and the bull banged heads. One of his horns was splintered. The splinter cut off my eyelid, left it hanging. Went into the sinus cavity of my skull, broke off and stuck there. The surgeon said I was lucky. The slightest pressure and it would have penetrated the brain."

Byrne has had broken ribs, terrible bruises, dislocated fingers and counts himself lucky to be still healthy and sound. That February, he told me, Rob Smets, four-time World Champion Bullfighter, had broken his neck in a bullfighting accident: it might take him a year to recover.

It was a sobering thought. "I don't take stupid chances," said Byrne after a bit. "I'll take the hit for a rider, but I don't do goofy stuff."

"Like jumping over the bull's head? That's a popular trick with the crowd, right?"

He grinned. "Yeah. Nobody wants to see a wreck but they sure don't want to miss it, either. Sure, I've done that plenty of times. When I think I can get away with it."

I blinked at this notion and asked what he liked most about his singular occupation. He told me how great it felt, what a rush it was, to save a cowboy from the bull. I remembered the black bull running toward me along the catwalk, that violent darkness, the wild bull, which symbolizes the chaos of death that all of us must face; the triumph of nature over man. The clown is the artist who cheats death of its prize—temporarily at least. That must be more than just a rush.

Byrne gave me a steady look. "People think bulls are stupid, but I believe they're quite intelligent."

"What do you say to yourself, when the bull is fast and smart?"

"Just that he's no better or worse than any other bull I've fought," he answered simply. But Byrne, a father of two boys, was cutting down on the appearances he would make that year. At twenty-nine, he was thinking about his family, about his wife, Kelley, and his sons who needed more of his time.

That night at Medicine Hat, he would supervise a bullfighting contest, the last event of the night. They would be Mexican fighting bulls; black as coal, fast and light on their feet at 1,200 pounds. Kelly LaCoste, the famous barrelman, would be there. Byrne was once Kelly's apprentice. "I travelled in his back pocket for a long time," he said with a smile. "Just about everything I ever learned, I learned from him."

A prairie city in the darkness appears to the traveller like a lake of embers lying under the stars. Some two thousand people were seated in Medicine Hat's red brick arena and perhaps 80 percent of them were from the countryside. Chernobyl green and toxic pink are as popular with ranchers and farmers as they are with urban joggers; the crowd was a day-glo sea of noise.

The clowns' room, a small cinderblock cell, was crowded and littered with duffel bags and clothes. Budweiser had provided refreshments set in tubs of ice; yours truly, of the thirsty Press, was grateful. Byrne and three other bullfighters were taping their ankles and buckling on kidney pads. Byrne put on a shiny moto-cross chest protector and endured good-natured heckling about his armour with a grin. "Put their names down there," he said, pointing at my notebook. "List them all under *A* for Asshole." A sweaty pair of socks thrown at him was their rejoinder.

Kelly LaCoste the barrelman was there. He turned out to be an avuncular, red-haired good-ole-boy from Louisiana and a long-time Medicine Hat resident. He was painting a white skull on his face, on which he would draw his clown mask. "I learned from the old guys," he drawled. "They never put on a pad until after they got hurt. These young guys are smarter than we were."

The other fighters were T.J. Baird, a young wildman from Castor, Alberta, and a former student of Byrne's; Raymond Goodman, a Manitoba boy; and Dwayne Hargo—the 1989 World Champion Bullfighter— a black American, and as hard and trim an athlete as one is likely to meet. A small pocket of neatness and calm surrounded Hargo. At one point he looked me over slowly and told me my exact height and weight.

Out in the arena the rodeo began with the traditional wild horse race: first you had to catch the horse; lots of neighing, bucking, kicking and dust. The crowd was roaring and the announcer's voice echoed through the hallway: "WHERE ELSE CAN YOU HAVE THIS MUCH FUN AND STILL KEEP YOUR CLOTHES ON?" In the clown room they talked about pulled muscles, the best way to tape an ankle; they talked about bullfighting. LaCoste grinned at their ambitions. "The real knack is to jump out of the barrel when a rider's hung up, and get to him just when he gets loose," he said in that hominy tone of his.

The bronc riding was announced and I followed LaCoste out to the arena. A roar from the crowd greeted him as he rolled his red barrel out into the sawdust. The announcer's voice boomed out a greeting, and LaCoste shouted a reply. They were soon kibitzing in the time-tested manner. "KELLY'S GOT FURNITURE DISEASE," boomed the announcer. "HIS CHEST HAS FALLEN INTO HIS DRAWERS." LaCoste reached into his voluminous baggies with both hands and pulled it back up, and the crowd roared again.

The bullfighting contest would be the last event of that first day. This is unusual. Bullriding is traditionally the last event at a rodeo. Anthropologist Elizabeth Atwood Lawrence has written that this "leaves both spectator and participant with the certainty that wildness remains a viable entity in their world. . . . All nature is not yet tamed." It may be a moot point which is wilder, though, man or beast, I thought, as I watched T.J. Baird painting big, jagged-edged stars over each eye. Baird had drawn a bull named Master of Disaster. I sensed, as he went into what looked like a sinewy yoga stretch, that he was going to try something very dangerous before the night was over.

At last the bullriding was announced. Byrne, unrecognizable to me now in his paint and costume, has transformed himself, his eyes concentrated on another world. He passes through the arena gate and runs out into that other reality, moving as lightly as a predatory cat. The announcer sings his praises and the crowd welcomes him back.

Kelly LaCoste is also ready at the mid-point of the arena with his barrel in position. He has set up a dummy on a pole; its face is a rubber mask of Saddam Hussein. There is a delay in the action. LaCoste goes into a striptease routine. He peels off his shirt and baggies revealing a truly frightening sight: he is wearing a pink tutu. He pirouettes coquettishly, letting his belly hang out. The announcer is disgusted: "KELLY, ON YOU THAT TUTU LOOKS LIKE A FOUR-BY-FOUR!"

Behind the chutes a Montana cowboy is getting ready to ride, stretching one arm up, stetching his legs, flexing his muscular buttocks from side to side. He finishes by slapping his chest, shoulders and then his face, very hard, with both hands about a dozen times. It seems the way to deal with pain is to first inflict it on yourself, and deny its power, the power of the bull that you will try to steal in eight violent seconds.

Twisting bands of dust curl up under the spotlights. The bulls come out from the red-and-white chutes, fierce and angular, twisting, bucking, rippling muscles under rolling sheets of hide, each with a human cross they cannot bear to carry. What they see first is Byrne's mocking mask; Byrne who has noted which hand the rider uses on the rope, which way the bull will want to turn; Byrne with the trickery of paint and colour, luring them away from the chute bars, out into the open, dancing away, making them twist and buck faster to follow him. Byrne whom they have seen and smelled before, so close, so tantalizingly close; if they can throw the rider quickly, they can turn and chase this lithe, colourful beast. To catch and throw it high, to pin it down at last, to beat it down into the dust.

"SO FAR THE SCORE IS LIONS FOUR, CHRISTIANS NOTHING," says the announcer after four riders are thrown without scoring.

Byrne is too fast, too smooth, too much a part of the action to make a spectacle apart from the bucking bull itself. Only when a limping cowboy gets up to shake his hand can the crowd begin to grasp what risk Byrne took, crammed in the corner with the rider hung up against the bars. Or when the bull attacks the barrel, with LaCoste hiding inside, and sends it rolling with Byrne behind it, letting it roll, running backwards but reaching out to tickle the bull under its foaming chops with one hand—then the crowd sees the beginnings of cosmic humour, the clown dancing with death on a banana peel of dust and fresh dung.

As they laugh, I remember him telling me, "I can't be funny out in front of a crowd. It's an art to make people laugh." But LaCoste, Byrne's teacher, says that after you get run over a few times you'll think you should try to be funny. Who knows, maybe Ryan Byrne's apprenticeship is not quite over yet; maybe there is one more face to find.

The spectacle would be provided each night—when T.J. Baird, during the bullfighting competition, finally jumped over the bull's head, and was hooked and flipped by a horn each time he tried it, helped dangerously in his leap that way. Or when the bull saw Saddam Hussein and sent him flying end over end: how the crowd would bellow for that one.

But when a black bull nearly caught Kelly LaCoste the crowd would be fatalistically silent.

I came into the clowns' room after the show one night, surprised to find it so quiet. The bullfighters looked dejected, the lips of the masks downturned, the eyes cold and hard. "I know how that shit goes," said Dwayne Hargo sadly. A thief had been into the lockers and Ryan, the only one who did not hide his money, had lost three hundred dollars. LaCoste felt bad: it's his hometown and he offered Ryan a loan. He wanted to call the police. Some town kids, non-rodeo types, have been spotted hanging around the hallways. None of the cowboys thought to warn them off.

I went outside for some air where the wind rattled through the leafless cottonwoods. There was a clanging of metal, and men shouting. Something heavy slammed into a parked truck, making it rock on its springs. A string of cuss words brightened the darkness. White eyes rolled coming out from the dark, and horns glinted in a streetlight's rays. A small herd of bulls was loose, big shadows rushing by. Moaning angrily, they ran heavily along, noses into the wind, smelling a promise of far distant cows, no doubt. Sparks trailed from horses' shoes as two riders went in pursuit, dodging among the parked cars, cutting off the vengeful bulls, who were following the wind uptown to raise hell.

It was 9:57 on Saturday night. I was weary after following Byrne back and forth between Balzac and Medicine Hat. My thoughts were on the students I had watched. The bulls had been hard on them. Their injuries so far included one collapsed lung, one severely bruised arm, one lacerated lip—"What really pissed him off," his chum had said, "was not that the bull stepped on his face, but that it stepped on his hat"—two groin injuries, one stepped-on ankle, several pulled wrist muscles, sore hands, sore guts, sore heads. Injuries to riders are not unusual; bulls are only very rarely injured. Sadly, a bull broke its leg during the Balzac school, and had to be put down. The incident had cast a pall over everybody for a while, but everyone I'd talked to thought the school was a wonderful success nonetheless. Ah, youth.

I glance up from my notes. Byrne is in one corner talking to some riders. The bullriding is over for the night, and LaCoste, at the far end, bends down to pick up parts of Saddam Hussein and other props. At that moment, a bull is released accidentally into the arena, something that is bound to happen occasionally. But this one charges immediately for LaCoste. It runs the length of the arena before someone breaks the spell and shouts a warning. I can see the surprise frozen on LaCoste's mask from the other end of the building as he looks up and sees the bull. He barely makes it to the fence, and dives right over it. The announcer is exultant. "THERE YOU HAVE IT, LADIES AND GEN-TLEMEN, PROOF THAT A BULL CAN TURN A FAT MAN INTO BEN JOHNSON."

In the clown's room afterwards, over two fingers of rye, I asked LaCoste if he'd been scared. He was rubbing baby oil on his face to dissolve the paint. "Scared? Woulda needed a hammer to drive a straight-pin up my butt. Hell yes, I was scared."

The party after the rodeo always starts in the clowns' room. They laugh a lot in the clowns' room, and their laughter draws a constant stream of visitors, cowboys and rodeo officials. "The best part of bull-fighting," says Dwayne Hargo, popping open a Bud Lite, "is when we all come back here to drink beer and bullshit about it."

They come in smiling and most of them have a joke, or a story to tell. And what are they laughing at, in there? Not at women, not at city people, and certainly not at the bulls. Themselves, in the final analysis, at their own bravado, at their own fear, which they oppose with action and overcome with laughter. Each one tells a joke or a story before they go. And when one man is talking the others listen. They know that the stories will be the only thing they have left when the dust has cleared, and the blood runs colder. And when they leave, reluctantly, they often say, "I'll see you clowns later."

And they exit, laughing.

15
POEM ON THE RANGE
~

June is usually a green month in southern Alberta, the month of rainfall, the blessing month that brings moisture to the fields sown in May. It is a season of relative calm, though sometimes the sidewinder of a hot wind snakes over the countryside like an invisible sponge and puckers the earth temporarily dry again. June is also the month of the Alberta Cowboy Poetry Gathering in Pincher Creek. Spring branding is over for most ranchers and the hay crops are not yet ready to cut. The poetry gathering is a time to celebrate the Cowboy Way; a time to celebrate surviving another winter on the northern range. Old friends spend nearly as much time visiting as they do listening to the western odes. When they part, one or the other may urge "Don't be a stranger."

It's an expression I've heard throughout the West. It means come see us some time soon, though it's possible to think of it as an admonition too: don't be someone we don't know; don't put a fence between us— unless there is a gate in it. Don't think too differently, act too differently or vote differently than we do. At least, not until we get to know you well enough to know you are no threat. If you are going to sing songs—

sing country songs, though you are allowed, like the band in the movie
The Blues Brothers, to play both kinds of music—"Country *and* Western." And if you are going to write poems, write cowboy poems. If you
have an entry in *The Oxford Book of Canadian Verse*—better keep that
to yourself, Slim.

The thing is, I don't mean to be a stranger. It just goes with the word-
slinger territory. So I had my reasons for being nonplussed when I was
invited to "say some poems" at the gathering. I can say poems, all right,
but I'd be stretching it to call myself a cowboy. Although I've made my
living at times on horseback, I've cleverly avoided learning how to rope
a steer—so far. And what would Dr. Juan Teran, mayor of Pincher
Creek, think of my presence in his bailiwick? Interviewed in *The Calgary Herald* this genius of *le bon mot* had labelled God-fearing citizens
like me as "tree-huggers" and "s.o.b.'s" for trying to shut down his pet
make-work project, the Oldman River Dam. I suspicioned that I might
say some swears right back at His Worship if I was to run onto him
sudden like. That could put a damper on the whole shebang.

But far more seriously than this, I didn't have a decent straw hat to
wear. My straw Armadillo was five years old. A dude might wear a
Diller; a cowboy wears a Resistol. So very vainly and warily on a Friday
morning in June I spurred my battered Jeep Cherokee past the sign that
says "Pincher Creek Welcomes You." That motto is emblazoned
between two pairs of gigantic hoof nippers or "pincers." I felt the merest twinge of paranoia. Try to stay out of trouble, warned a voice in my
head. It was the telephone voice of Blaine Pickard, who was then secre-
tary-treasurer of the Alberta Cowboy Poetry Association. Blaine's a veterinarian, and if you have horses, especially mares, a veterinarian is a
guy you tend to cultivate. I glanced again at the big nippers and imagined them snapping shut around my neck—or my wallet.

First stop was the Pincher Co-op, squatting on a bald-headed hill
above town. Speaking as a member, if they'd plant a tree there I would
hug it. But the view was superb. Spring rains had been generous for a
change. The hills were deep green, rolling south to the square brow of
Chief Mountain in Montana, west to the castellated front range of the
Rockies. This is cattle country. And there wasn't a BMW or a yuppy in
sight for miles in any direction.

I clapped the greasy Diller on my pate and moseyed on in to buy
some cassette tapes with which to capture this story. But how, I won-

dered, am I going to make sense out of thirty-two rugged he-men reciting poems? Who knows where the story will lead: a writer is like a pilot
fish beside a shark: the fish only pretends to know where the shark is
going.

They were playing Ian Tyson's new album on the Muzak, and I had
to stifle an urge to utter a barbaric yawp, or yodel. Then a suntanned
cowgirl swivelled past wearing a T-shirt with the words "BEAR BAIT"
printed thereon. Stay out of trouble, said that voice again but some rascal growled, hungrily.

She wagged a forefinger my way. "Watch it, cowboy."

I took her advice and ran into the door.

Cowboy poets don't have poetry festivals, they have "gatherings," as
in "Gather up them dogies, Slim." A gathering is not a competition, it's
more like a Scottish ceilidh or a big family reunion where they never
heard of the VCR. It's people with a common lifestyle and set of beliefs
taking turns entertaining each other. Cowboy singers and pickers are
welcome, but the spoken word, especially verses known "off by heart,"
is the essence of the gathering.

The most famous gathering of them all is held in Elko, Nevada. It
began in 1985 with a hundred poets and a thousand listeners. The
crowds have increased every year (swelling to 9,000 people in 1995).
Elko has become a major tourist attraction, one made famous by BBC
Radio and European television. That example inspired smaller gatherings in nearly all of the western states. In 1988, the Alberta Cowboy
Poetry Association organized the first Canadian gathering at Pincher
Creek. The founders were Blaine Pickard and two Medicine Hat ranchers, Valerie Schattle and her husband, the late Allen Schattle, who was
the founding president of the Association.

Blaine Pickard is a bear-shaped guy, built for comfort, not speed. I
asked him where they got the idea to hold the first gathering. He gave
his goatee a pensive tug and said, "I think we got it from a bottle of
Scotch we drank after a bull sale." The idea was a natural. In many
ways, the cowboy lifestyle doesn't recognize the border. The high plains
of Alberta flow naturally into the high plains of Montana. Cowboys
talk that talk and walk that walk the same old way, on either side of the
line; they drift back and forth somehow from job to job as if the
province and the state were all part of one big ranch.

The Pincher Creek Agricultural Society helped stage the event. Poets had come this year from all over western Canada and Montana. They'd say some poems Friday and Saturday, eat a barbecued steer or two and raise some dust at the Saturday night dance. There was also a display of western art, crafts and books of cowboy poetry, mostly self-published.

Allen Schattle provided a simple definition of what cowboy poetry is. "It's a poetic documentation of the cowboy's life." The versifying begins on top of a horse out under the starry quilt of the High Lonesome, and is traded from one rider to another around the campfire of nights. When Allan Lomax collected an anthology of cowboy songs back in 1919, he went out to the ranches and cow trails to find poems on the hoof.

A stage in the hall was faced with wagon wheels, hay bales and branding irons to add some atmosphere. There was a cowhide draped over the lectern, a tribute to the beast that makes cowboys possible. The room was a blur of running kids, fancy shirts and flashy trophy belt buckles. I saw cowgirls dressed much like cowboys and ranch women in traditional western-style skirts. (About 6 percent of the poets were female.)

The Friday crowd was in a celebratory mood. The range was lush with the promise of good hay crops, and the Rancher's Fun Rodeo was only two days away. The young cowboys were lean and cocky, the old ones crocked up and worn down from jousts with rough horses and ornery bankers.

As Lloyd Dolen, an oldtimer from Cochrane, Alberta, put it:

Old cowboys never die
Their bones just crack and squeak
And this is where you'll find 'em
Down in Pincher Creek.

A dismounted cowboy is a myth brought to earth, a booted, bow-legged anachronism among the stiff suits of town. But put a cowboy on his horse and see how true his outfit is to his profession. His high-heeled boots won't slip through the stirrups and hang him up. His big hat is a roof deflecting rain or shine. The "wild rag" (bandana) is his personal flag of valour. It also wards off melanomas of the neck, or acts as a dust filter over his mouth. He settles lightly into his seat, nonchalantly at home in the past, and leaning forward unafraid trots gracefully into the future, looking for trouble.

I trotted upstairs looking for a hat rack, and discovered the western art show: landscape paintings, silverwork, and a beautiful Chuck Stormes saddle, a sculpture carved from the finest leather. I also found Don Wudel, leather braider and cowboy "poet lariat" of Calgary.

Seeing Don's tooled leather eye patch and waxed moustache, I thought Long John Silver had been reincarnated as a buckeroo. Don had some exquisite braided reins and "mouth-closers" on display. He told me he was blind in one eye with 15 percent vision in the other, as the result of diabetes. He uses a magnifying glass for doing fine work. He doesn't cowboy full time any more. Yet he still manages to get out to the ranches, like one worked by fellow poet Bryn Thiessen, to do some riding and roping.

At thirty-three, Don is an active and very cheerful young man, but I wondered how he could rope calves given his poor vision.

"I go by feel quite a bit," he said laconically. "I can throw my hoof trap and catch 'em by the hind feet just fine. I don't neck rope 'em to check for pink eye, 'cause I can't see good enough. Someone else has to do that."

Wudel reminded me that "Cowboy Pride" is not just the title of an Ian Tyson song. Pain is an old acquaintance to cowboys. Don has had three broken bones in his career, and one thumb is just a round stub. He mashed it off between the dallies (turns of a lariat) and the saddle horn catching a mean old steer one time. But pride and love of the life keep him going back. He goes to be with his friends, to feel a good horse between his knees and a good rope whirling around his arm.

A loudspeaker sputtered as Blaine Pickard brought six nervous-looking cowboys to the stage. Things got off to a leisurely start. Each poet rose in turn to say his piece. The poet would sometimes begin by reciting an old broadside that he'd learned at a relative's knee, decades before. These were usually written by that favourite folk author, Anonymous, or else by revered forebears like Badger Clark or Bruce Kiskaddon. Then the poet would read a verse of his own composition.

Most of the men and women take pride in knowing a few of the "classics," as they're called. They're the stories of larger-than-life men moving through a vast and unforgiving landscape where the weak did not live long. Heroic cowboys rope a grizzly bear for a joke; they team-rope the devil, brand him and leave him with a knot tied in his tail: evil is met and bested by courage and by skill, and sometimes by prayer. The little kids would hush each other up whenever an old cowboy announced a title like "That Gol-Durned Wheel" (about a bucking bicycle) or "Hell in Texas," where Texas pride is satirized.

> The devil in Hades we're told was chained
> And there for a thousand years remained
> He did not grumble nor did he groan,
> But determined to make a hell of his own

God gives his fallen angel a stretch of land that was "too dry for hell," then throws in some sulphurous water to nurture it. But all it will grow is thorns, tarantulas and horned toads.

> Oh the wild boar roams the black chaparral,
> It's a hell of a place he's got for Hell.

Watching the crowd's delighted reactions, I thought of the old man in Calgary who collects bottles behind my son's place, shunned by most passers-by. Here in this far-flung family was a place where an oldster was still listened to with something akin to respect. Mike Logan, a big burly Montanan, put it simply for me: "They know things we don't know, and I like to find them out." In a poem about his own horseman father, Mike wears his heart on his sleeve without embarrassment.

> They'd not have said they loved them
> "I just like to see 'em go."
> Or, "All I want's the money!"
> But you knew it wasn't so.
> Hoof beats, I hear hoof beats
> In the dew moist Kansas air
> And I love to hear those hoof beats
> 'Cause I know my Dad is there.

One of the "visiting literati" (as Mike calls guys like me) once said to him, "You know, Harvard and Yale don't value cowboy poetry." "We're not writing it for Harvard and Yale," growled Mike. He might also have added that the literati are not exactly writing for the masses. The postmodernists, writing poems about other poems and gazing up their own yin-yangs in lieu of a moral imperative, have their own élite audience in mind.

Oblivious to literary trends, the cowboy poets entertained each other with sagas that had a beginning, a middle and an end. Gwen Peterson from Big Timber, Montana, assured us that "I am not, nor have I ever been a cow-boy." (Which led me to think maybe cowboy poets and cowgirl poets, being all cowpokes, need a nineties-type name: how about cowpotes?) Gwen, after listening to some of the boys slinging the bull for a while, concluded: "I figger you cowboys were put here on earth just to entertain us gals. Y'all do a fine job of it."

Taking a cue from her, I decided, when it came my turn to recite, to tell the story of a sunburned cowgirl who has a strange encounter with a black bear, whilst lying in a tent wearing nothing but Nivea Cream. It's a true story, and it seemed to go over fine. One elderly lady confided in me afterwards that a black bear was pretty tame compared to some of the men she'd thrown out of her tepee in days gone by.

No gathering would be complete without at least one tall tale about the west wind. Jim Ross, from the Bitterroot Valley in Montana, recited one of his called "The Day My Saddlehorn Blew Off." It could have been written about Pincher Creek. Part of it goes:

Crop rotation's no problem in Idaho
On the Snake's great watershed
Spud farmers don't rotate their crops
The wind moves the soil instead
After one trickle of air down the canyon
All the culverts were standing on end
And the railroad tunnel through the hill
took on a considerable bend

The poem-athon dragged in places, especially where the Lord got hog-tied to the plot with chains of rusty doggerel. In one poem, an entire family is wiped out in a series of bizarre accidents: a girl dies of snakebite, a son dies in a fall from a horse, two other offspring die in shooting accidents and another son is killed in the war. The punch line is that the heroine "never faltered even one day in the worship of her God." The audience sighed knowingly and applauded. It was too deep for me.

God is not only alive but very busy in southern Alberta. When not guiding cowboys through blizzards, God has to keep drought, hail storms, violent death and terminal diseases on the go to challenge his flock. But perhaps the Creator is just more believable to people caught in the round of the four seasons. These are people who depend on their muscles and physical skills to earn their living, and they know the cruelty of winter in the land and winter in the body that nothing but religion can console. When a poet from McGrath, Alberta, read a very personal poem about his faith, and his struggles with Parkinson's disease, the crowd got up and gave him a standing ovation. There were tears on some of those weathered faces.

It seems pointless to criticize this ingenuous event from outside the experience it contains. In the anthology *Cowboy Poetry: A Gathering*, Hal Cannon shows that the genre is based on "a language coded with insider's words, special phrases and meanings, and shared values. The general form of cowboy poetry is the four-line ballad of rhymed couplets, the same as that used by other popular poets of the nineteenth century such as Robert Service and Rudyard Kipling." But after listening to several hours of Kiplingesque couplets limping onward like the Charge of the Light Brigade, I have to point out one thing. Bad meter hurts the ears. Many cowboy poets would be wise to go and read some good verse and learn to count stresses before taking up their pens. Robert Service would not be a household name if he had followed "Oh the northern lights have seen strange sights, but the strangest they ever did see," with this: "Was the night on the edge of the Lake known as Labarge I incinerated that little varmint known as Sam McGee."

We hit a long patch of cowpotes reciting what they called "serious" poems, serious meaning religious in this milieu. The crowd was getting restless, and Don Wudel, acting as MC part of the time, was concerned. "Somebody should jump in and hit 'em with about three short ones that'd make 'em laugh and pay attention, and then we could run some more ninety-year-olds at 'em agin."

A moment later Don was up on stage throwing in some agricultural humour:

Mary had a little lamb
Her father shot it dead
Now she takes the lamb to school
Between two chunks of bread.

After a while, it occurred to me the idea of a cowboy as the strong silent type was just wishful thinking. I decided to put on the feed bag and catch up with Don Wudel and his friends at a local hangout later that night. Bryn Thiessen, who hails from Sundre, Alberta, was one of those present, and that brought back a memory.

*   *   *

Some years ago, when I was a "simple servant," a colleague and I were on a mounted patrol in the north end of Banff Park watching for poachers. After a week spent bucking a stiff west wind, we turned our horses around and drifted east thinking we would head for Sundre, and conduct an intelligence-gathering mission at a local watering hole where hunters congregate. I was nervous about the trip. There was rumoured to be a fellow living beside the road to Sundre who hated game wardens, which was not unusual. But this guy kept a homemade cannon in his attic. He'd been known to fire it through a loophole in the wall, usually when an official of some kind came around.

"Don't worry about him," said my partner. "We'll travel incognito."

Following his lead, I'd taken the badge off my hat, and had turned my uniform jacket inside out.

"Now we don't look like park wardens," he said.

He was right. We looked like a couple of Esso gas jockeys wearing identical roper hats. But we travelled at night, so it didn't matter.

The bar in Sundre looked like a set from *A Fistful of Dollars*. But there were always several empty tables near us for some reason, as we sat sipping our ginger ales. I knew the jig was up when a certain notorious party sashayed over and said, "Jeez I'm glad to see you guys here. Can you sell me a fishing licence?"

After looking at Thiessen, I realized all those tough-looking guys at the saloon were probably just cowboy poets out for a night on the town. Bryn has a gun-metal glint in his eye, probably of mischief, but his long, droopy moustache speaks of another era. He had on an old suit vest with a watch fob depending from one pocket, and a black hat. On his sleeves were something you don't see very often: leather roper's cuffs. They were popular in the twenties and thirties.

"They're good protection in the bush," Bryn explained, "and they stop the rope from whackin' your wrists. Kinda like a ring," he added. "You never take 'em off."

As I sat with the one-eyed Wudel, Thiessen and several of their pals that night, I thought, "Here's a bunch of outlaws, poetry be damned." A waiter appeared and said the Chinese cuisine was of the best.

"Is it Peking or Szechuan?" asked Don, innocently. Conversation stilled and the town folk turned and stared.

"I didn't know the James gang was gourmets," some wag whispered.

When the waiter asked him what he'd like to drink, Don fixed on him with his good eye. I thought, whiskey of course, you fool.

"I'll have a large milk," said Don. He had to turn to me just then. I was choking on my beverage.

We left the restaurant sober as judges that night: cowboy poets need their rest.

*   *   *

Saturday was more crowded and hectic. I found myself playing tag with the CBC's Don Hill, who kept trying to interview me while I was interviewing somebody else. I thought of what the media circus did for Elko. Blocks of tickets are now reserved for large numbers of outsiders to attend the gathering there. I asked Don Wudel if he thought hype and commercialism would ruin the down-home flavour of cowboy poetry in Alberta.

Don rubbed his bad eye thoughtfully. "Well, I think it'll be like any fire. I mean, it starts with a spark, and then it kindles, burns and fades down again. The thing is, it'll never go out. There's been cowboy poets for a hundred and fifty years and will be for the next hundred and fifty, but it may not have the prominence it has now." For Don, it's not prominence that counts; its authenticity, poems being recited by real cowboys about the cowboy life. The Calgary Stampede had approached him to organize a gathering there as part of the "greatest outdoor show on earth." He had mixed feelings about that: he didn't want this gathering of friends to get washed over in show-biz glitter. "But if I don't do it, I'm afraid they're gonna get someone who's not a cowboy poet, and the thing will get portrayed wrong for the public.

"So I'm hoping we're just fanning the flames a bit now," he said, wistfully, "and that it'll sorta die back down a bit."

Bryn Thiessen and I went out for some air that afternoon. Sitting on the tailgate of a pickup truck, I asked him if he ever felt like he was living in the wrong century. The question made him chuckle.

"Yeah, in some ways we're born a hundred years too late. In other ways we're a reminder of something in danger of being lost. It's an attitude on life maybe even more than the lifestyle itself. I think for the lifestyle itself" (of the old-time cowboy) "we are born too late. But we do have an advantage."

"What's that?"

"Well, we can almost go back to life the way it was, and still have what we have now, which would be hard to leave. I work alone a lot, in isolation. I'm to a point I can create my own world. And the government ain't figured out yet how to tax your mind, so they can't control it."

It's on these time travels that Bryn communes with the muse.

"See, cowboy poetry is a chance for the inside man to get to the outside. The things I hold inside are quite guarded. Partly by choice, partly by culture. So it gives me a chance to express the things I see in nature that cause me to think and feel. Here they seem to be able to hold and cherish it. Now if I did this on the street, well it's kinda like you take a part of your heart and hand it out. Here they would say 'thank you' and give it back. Out there, they'd crush it."

But at Elko, and even here in Pincher, Bryn has noticed a change in the crowd. Now it's not all working cowboys. The strangers don't get all the allusions to working stock or horses. "They're not livin' in the life," he says, sadly, "and their minds just don't draw those pictures."

k.d. lang's famous "Beef Stinks" campaign put the perils of vegetarianism to the forefront for a while in cattle country. Has anyone ever wondered what cowboys think of vegetarians? Bryn Thiessen got to musing about evolution and vegetarianism while doctoring some cattle one day. This led to a fifty-three-line broadside called "Edible Evolution." In it he notes how carnivores have eyes set on the front of their heads so they can see their prey, while herbivores have their eyes on the sides of their heads, so they can see the carnivores coming behind them. The cowboy poet confesses that he "might eat salad for its roughidual quality/ But a diet without meat seems 'most as bad as idolatry," and concludes:

> But if evolution is true, of which I have my doubts
> In a few thousand years there's going to be shouts
> There's going to be laughter, even downright derision,
> All because of an ancestry decision
> See, in a few thousand years, long after I'm dead,
> All those vegetarians will have eyes
> on the sides of their heads.

Bryn's analysis might ignore a few divisions of taxonomy, but it earned rollicking approval from the crowd. (They could smell the beef sizzling on the barbecue as he recited.)

Saturday night, after big platters of juicy beef had been consumed, Don Wudel got up to recite again. He did a comic song, a capella, about a cowboy who drops his glove in the mud. The cowboy gets off his horse to pick it up, trips over a stump and falls into the slime. His horse kicks his dog, the dog growls at his master, who gets back on the horse, breaks his thumbnail on the saddlehorn, and loses his hat into the mud this time. The crowd was rolling in the aisles; but something was bugging the little guy with the eye patch.

It seems a Calgary theatre group had done a cowboy poetry show, but they'd used actors instead of cowboys. The actors sat on imaginary horses, recited poems and knocked each other's hats off from time to time. Now to knock a cowboy's hat off is still considered a deadly insult in western Canada. Don didn't like it much, but the director felt that "cowboys are like that, just fun-loving guys."

The director was present that night. So Don recited "The Lost Pardner," an old classic by Badger Clark, to show there's more to cowboy friendship than mere horseplay. It's about a puncher who is killed when his spur is tangled in the cinch. You could hear a pin drop in the room when Don came to the lines:

We loved each other in the way men do
And never spoke about it, Al and me,
But we both *knowed*, and known' it so true
Was more than any woman's kiss could be.
We knowed—and if the way was smooth or rough,
The weather shine or pour,
While I had him the rest seemed good enough—
But he aint here no more.

What is there out beyond the Great Divide?
Seems like that country must be cold and dim.
He'd miss this sunny range he used to ride
And he'd miss me the same as I do him.
It's no use thinkin'—all I'd think or say
Could never make it clear.
Out that dark trail that only leads one way
He's gone—and left me here.

The range is empty and the trails are blind
And I don't seem but half myse'f today.
I wait to hear him ridin' up behind
And feel his knee rub mine the good old way.
He's dead—and what that means no man kin tell.
Some call it "gone before."
Where? I don't know, but—God! I know so well
That he aint here no more.

Late that night I left the noise and smoke of the dance floor and
wandered out under the kind of stars that a city dweller can't see. The
moon was full over the canyon and the wind was only a whisper
down the creek. There was a campfire burning over there where Don
and the boys were camped for the night, and moving a bit closer I
could hear the sound of a guitar and a mandolin. Earlier that evening
they'd all gathered on the stage for the finale to sing "Home on the
Range." But as I listened to their voices swelling and falling on the
breeze, I thought I recognized a newer anthem: Michael Burton's
song, "Night Rider's Lament."

The great elusive shark had swum away to hunt among the clouds for the silver moon, as usual. I drove home to the ranchette out west at Aspen Valley singing the answer, the chorus about how they've "never seen spring hit the great divide." And I yodelled the last part all the way home.

AT THE GRIZZLY'S DEN

16
SMOKEY THE MERRY MINION

~

When the big dog coyote, who has been sniffing around the barn of late, looks down from his den on that small hill in the middle of the valley, he sees our lives entire. His view takes in the house, barn and grove of trees. He can see our two horses grazing in the meadow, and watches them when they climb up to circle our ridge. He watches me and the dog leave the yard to walk north. He has followed our tracks, and he knows that we will make a circle, like deer, and go back south to our den before dark. Coyote knows how close he can let the dog approach him before he takes to his heels. The dog is no threat to him, though it is annoying and stinks of humankind. He knows that I have a mate. He knows that he can hunt grouse in my woods. He knows that if he sees me come out with that noise-stick poking up from my shoulder in winter, I may leave him something good to eat in the snow. Coyote doesn't know what the food chain is, but if he did he would know where he and I fit on it. Coyote knows what we are and where we belong.

In the parkland country along the mountain front, the December sky at twilight shows a tinge of palest violet. The faint new moon has already risen east over Terry's Ridge. I've made a circle north of the house, and come back from stalking my shadow through these hills. There is snow, jealously cupped from the wind among the long grasses. Each islet of snow is edged with an apron of ice from the warm wind's breath. As I near the ranchette, the dog lags behind, snuffing up the intoxicating musk of a badger's den. The evening is calm. But bend down and see the wind's calling card in the arched grass stems anyway. Each stem has been made to draw with its awn a perfect half circle in the snow, and now rests motionless in the groove like a compass foot. Now here's something starker: a spot of bright red blood on the white plate, and Coyote's tracks. Here is where he stood with his ear cocked to the snow. He sprang toward the sound of a hidden prey, and speared his front feet down through the white roof. He missed on the first attempt. But then from a round hole in the white the size of a dollar coin dart the tracks of a meadow vole. Flushed from its nest when its sanctuary collapsed. The tracks go one way; they end in that blood spot. Coyote is one of the many gods feared by mice.

But Coyote's eyes are bigger than his belly. He keeps an eye on Candy, our thirty-five-year-old white mare. She's been out to pasture since the summer day six years ago when she fell down, twice in quick succession, while carrying me over flat, safe ground. She is a bone-rack, though still healthy otherwise; a marvel to farriers and cowboys who have never seen a horse allowed to reach its own conclusion. The neighbours make bets with each other every winter that it will be her last. Coyote the fortune teller, who has been probing her dung with his nose, might predict her fateful day. We dread its coming: I wish her an instant heart attack, and pray she doesn't break a leg first. Because if a neighbour can't get here fast enough to spare me the grief of it, I will have to put a bullet through that wily, proud old head. I'll feed her substance to the life of these hills, rather than fatten some useless lapdog on her flesh—well, not fatten it really—exercise its jaws would be more like it, on canned whipcord and gristle. Hank Broda, who sold her to me, knows her time is not long. "Never you mind," he reassured me. "When the time comes, I'll slip down with the tractor and pick her old carcass up with my front-end loader. We'll put her out in a nice secluded spot."

For the coyotes, but also for the whiskey jacks, magpies, crows, ravens, golden eagles, bald eagles and turkey vultures. And her soul will take wing.

A rattle of metal tags and Mojo catches me up. She is a good-natured genetic invert who specializes in hair growing: she grows it in summer, and sheds it all winter. Mojo leaves a trail of black wool in the snow wherever she goes. She is my pal.

Just before the gate, absent-minded as usual, I break through the snow that covers a spring, one that never freezes; a thin razor of ice water kisses my ankle awake. Now there is mud on one boot. It always mystifies Myrna that like a muskrat I can find mud from December to February, here in this suburb of the Arctic Circle. Look up westward from the gate and see the alpenglow, unknown word to sodbusters, radiating from the mountain rim.

The most profound music of the day is heard on the distaff-side of the sun. The singer today is Raven, perched on the top of a distant fir tree, whose pebble-down-the-well song echoes briefly from ridge to ridge, announcing the night.

My boots squeak over a drift. Beneath the arches of willow boughs the fading light shows moose tracks and the frozen brown marbles of their droppings. The quarterhorse mares, Taj—Myrna finally got that horse—and Candy, poke their heads out from behind the barn to see who is approaching. (Dimples had other hearts to break, and went back home to the Brodas.) Some early mornings after I have fed them their hay, a big, dry cow moose will glide out of the shadows of this bush, step daintily over the barbed-wire fence (three and a half feet high) and amble over to the horses. They will jerk their heads up, hay dangling from their mouths, ears pricked at Ms. Moose. They back up, some-times quickly, sometimes slowly. When she reaches the hay, she drops her head down, and then shakes it up and down at the horses in a very horselike manner, which they understand. They like to pretend that she has never bullied them like this before, and while they run around the meadow, snorting and blowing, she picks over their hay, choosing the choice green stems at her leisure. I have a picture of a puppyish Mojo nose to nose with this largest member of the American deer family. It was Mojo's first moose adventure, and she trotted right up probably thinking it was just another horse. The moose reached out her nose to inquire of Mojo's intentions. Mojo lifted one leg and froze, and her ruff stood straight up, in horror. The moose took a gusty sniff, and suddenly shook her head up and down violently as if to say, that's close enough, cute little black coyote. Now piss off. . . .

Mojo follows me up to the Wheelhouse, would hold open the door for me if she knew how. She'll curl up in the snow like a wolf to keep an eye on her domain while I go back to work. Like Lion, her predecessor, Mojo doesn't like the indoors much; too hot.

And what is my work, just now, but remembering. Too many stories to tell them all. But there are pictures that stay in our heads. Myrna and I talk about them when the wood stove is blazing late at night. We open the oven door and rest our feet there. We sip a hot toddy. I never thought that I would ever enjoy such . . . tranquility. I know there's a war on, and I should be at the front, ruining some developer's day, but something in me needs these hours of peace. And those who would like to ruin mine will have to line up and get past her first. When the chips were down and I looked around for help, Myrna alone stood back to back with me. There is never a day when we don't have something new to talk about, or some old event to rehash. This is the humble glory of a long marriage, the everyday joy and simple comfort that this desperate western world, rushing from circus to circus, is so eager to shrug away from. Sometimes what I recall can only be confirmed by our shared experience. So many of the places we lived in together have disappeared under the wrecker's ball or the 'dozer blade. The life of a modern man is half hallucinatory: particular places are savaged, flattened, dissolved in a matter of hours. This is the North American Way, a life on the road, the human landmarks torn down, made over into some new and even more temporary concept than the last. But we refuse to forget what was lost, and refusing, decline to stamp a mindless approval on what has replaced it.

We reaffirm each other; we resist equally the right-wing hypnotism of progress, and the left's current obsession with victimhood. We prefer past ecstasies to today's titillation. We celebrate together the love that we have made together; we grieve over the errors made—or rather, I do, far too much. We exult in our children and try our best to help them still. We know that we are not unique in this, and that gives us hope, and so we keep on remembering.

Sometimes days will pass as I struggle with words and I get too preoccupied even to go for a hike. Then Coyote will come down to the edge of the yard at ten in the morning and make the hills echo with his madcap yodelling. I'll step out into the open then where he can see me, so he can be reassured. I'm touched by his interest, though I know there is no affection in it. Sometimes I will yodel something in reply. Coyote doesn't usually stop to answer; he has other calls to make, a congregation to subdue, a world to keep in order.

* * *

Thank you, Site 14A, *circa* July 1985, but who's counting, really. At a time when I tended to look back through rose-coloured binoculars at my old career, you threw cinders in my eye and broke the spell. And yet when I snapped out of it, there I was, back in harness you might say, this time with the Alberta Forest Service. In a summer of drought, I had taken a summer job: patrolman in the Porcupine Hills. It was Smokey the Pig revisited. But I never saw anything quite like Site 14A before, not even in Banff National Car Park.

The hills were not a park, though stretches of wild country seemed parklike. Facilities were few; there were no official hiking trails. The forest service cared little for tourism, and nothing for wildlife. That was another department. Logging and cattle grazing were the main economic uses. My tools were simple. A shovel, a polaski (fire axe) and a gieke can for putting out campfires, disinfectant for cleaning outhouses and picnic tables. I was a glorified janitor on the one hand, and on the other the acting mayor, fire chief and bylaw enforcement officer.

I always enjoy myself thoroughly when I can find a valid excuse for not writing (except when renovating). Every day I fuelled the truck from a forty-five-gallon drum at our place and headed for the hills to begin the day's rounds.

The Porcupine Hills rise north of Pincher Creek and trail off northward for thirty-six miles to Chain Lakes on Highway 22. The forest reserve encompasses the higher elevations of the hills up to 6,000 feet. The Hills were known to the Peigan as the Porcupine's Tail, hence the current name. Once they provided a protected wintering area to the tribe, which still maintains a timber reserve in the hills. Here and there are steep banks or short cliffs that were used as buffalo jumps by the tribesmen long ago. The hills shelter the same species that frequent my own back yard, and one addition—Merriam's turkeys—introduced some decades ago, which startle the wanderer with their astounded gibbering should you stray under a roost tree in the twilight.

Ah, but they are not the only wild turkeys in these parts. We know what we know, Site 14A. I know you will probably never read this, I doubt that you *can* read, frankly. There were no shreds of newspaper or charred magazines around the fire at your campsite among the other burnt offerings. Though granted you might have piled suchlike on top of the picnic table, along with the brand-new plastic lawn chairs, the new picnic cooler, the foamies and the sleeping bags—all purchased at Canadian Tire especially for the long weekend—before you poured gasoline on the pyre and touched it off with a smouldering Export-A. But there were no carbonized sentences scattered about; I myself was speechless. Are we to infer then that camping is not your thing? Smokey certainly hopes so. It was quite a piece of post-literate, deconstructionist sculpture you left behind for old Smokey to hose down, its base strewn with flowers of crumpled kleenex over every foot of ground. Oh how the merry stars of broken beer bottles sparkled under a confetti of cigarette butts, at the wedding of Ding and Dong. It wasn't a campsite, it was an ashtray; it was the inside of your heads exploded on the landscape.

I had a sheltered life, I see that now; I lived too long in the national parks. Then I tried to hide out in Aspen Valley for a while, brooding about man's fate. But you can't hide from Site 14A; you can't hide from an attitude. The only thing you can do with an attitude like this is shed light on it; flick it out from under its rock, and salt it with insights, hoping to see some changes.

In a green 4 x 4 I rode herd on platoons of dirt bikes and three-wheelers, checking for registration and insurance. I noted infractions of forestry, grazing or hunting regulations; but this time Smokey the Pig did not have full police powers. Arms folded, twitching spastically, Smokey growled as he watched the bikers rip and roar through the timber. They were a hazard to anything with eardrums. There was nothing in the regulations to say them nay, of course. This here's Al-bur-duh, bud. Where men are men and trees are nervous. In fact Bertie the Beaver, down at Blairmore, had given them his permit blessing. I told Myrna the opinions of a minion hath no dominion. I watched as they flayed the green hide off the belly of a virgin butte, leaving potential conduits of erosion, and future new creek beds aborning that nothing at all wanted. I tried to explain that simple concept to people whose engine displacements were inversely proportional to their cranial capacity. They grinned at me condescendingly as if I was mentally challenged. They could not relate to Smokey. I grinned back, searching for common ground. Guns, I thought. Smokey told the visitors about his hero, a Yellowstone Park ranger who, mounted upon a pair of snowshoes, blew away an illegal skidoo with his .45 when the operator tried to outrun him. That stopped the grins but not the motors.

"Have a really average day," I suggested, taking my leave. Rounding a corner a few minutes later, two riders shot across my path. I slammed on the brakes. They were mounted on shiny new three-wheelers. They went roaring straight up a dry wash set at a forty-degree angle, showering gravel and shredded willow leaves downslope. It was a dead heat. Near the top, both riders lost control: they jumped clear as their machines flipped over backwards. I watched in hysterical glee as the contraptions tumbled end over end for a hundred yards back down the hill and smashed into a rock pile. The engines hiccupped and stalled. The silence was golden.

That will teach you to laugh at Smokey. And I'm going to tell Bertie the Beaver on you, too.

The weather was hot and dry and lightning danced over the hills at night. The grass in the hills was gunpowder-dry, waiting for a fuse of lightning to ignite it. The fire lookouts grew jumpy up in their gondolas, mapping the strikes at night and watching for wisps of smoke by day. On July 11, a plume of smoke ascended above Tornado Peak, marking the Canal Flats fire in British Columbia. As the day proceeded, the smoke formed an ugly mushroom cloud five miles wide and five high above the mountains. I knew it was forty miles away, but I wondered what would happen if it jumped the Great Divide under a strong enough chinook wind. From the lookout, I could see the small white rectangle of our home at the foot of a forest, under the umbra of the great cloud.

The chinook wind during that summer of drought was a rough tongue in a hot, dry mouth dragged over any bare flesh it could spook out of the shade. It was the furnace wind my ancestors learned to hate in the nineteen twenties. As it toyed among the trembling aspens, their dried-out leaves rattled like castanets. Palliser's Triangle came creeping back onto the map. Farmers went to sleep dreaming about rain, but the next day, the clouds were "just empties goin' back." Then they woke up one morning and saw their prayers answered, as a dark cloud with an eerie yellowish tinge rode in on the wind's back. Yes, hallelujah Beulah land. Praise God. For this cloudburst of grasshoppers, devouring every green stem. Rattling down the stove pipe as in days of yore. Eating the clothes on the line; chewing on the straw broom left on the back steps, and turning the backroads into grease with their crushed corpses. Meanwhile, white ash from the distant fire fell as a parody of winter in a heat wave. Over in B.C., the main fire burned itself out of fuel but its outriders smouldered dangerously on in isolated mountain valleys.

*   *   *

I believe it was the black wind of drought, the rain of ashes and the infernal stuttering undertone of gasoline exploding in tiny cylinders, from dawn to dusk, that finally drove Tex, Guard Grouse of the Porcupine Hills, over the edge. God knows, he hated dirt bikes like poison.

Tex was a psychopathic male spruce grouse, a smoke-coloured bird with a fiery patch of orange over his eyes. He just materialized one day in the middle of the lookout tower road, all puffed up and looking for trouble. Tex, as Mike Williamson the towerman dubbed him, marched back and forth across the road; an angry strutter, high stepping, bobble necked. "Tut, tut tut," he warned, in a low, bad-assed manner. Tex attacked anything that moved, from field mouse to 4 x 4. Territorial imperative was his life's blood; the road was his Gaza Strip. "Watch out for Tex," warned Mike, watching Tex's antics through the big binoculars as he called me on the radio. "He's got an attitude."

The first time I went up to the lookout tower, Tex came running out of the bush, wings open like a cape, and pecked at the moving tires of my patrol truck. When I got out to investigate, Tex clacked away at my ankles like a pair of toenail clippers until I got back into the cab and drove away.

Mike and Laurie were not amused by Tex. Every time they put their baby, Riali, outside to play, Tex would come and chase her. They were afraid Tex might catch her on the eye. Laurie had a filly at the lookout that summer, name of Coyote. One time Tex came over clucking and gibbering, and went after Coyote. Mistaking the filly for a female spruce grouse, he flew up on her hindquarters to attempt fertilization. Coyote kicked Tex right over the woodshed.

Tex left Coyote alone after that, and shifted his attention to Mike. Mike was busy making a rope corral for Coyote one day when Tex

strutted over, mantled his wings in raptor-like posture to indicate possession of his turf, and hissed at Mike. At full fighting trim, Tex would
tip the scales at about two pounds, but in his own mind he was an
eagle. Mike had a coil of rope in his hand. He said something like,
"Tex, how'd you like to wind up in a frying pan with some butter and
maybe a few onions?" Tex flew at Mike's head. Mike swung the coil of
rope at Tex, scoring a base hit. Tex went sailing backwards and
bounced off a tree. But like a cowboy in a fist fight, punishment only
made Tex crazier. He circled for a moment to get his bearings, and came
after Mike again. Tex chased Mike partway up the tower ladder. "I
thought he might be rabid," explained Mike.

This easy victory went to Tex's head. One day the Jet Ranger helicopter came in for a landing. Seeing a strange bird on his turf, Tex came
running to attack, but the rotor blast swatted him back into the trees
like a shuttlecock. Nothing daunted, here he came again, mouth agape
with rage, though compelled to move in slow-mo. Meanwhile, Mike
was unloading supplies. At last Tex reached his enemy. He rapped
angrily on its metal landing skids until he forced the chopper to take off
again. At least, that's the way Tex called it. "Tut, tut tut," boasted Tex.
He did a war dance around the helipad, his breast feathers puffed with
pride, his tail feathers fanning the breeze.

It was his habit to leap up on the tailgate of the truck when I left the
lookout premises. Flapping up on the roof, he would ride with me for a
while to make sure I left. He banged away at that steel covering, trying
to drill a hole through it to reach my head. At the junction with the
Beaver Creek road one day, a squadron of dirt bikes had collected in a
rumbling rendezvous. I pulled over to answer a radio call, and forgot
about Tex, up on the roof.

"Hey Smokey," yelled one of the bikers. "Are you taking your dinner
home with you?"

They laughed, the mad fools, but not for long. There was a scrape of
talons on the roof and Tex launched himself at the bikers. The feathers
flew; arms flailed wildly and brave men and women swore with fear as
Tex gave them the full peckathon. Watching them fleeing back down
the road, motors snorting and popping, was a sight for sore eyes. When
last I saw Tex alive, he was rampant upon a helmet, pounding on it like
a feathered jackhammer as he rapidly receded from sight.

If only Tex had lived until skidoo season; he could have truly done the Lord's work. But he met his Waterloo—well, really it was a Toyotaloo he met—while working overtime one rainy night. Laurie was driving and didn't see him in the darkness. Perhaps he thought he was a great horned owl by then. We had hoped to collect his brain for science, but, alas, we could not find it.

*   *   *

Patrols were duller without Tex riding shotgun. In fact, driving around all day made me numb. I would park the truck, holster my portable radio, and take off hiking through the forest or up some ridge doing a smoke check. I loved to wander through the Douglas fir savannah, an open forest of giant trees a hundred feet in height and up to four feet in diameter, the largest trees in the province. A cross section of one of these Alberta giants is displayed in the Blairmore office. Its annual rings show it to be 330 years old.

Smokey was a merry minion, but Bertie the Beaver resented Smokey's freedom of movement. Bertie stayed close to the lodge, and he believed a ranger worked best in a sitting position, rising only to help plug information leaks in the red tape dam. Bertie suspected that any time Smokey was not driving around in the truck and jabbering on the radio, Smokey must be goofing off. When Smokey found a lightning strike in the old-fashioned way—using his nose instead of a space satellite—Bertie seemed to imply that Smokey had started the fire deliberately to justify his pedestrian habits. Bertie flew out from town in a Jet Ranger helicopter from which was suspended a monsoon bucket. The pilot scooped it full from a pond that was half water and half beaver shit. They came rotating in toward the strike. Bertie planned to empty that load on Smokey's head, but Smokey is telepathic. Also he knew Bertie from another movie. Smokey said look out. But four hundred gallons of beaver shit fell on Scott, a supervisor. His glasses turned black. Smokey had warned Scott that the woods can be dangerous, but he did not listen and now he was in shit, too. Scott shook the shit out of his radio and called, "Helicopter ATF, Sierra 62. Request you find some clean water for next drop. I need a shower."

*   *   *

Damage by all-terrain vehicles is just one of many cumulative assaults that are degrading the forest reserve and other Crown land in the east slopes of southern Alberta. Hereabouts, the problem lies in how the notion of multiple use of resources, a commendable idea, has been interpreted by politicians, to create what I think of as the Alberta Doctrine of Multiple Abuse. According to this pipe dream, you can have mining, cattle grazing, wolves, grizzly bears, big game hunting, clear-cut logging, gas wells, motorized recreation, cross-country skiing and resort developments all occurring simultaneously in the same habitat. And you can do this without conflict between the user groups, without loss of wildlife habitat and without declines in wildlife population. Most importantly, you can support these myriad activities, needs and species without impacting on the most important product of the east slopes: water.

You can defy ecologicial reality and satisfy every imaginable voter: you can eat your cake and have it too—providing you are deaf and blind and have the aesthetic sensibilities of a pocket gopher. I don't know what kind of medication the folks are on who believe in multiple use (probably Scotch and Coke), but they are in for some severe withdrawal pains one day.

In 1600 B.C., Emperor Yu of China said, "To protect your rivers, protect your mountains," but this ancient wisdom is too avant garde for the politicians of Alberta.

Clear-cut logging and road building in the watershed means that snow cover melts too fast, that soils are eroded, that water needed for grazing cattle and for irrigation runs off too fast. The government's solution, under the doctrine of multiple abuse, was not to limit logging, but to propose a dam project to retain the runoff, which would flood part of the valleys of three wild rivers—the Castle, the Crowsnest and the Oldman. It spent a million dollars on a consultant's report. The advice it received did not sit well with provincial politicians. It can be summed up thus: "More than enough water can be conserved by expanding your exisiting Keho Reservoir near Nobleford and upgrading your irrigation canals. A dam is not necessary, and the worst possible place you could build a dam would be at the Three Rivers site." The Conservative government, then in its monument-building phase, ignored its million-dollar advice and steam-rollered ahead with the $450 million Three Rivers Dam project. It proceeded, at first, without so much as a permit from Municipal District 9, where I am a ratepayer, or with a permit from the federal Department of Fisheries. The trophy trout fishery on the Crowsnest River is world famous, and part of it would be covered by the reservoir. The government broke the law and ultimately got away with it, though an environmental group, Friends of the Oldman River, took the government to court, and publicly humiliated it for its stupidity and arrogance. A federal environmental review commission did an impact study—after the dam was finished; they recommended that the dam be decommissioned. The recommendation was ignored.

Meanwhile, the government spent a few hundred million more dollars upgrading irrigation canals for its supporters in southern Alberta. Irrigation farmers, by the way, are subsidized to the tune of 85 percent of the costs of water resources. If farmers alone had to pay for those developments, they would never have been built.

Over the years, government spin-doctors have reamed off statistics to the public about the economic spin-off value of irrigation farming. There were twenty-eight farms and ranches in the path of the reservoir; some owners lost part of their land and others had to cease farming or ranching completely because the bulk of their land was appropriated. No studies were published about the cost to the town of Pincher Creek of shutting down entire farms whose occupants had been spending money in Pincher Creek for three generations. No government flak-catcher bothered to ask the farmers and ranchers what they thought about shopping in a town that was so eager to jump on the political space-shuttle, and trade long-term agri-dollars for short-term monument-building bucks. (Pincher Creek is hurting badly as I write this, with the dam now in operation, from high unemployment and customer losses to larger centres.)

As public fury over the flooding of three river valleys mounted, the government showed its environmental sensitivity. It changed the name to Oldman River Dam, creating the impression that only one river valley was being flooded. When the going gets tough, the tough change names.

*   *   *

There are 850,000 miles of seismic survey roads in Alberta. This is a province that *imports* toxic waste for local incineration, and whose taxpayers shell out $20 million a year to a private corporation to incinerate that imported toxic waste at a plant, the Swan Hills Waste Treatment Plant, that was built with tax dollars to begin with.

As the world contemplated the ominous destruction of its rainforests, this province was busy allocating its entire boreal forest, an area the size of Great Britain, to mega corporations like Daishowa and Alberta Pacific Forest Industries Inc. It approved the construction of megalithic pulp mills whose effluents drain into the Mackenzie River, thence to the Arctic Ocean. And it threw in $1 billion in loan guarantees and government assistance to the industry just to sweeten the deal.

Dear Minister of Forestry: Ask not what our forests can do for us, but rather what we can do for our forests. Will we still be logging at the present crack-brained rate ten or twenty years hence, when your own data tell you that 38 percent of logged areas have not, for various reasons, regenerated? Will we be logging at all twenty years from now? Dear Minister of the Environment: The forest is the principal in the environmental savings account; the logs, the potable water, oxygen and wildlife—this is the interest the forest/principal produces. You have let your multinational cohort carve up the lion's share of our public principal. Virtually every publicly owned tree in Alberta is earmarked for cutting. You will leave us with an environmental deficit, which will translate into an economic deficit in lost jobs, lost recreation opportunities and losses in air and water quality that no one can even measure in dollar bills.

An environmentalist in Alberta feels like a boy scout in hell. Better learn to love being abused. For a decade now, we have had to put up with a succession of environment ministers and politicians who know as much about ecology and environmental issues as I know about nuclear physics, and whose main means of communication lies in opening their mouths to change feet.

Blame it on the electorate.

Canadians do not have heroes; they have hockey players. Similarly, Alberta's blue-chip élite prefer their conservative politicians to be smaller than life, and hence easier to influence. And voters here think at least once before voting for anybody perceived as an intellectual. Unfortunately, once baptized with the holy water of notoriety, our environment ministers in particular tend to swell up like freeze-dried ham. And as their aides wince in horror, they begin to share their thoughts.

The Hon. Ken Kowalski was a man whose grasp of environmental issues in no way exceeded his reach. He operated as if he was minister of public works, and rammed through the Oldman River Dam project over all objections, including the objections of Friends of the Oldman River (FOR) and the 8,000-plus people who came out for Ian Tyson's Oldman River Dam Concert in 1991. It was Kowalski who first called environmentalists dope-smoking "social anarchists," and it was a courageous Kowalski who shocked the fashion industry by pointing out that bra-less women were known to be environmentalists.

Pincher Creek, Alberta, located a few miles from the Oldman dam site, was one platform where Kowalski delighted the credulous ears of Alberta's staunchest Conservatives with his scintillating wit. Squeals of approval greeted his notorious remark that real environmentalists are "people like yourselves who come to meetings wearing suits." It was the fashion-conscious Kowalski who told True Blue Suits that the other environmentalists always wear patched jeans and wire-rimmed glasses and sport long, tick-infested hair. According to Kowalski, when these hirsute imposters go hiking suitlessly into the foothills, "they maybe even discovered some grass they never heard of, because when they seem to come down, they sure get pretty high."

The reign of the ecologically challenged has continued to this day. Recently, citizens have objected to the wholesale stripping of timber from privately owned land without any environmental controls, because this land is often an important additive to watershed quality and wildlife habitat. The loggers have moved in from British Columbia where the New Democratic Party government has imposed quotas on logging. Ty Lund, current minister of the environment, was not about to suggest to landowners that they should submit to regulations and controls. Instead, at the height of the boom, while three million dollars worth of logs and potential sawmill jobs left the province every 48 hours, he blasted the socialist government across the mountains for allowing the loggers to drive their trucks into Alberta.

Should Ty Lund ever dry up and blow away, like the banks of the Oldman River Reservoir in a chinook wind, MLA Lorne Taylor can take his place. Mr. Taylor, who apparently commutes to Edmonton from the eighteenth century, believes the idea of preserving a piece of wilderness from all and any development "is an idea of eco-terrorists." It is, I believe, also an idea entertained by H.R.H. Prince Philip, international president of the World Wildlife Fund, a very conservative conservationist indeed, who lives in the twentieth century with an eye on the twenty-first.

I recall so many of the fights that conservationists have waged to save old growth forests and set land aside for wildlife, and how they have lost nearly all of them. But in southern Alberta, the Oldman River Dam fight was one that tempered their mettle. The fight to save a lesser mountain known as Prairie Bluff was the one where they finally realized that something more than well-written briefs and reasoned, scientific argument would be needed if we are to defeat the ecologically challenged, boom-and-bust culture of destruction that powers this province.

There came a moment when I had to acknowledge the truth that I had been pushing away for a long time—that no place is safe from the developmentalists. If you do not help to fight them, you will wake up one morning like the Indians in the rainforest, surrounded by bulldozers. This reawakening of the will to resist came to me in 1987.

It started, as many stories do in this era of instant communication and delayed action brains, with the ringing of a telephone. . . .

17

HEADLIGHTS AT THE
GRIZZLY'S DEN

~

Mike Judd never flat-out asked me to go up on Corner Mountain to help stop the lions of progress from clawing a road up Prairie Bluff, a 7,000-foot-high plateau southwest of Pincher Creek. As a matter of fact, it was his former wife, Wendy, who had phoned me one evening in early November. I could hear kids yelling in the background as Wendy explained how Mike (a guide and outfitter at Beaver Mines), along with James Tweedy (a local cabinetmaker), had discovered Shell Canada bulldozers building a road up the bluff, which is Crown land. They were not surprised by the discovery. Mike and James are long-time members of the Alberta Wilderness Association, and the AWA had appealed to the Energy Resources Conservation Board (ERCB) in September to deny Shell a gas well drilling permit on the bluff. Their request was denied, as usual.

Mike and James had done something that marked a first for the AWA: they went and asked the work crews to stop the destruction. The men shut down their machines, and Shell called the police. Mike was warned that he could be charged with "public mischief" if he got in Shell's way again. That's what they call civil disobedience in the province where I was raised.

Prairie Bluff is Crown land located in the Alberta Forest Reserve. Corner Mountain (7,396 feet) rises from the north end of the bluff, and Victoria Peak (8,400 feet) rises from the south end. These are part of the chain of front range mountains that form the magnificent skyline between Pincher Creek and Waterton Lakes. The range is interrupted by steep-sided canyons, the headwaters of trout streams, canyons that funnel the chinook wind out over the adjacent prairie. Every one of these valleys contains roads, pipelines and gas wells. These mountains were once part of Waterton Lakes National Park, and I wish to hell they still were, because then somebody would protect them. This is valuable winter range, always in short supply, for a herd of bighorn sheep. It is part of what biologists refer to as the Crown of the Continent Ecosystem, which takes in mountainous country from the Bob Marshall Wilderness of Montana north to the Crowsnest Pass. This expanse of land is vital for the survival of wolves, grizzly bears and other predators that move back and forth across both international and provincial boundaries. Since 1950, 290 miles of roads have been built in the surrounding mountain area, resulting in a 45 percent loss of elk habitat and a decline in elk and grizzly bear populations, according to the Castle-Crown Wilderness Coalition.

The summit of Prairie Bluff offers a panorama east over the prairies and south to Chief Mountain that is stunning to behold. The bluff is windswept, the plant cover is scarce and slow growing and the alpine habitat it encompasses is not only fragile but is itself a very small portion of the Alberta land mass. These surrounds of mountains and river valleys offer 120 rare species of vascular plants, three times more than are found in Banff National Park.

The government had approved Shell's application to bulldoze roads and drilling pads on the bluff, build a powerline and drill for gas even though the sites were in a high-altitude "Prime Protection Zone" described by the Department of Energy and Natural Resources as a zone to "preserve environmentally sensitive terrain and valuable aesthetic resources." It was an unjust decision that would finally provoke normally restrained and cautious conservationists into direct action against the developmentalists.

If you live on the east slopes of the Rockies, and you love the mountains, you are just bound to wind up wrestling with oil company behemoths, and these companies, always on a tag team with the provincial government, seldom lose the match. This perception is shared by a lot of people who care about publicly owned land. Mike Judd summed it up this way: "The government and the oil companies are the same thing." You might say the government is a company's major shareholder, since it stands to scoop up millions of dollars in royalties from natural gas sales. (How many millions I can't say. Alberta Energy wouldn't tell me what our government received from Shell. The information was confidential.)

I wasn't sure if I wanted to take another psychic mauling from these two giants just then. I told Wendy I would think it over. I went to bed and lay awake for a long time. I told myself it would be crazy to go and stand in front of a bulldozer driven by a perfect stranger. It's not a good way to get acquainted. But then I started thinking about other things.

I thought about dirt bikes, skidoos and 4 x 4s running amok, about hunters chasing elk on opening day in the Porcupines that year in a 4 x 4 truck, shooting rifles out of the window. I thought about all those oil company roads, out there in the darkness, groping around in nearly every valley along the east slopes. Headlights at the grizzly's den.

"I wonder if Mike's asleep yet," I said out loud.

"Of course he's asleep," said Myrna. "Just like I was until you woke me up."

I phoned Mike and woke *him* up. It seemed nobody else was available at dawn to go up on the mountain. Mike was worried about going back there by himself. "I wouldn't ask anybody to go along on a thing like this," he said quietly.

"Well, I'll go with you. I'd like to try and write something about it for the funny papers, to at least let people know what's going on."

That's how Mike and I wound up at Shell's upper well site on Prairie Bluff in the chilly hours before dawn one November day. A narrow valley here leads to the summit of the bluff. I pulled my old Dodge Coronet off to one side. The venerable landship let out a long gurgling sigh of relief, and assumed a position of neglect.

"You don't think they'll sort of 'doze the landship off the mountain, do you?" I asked Mike as we pulled on our packs.

"They'd better not," he replied encouragingly.

The well site, flooded with artificial light, was full of men and equipment. There were several large bulldozers, and a number of Rota-screw rock-drilling machines ready to screw the earth. Men were scampering around their rumbling charges looking efficient and keen to get on with the legalized assault on Prairie Bluff. Down below us, near the company field office, we could hear the whine of helicopter engines warming up.

The first light of dawn crept arthritically across the vast prairie below the mountain foot. It gleamed on the towering smokestack of a gas plant a few miles to the east. Fireflies of light streamed down the roads that radiated out from the plant like the glimmering tentacles of an octopus. A company supervisor came roaring up the road in an expensive-looking car. He eyed us suspiciously, slapped leather and drew his cellular phone or whatever. But he didn't try to stop us as we started walking up the mountainside.

"He'll be calling the Mounties, I imagine," said Mike.

We walked in silence for a while. I was feeling queasy about taking on the law. As a former park warden, I had been a bona fide peace officer, and I'd stood back to back with the Mounties on occasion to fight off platoons of rioting drunks in the park campgrounds. That was many dead Tories ago, but I still felt strange, as if walking up the trail into willful exile. Both of us live on a shoestring budget. As a guide and outfitter, Mike cannot afford to place himself in a confrontation with government agencies that regulate where and how he does business. But those same agencies had presided over the destruction of far too much of the wild terrain he needs to stay in business. Tourists are funny. They don't enjoy trail riding through clear cuts, seismic lines, powerlines and gas well sites. Underneath Mike's calm exterior, he was starting to do a slow burn that would lead to an explosion.

I glanced at him. "How many people will be coming out to protest this thing?"

Mike grinned. "There'll be at least four here from the AWA by 10:30."

Four!

Surveys have shown that 80 percent of Albertans think our wildlife should be conserved. Wildlife needs wildlands. There are thousands of people in this province whose incomes depend on the existence of wildlands: photographers, mountain guides, biologists, outdoors writers—the entire tourism industry. What about all the storekeepers who sell cross-country skis, hunting and fishing equipment? What about the thousands of backpackers, hunters, skiers, the rangers, wardens, professors of environmental science—an endless list of potential defenders, and we had five protestors and one writer. No wonder we're being eaten alive by "progress."

It was 7:30. Mike was going to try to hold off the lions for three hours. He had only one card to play.

A cold wind, a hard wind that whipped particles of shale against our faces like buckshot, was coming down the little valley. I could see a narrow white scar leading up the mountainside, an old trail partially drifted in with shale. It was built twenty years ago to install a radio tower on Corner Mountain. The summit of the peak, at 7,400 feet, was up there beyond the red rock bands of Prairie Bluff, which forms a high plateau at its base. Up above us on the summit of the bluff were the two drill sites. The bulldozers would widen this road to get to the sites, towing the rock drills behind them. This old trail could not be made safe for permanent use, according to Shell Canada, but opening it temporarily meant they could start work on their drill sites right away. Once on top, the crews would begin cutting their way through the fragile meadow, going deep enough to grade out a level spot on the steep slope. They would have to push aside a thin soil cover in the Prime Protection Zone that had taken 10,000 years to accumulate. One operator would work his 'dozer down from the summit, following Bar Creek to the south, building a section of the new road, and eventually meet up with the one Mike and James had confronted on November 1. That 'dozer was now stopped by a rock spur that would have to be blasted out with high explosive.

When Shell were finished building on Prairie Bluff, the ram pastures there would be an industrialized landscape. There would be a new road up the tiny perfect valley of Bar Creek, blasted through rock spurs on forty-five degree slopes. Shell promised to install a gate on the new road to deter 4 x 4s.

Gas wells on the mountain tops! At least Shell does not tolerate any litter around their gas wells, and they keep their pipe mazes well painted. Royal purple was one of their favourite colours at that time.

The wind that first morning was gusting hard enough that we had to brace both feet to stay upright. We got down behind a stand of dwarf-like bullpine, and instantly found ourselves in a little pocket of calm in which to wait for the bulldozers. While the sun's first rays arched over the prairie, we sat mulling over the events that had brought the AWA to this confrontation with a multinational corporation. Of the 4,500 drilling permits requested by the industry so far that year, these two permits were the only ones that conservationists had contested, because they were in the Prime Protection Zone.

Now one of the things that deeply troubles some Albertans is that permits like Shell's can be issued without a full environmental impact assessment (EIA) being undertaken. That is a survey of effects not only on recreation but on many other features, including wildlife, soils and plants as well as the social and economic effects of development. The AWA had been attempting for over a year, without success, to get the Department of the Environment to do an EIA of Prairie Bluff. Such an assessment is admittedly expensive, but the government does have employees and resources for doing such work, and the oil companies should help to foot the bill for it, in my view. After all, the gas that Shell wanted to produce on this publicly owned mountain was destined for export. The main beneficiary, after royalties are paid, was a foreign-owned corporation, Shell Canada, that generated $5.3 billion in sales and operating revenue in 1985. Shell hoped to recover 20 billion cubic feet of gas, worth about $300 million, from these new wells. Even a million dollars for an EIA would not be out of line. To Shell's credit, they employed a biologist to do an inventory on the bighorn sheep population on the bluff (at a cost of $75,000). Still, in the United States, an EIA would be mandatory in a case like this. Our government has no policy requirement that EIAs be done for any project, even when they take place at the source of our drinking water supplies.

The bluff provided vital winter range for bighorn sheep habitat in an area often cited as the best bighorn sheep habitat in the world. At a September hearing, Shell's biologist testified that the development shouldn't interfere unduly with bighorn sheep use of the bluff for winter range and mating activity. Shell would restrict its activities to "windows" of use. They had until November 30 to complete their construction. Then the bighorns could return until drilling activity began for the May 1–November 30 window. Shell was trying to show good will to the bighorns. But wait a moment; weren't there other mammals living on the bluff—deer, bears, wolverines etc.? What about them? And what about the rights of Alberta citizens who don't enjoy hiking, riding and experiencing wildlife right next to an industrial development, on publicly owned land? Such concerns went unheeded.

As we sat sipping our coffee that morning, we could see a huddle of men down below us obviously confused over what to do about the two "crazies" up on the mountain trail. It was then I spotted the police car wending its way up the switchbacks down below. Sure enough, one of the bulldozers idling at the foot of the trail finally came to life with a metallic scream and started grinding its way up the steep slope toward us. The cruiser pulled into the parking lot below. We stepped out on the trail in the dim morning light. The huge orange machine crawled closer, closer. I could see the operator huddled over his controls as the shiny blade lifted higher, the cat tilted up, the blade hung suspended in mid-air.

"Just stand your ground," ordered Mike.

"Uh, Mike. Remember I'm here as a journalist."

Mike laughed unpleasantly. He glared down at the well site below us, and muttered an outdoorsy saying or two. The blade slammed down into the gravelly trail. There was a hummock of gravel and a shallow ditch that was supposed to deter dirt bikes from roaring up the mountainside: it never has. The big blade bit into it, and shoved the pile toward us, flattening it out. A few stones rolled to a stop in front of us. I made like a reporter and took some pictures. The operator stopped the machine and stared at us. I thought, here we go. Now he's going to blade us right off the mountain. Instead, he just shrugged his shoulders and grinned as if to say, "I just work here," and sat back in his seat to wait for instructions from his foreman.

"Keep him here," said Mike suddenly. "I'm going down there to talk to them."

I swallowed nervously. "Why, what's up?"

He hurried over to talk to the operator. He was going to play his one card.

"Have you got a permit to go up here?" he shouted over the engine noise.

The operator shrugged again. He had his orders.

Mike turned to me. "They need a letter signed by Art Evans to go up this trail."

I stared at him, catching his drift. Evans was the Chief Forest Ranger for the area, based in Blairmore, Alberta, some miles to the north. Without a letter from him Shell had no legal right to begin work here, and any citizen certainly had a right to ask them to stop.

Mike went tearing down the hill to talk to Shell's foreman. I went over to talk to the operator, get his point of view. He said it's too bad that we have to do this, but I just work here, or words to that effect. The policeman was standing by his cruiser just then, watching events unfold. Everything was too well orchestrated, like a badly scripted play. In a few minutes Mike came panting back up the trail.

"They don't have it!" he cried, elated. "Can you believe it! They never even bothered to get that letter. We've got 'em."

The victory was short-lived. A forestry truck soon appeared on the scene. We watched as the Mountie went to confer with the new arrivals, a forest land use officer from Calgary and a forestry officer from the Blairmore office.

"They're cooking up that letter right now," I warned Mike.

"They can't do that!"

I didn't say anything. I had some experience in these matters. The forest officers could act for Evans if he gave the word by radio, and I didn't see how anyone could do much about it.

We stood in front of the 'dozer, the hard wind blowing at our backs, getting down the back of our necks, getting closer to the bone. Pretty soon a small knot of men started climbing up toward us. One of them clutched a scrap of paper in his hand. It's always amazed me how much damage can be done to entire mountain ranges just with a few words scribbled by a ballpoint pen.

I looked at Mike, a tough, medium-sized man in a black wool cap, a pack on his back, worn climbing boots on his feet. He is a horseman, and has the right build for the trade. Behind him the mountain loomed, a threatened giant, an elephant guarded by a pair of ants. By 9 a.m. that morning, it would be all over but the shouting. We would have to stand back and watch as the 'dozers bit deep into the side of Prairie Bluff and the falling rocks went rattling down the shale slope.

We left the mountain shortly afterwards. By the time we returned later that morning with Vivian Pharis, president of the AWA, executive director Diane Pachal and two other members, the old trail had become a road once more. The 'dozers were already starting work on the drilling pads on the summit of the bluff.

That was the beginning of a week-long confrontation between the

AWA and Shell that only subsided when Shell got an injunction to keep the AWA and everybody else out of the working area. The AWA managed to slow down some of the work before the injunction came into effect. Members would walk in front of the 'dozers carrying picket signs. News media from Calgary and Lethbridge filmed some of the action. So did Shell.

To some of the operators, the pickets must have seemed like members of a union, manning a line that they, as fellow workers, should not cross. As one man said to Mike Judd, "That's okay, you have a job to do I guess." He was nonplussed when Mike explained, "Hey, I don't get paid to do this." It was puzzling for the workers. I think they started resenting the protestors after a while for expecting them somehow to be better than they were able to be, to suddenly develop the elegant principles of conservationists when they were working men with families to feed and not predisposed by habit or inclination to spend time informing themselves on complex environmental issues. They had to make a living. Here you are, working away, proud of your skills at cat skinning or blasting, and those bozos keep waving their signs at you—"Save the Bluff"—as if what you are doing is somehow evil. This makes you irritable, and on two occasions the protestors felt the earth move before an overzealous operator backed off. But it was obvious that Shell was determined not to make martyrs of the opposition.

There were some bizarre moments that week. The sight of news reporters climbing up a mountainside in shiny patent-leather shoes and trench coats was good for comic relief. Mike Nikotuk from the Canadian Broadcasting Corporation conducted one of the strangest interviews I've seen in a while. By that time there were five protestors on the bluff, and more were on the way. Three bulldozers were blading up the heather at one site. Three hundred yards to the north, crews had already stripped the topsoil for another pad just below the summit of Corner Mountain after pushing a trail through the forest to get there. I'm not sure that Nikotuk grasped the terrible damage that had been done to the fragile soils of the mountain. He gathered the little knot of protestors together and began firing questions at them. Nikotuk, recently arrived from the west coast, wanted to do a new angle on the AWA. His view seemed to be: If this were Vancouver, there'd be thousands of demonstrators here. Obviously the people of this province don't agree with your position, so why do you bother protesting?

Nikotuk hit a sore point. Diane Pachal pointed out that there are 2,500 members in the AWA alone. I couldn't help wondering myself where the hell they all were right then. They couldn't all be working, out of the country or having babies at that moment. Of course, this is the problem with leaving environmental police work to volunteer organizations. Somebody working for an oil company as an in-house "social anarchist" (i.e., Environmental Co-ordinator) was making forty to fifty thousand dollars a year from environmental issues. They need an aroused citizenry to keep them employed. It is the AWA and other organizations that arouse the citizenry who don't have time to track every environmental outrage going on in this province on any given day. Those who try to stop developments like this have to take time off work and pay their own expenses in order to do the work that well-paid civil servants and politicians are supposed to be doing for us. Eventually, this cripples you both financially and psychically. But Diane Pachal probably gave the best answer that day on the bluff. She swept her arm around to indicate the beautiful plateau, the prairies to the east, the towering wall of Victoria Peak behind us. "I believe there are thousands of people who support our stand here. But even if I was the only person in Alberta who cared about this beautiful landscape, I would still be here. These mountains demand it of us."

My thoughts went back to the first day of the picket, when Mike and I had been alone. We stood in the howling chinook wind that blew down from the summit of the bluff. Constable Foster of the RCMP told Mike he would have to stand aside and let the bulldozers come through. Backing him up were the two Forest Service officers, Shell's foreman and several other employees. I exchanged ironic looks with the forest rangers, who were known to me. No words were said, but I knew that, hard as it might be on Bertie the Beaver, he was going to have to struggle along without yours truly.

"Where's the letter from the Chief Ranger?" demanded Mike.

One of the rangers produced a sheet of paper with a handwritten note, and handed it to Mike.

Mike glanced at it and handed it back. "That's not good enough. That's not signed by Art Evans."

Constable Foster, a neighbour of Mike's and a man he likes and respects, said quietly, "Mike, it is good enough. And I'm telling you, you'll have to accept it."

As they spoke, the wind howled in stronger protest. It struck Mike in the back and threw him forward, as if urging him into the fray. I caught him by one arm to stop him from flying into the opposition. We were all holding on to our hats, our opponents leaning forward and moving their legs as if on a treadmill to hold their ground, while Mike and I had to lean backwards and shuffle uphill. One of the men tried to explain how Shell was going to repair all the damage they would do on the mountain when the gas wells on the bluff went dry. I believe he was sincere, but the wind blew the words back down his throat.

That's when Mike finally let go some of the bitterness that had been building up in him over the last decade of exploitation in these mountains. He had been to so many east slope policy information sessions and hearings, had swallowed so many paragraphs of bafflegab promises and buzzwords from government flak-catchers and industry mouthpieces while the bulldozers and chainsaws did their deadly work, that he was full to the brim with it all. Now he spat it all back up, and cut to the heart of the issue.

"Look at that road behind us!" he yelled over the roar of the wind. "That was done twenty years ago and the scar will last hundreds of years. You'll be gone from here in twenty years, and this is what we'll be left with! This is the best bighorn habitat in the world. You'll never put it back, you'll never make Bar Creek like it was. You can't do it! You—"

Mike's voice was partially drowned out as the wind hit him again, throwing him forward. He was yelling some pornographic descriptions about his opponent's lineage. I caught him again. The wind pushed us all down the steep slope as if we were sailors plunging through a gale.

Constable Foster tried to comfort Mike. He put his arm around him, his other hand anchoring his hat. "I know how you feel—"

Mike shrugged off the gesture. The wind spun him round and nearly knocked him to his knees. He said what we all say in that situation. "No you don't! You don't know how I feel." Mike was the loneliest thing in the world at that moment, except for the mountain brooding over his shoulder like a beast at bay. "It's greed!" he yelled. "That's all it is. After all the bullshit, it just gets down to one thing; just greed!"

The other men looked away, embarrassed. Albertans hate making a scene while they are trying to eat. Whether Shell realized it or not, it was the brave notion of the Prime Protection Zone, it was the very idea that something should be allowed to exist that wasn't generating money—that idea was what it had come to eat that day.

The bulldozers were lining up below now. Tons of iron and steel, thousands of horsepower. The helicopter was lifting off its pad. One fierce-hearted man stood in front of them for a final moment, and Prairie Bluff, sending its winds in protest over the ram pastures and the coloured shale, over the weathered little fir trees and the tough wisps of flower stalks, awaited its fate.

Mike stepped aside and climbed up the mountainside. He sat down, fighting back bitter tears. In a few minutes he would apologize to those minions of the law and progress for his rough language. The people who should have been there to get the benefit of his rage were safely hidden behind steel towers in Calgary and Edmonton, Toronto and London, or in the helicopter that would soon be circling overhead, watching our every move.

High above Prairie Bluff, on a ridge of Victoria Peak, there is a dream bed: a circle of stones, a lichen-covered cairn. For 12,000 years, maybe longer, young warriors came to this place to gaze over the prairie and stare at two great spiritual landmarks: Chief Mountain to the south, Crowsnest Mountain to the north. They fasted and prayed for a spirit guardian to visit them in visions, to grant them the secret of its power. They prayed mainly for courage, so they could flourish in a dangerous world armed with stone knives and spears, long before the bow. Often the spirit guardian took the shape of a bird or animal: an eagle, an elk, a grizzly bear. They would be directed to obtain an eagle feather, an elk tooth, a bear claw—some such totem of the spirit's power to keep in their medicine bundle. This eight-foot circle of lichen-covered stones, sunk into the mountain earth, is the memorial of all those generations. That is the total impact of the ancients on this piece of mountain earth.

That day, a magical thing had happened below the dream bed. Huge roaring beasts the colour of paintbrush flowers in the summer were devouring the earth of Prairie Bluff, sending up clouds of dust and smoke. They had only been there for a few hours, but they had transformed the mountain in those few hours, forever.

Goodbye, Prairie Bluff.

*   *   *

The wind blows and it spreads the news. I know that my neighbours have grandchildren visiting today, and I know that one of them lost his jacket this morning because I found it hanging on the barbed-wire cross fence of the horse pasture where the wind had left it. I knew when an "outsider" (as they call strangers here) bought a quarter section upwind from ours even before the Local Oracle told me about it. I knew that the new owner was from the city, because when I went out to feed Candy, she was staring down at a sign lying in the snow that said "NO TRES-PASSING" in bright red letters. It was the only No Trespassing sign in the valley back then, and the wind had torn that sign off his fence and wafted it over the top of our hill like a plywood frisbee to land in the corral. I am glad to report that he has not put the sign back up.

Down south along the North Burmis road there is a small memorial to man's hubris and the wind's power. On a stark, bare promontory, completely exposed to the elements, there is a cement pad where a stranger intended to build a house. If he had asked around, he would have discovered that it is probably the windiest place in the valley, and outside of Blow Me Down in Newfoundland, where we once camped, and duly had our tents blown down, that little spot below Cirque Peak may be the windiest spot in Canada. When the chinook came calling, it lifted up that entire supply of building boards and scattered them all over the range. The stranger quit his project in disgust.

A local rancher gleefully collected the boards and built himself a nice little barn with them. But it seems the wind has a law against that too. It was not long after that barn was built, and this neighbour was proudly surveying it and congratulating himself on his good luck, that a cyclone took shape in an unusual spot—right at the foot of the mountain, just one mile west of the celebrated barn. No one in the valley can recall a cyclone occurring here before; it is a phenomenon associated with the prairies a few miles to the east. But that cyclone came dancing across the valley as if an invisible hand smoothed the treetops in a long line, and it headed straight for the new barn. When it was done, the boards were scattered all over the hills again, though the rest of the place was barely touched.

*   *   *

Change is the cyclone that has caught up to Municipal District 9. Gravel roads discouraged city people from exploring our valley. But

Change came with the paving and widening of Highway 22. We have been "discovered." Country properties are being snapped up at unheard-of prices, but prices that seem cheap to those people who know what land costs near the major centres.

The traffic has mushroomed on 22, peaking on weekends. It consists of folks in fast cars whose lives are ruled by schedules—the most dangerous people on earth. Ranchers don't stop in the middle of the road to visit any more. Now you either adapt to the new agenda, which is the old Boomer agenda with more horsepower, or die. Highway 22 connects Calgary with ski hills and summer resorts in B.C. and Montana. This is not good. Skiers in muscle cars had missed killing me by inches on a number of occasions in Banff National Car Park. I hate to see them on our highway, but now they own it. Alberta petrobucks are flowing heavily again.

A local rancher saw the chance to convert a quarter section into cash, and did so. Another, who was not beloved of his neighbours anyway, was inspired to do more. He divided off as many chunks of his property as he could, and he cashed in on the demand for "recreational" property. Then he pulled out, left his neighbours to contend with the new reality. Almost overnight, we find that five city couples have bought property here.

Newcomers are not by definition a detriment; far from it. This is a place where you are still a newcomer after ten years of residence. They will have to see how your grandchildren turn out before they consider you tenured. There are a few founding families, noted for their arrogance, that like to hammer you with "My family's been here since 1885." To which you might be tempted to reply that in some cases the undesirables got here first. So a person who buys a small piece of property here to visit only on the odd weekend may prove an asset yet. He or she pays some taxes; he enjoys the fly fishing; the pleasure she takes hiking the hills brushes off on the locals.

But the greatest thing the ranching lifestyle can offer is freedom of movement. Though I live on a small property, I have access to thousands of acres of neighbouring land on which to go riding, hiking, hunting or camping. All I have to do in return is keep up my own fences and close the gates behind me so the cattle cannot escape. This little world was in balance, because change had come very slowly.

When the first city people come, they bring their city mindset along.

Some, not all thank heavens, immediately nail up No Trespassing and No Hunting signs. Next they may chain and lock all the gates, including those giving traditional access, shortcuts from one piece of land to another, or to the forest reserve. There is little consideration for local ways of doing things; no notion, I suspect, that this might be a community, that such a thing as a land use ethic might already exist among these rustics.

We still don't lock our doors at night in Aspen Valley.

I fear the day when we are all confined within the borders of mere property, when our interests become narrower and narrower and we have less and less of a common purpose, less and less responsibility to the land, and to each other; the day we start locking our doors. I put the thought from my mind with a shiver.

What we risk losing here is the very thing that makes our valley the Great, Good Place: that delicate flower of trust, like a cowboy poem proffered in work-calloused hands between neighbours.

The oldtimers grumbled about the invasion but they tend to resign themselves to things a bit too easily, in my opinion. The last straw came, however, when some newcomers bought some bottom land zoned A-1 (agricultural land), then immediately turned around and applied for approval to subdivide it into smaller pieces, and to cut off the customary access road used by an old-time family. The M.D. 9 Council and the Oldman River Planning Commission (OMRPC) granted approval. This type of subdivision is contrary to the intent of our local bylaw, and the folks sat down and scratched out some pained letters to appeal the decision—but all to no avail. The appeal board ruled against us.

The OMRPC was once a public body answerable to government, but under the current Ralph Klein regime, it was cut back to the point where it became a privately run corporation, a private institution making public land use decisions under contract to municipal governments such as M.D. 9. In 1994 the OMRPC received $250 for each application to subdivide, $300 for each subdivision it granted and $150 for every land title it endorsed. It was contrary to good business for it to turn down applications. It was a go-ahead outfit; it was making money on land use decisions, all part of the skewed logic of our Brave New Alberta. Under this government, a mob of free market libertarians by any other name, there are wolves running every chicken coop. Another screwball decision is made, which means another battle for the citizens, another appeal to lodge with the Alberta Appeal Board; more of our diminishing time must be wasted to defend our own zoning laws, laws that we do not want changed in the first place. More of our hard-earned dough will have to be spent to hire lawyers to defend us against the acts of our own officials and politicians.

What is needed is the political will to protect large tracts of agricultural land, including grazing land, from falling into the hands of speculators. The incoming acreage owners need not destroy the economic balance if their purchase is limited to a few acres. But if they start buying quarter sections to speculate on, their money fuels land price rises that the young rancher cannot compete with. He cannot pay a thousand dollars an acre for land that is only worth three hundred in terms of production.

As the speculators take hold, they keep applying to subdivide their holdings into smaller pieces, and more and more people move in. Inevitably, there comes a time when they outnumber and outvote the agriculturalists. They will want to change the agricultural zoning that protects the farmer's operations—"That feed lot, my dear, you can't imagine the odour!"—and protects this place from commercial exploitation. The golf courses and condominiums will follow. No need to worry about hunters then; there won't be any game left to hunt, no room to roam without fences. But we can import the beef, the produce, the grain from Mexico. The rancher's kids can get a great minimum wage job riding a lawnmower.

And what starts this ball rolling, of course, is the rancher or farmer who sells the first big piece of recreation property.

Ranchers and farmers think of themselves, usually, as conservationists. In M.D. 9, many ranchers resented the environmental activists who came to protest the Oldman dam construction. They did not like outsiders lecturing them or their politicians on the environment. But locally, only these agriculturalists and their economic cohort have the political clout to rock the Conservative government; since they are its staunchest supporters. They have the power, if they choose to use it, to enforce agricultural zoning laws and protect their own interests. What defeats them is their own stubborn individualism, their dislike of not having total control, without regulation or caveat, over their property. This stubbornness is appealing, in many ways it is commendable, but it cannot be sustained in the face of development. Soon they must decide to either stand together, maintain a common front as a community and protect the agricultural zoning, or prepare to fall, one by one, until the names of the founders disappear from the M.D. map.

*   *   *

Every once in a while, thanks be, our species does something endearing. Man the inventor has solved some of the problems inherent in wind-generated electricity. There are braking systems in place now that will shut down wind turbines at 65 m.p.h., when the big wind gets too rough. They have better towers, better lubricants, interior heating systems to keep control parts from freezing up. There are now fifty-two of these modern wind machines sitting on the Cowley ridge, raking the sky with twenty-six-foot-long blades on eighty-foot-high towers. They are impressive, and though ugly, they seem less so when you realize that they produce a combined total of eighteen megawatts of electricity, and the air that blows through their blades is clean both coming and going. And they offer something else, for those who are bored gazing at one of the most sublime mountain views on earth, which these machines have now upstaged, stuck up there on the skyline like the spur rowels of buried cowboy deities, raking the sky. As a certain local lady put it, "At least now we have something interesting to look at from Cowley." If only the power from them could be used locally to lower our power rates, instead of going into the grid for allocation in the United States; now that would be a real green development.

Sometimes I feel like a Martian; either that, or the Martians have landed and I am the only Earthling around. They tell me at the local Economic Development Board that I am the only person in M.D. 9 who felt the Cowley windfarm detracted from the mountain view. But I don't believe that; it would make me crazy if I believed that I am the only person in M.D. 9 who is not blind.

*   *   *

God save Alberta from Men and Women of Vision, with which the place is positively brimming, these days, according to what I see in the funny papers, meaning the newspapers Myrna brings home from Pincher Creek. Vision is the most overused word in creation just now, along with network, mentor and the F. word. In Alberta, when a Man of Vision looks at a 10,000-foot-high snow-capped mountain, he sees a golf course. Elsewhere, these folks are called certifiable and consigned to the grin-bin for treatment. Here they are called visionaries. William Blake, the poet, had visions. If your typical real estate developer or right-wing politico had one vision a tenth as powerful as one of Blake's, he would be catatonic for the rest of his life.

I know they are "visioning" a free-market heaven on earth. But one man's trickle-down-effect heaven is another man's hell. Here in the bible belt, there are many eccentric visions of heaven. My ancestors thought it was a field of yellow grain undulating in the breeze. The Nitsitapii preferred a field of undulating buffalo. When I picture heaven it looks like this: a clear-cut logger leaving Alberta, with a Man of Vision under one arm and the incumbent Conservative environment minister under the other. Off to slash and bulldoze a glory hole in the Great Somewhere Else that will reveal that heaven they are destined to inhabit for ever and ever.

Amen.

18
THE SWEAT LODGE

~

To ruminate on the environmental body politic of Alberta can make for an unhappy camper at times. Or as one of my friends put it, "Jeez. Who pissed in your cornflakes?" And Dave suggested that what I needed was to come with him, come and sweat with the Piikani, and get rid of some of the political toxins that kept thunderclouds on my brow. The idea struck a chord within: for some time I have wanted to undergo that initiation, the key to many aspects of Blackfoot religion, another piece in a fascinating puzzle called western history.

*   *   *

The sweat lodge, made of a willow framework covered with old canvas and blankets, stood in a clearing on the river terrace. Through the cottonwood trees I saw the blue eye of the Oldman River, forever marking the home of the Piikani people. The dome of the sweat lodge is said to represent the sky, and the floor is Mother Earth. The lava rocks, called Grandfathers, were in a red hot pile amid the flames of a bonfire that I had been asked to start earlier in the day by Melvin Potts, whose land it was. A certain number of rocks are selected, according to the traditions known to the celebrants like Melvin.

The clearing was ringed with trucks and cars. Some Kaina people had come from Stand-Off to join Peigan residents from Brockett to take the sweat. In talking, the people say, "Did you ever sweat with So-and-so? Man, he likes it hot." It is a compliment. We were there to sweat with John Day Rider, a Holy Man from Browning, Montana. We were there to sing the songs of praise, and to pray for help for ourselves or our loved ones.

As one of only two whites present, I felt self-conscious as I stripped down to bathing trunks and bare feet with the other men. I knew one of the men and one woman who had been a student of Myrna's in an adult education course Myrna taught in 1987. Myrna knows more of the Piikani people than I do. They come and go in Pincher Creek, keeping mainly to themselves. The whites in Pincher are notorious for doing much of their major shopping in Lethbridge. Some of the business people in Pincher will tell you frankly that if not for the Peigan's patronage, they could not stay in business.

But although there was a little coolness, a little wariness shown to me at first by some of the younger men present, there was no unfriendliness offered to this pigmentally challenged Napikwan, a member of the tribe of white Seizers.

Glancing around, I saw that one young man, Robert Crazy Bear (not his real name), was a traditionalist of the kind that we sometimes heard rumours about. There were sundance scars on his chest and back, livid, purplish-white worms of scarified tissue. They marked where wood skewers had been pushed through his flesh. The skewers in his chest had been tied to leather thongs fixed to the top of the Sundance Tree, a cottonwood log cut especially for that purpose and stood upright like a maypole. Robert had danced around that tree, offering his pain as a sacrifice to the Sun, singing and praying most of a hot day until the skewers were torn loose from his flesh. He had done this on two separate occasions, scarring his chest at one sun dance, and his back at another, when he had danced "dragging his buffalo skulls," as they say, behind him.

On such occasions, the initiate often has a loved one or a friend in need of spiritual help, the kind of help that can only be obtained through great sacrifice. There is some controversy among the people over the resurgence of this rite from buffalo days. At any rate, Robert's scarred body was a testament to his faith in the old ways, the old religion of the sun worshippers. Looking at his scars made me wince: I felt my hands move involuntarily to my chest, in a protective reaction. Crazy Bear's body looked hard and muscular and his eyes burned with the fierce intensity of a warrior soul.

The sweat bath is a ritual as pronounced and deliberate, as charged with symbolic vessels and artifacts, as high mass in a Catholic cathedral. It is not ethical for Napikwan, as a guest at the feast, to describe each step or item, or the particular ways of belief practised by the Holy Man who had come so far to offer this sweat. I will confine myself to things that are already generally known about this rite, which has long been a vital part of Blackfoot culture and spirituality.

The Holy Man and his assistants had entered the lodge; they had burned sweet grass (vanilla grass) and other incense to purify the lodge, and they had prayed for the success of the ceremony before the people were invited to enter. There is a certain way of entering the lodge, and if you do it incorrectly, you must start over.

There is not enough height to stand upright in the lodge, which is only about five feet high in the middle and some fourteen feet wide. Some twenty-five people were crowded into this space, so there was barely enough room to sit, with ankles crossed, on some old blankets and rugs spread on the earth. I found myself at the forefront, close to the pit. And although I only know a few words of Blackfoot, I knew by the sly chuckling that I had been given a hot spot on purpose.

The women, clad in loose-fitting shifts, sat on one side, and the men on the other. The Holy Man and his assistants faced us; the pit that would hold the Grandfathers was in the centre of the lodge.

Robert began things by praising the life of the Holy Man at length and thanking him for coming to share his power with us. The Holy Man prayed then to Creator Sun and to Mother Earth, asking them to hear our prayers.

In the dim light, with the flap of the lodge open, each person spoke in turn to reveal what they had come to pray for. One woman had come to pray for a child who was sick with an unknown malady that the white doctors had yet to diagnose. The child sat with her, restless and out of sorts. One man had come to pray, as far as I could tell, for a relative who was addicted to drugs and unable to cope with life. There were a wide variety of troubles, some described in English, some in Black-foot. Not every Peigan is fluent in the native tongue, though there is increasing interest in learning and preserving the language.

My turn came. I said I had come to pray for friendship and under-standing between our races, an understanding that has eluded us so far. I said I was sick of the violence and hatred in the men on the earth, and I was tired of the hostility that was present in myself because of the frustrations I was feeling as one who wished to help Mother Earth to stay whole. I spoke slowly as the others had done, avoiding the white habit of amplification, hewing to the truth. As I spoke, there were polite cries of encouragement from the people—"Eeeh, Eeeh"—to show they were listening and thinking about my words. Then I handed the offering of tobacco I had brought along to the Holy Man, which would be a sac-rifice to the spirits.

We all shared a symbolic meal of imported salmon and local berries, handing the ingredients around the circle, eating with our fingers. It was time for me to be surprised, since ethnologists maintained that the Blackfoot did not eat fish, which they considered to be unclean. Well, they eat it these days.

The Holy Man prayed aloud, talking to the Creator about the things we had asked for, and asking for His help. Robert translated for the benefit of those who did not understand the Blackfoot language. "Oki. He says we are going to do good things together here: we are going to talk to the Creator, but we are going to have a good time together also. Oki. He says he is glad to see some white people have come to sweat with us. Maybe they will learn something today. He will do his best to use his power to help the white people today."

The sweat would purify us and heal our hurts, and the spirits would help us. Balls of sage were passed around, and we rubbed them on our bodies to make ourselves more pure in the sight of the Creator. The Holy Man dedicated the first round of the sweat to the woman whose little girl was sick. He urged us to pray for her and ask the Sun and Mother Earth to heal her.

The first pile of red hot Grandfathers, welcomed by the Holy Man, was slid into the lodge on a board and into the fire pit in the middle of the lodge. The hot stones and the pit represent the marriage of Creator Sun and Mother Earth. Their union is the medicine that makes the sweat.

The flap of the lodge door came down and we were in total darkness.

There came the sound of a rattle, then a hand drum spoke in the darkness and the singer began, a disembodied voice filling the lodge, in time with the drum.

"Hey hey ya ho, ya hey, ya ho, ya hey hey ya." And as he finished a phrase, the people's voices swelled up on the next heartbeat of the drum to answer him. The song was all enveloping in that tight space. Bare arms and shoulders and legs were pressed against my own. The sweat stood out all over my body; the darkness was a womb where we swam, singing.

"Hey hey ya ho, ya hey, ya ho, ya hey hey ya."

"Whoosh" went the steam, as the Holy Man plied his ceremonial dipper; the heat billowed outward, enveloping us. The Holy Man was there, among other things, to make sure our singing and prayers were sincere. If he sensed we were lagging, we would hear the angry hiss of the steam more and more often. Fighting for air, we gasped and sang with greater power, following the singer's lead. One had to listen carefully to his inflections, and imitate them at full voice, and get them all right. The chant was endlessly variable and beautiful, impossible to describe in words. Its force carried us through the ordeal of the heat.

After each round, the flap was opened to allow us cold air to breathe. We sat still mostly, pouring with sweat. One or two of the men lay flat, giddy from the heat. A calumet was prepared and handed to the Holy Man, who presented it to the four directions. He took several whiffs and passed the pipe on. It would be circled through the men and returned to him again. Tobacco, out of favour with many white North Americans nowadays, has long been a sacred plant to the First Nations. Each of us smoked in turn; and then we prayed, aloud, making a tumult in the lodge with our voices. The smoke of the calumet would carry our prayers upward to the Creator Sun.

Then more red hot Grandfathers were slid into the pit by the Holy Man's assistant. The light revealed that all of us were streaming wet from the heat. The last round began, and the singing reached another pitch of intensity; the water flew on the rocks like whiplashes until I felt that I could not stand another minute. For long moments, I fought off a wave of panic, of claustrophobia, an impulse to bolt out through the flap into the daylight and the cool air of May. I closed my mouth against the heat and steam, and my ears were ringing, my eyes bulging.

But the voice of the singers swelled on. Pressed shoulder to shoulder with the men, I felt the life force of the people surging through me again. If they could breathe steam and sing, surely I could. I willed myself to open my mouth, and just let the saturated air fill my lungs. I sang with all my power, and Crazy Bear gave me an approving nudge on the shoulder. The power of the tribe lifted me with the song. I let my sense of my own boundaries drift, drift. Until I no longer felt alien and separate. I concentrated on the singing, committed now to the effort we were making together, in worship, in prayer, in a human family that was hurting, and crying out to its Creator for assistance. It was as sincere, as devotional as any church service you can think of—and more sincere than some I have attended.

Its effect on me that afternoon was to break down the racial barrier between myself and the Peigan. They are not nearly so distant to me any more, not since we sweated together, prayed together. Perhaps we should put up sweat lodges in every city in the nation, when it comes time to talk about the rights of the First Nations, the first Canadians. Put the white politicians in to sweat with the elders and pray together for guidance before they begin to negotiate. It would be an archetypical Canadian experience uniting the whole multicultural *ménage*; let's put sweat lodges in shopping centres from coast to coast, starting with that mother of all malls, the West Edmonton Mall.

Afterwards, some of us went down and waded out on the gravelly bottom of the river to wash off the salt. There was a feast awaiting us of tasty stew, Indian fry bread—which I can never get enough of—and tea.

Crazy Bear stared at me intently. "Did you see the lights?"

"The lights?"

"Of the spirits. Moving around through the lodge. Didn't you see them?"

"No."

He nodded sympathetically. "That's too bad," he said.

But I was not disappointed. Crazy Bear had earned the right to see spirits; I had not. I felt clearheaded and renewed after the ordeal, as if my prayers had been answered. My circle had been expanded; I had taken a step I had wanted to take for a long time. The feeling lasted quite a while; it comes back to me as a dream of singing. When I pick up the guitar it is there inside the sound board. I hear it in my own voice, and in the voices of my family and friends, lifted in song.

*　　*　　*

I cannot now remember the exact moment when I realized that nature does not need to be redeemed by man. Perhaps it was when I saw the teardrop of blood on the mourning dove; perhaps it was when I discovered that the fruit of the pincushion cactus is the sweetest fruit of the prairie. Or maybe it was watching my Uncle Jack kill a rattlesnake; or the first time I felt wet sand between my toes in the shallows of the South Saskatchewan; or the moment when I saw my infant son's head emerge from his mother's womb: one or all of the above.

Looking back at what was exhausted in blood and treasure, looking at what has been done to pave a way for us in the earth that Crowfoot once said was not his to sell, I have to wonder sometimes if we are worth it, G.K. Chesterton's "small arrogant oligarchy that happens to be walking around." And yet, so much continues to be notable, to be itself with or without our interest, like the migrating rosy finch that landed on Myrna's shoulder this morning, that lingered a few seconds, a greeting from another sky, then flew away.

Even at this late hour, there is nothing, really, that we can take for granted. The cyclone is ambushed everywhere, waiting, watching. There is no pact we can make with fate: fate is the flesh of a mammal meeting hazard, breaking down. And nothing needs us, but something wants us to continue, though in a different way, in a way that sustains life. This is the good, to persevere and try to live better; to become less toxic to the systems that sustain us; this is the goal that must be rationalized within the framework of the various catechisms, if we are to continue.

I remember a night in March 1992. We had been away from here for quite a while and we were eager to return home. It happened the boys were with us that night, hitching a ride back home from their rented house in the city. The moon had risen over the Porcupine Hills when we turned off on the Aspen Valley road, as we had done so many times before, as a family of four. A high band of clouds extended over the mountains out to Buffalo Butte. We rounded the corner of the butte, and entered without warning upon a sublime spectacle the like of which we had not seen before.

In the limpid moonlight, the pearly edge of the Chinook Arch cloud glowed in a translucent border over a belt of deep violet sky, studded with brilliant stars. The serrated mountain ridge had been smoothed out under a white outpouring of cap cloud, from which rocky summits protruded here and there, the cap cloud seeming to plunge toward us as a fantastic surf, breaking over the mountain in an endless waterfall of vapour. That would have been enough to stop us in our tracks, to pile out of the car, but there was more.

Moonlight picked out the distant shape of our house. Against the backdrop of the black forested mountainside there was another arch, an echo of the greater one above. It was a prismatic arch of rainbow colours rising directly out of our distant yard, out of the barn roof. It shot upward, and curved across the valley to descend at the foot of Coyote Bowl to the south. We had blundered upon the mating of two legends.

We stared at this amazing creation made from moonlight, mist and chinook whimsy. Myrna named it correctly: "It's a moonbow!"

"There's no such thing," said Paul, piqued with her for finding the right name without even reflecting on it. He reads books on physics as entertainment and considers us woefully behind the times on that score. "But I see it," he finally admitted. "It must be."

Indeed, moonbows are extremely rare. By chance, I happened to know about them: I had just reviewed a book, *Natural Attractions*, by John Thaxton, in which they are explained. They are caused by the same principles of refraction that create rainbows, except the full moon replaces the sun as the light source. The best-known recurrent moonbows are formed in the mist over Victoria Falls in Africa, and Cumberland Falls, Kentucky. The moonbow at Cumberland Falls is thirty feet long. Ours was a thousand yards long, and it was formed by a fall of vapour flowing over the top of the Livingstone Range.

What a privilege it was, standing in our storied land at that moment, feeling the wind rushing into my arms as I stood in the arms of the family again, the wind bringing us greetings from the sounding sky. Knowing the gold at the end of the moonbow was nothing more or less than the montane earth, the home of the people. The Blackfoot did not know they were the Blackfoot when they said they were the real people. We are real people, at that moment of epiphany when we hear the earth singing for us and know that something wants us here. As for me, something urges me to be the voice of the inchoate. Perhaps someday the moonbow will return, and by then I may know why this is so.

*   *   *

Last October, I went for a walk up on the Livingstone Range. There is a cirque up there that I had somehow failed to visit over the years, and I wanted to remedy that before another winter set in. A small creek flows from the cirque, and I am ever hopeful of finding in such places a little tarn, too small to be found on the map, but big enough to make its own magic with rock, dwarf trees and moss.

I followed an old gas well access road that has grown over enough now to make a fine riding or walking trail, and that consoles me in a country so marked by roading. It wound up through sombre spruce and fir forests, quiet now in an absence of birds, gaining altitude in a series of long graceful switchbacks.

The world is transformed endlessly of itself, and in our minds. Nonfiction cannot keep up with reality. I used to think the big Douglas fir trees hereabouts were the oldest in Alberta. I used to think I knew something about drought and bullpines, two apparently unrelated topics. Recently I picked up the *Globe and Mail* and learned from Science Reporter Stephen Strauss that a geographer, Glen MacDonald of McMaster University, has been out in my bailiwick sampling bullpine tree rings with a tiny drill—and just a few miles from where I live, too. The nerve!

And the oldest one was 526 years of age.

MacDonald calibrated yearly growth ring size against known meteorological records. One of his conclusions was that the drought of 1916–1926 was worse than the 1930s, which would not have surprised my grandfather's generation. More importantly, we westerners who know the black wind of drought and think we know about heat have not experienced the worst this country can produce. That drought occurred long before the settlers arrived, in the 1790s, when only eight inches of rain fell one year. It was 1793 when Fidler came nigh this place, and saw great fires burning in the middle of the winter. Ever after, Fidler referred to this country as "barren grounds." According to MacDonald, if there had been farmers here in the 1790s, "that drought would have essentially moved the people all off the land."

So all these centuries the bullpine, standing in the thin soil and bare rock, safe from our plows and runaway campfires, too gnarly and twisted to be worth logging, has maintained a living archive, a coniferous winter-count of rain and snowfall in the country it stands in, waiting for a questioning mind to hear the news from the earth.

But is the worst drought over, or yet to come? And if it is yet to come, if we can predict its coming, how can we prepare ourselves, and how protect the land? What steps should we take now, what seeds should we sow that would pacify the great chinook and keep the black blizzards at bay?

The trail ended, and I found myself in the bottom of the old ice-carved cirque at the foot of a slide path, with timbered slopes on either hand. There was no tarn. The old road ended in a small cleared area that once had held a test site for a drill rig, two decades earlier. The drill pad in this sublime setting was a sacrilegious mess of exposed shale, and push-off piles of overburden, not redeemed, though cheered, by an ice-cold spring that made a pool on one side of it. The mountain earth had not begun to heal, unlike the road below. But when I looked up the mountainside some two thousand feet higher, I was thrilled to see the white forms of two mountain goats threading between gendarmes of rock on the slopes below the summit.

This range was long the home of bighorn sheep, who survived here when other species were driven out by fires in 1885. Mountain goats—which are actually not goats at all but members of the mountain antelope family—were once native to this range, but it is marginal habitat for them. This species cannot tolerate the kind of hunting and poaching pressure that comes with roading—seismic roads and logging roads, that is—and hunting soon decimated their numbers or drove them farther west. The golden eagles that are common here, which can snatch a kid from a ledge, along with cougars, are all the predators this species needs to keep them in check. The two I observed were part of a group of four goats that had been reintroduced to the range the year before by the Fish and Wildlife Division. They replaced a small herd that was relocated here a few years ago—and that was immediately wiped out by poachers. Kudos to the men in green for persevering. These grave, deliberate beasts, working their way across a mountain face, are a pure pleasure to observe.

I heard a rock rattle nearer at hand. Looking up, I was elated to discover a bear, six hundred feet above me, digging roots out of an old slide path. Seeing a bear outside the confines of a national park in this part of Canada is always a big event; they pack such a visual and visceral wallop. Even black bears are infrequent these days, so imagine my delight when I put the glasses on him, and beheld a small grizzly, probably a two-year-old not long parted from its mother. The bear sat up on its haunches, rocking back and forth, scratching its back on a protruding rock. It dropped to all fours and stared in my direction. It had seen me before I saw it—bears, we have discovered, see a lot better than we used to believe. This one was young and inexperienced with man, I felt. But it had read my body language somehow, decided I was not a threat and continued its foraging.

A few years ago, Frank Halek had spotted a grizzly bear with cubs passing through this country, the first time a grizzly had been spotted here for decades. About that time, I heard the hunting songs of wolves for the first time ever at the head of the valley.

Since 1987, Canadian and American biologists have been observing the recolonization of the grey wolf in the front ranges and interior valleys of the Rocky Mountains, an area that had been empty of wolves for half a century. By 1994, some forty-five to sixty wolves ranged from Banff National Park south to the boundary, while another fifty to sixty wolves haunted adjacent mountain valleys in Montana.

Ranged is the operative word. A wolf radio-collared by Montana biologist Diane Boyd in Montana's Glacier National Park travelled five hundred miles in seven months—before being shot by a farmer in Dawson Creek (who thoughtfully returned the collar to her).

The wolves I heard are part of a larger pack hunting near the headwaters of the Oldman River. Last summer, rogue members of the pack killed sixteen head of cattle, and carved up a number of others. Local ranchers demanded the government account for their cattle killers. Out of fifty wolves roaming in mountainous southern Alberta in 1994, thirty-five were shot, trapped or poisoned. And now brickbats to the same boys in green, because they have poisoned four of the Oldman River Gap pack with strychnine, and they really have no way of knowing whether or not they have killed the "guilty" wolves.

On the same day we heard that news, we learned that three stray dogs had killed fifty head of prize sheep at a farm near Dewinton, Alberta. South of Pincher a rancher has lost six calves to a roaming pair of pug-faced mutts. The owner's motto is deny deny. He refuses to tie the dogs up. Nobody advocates setting out strychnine for stray dogs. Dogs are owned by voters: voters would be enraged, watching their dogs, or anyone's dog really, convulse and writhe in pain. Wolves are owned only by themselves: they die in the heart of the country, unmourned except by the wild pack.

Alberta is supposed to have a program for managing cattle-killing wolves and conserving other wolves, but it is a bad joke, because any Alberta resident can shoot wolves on sight, without so much as a licence, for nine to ten months of the year. Fortunately, not every rancher shoots wolves on sight. If they did, there would not be one wolf left alive in southern Alberta. It is up to the government, not the ranchers, to abolish the notion that wolves are little more than animated rifle targets.

If wolves were more "humane" predators (for want of a better word) they would not be quite so reviled by herdsmen. The mutilation they cause to stock they do not quickly kill is an outrage to ranchers.

A neighbour of mine is missing four head of cattle that may or may not have been taken by the Highwood pack in the Livingstone Gap area. What disturbed him a great deal was the rogue wolves' tendency to eat living flesh—a football-sized hole in the case of one of his heifers—out of the rectal area, leaving it to live or die as nature dictates. Despite this experience, he says, "I don't want to knock them off the face of the earth. It's sensible if we are in the forestry that we have to accept some losses." He added, "If I knew I would only lose one or two a year—I could live with that."

I know other ranchers who realize that this financial plum called grazing rights, though of long standing in the West, is resented already by other sectors of the public who would like to see it dissolved. If all the potential defenders of the wolf and other wildlife out there organized their forces and lobbied the politicians to put the interests of wildlife ahead of grazing on public land, the ranchers' whole tenure along the east slope would be threatened. It may be time for ranchers to eschew their usual shoot-and-shut-up predator management technique and take a bold leap into the twentieth century—five more years and counting. . . .

This narrow band of foothills and montane forest is merely fringe habitat for wolves and grizzly bears. Their main range is closer to the Great Divide, west of here, where the vegetation is lusher and human settlements uncommon. That they are able to utilize this habitat at all could be seen as a hopeful sign, considering the changes made by roads, logging and grazing. But it might also only mean that the prime habitat is threatened by clear-cut logging, roading and petroleum development. It could be that a wolf's or a grizzly bear's presence here is a sign of desperation. For now, I choose to see it as a sign of hope; without hope, we are done.

As darkness settled in, I made my way back home elated, inspired by the sight of mountain goats and a grizzly bear within a few miles of my house. A country that can still maintain animals like this is worth celebrating, and worth protecting. Outside of the national parks, this foothills ranching country still offers the only chance we have for a buffer zone, a place of accommodation and balance between wildlife and humans in Chinook Country. The land use decisions we are making now are absolutely vital for the future of wildlife and wild country in southern Alberta.

*　　*　　*

I dreamed about the sweat lodge last night. I felt again the surge of power from twenty-five souls willing to suffer together, to be redeemed together. I felt again the circle of energy flowing through the celebrants. If our own community could be energized like that, we could do some fine things to protect our small Shangri-la. There is no real equivalent of the sweat lodge and its healing circle in the community where I live. We are too obsessed with individuality here, and it undercuts our ability to safeguard the community of plants, animals and people that sustains us all. So the conservative politics of most of the ranchers here preclude them involving themselves with a non-believer like myself, even if they secretly agree, in principle for example, that subdivisions threaten their livelihood and I'm on the right track in opposing them. It's just that I'm the wrong person to be opposing them, from the ranchers' point of view. On accounta my politics. Is that clear enough? Is that eccentric, short-sighted and parochial enough? Because I'm not even revealing one-quarter of its stubborn bullpine craziness. And yet, despite our differences, I would not hesitate to pick up the phone and call the staunchest Tory among them if I needed help in an emergency. I know he or she would come roaring down the road in a moment, and they know that I would do the same. We don't, any of us, hate each other's guts, at least not yet. As far as I know. And even if we did, we would help each other anyway. Because if we didn't, we would never hear the end of it from the Local Oracle. The LO is the kind of guy who, while driving by with his tractor on a winter day, will turn in and plow your driveway out, without being asked. Just because he can see it needs doing, that your small car will not get out to the road without it.

Ultimately, the newcomers will discover a few things like that about the oldtimers here, and I think they will value that generosity as much as I do; perhaps be deeply touched by it, as I am. Maybe some of the new people are here to become the links that make us a circle after all; I have to hope so. But I have taken on the social characteristics of the people hereabouts over the years, and so I am inclined to wait and see what the "outsiders" do when the wind finally hunts them out of cover: I have to see if they hunker in and put their roots into the rock, or just unreef their Gore-Tex windbreakers or their brand-new Koolha saddle-coats like sails and blow back to where they came from.

We are raised in joy, nurtured by love, deranged by pain, nurtured by love again. Thus we go on, and I am grateful for the chance to live one moment perfectly, and to live even one day successfully, to give thanks. I don't want to forget what was spilled and what was lost; it would cheapen the sunrise, it would hasten the night. And I will fight, and teach my sons to fight to keep the land whole. That is what we can learn from the Nitsitapii, but our way now must be to war with words, to war without violence.

I think that I am fated to be a curmudgeon. I certainly hope so, but only if I can keep finding the funny bone among all the bones scattered on these hills. The funny bone is the only weapon that makes sense. I learned that at my mother Jesse's knee, and from my Uncle Oscar and from Orland on his best days, his sunshine days.

I think about my grandfather J.C., of his coldness and of his warming up too late. His tragedy was that he had succeeded, but did not recognize where his success lay—in his family, his wife and children. What he taught me was to beware of doing the same, and yet I have come very close at times to repeating the same mistakes, prey to an ambition more grandiose than his own. I think we are successful if we can learn from our ancestors, if we can improve on them, where that is needed, live up to them in our own way where they excelled and celebrate whatever good we see in them. We will all be forgotten eventually, but it is sad to be forgotten by your own kin. Remembering is its own thank you for a life given.

Tonight, mountains shrug their cold white shoulders up out of the robes of black forests. In the alpenglow, bullpine on the ridge are a black intaglio etched into a mauve sky. There will be a full moon tonight.

A major chinook gave way to a cold front that dropped ten inches of snow along the mountains. Now the weather has cleared again, and the mercury drops to –30°C. After sundown, the Livingstone turns deep violet, its edge sharply drawn against a burnished pewter sky fading into ultra blue several miles higher in the heavens. Now something strange happens: smoke, amber-hued, rolls up in waves from Cirque Peak. It looks like the cone of an awakening volcano done in rotogravure. But this illusion is only the product of the wind kicking up on the ridge of the mountain, throwing up waves of snow off the summit to be backlit with faint rose by the last rays of the sun, a sun that is too faint and hidden now to be seen from this cabin.

Poplar logs burn silently in the heater and quickly turn into a sediment of bitumen. They remind me of the soft coal, the "luggit," my grandfather used to burn, dug from the banks of the South Saskatchewan with a pick and shovel to keep his family warm. Life, survival, is reduced to the warmth of this small cave of wood, that small black barrel of iron glowing to red at the edges with the trademark on the door that reads "Alberta."

Alberta, word of glory, freighted with promise to my ancestors. And I have learned, in a story told me by my American cousin, a secret that Aunt Sis keeps locked in her birdlike chest, why great-grandfather Robert, fifty-five years of age and with an ailing wife, came west to exile in the desert drylands of an unknown country.

As a lawman in the States, it fell his lot to preside over the execution of a convicted murderer. Call him Joe; his name's forgotten now. By the gallows drop Joe insisted, over and over again, "You are hanging an innocent man."

Time passes; then one day Robert receives grim news. Joe had spoken true: a condemned man in Colorado had confessed to the murder.

The women all liked Robert. He was the only man they knew who would don an apron and help out in the kitchen, joking them up and laughing with them when his frail wife could not pitch in. He was the gentlest of men, they said; kind, but strong too. In my picture of him, he looks like an old, bent professor. Bending to gaze, with puzzled affection, into his wife's smile. He built his home where he could watch the back trail to Montana, an old lawman with enemies. And he turned to address the *tabula rasa* of the bald-headed distances. I said he had the soul of a poet. I think he could not afford to make another mistake: his soul would not abide it. The soul of a poet can turn on itself. And that is why he said, "They never gave it a chance. A man could make a fortune here." And his heart, which was broken, mended itself for very pity.

Faint flame, light the word Alberta. The smoke of my fire blows by the window in raven's wings against the darkening winter sky. The flames die down, but suddenly something scrapes violently against the corner of the Wheelhouse. I stare out the window and see in the moonlight the ghostly shape of the old white bell mare, outlined against the mountain.

I have been worried about her; does she know it? Is this her reassurance—more likely just an itchy buttock. Yesterday as I was crossing to the house, she was working her way carefully down the hill. The last part is the steepest, and it was patched with ice. Suddenly she fell heavily on her side. She rolled back up, slowly but efficiently, planted her front feet and got up. But in one more cautious step, she fell down hard again, making me groan in sympathy with her. She lay there looking at me for a moment, winded. I thought, this might be it, the heart attack; the fatal stroke.

This is a quiet horse. Her only sound is a throaty whicker when she sees me coming with some oats. Slowly, she had gotten to all fours again. She worked her way down, passed me with measured dignity, and stopped at the stable door. Then she turned her head back, showed me those dark eyelids set in white hair that gives her old goat-like head its special charm, and gave me the low, soft whicker, the old coquette.

Her end is drawing near; she moves more slowly by the day, afraid of slipping again, like an old woman terrified of breaking a hip. Last night I dreamed of her death: it was perfect, serene and quick. I woke up and wrote words spoken in the dream, rough notes for a future poem:

Her dream flesh was desert dry
I touched her head, and it fell away like shale
in layers, that were years of questions
The outline of her body turned to quartz
giving the stars back to their constellations
This was the wish of the ground

her shoes struck fire from
And all the grass cried out
for her salvation

I looked out the window again later that night. I saw something goat-like gliding up the edge of the hill, outlined against the sky that had now gone to royal purple. It was the white mare. I could not see her feet move in that light over the whiteness of snow, the white mare in the moonlight on a white page. She seemed to float upward, onto the rimrock, into the dome of the sky where she bent to take a drink from the Little Dipper, then whirling away as the wind lit down again to argue with the bullpine, she disappeared among the Northern Lights.

BIBLIOGRAPHY

~

Alt, David, and Donald W. Hyndman. *Roadside Geology of Montana.* Missoula, Mont.: Mountain Press Publishing, 1990.

Anderson, Frank W. "Wagon Train Massacre." *Sagas of the West* (winter 1972).

Beaty, Chester B. *The Landscapes of Southern Alberta: A Regional Geomorphology.* University of Lethbridge, 1975.

Berry, Gerald L. *Whoop-Up Trail: Early Days in Alberta-Montana.* Edmonton: University of Lethbridge Production Services, 1953.

Brado, Edward. *Cattle Kingdom: Early Ranching in Alberta.* Vancouver: Douglas and McIntyre, 1984.

Buckler, S.J. "An Analysis of Meteorological Conditions During a Case of Severe Turbulence." Canada, Department of Transport, Meteorological Branch, CIR 4211, TEC 563, 1965.

Butler, William F. *The Great Lone Land: A Narrative of Travel and Adventure in the North-West of America.* London, 1873.

Canada, Department of the Interior. "The Last Best West." Ottawa, 1905.

Canada, Indian and Northern Affairs, and Parks Canada. "Cypress Hills Massacre" (pamphlet). Ottawa, 1978.

Cannon, Hal. *Cowboy Poetry: A Gathering.* Layton, Utah: Gibbs M. Smith Inc., 1985.

Chandler, Raymond. "Red Wind." In *Trouble Is My Business*. New York and Toronto: Random House, 1992.

Clark, Charles B., Jr. "The Lost Pardner." *Pacific Monthly*, April 1908. In Folk Coll. II C26. Fife Folklore Archive, Utah State University, Logan.

Conway, J.F. *The West: The History of a Region in Confederation*. Toronto: James Lorimer, 1983.

Dary, David. *Cowboy Culture: A Saga of Five Centuries*. Lawrence: University Press of Kansas, 1981.

Dempsey, Hugh A. Letter to Mr. Leon Levesque, July 9, 1984.

Denny, Sir Cecil E. *The Law Marches West*. Ed. W.B. Cameron. Toronto: J. M. Dent, 1939.

———. "Traders of the Early West." *Alberta Historical Review* (summer 1958).

Douglas, R.J.W. *Geolgical Survey Memoir 402. Callum Creek, Langford Creek, and Gap Map-Areas, Alberta*. Hull: Canadian Government Publishing Centre, Supply and Services Canada, 1981. (Reprint of Memoir 255, 1950.)

Ewers, John C. *The Blackfeet: Raiders on the Northwestern Plains*. Norman: University of Oklahoma Press, 1958.

———. *The Horse in Blackfoot Indian Culture*. Smithsonian Institution, Bureau of American Ethnology Bulletin 159. Washington, 1955. Reprint, Smithsonian Institution Press, 1980.

Fidler, Peter. "Journal of a Journey over Land from Buckingham House to the Rocky Mountains in 1792 & 3." Hudson's Bay Company Archives. Provincial Archives of Manitoba, E.32 fos. 2–36.

Fletcher, Roy J. *Winter Atmospheric Ionization in the Chinook Area of Southern Alberta*. Current Research by Western Canadian Geographers, University of Alberta Papers. Edmonton, 1986.

Francis, R. Douglas. *Images of the West: Responses to the Canadian Prairies*. Saskatoon: Western Producer Prairie Books, 1989.

Geist, Valerius. "Pronghorns, Fires, Fossils." *Alberta* 1, no. 1 (1988).

Goodloe, Abbe Carter. "At the Foot of the Rockies." *Alberta History*. Vol. 34, No. 2, 1986.

Gray, James H. *Men Against the Desert*. Saskatoon: Western Producer Prairie Books, 1967.

Hamilton, James McClellan. *From Wilderness to Statehood: A History of Montana, 1805–1900*. Ed. Merrill G. Burlingame. Portland, Ore.: Binfords and Mort.

Hardy, W.G., ed. *Alberta: A Natural History*. Edmonton: MisMat Corporation, 1967. Reprint, 1977.

Hedges, James B. *Building the Canadian West: The Land and Colonization Policies of the Canadian Pacific Railway*. New York: Macmillan, 1939.

Henday, Anthony. *Journal of Anthony Henday*. Annotated by L.J. Burpee. Ottawa: Royal Society of Canada, 1907.

Henry, Alexander (The Younger). *New Light on the Early History of the Greater Northwest, Journals of Alexander Henry*. Annotated by Elliot Cues. New York, 1897.

High River Old Timers' Association. *Leaves From the Medicine Tree*. High River, Alberta, 1960.

Hill, Alexander Stavely. *From Home to Home: Autumn Wanderings in the North-West in the Years 1881, 1882, 1883, 1884*. London, 1885.

Historical Society of Alberta. *"We'll All Be Buried Down Here": The Prairie Dryland Disaster, 1917–1926* . Ed. David C. Jones. Calgary, 1986.

Hooker, William Francis. *The Bullwhacker: Adventures of a Frontier Freighter*. Ed. Howard R. Driggs. Lincoln: University of Nebraska Press, 1988.

Ings, Frederick William. *Before the Fences: Tales from the Midway Ranch*. Ed. Jim Davis. (Published by the family) Nanton, Alberta, 1980.

Ives, Ronald L. "Frequency and Physical Effects of Chinook Winds in the Colorado High Plains Region," *Annals of the Association of American Geographers* 40 (1950).

Jones, David C. *Empire of Dust*. Edmonton: University of Alberta Press, 1987.

Kelly, L.V. *The Range Men: The Story of the Rangers and Indians of Alberta*. Toronto: Coles Publishing Company Limited (Reprint), 1980.

Kerr, Richard A. "Chinook Winds Resemble Water Flowing over a Rock." *Science* 231 (March 1986).

King, D.R. *Alberta Archaeology: A Handbook for Amateurs*. (Self-published) High River, Alberta, 1968.

Lester, Peter F. *Turbulence: A New Perspective for Pilots*. Englewood, Colorado: Jeppesen Sanderson Training Systems, 1993.

Logan, David Michael. "Hoof Beats." In *Bronc to Breakfast and Other Poems*. Helena, Mont.: Buglin' Bull Press, 1988.

Long, Philip S. *Jerry Potts: Scout, Frontiersman and Hero*. Calgary: Bonanza Books, 1974.

McDougall, John. *On Western Trails in the Early Seventies.* Toronto: William Briggs, 1911.

McHugh, Tom. *The Time of the Buffalo.* Lincoln and London: University of Nebraska Press (Reprint), 1972.

Mackenzie, Sir Alexander. *Voyages from Montreal on the River St. Lawrence Through the Continent of North America to the Frozen and Pacific Oceans in the years 1789 and 1793.* Philadelphia, 1802.

MacLeod, Margaret A. *Songs of Old Manitoba.* Ryerson Press, Toronto, 1959.

Macoun, John. *Manitoba and the Great North-West.* Guelph, 1882.

Marsh, John Stuart. "The Chinook and Its Geographic Significance in Southern Alberta." Master's thesis, University of Calgary, 1965.

Nix, J. Ernest. "Button Chief a Native Hero." *Alberta History* (winter 1981). Original letters in 86.279C, John Maclean Papers, United Church Archives, Toronto.

Nkemdirim, Lawrence C. "Chinooks in Calgary." *Pika* 8 (1988).

Oard, Michael J. "A Method for Predicting Chinook Winds East of the Montana Rockies." *Weather and Forecasting* 8, no. 2 (June 1993).

Ondrack, Jack. *Big Game Hunting in Alberta.* Edmonton: Wildlife Publishing, 1985.

Osmond, H.L. "The Chinook Wind East of the Canadian Rockies." *Canadian Journal of Research* 19 (April 1941).

Overholser, Joel. *Fort Benton: World's Innermost Port.* Fort Benton, Alta., 1987.

Palliser, John. *Journals, Detailed Reports and Observations Relative to the Exploration of British North America.* London, 1859.

Prest, V.K. "Map 1257A. Retreat of Wisconsin and Recent Ice in North America." Ottawa: Geological Survey of Canada, 1969.

Robertson-Ross, Colonel P. "Robertson-Ross Diary, Fort Edmonton to Wildhorse B.C. 1872." Ed. Hugh A. Dempsey. *Alberta History*, Vol 9, No. 3, 1961.

Ross, Jim. *Saddle Up and Ride.* Stevensville Mont., 1980.

Schultz, James Willard (Apikuni). *Blackfeet and Buffalo: Memories of Life Among the Indians.* Ed. Keith C. Seele. Norman: University of Oklahoma Press, 1962.

Schwartz, Eric. "Ill Winds That Can Make You Sick." *Saturday Evening Post*, March 1982.

Stark, Malcolm. "Soil Erosion Out of Control in Southern Alberta." *Canadian Geographic.* December 1987.

Thaxton, John. *Natural Attractions.* New York: Warner Books, 1987.

Thompson, David. *David Thompson's Narrative of His Explorations in Western America, 1784–1812.* Ed. J.B. Tyrrell. Toronto: Champlain Society, 1916.

Troper, Harold Martin. *Only Farmers Need Apply: Official Canadian Government Encouragement of Immigration from the United States, 1896–1911.* Toronto: Griffin House, 1972.

Webb, Walter Prescott. *The Great Plains.* New York: Grosset & Dunlap, 1931.

Wiese, Ursula. *Stalking the Mountain Wave.* Claresholm: Alberta Soaring Council, 1988.

Woods, Lawrence M. *British Gentlemen in the Wild West: The Era of the Intensely English Cowboy.* New York: The Free Press, 1989.